DENNY
THE STORY OF
McLAIN
STRIKEOUT

DENNY
THE STORY OF
McLAIN
STRIKEOUT

BY DENNY McLAIN
WITH MIKE NAHRSTEDT

Published in the United States by THE SPORTING NEWS ▼▼ A Times Mirror
Publishing Co., 1212 North Lindbergh Boulevard, ◣ Company
St. Louis, Missouri 63132.

Library of Congress Catalog Card Number: 88-60160

ISBN: 0-89204-234-6
10 9 8 7 6 5 4 3 2 1

First Edition

C O N T E N T S

For my Sharyn.
I love you and I thank you.

ACKNOWLEDGMENTS

From the bottom of my heart, I want to thank the following great folks for all their help and support, not only with this book, but also in my life:

Judge Mike Schwartz, for keeping my family alive while I was in prison and for going out on a limb just by being my pal. He's an elected official, but he refused to let my conviction get in the way of our friendship.

Arnie and Gail Levine, for all their help, not only in my defense and successful appeal, but also for their kindness to my wife, Sharyn, and our children.

Steve Northcutt, Arnie Levine's partner, for devoting months of his life to the preparation of my winning appeal.

Gary Leshaw, the Atlanta attorney who has done an exceptional job representing the Cuban and American prisoners in the U.S. Penitentiary in Atlanta. His friendship and assistance made it possible for me to do my investigative work in Atlanta and then to write about it later.

Harold Warren, a pal for many years who helped my family financially, but more importantly, stood by me through thick and thin.

Walt Olender, a pal from New Jersey who came through when asked. He sent me money for my commissary needs in the slammer and was solely responsible for my being freed from prison on September 4, 1987.

Buddy Leake, my insurance man in Oklahoma, for paying all of my insurance premiums while I was in prison. I'm sure glad Sharyn didn't have to collect on anything while I was away.

Jack Ross, the landlord in St. Petersburg who looked the other way when rent checks arrived late or never at all.

Jim Campbell, president of the Detroit Tigers, for his support and for the money he gave Sharyn when she needed it.

Frank Slocum, who was involved in the early stages of this book, for his support as director of the Baseball Alumni Team. B.A.T., which helps former major league players in dire straits without asking questions, is a real major league group.

Sister Veronica, for keeping me close to God and helping me understand that God is not responsible for the many mistakes in my life.

Such kind friends as Mickey Herskowitz, an author who helped my family; Brooks Robinson, for his gift to my family; Dan Ewald, public relations director for the Tigers; the entire staffs of Metropolitan Detroit magazine and the Sports Fans Journal in Detroit; Don and Alice Mathews; Dr. Bert Carnera; Dr. Craig Maguire; Warren and Rose Fata; Pete and Anne Sark; Jim Powers; Dan Scenga of Dan Scenga Chevy/Olds in Richmond, Mich.; Bernie Nelson of Bernie Nelson Chevy/Olds in Huntington, Ind., and Don Bartrom, who personally made the Christmas of 1987 my most memorable ever.

Denny Meadows of the U.S. Probation Office in Fort Wayne, for helping me make the adjustment back to the free world.

The following Bureau of Prison cops: Gene Webster, Pat Reams, Roger Colley, Jim Fleagle, Ed Cochran and Dale Dombroski, the aspiring radio announcer. These guys have tried to make the system better, despite the system working against them.

The many baseball fans and other letter writers whose kind words kept me going.

Richard Waters, president of The Sporting News, who had the guts to print this book when others had said no.

Mike Nahrstedt and Ron Smith, the two guys who have spent months of their lives with this book. They have written, edited, rewritten and re-edited this book so many times, their recall about my life probably is better than mine. There have been tense times and a few arguments along the way, but I consider the confrontations educational and I value their friendships more than anyone can ever understand.

Bill Perry, Mike Bruner, Gary Levy, Steve Gietschier, Craig Carter, Anne Files, Carolyne duNard-Phillips, Rich Pilling and Lesley Damewood of The Sporting News.

Paul and Barbara Golaszewski, my brother-in-law and sister-in-law, for their strength and kindness.

Jimmy and Louie Boudreau, my brothers-in-law.

Lou and Della Boudreau, who have stood behind me and Sharyn despite being embarrassed by my ridiculous conduct at times.

My children—Kristi, Denny, Tim and Michelle. Thank you for loving and believing in me. I'll never let you guys down again.

And my lovely, beautiful and tolerant Sharyn. Without your strength, I never would have survived the ordeal. I am truly sorry for all the hurt I have caused you. I love you.

PREFACE

Another autobiography by a former baseball player? Yes, but with a different twist. My story is not your basic collection of ball-yard humor and clubhouse mischief, though sometimes I wish it was.

"Bizarre" is a good word to describe life after baseball for Denny McLain. I've been involved in a lot of business deals through the years, and some of them have definitely been bizarre. Some also caught the attention of federal and state law enforcement authorities. Though my connection to the shady end of these deals was remote, I was indicted and wrongly convicted for racketeering, conspiracy, extortion and cocaine possession with intent to distribute. That led to a 23-year prison sentence, 2½ years of which I served in the U.S. Penitentiary in Atlanta—site of the 1987 Cuban riots—and the Federal Correctional Institution in Talladega, Ala. That's how long it took to get my conviction thrown out on appeal.

It's not exactly the Tom Seaver story. But it is worth telling.

Why? Because it's relevant. I have learned things about our criminal justice system that will make your hair stand on end. I saw a federal prosecutor abuse the grand jury process. I saw a federal judge make a mockery of the criminal trial process. I saw a prison system that stripped men of their dignity, brutalized them and did everything but rehabilitate them. This book is not an indictment of the many lawmen, lawyers and jurists who do their jobs honestly and fairly, but my experience certainly was not unique. Injustice happens every day, to regular folks as well as famous ball players.

I have another reason for telling my story: To set the record straight. People have been writing and talking about me for years, but it's amazing how seldom the facts are right. Once and for all, I want everybody to get the story straight from the horse's mouth.

It won't be sugarcoated. I let myself get in some messy situations, and retelling those stories is, out of necessity, a dirty job. I won't always come out looking too clean myself, but that's my own fault. When you hang around with scum, some of it is bound to rub off.

But understand this: While I'm no altar boy by any stretch of the imagination, I'm not Al Capone, either. The government tried to portray me as Public Enemy No. 1, which simply was a false characterization. When you read about my trial and the people who implicated me in crimes, you'll see why.

I'm bitter about my experiences with our system of justice, but that's not my overriding emotion. More than anything, I'm grateful. That's because through the whole ordeal, my wife and friends never deserted me. They had plenty of opportunities to say, "To hell with you." My wife, Sharyn, especially put up with a lot. But when I walked out of prison, I was welcomed back with open arms. Most guys aren't that lucky.

But then, I'm not like most guys. I won 31 major league baseball games in one season and later served almost as many months in prison. It took quite a series of bizarre events to accomplish that. There's that word again. If nothing else, my life has been eventful.

I hope that it also has been and will be instructive. I'm certainly in no position to preach, but I think I can offer some valuable insights about life. During 29½ months of self-examination, I learned some lessons. Finally.

CHAPTER 1

A Look In the Mirror

September 14, 1968. March 16, 1985.

Those are the two most significant dates in my life, and that's really saying something. On the first, I became a 30-game winner for the Detroit Tigers. On the second, I was pronounced guilty by a jury and sent to prison. Talk about a slide! From the top of the world to the lower reaches of despair.

One day I'm matching wits and athletic skills with the likes of Mickey Mantle and Reggie Jackson. The next I'm fighting for my sanity in a federal prison system that goes out of its way to beat you down.

How do I justify the convoluted life style that led to my downfall? I can't. What I can do is try to explain what can make a man who had the world in the palm of his right hand go from No. 1 to a different kind of number, 04000-018, in just 17 years.

If I'd been as careful off the mound as I was on it, I'd probably be writing a different kind of book. When I was at the top of my baseball career, no one in the world had better concentration than I did. On the mound, my mind was focused on one thing, and one thing only. The batter. People in the stands could be calling me every name in the book and fireworks could be going off all around me, but I wouldn't see or hear any of it. The only thought running through my head was how to get that batter out. I didn't like to mess around out there, either, so even if I got two quick strikes, I wouldn't waste a pitch like so many guys do. I'd go straight for the jugular. The batter would either have to beat me right then and there or take his seat back in the dugout. Call that cocky, but I knew what I was capable of doing. It was just a matter of concentrating and getting the job done. Usually, I did.

When I wasn't pitching, however, my concentration wandered. Until the U.S. government gave me an extended opportunity to think things over, I never analyzed anything in the real world as carefully as I analyzed a batter. If a business proposal looked intriguing, that was good enough for me. People would say, "Denny, have I got a deal for you," and I'd say, "Great, let's be partners." Usually it wasn't so great and I'd wind up paying the price. Looking back, I realize I should have shaken off some of these schemes, just like I'd shake off Bill Freehan's sign for a slider when I knew I could blow the guy away with my fastball. I was in control on the mound; unfortunately, I was overmatched when it came to making important decisions in my life.

To say that I was not blessed with the ability to make sound judgments is like saying that Florida gets warm in the summer. A massive understatement. To put it bluntly, my judgment stinks, especially when it comes to sizing up other people. I like people, and when I meet somebody for the first time, I'm usually blinded to any negative vibes that may be slapping me right in the face. I'm too quick to trust. Read resumes? Check references? That's not my style. Later, when I finally realize what I'm dealing with, either I don't have enough sense to say adios or I'm already up to my neck in alligators.

Here's an example. During my playing days, I got involved with an attorney who said he'd straighten out my financial affairs. I was pulling in a pretty hefty income, and I needed financial guidance. This guy impressed me, so I gave him control of my money and told him to keep track of everything. It wasn't long before he started telling me all the wonderful things he could do for me. "Think big, Denny, think big," he said. Well, when it comes to dollar signs, I can think as big as anybody. In no time at all I had a minor business empire that, quite frankly, I really didn't know much about. It was great. I was playing ball while my attorney was running everything, making me money. No problems, at least not until we started hearing from creditors who wanted to know when we were going to pay up for some little things, like our house and electricity. When I called to find out what the problem was, my attorney was gone. He'd taken off with my money and left me the bills. A few months later I filed for bankruptcy.

Dumb? I sure was. I put all my eggs in one basket and handed them over to a fox. I was left with nothing. The media portrayed me as a real jerk because a lot of people who had loaned me money or extended me credit never got paid back. I was sorry, but what could I do? I made a bad decision and got burned. It was one of my many bad decisions that were blurred by my desire to live in the fast lane.

That desire fit nicely with my interest in making money, lots of money. It's interesting that as I look back over the years and try to figure out how my life turned out the way it did, the topic of money keeps coming up. Samson had his Delilah, McLain had green pieces of paper with pictures of presidents. I guess money is one of the constants in my life. I've always wanted it, and when I had it, I wanted more. Don't ask me why. It's my addiction. Some people use drugs or booze or gambling to get high. I get off on making money.

I remember a game I pitched at Minnesota back in 1969. It was a Saturday afternoon, and NBC was televising the game. After eight innings we had a 6-0 lead, so I was shaping up as the "star of the game." That was significant because NBC had a crisp $100 bill waiting for the player it selected to appear on its postgame show. The only other serious candidate for the interview was our first baseman, Norm Cash, who had collected a home run and a single in four at-bats at that point. Norm wanted that $100 as much as I did, and when he went to the plate in the top of the ninth, he figured one more hit would give him a good shot at it.

Well, I didn't want Norm stealing my C-note, so I started hollering instructions to the Twins' catcher, Johnny Roseboro, on what pitches to call—the ones Norm couldn't hit. Sure enough, Norm flied out. I went out there in the bottom of the ninth and got the Twins out, one-two-three. It was the best inning I'd pitched all year. As expected, NBC invited me to appear on the postgame show. When I walked back to the clubhouse, I had that $100 bill pasted proudly on my forehead, where everyone could see it. Norm didn't appreciate that too much.

Did I need that $100? Yeah, like Suzanne Pleshette needed beauty tips. We both could get by without just fine. At that point in my career, $100 was pocket change. But with that money dangling in front of me like a carrot on a stick, there was no way I was going to let Norm Cash beat me to it.

Don't get me wrong: Money is great, but it's not my god. Money doesn't make the world go around for me, though it does make it spin a whole lot smoother. It certainly is not as important to me as my family. That may be hard to believe when you read my life story, but everything I've ever done has been in the interest of taking care of my family. That's easier to do if you have money.

I think everybody wants their family to have it better than they had it growing up. When I was a kid, we never went hungry, but it was always a struggle. My father always worked two jobs to provide us with enough food and clothing, and even then we were cutting it close. I'm convinced that all those 16-hour days are what killed my dad at the age of 37. After seeing him work himself to death, I promised myself that I would do things differently.

And I certainly have lived up to that promise. More than anything else, money has given me freedom, freedom to do what I want to do and be what I want to be. If I need to go out of town on business, for example, and have to drive or take a commercial flight, several hours of my time are wasted just in transit. But with money, I can buy my own plane, get to my destination in less than half the time and have fun while I'm at it. Then I can do my business and be back home in time for dinner. I like that.

My father's early death also put the idea in my mind that I'd probably die young, too. Maybe that explains why I've jumped into ventures that promised a quick buck. I guess I wanted to do it up proud before I left this earth, plus I wanted to make sure my family would be well taken care of after I was gone. Well, I haven't died yet and I still like making money, so there must be more to it than that.

As you've probably figured out by now, I've never been too particular about how I make money. As long as it's not criminal. Notice I didn't say "illegal." To me, there's a difference, and I must admit that this philosophy has created serious problems all my life. I've been a gambler most of my life and, on a couple of occasions, a bookmaker. Now, neither of these career choices is legal unless you're in Nevada or Atlantic City, and I've never lived in either place. That means I've broken the law. So be it. As far as I'm concerned, gambling and bookmaking may be crimes, but they're not criminal. They're victimless. The people involved can hurt only themselves, and if they do, it's only a financial hurt. Sure, I've heard of Gamblers Anonymous, and I know a guy with a gambling problem can hurt his family. But he's no different from a guy with a drinking problem, and as far as I know, drinking is still legal in this country.

Gambling should be, too. Is there anybody out there who doesn't gamble, be it Sunday football or the office pool for the NCAA basketball tournament? Hell, gambling should be controlled by state governments. They'd put bookies out of business, and all the money bookies are making now would wind up in state treasuries. Then make the gamblers pay taxes on their winnings and put the money to good use—hire more teachers, build better roads, whatever. There's nothing wrong with letting gamblers have their fun and improving life for everybody else at the same time.

Prostitution? Another victimless crime. It's also an unstoppable crime. Sex is one thing people will get one way or another. Why not legalize it? If the government controlled the industry—and that's what it is—hookers could be given regular physical examinations and health risks could be minimized. Risks would still be involved, but the situation certainly would be better than it is. Now I'm not saying we should go open up brothels and everybody should start banging their eyes out. Everything in moderation. But you might as well do something to legalize the oldest game in town.

Where do I draw the line? The way I see it, an act is criminal if somebody gets hurt. Stealing is criminal. Arson is criminal. Embezzlement is criminal. Selling drugs is criminal. Murder is criminal. Gambling and prostitution are not.

I would never do anything criminal to make money. You might be wondering, "If he didn't do anything criminal, how did he wind up in prison?" Good question. Well, it goes back to my poor judgment. A few years ago, I went into business with some scum-bum people. One thing I've learned is that scum attracts more scum, like a magnet. Before long I was wallowing in it. I didn't realize, of course, what I was getting into. Remember, I'm no King Solomon. People don't come to your door with a sign around their neck that says, "Beware, I'm a slimy snake that you want no part of." Lord knows, I wish they did, because I could use the help. Anyway, these guys seemed OK to me, and I got involved with them through some legitimate business deals I had going. Before I could say "not guilty," they were off telling a grand jury—after being granted immunity against prosecution themselves—that I was involved in their dirty deals. That was a crock, but the grand jury believed it and so did a trial jury, which is all it took to put me away.

Many of my problems through the years probably can be traced to the fact that I have a little bit of a rebel in me. I'm no James Dean, but I've never been one to deal meekly with authority, either. As a youngster in Catholic grammar school, I hated wearing a bow tie to class. Think about it. What sense was there in making a 12- or 13-year-old kid wear a tie? Except to teach a kid discipline— and I question whether kids really learn discipline that way—it's pointless. Naturally, I rebelled. I remember one day I ripped the tie off just moments before the final bell was about to ring. One of the nuns saw me and told me to put my tie back on.

"I'll be damned if I'm going to put it back on!" I yelled.

An unfortunate choice of words. The sister didn't care for my remark and proceeded to scare the hell out of me as she marched me down to the principal's office. The reception I got there wasn't half as bad as the one I got from my parents at home. My rear end still smarts when I think about that episode.

That wasn't my first run-in with an authority figure, and it certainly wasn't my last. I became more rebellious after my father died. He was a strong disciplinarian and he pretty much kept me in line. But when my mother remarried less than a year after my dad died, that was extremely tough for a 15-year-old kid to take. Not only was another man sleeping in my father's bed, but my mother had invited him in! I wasn't about to take orders from a woman who, in my mind, had that little respect for my father. After that, no one could tell me what to do.

What it boils down to, I guess, is that I like to decide for myself what I can and can't do. Don't tell me I can't make a certain business succeed. If you do that, I'll just go out there and try to prove you wrong. If I fail, I'm fully prepared to take the blame. But if I succeed, then I expect to be congratulated. To me, the accomplishment of the task is sweeter than the money I make in the process.

That's why I liked pitching so much. It was a one-on-one confrontation, just me against the batter. The guy standing out in right field might be in on three or four plays all afternoon, but as a pitcher, I was in control of the game. If I won, I did it on my own. If I failed, I did that on my own, too. I like golf for the same reason. It's just me and the ball against the green.

The popular image of me as a rebellious baseball player has some merit, but not much. Most of what you may have heard was blown way out of proportion. I'll admit, though, that some of it was true. The first summer I played professional baseball, I left my team in Clinton, Ia., against orders about three times to drive back to Chicago to see my girlfriend. Each time the manager found out, and each time he fined me. The fines bothered me, but I wasn't going to stand for some minor league manager telling me what to do—especially when a woman was involved.

My attitude improved when I advanced to the major leagues, although I still managed to cut corners. On days I wasn't scheduled to pitch, I sometimes wandered into the clubhouse 15 or 20 minutes before game time. Other times I might not show up at all. But you know what? I had the club's permission. My manager knew what I was doing and he said OK. But the way the Detroit media wrote about it, you'd have thought I was getting away with murder! The fact of the matter was that as long as I was winning, nobody on the Tigers worried too much about how I budgeted my time.

I'm still not too comfortable with authority figures. Judges, for instance. The judge in my trial exercised her authority over me in a way that was downright sickening. She allowed things to happen in her courtroom that were unfair, and the sentence she gave me was completely outrageous. Just unbelievable. And the 11th Circuit Court of Appeals confirmed her outrageousness. I wasn't too crazy about having to answer to guards and wardens in prison, either. At least they were just doing their job. The judge was abusing hers.

As you've probably figured out by now, I have a bit of an inflated ego. Well, maybe more than a bit. I mean, would any other 18-year-old kid repeatedly run out on his team in his first year of professional baseball—and expect to get away with it? Only Denny McLain. And lo and behold, I got away with it. I learned long ago that when you have a highly sought talent, you can write your own ticket. I was a damn good pitcher, and I knew it. Unless I became intolerable, teams weren't going to discipline me much for breaking a few rules. That's exactly what happened in Detroit. I could've starred in a weekly TV show and served as ambassador to Ireland while I was pitching for the Tigers, and they wouldn't have cared, as long as I was around to pitch every fourth day. And to win, of course.

So, I took my share of liberties and won lots of games, and everyone was happy. Until 1970, that is. That was when everything went wrong and the Tigers were forced to call me on the carpet. But by that time I'd had it with Detroit anyhow and was glad to part ways with the Tigers. Little did I know the grass isn't always greener in other major league pastures.

I can see the gears turning in your mind. You're looking beyond my baseball career and thinking that if I have such a big head, I probably consider myself above the law and so I probably was guilty of the charges that put me in jail. Well, you're wrong. I know what I'm good at—selling things, promoting things, drumming up business—but I don't consider myself above the law. I never have. I may not always agree with the law—Exhibit A, my stand on gambling—but I respect it. I knew that if I got caught breaking the law, I'd have to pay the price, and rightfully so. And I sure as hell wouldn't expect to get away with extortion and selling drugs, which I do consider criminal, just because of who I am. If anything, being Denny McLain is what got me in trouble. I was a legitimate businessman. I was greedy and I just got tangled up with some of the wrong people. They implicated me, a high-profile guy, in their moronic schemes just to save their own skins.

I've blamed the media for a few of my problems over the years, so it should come as no surprise that I blame sportswriters in part for giving me the big head. Ever since I was a teen-ager, newspapers have run stories about how great a pitcher I was. That was nice, but the problem was that I started to believe what I read. And the more they wrote, the more I believed it. My ego grew to a proportion that was out of whack with reality. After my baseball career ended, my ego didn't just disappear. Once you've been successful in a big way, like I was in baseball, you want it to continue no matter what you're doing. You want the applause, the pats on the back, the awards. Unfortunately, the only real award in the business world is the bottom line—the net profit. Maybe that's another reason why I've always felt pushed to make money. It's a boost to my ego.

As you might guess, my ego took a beating when I went to prison. I considered it a tremendous injustice that I was sentenced to 23 years, and I certainly didn't consider myself a criminal. But that didn't change the fact that I was convicted, separated from the rest of society by guards and walls and barbed wire. I had to eat the same slop, sleep on the same concrete slabs and endure the same humiliation as any other convict. I came out of prison a lot humbler and, I hope, wiser.

The saddest part of all is that I could have been a whole lot wiser a whole lot sooner if I'd ever listened to the advice of one specific person. In this book you'll read about a lot of guys I would have been better off never having met, and in almost every case this person had warned me to steer clear of them. But I thought I knew better, and so I didn't really respect that advice. Big mistake. As I discovered too late, the person who really knew better was my wife, Sharyn.

Sharyn is a saint. A true saint. She is everything I could possibly want in a wife. I realize that sounds like a guilty conscience's plea for forgiveness, and that certainly is part of it. I've put Sharyn through more hell than any person should have to endure in a dozen lifetimes. Yet, somehow, she's stuck by me all these years. That's the greatest miracle in my life. A friend of mine once told me, "You've said an awful lot of dumb things in your life, Denny, but the smartest thing you ever said was 'I do.' " He was right.

Sharyn is a beautiful lady. She's a lot of fun to talk to and to be with, and she has a good head on her shoulders. She's also a terrific mother. We have two boys and two girls. Our oldest child is Kristin, who was born in 1965, two years after we were married. Then we have Dennis (born in 1967) and Timothy (1969), both of whom we adopted as infants. Our youngest is Michelle, who came along in 1972. I'm more proud of my family than I am of any baseball award I ever won, and Sharyn is primarily responsible for that. If somebody gave out a Cy Young Award for wives and mothers, she'd win it every year.

While I was in prison, a fellow inmate asked me if I had learned anything from the whole experience of being arrested, convicted and incarcerated. I told him I'd learned a lot about my wife. I loved her very much, and I always had, but I never really learned how wonderful she is until I went to prison. She's my best pal.

I always considered myself the strong one in our relationship. I had the typical male chauvinist's attitude that it was the man's job to bring home the bacon and the woman's job to cook it. I didn't think women were capable of making major decisions, so I made them all myself. As boss of the household, I did pretty much whatever I pleased and expected Sharyn to just live with it. During the early years of our marriage, I did a number of things that could have driven her away. I gambled a lot, spent money frivolously, ignored her at times and, worst of all, I abused her trust. For the most part, she put up with all my crap, and I guess I took that as a sign of her weakness, her inability to make it without me. It was a sign of love, but I was too dumb and too vain to figure that out.

Then I was convicted and everything changed. Suddenly, I was in prison with no source of income and Sharyn was left to fend for herself and the kids. We had no money. She had to deal not only with the indignity of her husband being sent to jail after a highly publicized trial, but also the reality of paying the rent and putting food on the table. Sharyn got a job. The kids helped out, too, but they could earn only so much. Some friends of ours loaned us money, which was a miracle in itself. It takes a real friend to loan money to someone who might not be able to start paying you back for 23 years. We also got some help after the formation of the Baseball Alumni Team in 1986. That's a group of former players who help out other former players in need. For part of the time I was in prison, B.A.T. made arrangements to pay the rent on the apartment where my family lived. I'll never forget that.

For 2½ years, Sharyn had no husband, no money, a ton of responsibilities and little hope. Why did she stay? Why didn't she just pack up and get out while the gettin' was good? As I finally learned, she stayed because she's strong —a lot stronger than I am. On nights when those jail walls would be closing in on me, when I would have fits of depression that made me seriously question whether or not I wanted to keep on living, she was my strength. I'd call her, and she was a rock. Instead of her breaking into tears, she was the one consoling me while I sobbed like a baby. I went to prison thinking I was the strong one, but I know now that if it hadn't been for Sharyn, I literally couldn't have survived my prison term. She saved my life.

This book is the story of a guy who made mistakes. Lots of them. I'm sorry about some of the things I did, and I'm not sorry about others. I wouldn't want to do it all over again, but the biggest reason for that is not because I'm afraid of returning to prison. My biggest regret is the hurt I inflicted on a woman whose only crime was loving me. Women with her determination, her devotion and her class are much more rare than 30-game winners.

This book also is the story of a guy who has known some pretty good times, but whose best years may still be ahead of him. I can't predict the future, but with Sharyn by my side, I like my chances. For now, let me fill you in on the events that led me to the pinnacle of baseball success and the depths of the federal prison system. I didn't rush into my life story in this chapter because I wanted to introduce myself first. I wanted you to know a little bit about what makes Denny McLain tick. I guarantee you that without that background, you wouldn't believe I actually did some of the things I did. Like they say, truth is stranger than fiction.

My life is proof of that.

CHAPTER 2

Growing Pains

On March 29, 1944, Tom and Betty McLain of Chicago became the proud parents of their first child, Dennis Dale McLain. Little did they know! My brother, Tim, was born two years later and we lived six or seven uneventful years on Chicago's South Side, not far from Midway Airport, before moving to Markham. It was in Markham, a suburb on Chicago's South Side, that Tim and I grew up.

My dad, mom, brother and I were pretty close. We had a lot of relatives in the Chicago area, but didn't socialize with them a whole lot. We'd get together with my aunts, uncles, cousins and so on for weddings and that kind of thing, but that was about it. My family, as I saw it, was limited to the four of us in our little two-bedroom frame house, isolated at the top of a hill in Markham.

My dad was a very honest, hard-working man. But he also was a classic victim of the daily grind and the work ethic, even though he had some interesting talents. At various times in his life he worked as a truck driver, an insurance adjuster, a factory worker and even an organ and piano teacher and player. But times were tough and he often had to work two jobs to make ends meet. Putting food on our table, a roof over our heads and decent clothes on our backs was his No. 1 goal and, judging by those standards, he was a spectacular success.

My dad started me on the organ when I was 8 or 9, and I've been playing it ever since. A lot of my friends thought the organ was for sissies, but I loved it. I got teased a little bit, but that didn't stop me from practicing two or three hours every day. I took lessons for several years from various tutors because my dad decided his opinion of my ability was too subjective. A prodigy I was not, but I eventually became talented enough that people paid me to play. My entertainment career was directly related to my baseball popularity and pretty much fizzled out after I hung up my spikes. My most recent organ performances were of a different nature; I played at Mass in prison. It wasn't exactly Vegas, but I did have a captive audience. I still enjoy the organ very much, especially picking up a sheet of music I've never seen before, reading it and playing it. People don't believe this, but most of the time I enjoyed playing the organ more than playing baseball.

I learned a lot about baseball from my dad, too. When I was 7, he tried to get me onto a team for 8-year-olds in the nearby town of Midlothian. The manager let me try out, and my baseball debut was nothing short of spectacular. I played right field and went 5 for 5 in a six-inning game. The manager was ready to give me a long-term contract until he found out that we lived in

Markham. Bad news. This was a Midlothians-only league, so I couldn't play.

My dad was more disappointed than I was. "Well," he said, "we'll just have to start our own team in Markham." And that's exactly what he did. The American Legion sponsored our team, which later that summer got the chance to play the Midlothian team three times. To say that my dad really wanted to beat those guys was an understatement. And beat them we did. We creamed them the first two games and won the last game by a run. I was the reason the last game was close. I had to play first base when another kid didn't show up, and I couldn't field a ground ball that day if my life depended on it. I made seven errors and it got so bad that the kids on the other team were yelling, "Hit it to the first baseman!" After my seventh error I started crying, like any other 7-year-old kid would. The same thing happened in our last game of the year— seven errors at first base and I ran off bawling. It was a good thing that was our season finale because as mad as my dad was, I sure as hell wouldn't have played another inning that year.

My dad, who had played shortstop on a semipro team in Chicago for several years, continued to manage all my Little League teams. When I was 9 or 10, he let me start pitching. He recognized that I could throw the ball harder than anybody else in our leagues, and he taught me two things that helped make me a successful pitcher. No. 1, throw strikes. If you don't walk people, you'll do OK. No. 2, throw as hard as you can as long as you can. It was power, power and more power—no curveballs. It was a very basic philosophy. You should leave with the same girl you took to the dance, even when you get in trouble, and that was what he was saying about pitching. Both pieces of advice stuck with me and helped me through the years.

My brother picked up a few pointers about baseball from my dad, too. Timmy was my catcher on a couple of our Little League teams, but he developed into a pretty good pitcher himself. He was a righthander, just like me, and we became fairly competitive.

Timmy was considered a pretty good pro prospect for a while, and the Chicago White Sox signed him to a minor league contract in 1965. But Timmy just couldn't throw the ball hard enough, so he tried to get by with a curveball, which is hard to do in the minors. His baseball career ended a couple of years later when he suffered a pinched nerve in an auto accident.

Timmy and I both discovered early on that when it came to discipline, my dad believed in using a firm hand and a long strap. The incident I recall best was when I was about 11 and I decided to run away from home. I wasn't unhappy, but I had missed my curfew, which was a mortal sin in the McLain household. I had been out playing ball and was supposed to be home by dark. But here I was, arriving back at my street well after 9 p.m. It was pitch black and I knew what was waiting for me.

I didn't run too far. They were building some houses about half a block away from our house, and I hid in one of those until about midnight, trying to decide what to do next. There had been some activity around the neighborhood with cars coming and going and people yelling, and then all of a sudden, a bunch of police cars pulled up to my house. When the cops started combing the streets, I knew what was going on. Three young boys had been viciously murdered in Chicago. The "Schuessler murders"—two of the victims were brothers named Schuessler—was big news around town because the killer hadn't been caught. When I didn't come home, my dad and the entire Markham Police Department thought, "Oh my God, Dennis has been killed."

A bad situation had gotten worse. I knew they were looking for me, so I figured I'd better get home and face the music before my parents worried themselves to death. When I straggled in, I told my dad, crying, that I had run away because I thought nobody loved me. Well, that was a big lie. I was running away because I'd missed my curfew and I knew I would get my ass tanned. And I wasn't disappointed. I got a tanning that night that nobody should ever get. I mean, sitting was out of the question for a week. It was that bad.

My dad was stern, but he was always fair. Our relationship certainly never suffered because of it. We were very close. I loved him and he loved me. He took an active interest in whatever I did, and I learned a lot from him.

When he was around, that is. I hated the way he was always working. It was like he was only a part-time father, a guy I'd see on weekends. I resented that.

Actually, I resented my mother for that. I think she pushed my dad to work so much. If he'd had a choice, I don't think he would have worked two jobs. As a result, my mother and I didn't always get along. And whatever we had by way of a relationship was destroyed after my father died when I was 15.

On May 4, 1959, I pitched a game for Mount Carmel High School. My dad never missed one of my games—he always arranged his work schedule so that he could get away for a couple of hours. So I naturally looked for him up in the stands. No sign of him. When he still hadn't showed up by the end of the game, I started to feel a little uncomfortable. I figured he'd been tied up at work or in traffic or something, so I hung around at the ball park and waited for him to come by to give me a ride. After waiting about an hour, I finally took a bus home.

When I arrived in front of our house, I knew something was wrong. I saw some of my relatives going inside and I noticed my father's car parked out front. I went in and saw my mother.

"Your father is dead," she said.

That was it. There was no compassion, no tears, no putting an arm around me, not even an "I'm sorry." No big deal, just like she was telling me dinner was ready. "Your father is dead." While driving to my game, my dad had suffered a heart attack. He died right down the street from Comiskey Park.

I was shattered. No one in this world meant as much to me as my dad, and he was gone. I was left with my brother and my mother, and after the way she told me about my dad's death, there was no way we could ever be close.

We haven't gotten along since. Our relationship, if you can call it that, got worse when she got married again—to a guy named Tom, of all things—less than a year after my dad died. I had a lot of trouble dealing with that, so I'm partly to blame for our not getting along. I can understand now that she was entitled to go on with her life, but that sure didn't make any sense to me as a teen-ager. All I knew was that some guy was sleeping in my father's bed, and I didn't buy it. There's no question that when they got divorced a couple of years later, one of the big reasons why was me.

My mother and I haven't communicated much since I began playing professional baseball. She has reappeared in my life here and there, but not too often. We had a truce of sorts in 1968, when I was winning 31 games and leading the Detroit Tigers to a world championship. And when she decided to get married again sometime after that, she let me know that they wanted to buy a house in Plant City, Fla. I helped arrange the financing for that house. That doesn't entitle me to take any bows; she was my mother, after all, and I'm sure she made a few sacrifices for me that I never heard about. Besides, you have obligations and duties to your mother, even if you don't see eye to eye. But when I got into trouble and was sent to jail, she was still living in that house in Plant City—not 30 miles from where my family was living—and she never came by, never called Sharyn, never even sent her grandchildren a Christmas card. I can't forget, or ignore, that.

It's important that you realize I don't blame my mother for what has happened to me the last few years. I can't respect people who get into trouble and try to blame all their problems on their parents. It doesn't work that way. Make no mistake, my mother didn't put me in jail any more than she made me a Cy Young Award winner. I'll take the credit and the blame. But it occurred to me that since I'm a comparatively young man and my mother is alive, you might wonder why you don't read much about her in this book. Now you know.

Not long after my dad died, the guy who ran the barbershop in Markham gave me chance to make some money. I worked part-time at a grocery store, but this was different. Poppa, as he was called, asked me one day if I would do him a favor. We lived near Route 6, a big trucking highway, and he asked me to carry a package over to the truck stop. For this small service, Poppa gave me $5—not bad money at all. He asked me to carry another package to the truck stop the next day, then the next day, the day after that and so on. After about a week I not only had $35, but I also knew why.

Poppa was running a numbers bank. The truck stop was just one of many places in town where people could place a bet on the number. All the bets from around town were sent over to Poppa. After the winning number was announced, Poppa would send some of that money back to the truck stop and the other betting places, where the winners collected their money and the people who took the action got their percentage. The man in charge of transporting all this money was yours truly.

It took me only a week or so to figure out what was going on. Not that it bothered me. Poppa increased my wages and my responsibilities before long, and that suited me fine. Besides the truck stop, I had eight or nine regular stops. For this I made $10 a day.

Why me? Well, I don't think Poppa was using me as a patsy. A patsy is someone who gets conned into doing something illegal, or at least looking like he is, to protect the real criminals. In other words, a sucker. Drug dealers often use patsies. They'll give drugs to 10- and 12-year-old kids to deliver for them because if the kids get caught, they won't get sent to jail. If that sounds slimy, consider this: Some of those dealers pay the kids off in drugs, too. It's sick.

I learned all about being a patsy long after I had left Chicago. At my trial, my lawyer told the jury I was "a perfect patsy," and it was the truth. All these guys around me had been breaking the law, and when they got caught, they set me up to take the fall for them. Great guys!

No, I don't think Poppa was using me as a patsy. I think he picked me to be his numbers runner because he felt sorry for me. He knew I was upset about losing my dad, and he knew my family could use the money. It was illegal, of course, but I really think he was just being nice. I was grateful.

Running numbers didn't make a gambler out of me. I don't know what did, but it wasn't numbers. As I've already confessed, I'm no nuclear physicist, but even at 15 I was smart enough to figure out that playing the numbers is a bad bet. You bet on a combination of three numbers. These numbers are determined by different methods in different places. Anyway, if your number comes up, you get back $600 for every dollar you bet. Sounds great, doesn't it? Problem is, the odds aren't 600-to-1; they're 999-to-1. (You can bet 000, too.) You don't have to be Albert Einstein to figure out that if you're paying 600-to-1 on 999-to-1 shots, you're going to make some serious money.

Why do people play the numbers? The biggest reason, I guess, is that it's a poor man's game. You can bet a dime, a quarter, whatever you want. Also, the state lotteries, another poor man's game, weren't around then like they are now.

The lottery is another gamble that doesn't appeal to me. They say you can bet a dollar and win a million in the lottery. Not really. You bet a dollar and win some of the interest on a million. They don't hand you a check for $1 million. You get $50,000 a year for 20 years. If they gave you $1 million up front, you probably could pay your taxes, get the rest in tax-free bonds and still have the $1 million when the 20 years were up. If you win, of course, it's great. But the bet still doesn't make sense because the odds against winning are enormous.

Running numbers was an easy job. I knew all the stops and most of the people who were handling the bets. They knew me, too, because everybody knows everybody in a small town like Markham. One of my stops was St. Gerard Majella, the parish where I went to school through the third grade. No, the priests and nuns weren't playing the numbers. Many of the parishioners did, though. They would drop off their bets with the caretaker, and I'd pick them up from him. Another stop was a liquor store, and one of the biggest was the VFW Post.

I remember really being scared in there one day. I walked in with a paper bag full of money and heard someone say, "Hello, Denny." It was a cop who knew me because I played softball on the Police Department's team. I said hello and tried to stay cool. We talked baseball for a few minutes, and he went on his way. That shook me up, but not half as much as a similar episode more than two decades later. In 1982, a passenger on my airplane spotted a couple of cops walking toward the plane and told me he had a pound of cocaine in his briefcase. Now that's beyond scary. That's heart-attack time.

You might wonder whether I was ever tempted to steal some of that numbers money I was carting around town. In all honesty, I wasn't. I was getting paid well for a very simple job, so why jeopardize it? In fact, the thought never even occurred to me. But I couldn't have stolen the money even if I'd wanted to. Every day, Poppa gave me a taped-up paper bag. I couldn't have disturbed it without leaving traces. At the other end of my route, the guys taking the bets usually gave me an envelope to take back to Poppa. They scribbled all over the back flap and onto the rest of the envelope. It would have been impossible to unseal the envelope, take out some money and reseal it without disturbing those marks. I tell you I was honest by choice, but I admit I really didn't have a choice.

I ran numbers for about a year and then quit. I went back once for about six weeks, but I had to give it up because I was too busy playing baseball. I'd like to say my conscience could no longer bear the guilt associated with my role in this illegal game, but that wasn't the case at all. In fact, I had done something else illegal in the interest of my ball-playing career. I lied about where I lived.

Back then, there was nothing bigger than Babe Ruth League, a national baseball program for teen-agers. But there was a problem. We didn't have a Babe Ruth League in Markham. They had one in Harvey, which was about 15 miles away, but you had to live in Harvey to play in that league. It was the Midlothian situation all over again. This time I decided to work around the problem. I had an aunt who lived in Harvey, so I used her address and played in the Babe Ruth League there.

Even at that age, I was a heck of a player. I could throw the ball harder and hit the ball farther than anybody. When I wasn't pitching I'd play the outfield, although my first love, besides pitching, was shortstop. Unfortunately, I fielded ground balls more like Ozzie Nelson than Ozzie Smith. That didn't matter, though, because it was quite clear that my arm, not my glove, would be my ticket to the major leagues.

In the summer of 1959, just a couple of months after my father died, I got the biggest break of my life while playing in a Babe Ruth League game in Harvey. Ironically, my good fortune was the result of me striking out. After the umpire had called me out, I got so mad I threw my bat. It flipped end over end into the first row of bleachers, where it hit a girl on the leg. I ran right over to apologize and to make sure she was OK. This petite little girl with a pretty smile and a brunet ponytail was wearing blue Bermuda shorts, a white blouse and white tennis shoes, and she was absolutely the most stunning thing I'd ever seen.

Actually, this young beauty had been pointed out to me before the game. You see, she was related to the No. 1 citizen of Harvey, Lou Boudreau. Lou had been a big college star at the University of Illinois in both basketball and baseball. He went on to play major league baseball with the Cleveland Indians. On top of being an outstanding shortstop, Lou was named manager of the Indians at the incredibly young age of 24. In 1948 he led Cleveland to an American League pennant. He later went to Boston and managed the Red Sox, but by the time I was playing in Harvey he had retired from the field and was broadcasting Chicago Cubs games. The girl I had hit with the bat was his daughter, Sharyn.

Before I go on, I want to say something about Lou Boudreau. I've put him through a lot of grief. No father likes it when his son-in-law makes his daughter unhappy, as I've done way too many times, or makes national headlines and eventually goes to jail, as I've done once too often. It's especially tough when both men are in the same business and know many of the same people.

I've given Lou plenty of reasons to picture himself taking a baseball bat and seeing how far he could hit my head. But he has been supportive of Sharyn and the kids, if not always me, and he has done it with a lot of class. He's a Hall of Famer in more ways than one. I hope and pray that I've embarrassed him for the last time.

Back to Sharyn. As soon as that game was over, I went looking for her. I wanted to tell her again how sorry I was for hitting her with the bat. Hell, I'd apologized enough already; what I really wanted was an excuse to talk to her again and, frankly, to get another peek at those Bermuda shorts. Unfortunately, she already had left.

For the record, Sharyn remembers that day a little differently. She says we met after a pitch I threw while warming up got past the catcher and hit her in the leg as she was walking behind the plate. I still say it was a bat I threw in anger. We've been debating this point for years, though it really doesn't matter. Whatever I hit her with, it was the most fortunate accident of my life.

I didn't see Sharyn again for a few weeks. My team went on to win the Babe Ruth League state title, and after the championship game in Mattoon, Ill., we drove back and had a big celebration in Harvey. The master of ceremonies for the event was Lou Boudreau. Even better, Sharyn was there, too. She congratulated me and we talked briefly, but that was about it. I was starting to develop quite a crush.

A few weeks later, I got up the courage to go visit Sharyn in Harvey one afternoon. Harvey was a pretty good ride from Markham on my Schwinn three-speed racer, which was the only source of transportation available to a kid who was still a year away from getting his driver's license. I pedaled like mad to get there as fast as I could, and the trip still took me more than an hour. But it was worth it when I walked up to her front door and Sharyn showed up wearing those same tight blue Bermuda shorts. She had the best-looking legs and bottom I had ever seen in my life, and I have to tell you, she still does.

Sharyn came outside and we sat together on the front porch, just talking. I was in heaven. This gorgeous creature, who was a year ahead of me in school no less, seemed interested in me! But about 10 minutes later, my bubble burst. A guy driving a '57 Chevy pulled up in her driveway. He was wearing a leather jacket with a rolled-up collar and blue jeans, and his hair was combed back in a ducktail. An honest-to-God greaser! This was the kind of guy that jocks like me and nice girls like Sharyn did not hang around. I figured he must've been lost.

No such luck. Imagine my surprise when he got out of his car and Sharyn called him by name!

"This is Louie," Sharyn said to me, "and we've made plans to go get some ice cream. We'll be back in an hour. If you can, come back then. I'd like to talk to you some more."

With that, they were off in the '57 Chevy, and I was left standing in the driveway, holding my bike and scratching my fingers through my crewcut.

I couldn't believe it. Why in the world would Lou Boudreau's daughter, of all people, be more interested in a greaser than the star of the local baseball team? It didn't make sense.

Well, I figured it couldn't have been me, so it must have been the car. He had one and I didn't. That was the only logical explanation. So, with lust in my heart (love would come later), I tried to think of a way to impress Sharyn.

To kill time, I rode my bike about four blocks to the Babe Ruth League ball park. One of my coaches, Les Duncan, was there with a few of my teammates for an informal workout. I quickly spotted Les Duncan's car—a beautiful white Edsel! It was a convertible, and the top was already down and the keys were in the ignition.

My mission was clear: Borrow Les' Edsel.

It took most of the hour that Sharyn said she would be gone to persuade Les to loan me his car. He knew I was 15, but after convincing him that I knew how to drive, he said OK.

Sharyn and her friend wheeled into the driveway just as I drove up in the Edsel. I parked on the street so the guy could let Sharyn out and be on his way. And that's just what he did. He backed out of the driveway, and if looks could kill, I would have been dead. He stared at me, gunned his engine, spun his tires and screeched off down the road.

As Sharyn walked over, I was as nervous as a whore in church. I was driving without a license and I didn't know what she would think of that. She liked the car all right, but she nearly exploded when she found out I was too young to drive it.

"You take that car back to Les this minute!" she yelled. "Then you come back and we'll sit down and talk."

You'd have thought I was selling secrets to the Russians or something! I was just trying to impress her. But I knew better than to argue. I pumped the accelerator and, wouldn't you know it, the car wouldn't start. The engine was flooded. I finally got it going about 30 minutes later. Talk about embarrassed! I felt like sinking into the seat.

By that time I had no intention of coming back to her house that night. I could only imagine the next thing that would go wrong. Sharyn suggested that we try it again sometime, but we didn't. We went to different high schools that were several miles apart, and it just never worked out. I ran into her around town every now and then and I never forgot how pretty she was, but I didn't try to date her. More than three years went by before I pursued Sharyn again.

Meanwhile, I kept playing baseball. It became increasingly apparent that I had professional potential. In my four years at Mount Carmel, I won 38 games and lost seven. Not bad, huh? Academically, I was getting by with Cs. I probably could have done better, but school just didn't interest me. I enjoyed writing classes, where I could express myself, but algebra, geography and all that other stuff just weren't my thing. I didn't even consider going to college on a baseball scholarship—not with the scouts coming around and talking about paying me to do what I liked best.

The White Sox offered me a $17,000 bonus to sign a minor league contract with them, and in May 1962 I gave them my autograph. They gave me $10,000 up front, with the rest to be delivered in contingency bonuses based on my progress. I thought I was rich. I promptly went out and bought two cars, a Pontiac LeMans convertible for myself and a LeMans hardtop for my mother.

I didn't waste any time waiting around to launch my baseball career. Three hours after my high school graduation, I was on a plane bound for the minor leagues. It was the first airplane trip of my life, and I tell you, it sure wasn't love at first flight. I was scared to death.

The plane's destination was Knoxville, but my destination was Harlan, Ky., where I would play with other rookies in the Appalachian League. As I rolled into town on a Greyhound bus and checked into a hotel, it became quite evident that regardless of what the geography books indicate, you can't get much farther from the big leagues than Harlan, Ky. This place was miles from nowhere, a real hick town down where Kentucky, Tennessee and Virginia all meet. It didn't help matters when someone told me that there had been a shootout on Main Street just the day before. Wonderful, I was starting my career around the corner from the OK Corral.

I encountered some deplorable conditions in prison, but only Atlanta was worse than that rickety old hotel in Harlan. At least the prisons had toilets. In Harlan, the room I shared had two single beds and a wash basin. That was it. The toilet and shower, complete with rusty water, were down the hall. You had to wait your turn. It took less than a day to dispel any misconceptions I had about the glamour of playing minor league baseball. After sitting around the hotel for three very lonely hours with absolutely nothing to do, I knew I wanted to get the hell out of Harlan as soon as possible.

The major leagues seemed like light-years away as I took the mound for my professional debut a few days later. Think I was nervous? I guess I should have been. After all, I was away from home for the first time in my life, which was traumatic enough, and this was my first game ever against people who played baseball for a living. I was lonely, depressed and disgusted. But I sure as hell wasn't nervous about throwing a baseball. I was so confident, in fact, that I pitched a no-hitter.

Isn't that something? First time out of the gate, a no-hitter. Hell, I'd never even pitched nine innings before. And I did it with nothing but fastballs. At the time, it was the only pitch I knew. I never pitched another no-hitter, but it was a hell of a way to get started.

One of my teammates in Harlan was Ronnie Boyer, a third baseman just like his brothers Ken and Clete. Imagine that, a mother and father put into this world to breed third basemen. Anyway, I thought I was hot stuff after throwing the no-hitter, and since we didn't have a game the next day, I borrowed Ronnie's car and drove home with another guy on the team. That's right, to Markham, where I just knew this redheaded gal I'd been dating would be so happy to see me. It didn't look that far on a map—only about 10 inches, as I recall—and I figured it would be a snap to cruise up to Markham, spend the evening with the redhead and hustle back to Harlan in time for practice the morning after the off-day.

Little did I know that 10 inches on the map translated to 17 hours in the car. A slight miscalculation on my part. That meant that by the time I arrived in Markham, the only way I could make it back in time for practice was if I turned around immediately. Even then I might not make it, especially since I'd have to stop somewhere and get some sleep. Well, I figured I'd come all that way to see my girlfriend, so I might as well stay.

It's amazing how quickly your star can be brought back to earth. When my teammate and I didn't show up for our next practice, Glen Miller was boiling. Miller was the director of farm clubs for the White Sox, not to mention the man most responsible for my getting a pro contract. He got on the phone and finally reached the redhead, who relayed this message: "If Denny is not in Harlan by game time tomorrow night, he need not show up at all. And I'll see to it that he never plays pro baseball again."

Now is that any way to talk to a guy who just threw a no-hitter? I thought not, but I also thought I'd better hightail it back to Dodge City. I picked up my teammate, drove like hell and arrived in Harlan by noon the next day, cutting three hours off the time of my trip up there. As expected, the manager bawled me out and said that I'd better not pull another stunt like that again. I didn't, either—not for a couple of weeks, anyway.

And what about the guy who made the trip with me? He got released.

I lost my next time out, but I gave up only two unearned runs in another complete game and upped my strikeout total to 32. That's almost two an inning! The White Sox decided that even if I wasn't overly bright, I was talented enough to move one rung up the minor league ladder. They sent me to Clinton, Ia., in the Class-D Midwest League.

That may have been the sensible baseball move, but in terms of trying to keep me away from temptation, it was awful. Clinton was only 3½ hours away from Markham. A mere 3½ hours between me and that pretty redhead. And I didn't have to worry about borrowing a car, either, because I took my new convertible up to Clinton with me. It was time to make some more unauthorized trips home.

Ira Hutchinson, my manager at Clinton, had warned me about going AWOL, but I couldn't resist. One night shortly after I arrived in Clinton, I hopped in my car, crossed the toll bridge over the Mississippi River and boogied over to Chicago. I came back the next afternoon around 5 p.m., just in time for batting practice, and walked into the clubhouse.

"That'll be 100," Ira said.

"What are you talking about, Mr. Hutchinson?"

"That's $100 for going over the bridge. I told you not to leave town. Don't do it again."

How did he know I'd gone to Chicago? I couldn't figure it out. But I was making only $500 a month, so that fine really hurt.

About a week later, I got the urge to try it again. I went over, saw my girlfriend, came back the next afternoon and went straight to my locker.

"McLain." It was Hutchinson again.

"Yes, sir."

"That's 200."

My jaw hit the floor. "Come on, Mr. Hutchinson, I can't afford that."

"Then you can't afford the bridge. Forget the bridge."

Two hundred bucks was serious money. Add that to my other fine, and my first paycheck in Clinton was next to nothing. That kept me grounded for a while.

Then came the last week of the season, and once more I felt compelled to take off. But I thought something funny might be going on at the bridge crossing, so this time I drove about 15 miles north to the next toll bridge and crossed there. If Hutchinson had an informant working for him at the bridge, I was one step ahead of them both.

When I returned the next afternoon, I figured I was free and clear. And then I saw Ira walking toward me.

"McLain, that's 400."

"You're crazy!" I yelled. "How, Mr. Hutchinson? How did you know? How?"

"Let me tell you how," he said. "You know that guy in the toll bridge the first two times you went across?"

"Well, I had a pretty good hunch," I said, "but this time I went to the other bridge."

"Guess what, McLain. He got transferred."

I couldn't win.

On the field, either. I went 4-7 in 16 games at Clinton, but I still averaged just over one strikeout per inning. Part of the reason I struggled was because Hutchinson was trying to teach me to throw a curveball. He said one-pitch pitchers don't last long, which is true, but as nice a guy as he was, he wasn't much of a teacher. And I wasn't much of a student because I resisted the change, remembering what my dad had said about sticking with the fastball. I learned the curve and a couple of other pitches down the line, but it just messed me up in '62.

After the season, the White Sox rewarded me with a major league contract. That was pretty big news back in Markham and Harvey, where Sharyn Boudreau heard about my good fortune. She must have been pretty impressed because she wrote me a letter to congratulate me. At the time, I was playing in an instructional league in Sarasota, Fla., and I was pleasantly surprised to hear from her. I did the obvious thing and wrote her back. The correspondence began to build, and before we knew it we couldn't wait for the mailman to arrive each day. So, we started calling each other. Over the next few weeks we spent a fortune on long-distance phone calls. But boy, was it worth it. Just like all the calls I made to Sharyn from prison were worth the cost. Without those calls, I'd have gone loony and they'd have put me on the funny farm.

Just before Christmas in 1962, I returned to Chicago. I picked up Sharyn at the bank where she worked and we went to a diner in Harvey. On New Year's Eve, while watching the movie "West Side Story," I made the smartest move of my life and she made the dumbest. I asked her to marry me, and she said yes. We spent much of the next few weeks going to movies and getting to know each other a little better.

The White Sox invited me to spring training in 1963, but they had a problem. I was one of three young bonus pitchers in their organization that year and in those days, a club had to either put a bonus player on the major league roster after his first year or leave him unprotected, thus giving other clubs a chance to acquire his contract. The problem for the White Sox was that they had room on their roster for only two of the bonus pitchers. One of us had to be left unprotected. The commissioner of baseball, Ford Frick, already had ruled that one of the other guys would have to be protected, so it came down to me or the other guy. The White Sox decided to keep the other guy and risk losing the $17,000 they already had invested in me. That's the way it goes in baseball.

One of the two pitchers the White Sox kept went on to become a genuine superstar—but not in baseball. Dave DeBusschere won three games and lost four in his brief career with the White Sox before settling on basketball, a sport in which he became a Hall of Famer, playing first with the Detroit Pistons and later the New York Knicks. The other guy they chose over me, Bruce Howard, went 25-25 for Chicago from 1963 through 1967 and then was traded to the Baltimore Orioles for the 1968 season, his last in the majors. He now is in the insurance business in Florida.

In baseball terminology, the White Sox placed me on first-year waivers. That meant that any other club could acquire my contract by paying the White Sox the going waivers price ($8,000 back then). Would anybody want me? Well, I'd pitched pretty well in 1962, so it seemed quite possible. I had been excited about the possibility of pitching for one of the teams in my hometown, but it looked like I might have to leave.

Let me back up a few months to set the stage for what happened next. Back in 1962, Ed Katalinas, the chief scout for the Detroit Tigers, was on the road looking at minor league clubs. He was driving through Iowa one day when he came to a fork in the road. One road led to Burlington, where the Pittsburgh Pirates had a farm team in the Midwest League, while the other led to Clinton. It didn't matter to Katalinas which road he took; he'd get to both cities eventually. For no particular reason, Katalinas decided to go to Clinton. That decision was to have a tremendous influence on my life and the lives of a lot of other people, particularly those who were baseball fans of the Detroit Tigers.

It just so happened that one Denny McLain was pitching for Clinton that night. Bear in mind that Katalinas didn't come to see me pitch. In fact, he'd never even heard of me. It was just a coincidence that I was scheduled to start that game. As it turned out, I pitched well and caught Eddie's eye. He then made a point of telling the Tigers that if my name ever showed up on a waivers list, they should grab me. And that's exactly what happened at the end of spring training in 1963. Detroit picked me off the waivers list and I became a Tiger.

That's what I call lucky. If Katalinas had taken the other road at that fork, he might have seen Clinton some other night when I wasn't pitching. Or he could have seen me pitch a bad game. My ego is big enough that I believe I eventually would have reached the big leagues anyway, but I can't be sure. I've seen some pretty talented ball players who never made it for one reason or another. It's also possible that some other club could've picked me up, perhaps a weak-hitting club. Even with my ego, I know that my big years with Detroit were the result of excellent offensive support as well as my pitching.

My first reaction to being a member of the Detroit Tigers organization was negative. I called Sharyn after hearing the news and informed her that I was going to quit if I couldn't play for a Chicago team. She screamed and yelled and told me there wasn't any room for quitters in her life. I listened and thus took my first big step toward baseball immortality.

The Tigers had to like what they saw me do in 1963. First they sent me to Duluth-Superior in the Class-A Northern League, where I posted a 13-2 record and registered more than three times as many strikeouts as walks. The Tigers saw that I was a man on the move and promoted me to Knoxville in the Double-A South Atlantic League, where I went 5-4. Impressed by that combined 18-6 record, the Tigers brought me up to Detroit in September to finish the year.

I made my major league debut September 21, 1963, at Tiger Stadium, and it came against, of all teams, the White Sox. Needless to say, I was plenty fired up to beat the team that had seen fit to let me go just a few months before. The adrenaline must have been pumping pretty fast because I hit a home run that afternoon, something I never did again as a major leaguer. That homer helped me post a 4-3 victory. I went on to win one more game and lose one in my only three games with the Tigers that fall.

Sharyn and I had seen each other no more than half a dozen times during that season, but we didn't waste a minute getting reacquainted. We had wedding plans for immediately after the season ended. Lou Boudreau had picked up a pretty big wedding tab for another daughter a couple of years earlier, and he wasn't crazy about doing it again. He asked Sharyn and me how we felt about eloping. It didn't matter to us, so we accepted his gift of $1,000 and took off for New Buffalo, Mich., which is just across the state line from Indiana. I was only 19 and Sharyn was 20, which was old enough to get married in Michigan without parental consent, but not in Illinois or Indiana. And my mother wasn't about to give her consent.

It had nothing to do with Sharyn. My mother was opposed to any woman entering my life at what she considered my tender young age. People were saying some very positive things about my potential as a baseball player, and she didn't want anyone or anything blocking my way. Maybe she was concerned for my sake, maybe she wanted a piece of whatever I stood to make down the line, maybe both. I don't know. But she was absolutely opposed to our marriage. Thus, the trip to Michigan.

We drove up to New Buffalo on October 5, 1963, along with Jack and Marie McLain and a girl named Marci, who worked at the bank with Sharyn. With Uncle Jack as my best man and Marci as Sharyn's maid of honor, we were married that day by a justice of the peace. Sharyn wore this cute little white dress, and I remember as we drove back to Chicago, I could hardly wait to get to our downtown hotel. Sharyn's mother had given us a bottle of champagne, but we didn't open the bottle for years. We had other things on our mind that night.

The next day, a Sunday, we held a reception for both sides of the family. Needless to say, my mother didn't come.

We had to squeeze that reception in right away because on Monday, I was off to play winter ball in Dunedin, Fla. Our honeymoon was short—two nights—but believe me, we made the most of them. As a result, I wasn't too excited about playing ball right then. Oh, I was happy about the opportunity to impress the Tigers some more. With any luck, maybe they'd put me on their opening-day roster the following spring. But remember, I was a 19-year-old newlywed and my mind was on Sharyn.

We were apart only six days when Sharyn joined me. She had given her boss at the bank two weeks' notice that she was going to quit, but she decided she couldn't wait that long. I was glad she came down early because until I first went to prison, those were the longest six days of my life. I don't have to tell you what we did when she arrived in Dunedin. Just use your imagination.

Unfortunately, I had to pitch the next day. I was kind of looking forward to it because I wanted to strut my stuff for Sharyn, but I did more ducking than strutting that day. Batters were spraying my pitches all over the field and I got knocked out in a hurry. I obviously had left my fastball in bed. When the manager, Bob Swift, came out to the mound and signaled for a reliever, I was standing there with a big smile on my face. You can imagine how well that went over with Swift.

Many theories have been proposed about athletes and sex. One theory is that sex actually enhances athletic performance. Competing in front of big crowds can build up a lot of tension for an athlete, and sex is supposed to help you relax. As much as I'd like to believe that theory, I don't. When I was pitching, sex always left me completely drained. If I had to pitch the next day, I guarantee you that I wouldn't last too long. I was too tired. If I hadn't abstained from sex before my starts with the Tigers, the Detroit bullpen would have been worked to death and my major league career would have been a lot shorter. I don't want to take anything away from Dr. Ruth, but the fact of the matter is that while sex may be great for muscle tone, it's hell on your earned-run average.

Sex is tougher on the athletes who work harder—fighters, for instance. Pitchers work harder than anyone else on a baseball team, so they have to be most careful. That was never easy for me because I always seemed to have the biggest appetite for sex the night before I was scheduled to pitch. You know how it is when you know you can't have something; that's when you want it most. But at least I knew when I was going to pitch, which is more than relief pitchers can say. They never know when they'll be called into a game. On the other hand, relievers don't usually pitch more than two or three innings anyway. I don't know how relievers—or everyday players, for that matter—handle this, but I can't imagine they are celibate from opening day until the season is over. That's a good way for a married guy to wind up single. But I know that after the experience in Dunedin, I was careful to avoid sex the night before I was scheduled to pitch.

Remember that big smile I had on my face when Swift took me out of that game? Well, it was gone a few months later when I opened the 1964 season in the minors. But that was only a minor setback. The big time was right around the corner.

CHAPTER 3

The Glory Years

Long before flip-top cans and twist-off bottle caps, I was a charter member of the Pepsi Generation.

I love Pepsi-Cola. Always have. And I've been addicted to the stuff since I was 15.

I mean really addicted. Some people are addicted to cigarettes, some to booze, some to drugs. I'm addicted to Pepsi.

My dad used to drink 10 or 12 Pepsis a day. He'd drink them all day long, and it didn't matter if they were warm or cold. I would have done the same thing if he had let me. But I was only allowed one a day; that was my limit. He thought too much Pepsi would ruin my teeth and eat away at my stomach.

After my dad died, I went on a Pepsi binge. With him no longer around to tell me what I couldn't do, I started putting away about a dozen a day, just like he had. And it didn't seem to matter. I was outside playing baseball, basketball and football all the time, so I didn't have to worry about gaining weight. My metabolism took care of that.

By the time I made my major league debut in 1963, I was drinking 15 or 20 bottles a day. I'm talking Pepsi by the gallon. I'd start a bottle, leave it by my bed overnight and finish it the next morning. Warm, cold, in between—it didn't matter. My habit got even worse as I became a better pitcher. I don't know if there's any connection between the two; if so, watch out. The whole world will be drinking Pepsi and Michael Jackson will be out one hell of an endorsement.

My affinity for Pepsi became public knowledge when Joe Falls wrote a big article about it in the Detroit Free Press. Ed Schober, a vice president in charge of marketing for the Pepsi-Cola Co. in Detroit, picked up on that, and I was glad he did.

"Listen," Ed said, "we want to give you Pepsi-Cola. We don't want anything out of you. No advertising, no nothing. Just go ahead and take as much as you need."

"Don't mind if I do," I said. After that, a guy named Max made weekly deliveries to the McLain household. A dozen or more cases of Pepsi. I gave some of it away, but the vast majority I drank. At least a case a day.

Ed eventually hired me to work for the Pepsi-Cola Co. Officially, I was involved in public relations, but it really was a sweetheart deal. They paid me $15,000 a year just to show up at an occasional luncheon or dinner and tell everybody how much I loved Pepsi. It was easy money for me and great PR for them.

I quit working for the company after about four years, but I never quit drinking its product. The only difference now is that I'm drinking Diet Pepsi. The transition was tough. I thought the stuff was raunchy when I first tasted it, but I needed to drop a lot of weight, so I got used to it. Now I'm drinking 12 or 14 cans a day. I must admit, Diet Pepsi has opened up a whole new world for me. Now I can drink Pepsi and eat Twinkies at the same time without risking a sugar overdose. Pepsi and Twinkies. What a way to go! And I guess that possibility will always exist, at least until Hostess comes out with a Diet Twinkie.

When I went to spring training with the Tigers in 1964, I was just another face in the crowd and my Pepsi addiction was unknown. Nobody paid much attention to rookies, although I was fortunate that Frank Lary noticed me. Lary, known as the Yankee Killer, took pity on me and taught me the mechanics of the overhand curveball. Most guys throw a curve with two fingers on the seam, but that never worked for me, and Lary taught me how to spin the hell out of the ball with just one finger. That pitch was one of the big reasons for my success in the major leagues, although it didn't help me much that spring. I was less than sensational and the Tigers sent me to their top farm club, Syracuse in the Triple-A International League.

My stay there was short. I posted a 3-1 record with a 1.53 earned-run average and the Tigers requested my presence in the big leagues at the end of May.

The manager in Detroit at that time was Charlie Dressen. As I quickly found out, Charlie was a disciplinarian. He loved curfews, bed checks and team meetings. He was the type of guy who would hide in the bushes outside our hotel just to see who was coming in late. When things started going bad, he'd impose even more rules.

I'll never forget my first night with the Tigers. We were playing awful, and Charlie vented some steam. Everybody got singed.

"You dirty rotten bastards are going to start coming in on time," he screamed. "From now on, I'm going to check everybody's room. No more breaking curfew. I'm tired of you guys sneaking in late. I'm tired of you guys playing cards all night. I'm tired of you guys screwing around all night. That's why we're in fifth place, and I'm not putting up with it anymore."

Then Charlie really got nasty. Sailors would've blushed if they'd heard the language he was using. He called each player every name in the book and then informed us that we'd be required to attend a workout the next morning at 9 a.m.

"Any questions?" Charlie bellowed.

Norm Cash stood up. "Charlie," he said, "it's virtually impossible for me to get to the workout by 9 a.m."

"Dammit Cash, why?"

"Because I'm not done throwing up before 10."

Greatest line I've ever heard.

Dressen liked his rules, but he also liked his young players. For me, that was great. I needed the discipline, and I learned a great deal from Charlie, not the least of which was how to throw the overhand curve. Lary had taught me the grip, but he was sold to the New York Mets shortly after spring training in 1964, and it was Charlie who really taught me the ins and outs of how to throw the pitch.

I always liked Dressen. Most importantly, he believed in me. As soon as I joined the club, he handed me the ball and told me to show him what I could do. I didn't show him much at first, but he kept sending me out there. I fought off some injuries and pitched in 19 games for Detroit in 1964, starting 16, and finished with a 4-5 record and a 4.05 ERA. It was a pretty mediocre performance, but Charlie told me not to worry and to keep plugging.

After the '64 season, the Tigers sent me to Mayaguez, Puerto Rico, to play winter ball. Talk about fun! I took Sharyn down with me and we had a super time. When I wasn't playing ball, all we did was lie in bed, order room service and try to make a baby. In fact, we spent Christmas in St. Thomas in the Virgin Islands, and we're pretty sure that Kristin was conceived there. Even if I'd lost every game I pitched that winter, the trip to the islands was worthwhile.

As it turned out, my performance on the diamond was equal to my performance in St. Thomas. I won 12 games, lost only four and posted a 1.92 ERA while our team won the league championship. I learned a lot about pitching that winter, and my success carried over to the 1965 season, when I became the Tigers' ace. I had a 16-6 record, 192 strikeouts and a 2.62 ERA, tops among the team's regular pitchers. In one game I came in as a reliever and struck out 14 batters, including the first seven I faced. Dressen had worked with me on a changeup to go along with my fastball and curve, and the combination of those three pitches made me very effective. At 21, I already was starting to look, and feel, like an established big leaguer.

I was starting to establish myself in a few other fields as well. I already was doing year-round PR work for Pepsi-Cola, and I filled my off-season with speaking appearances and organ-playing engagements. Not only was I appearing three nights a week at a Detroit lounge, but I also was giving lessons to about 40 students a week. I really enjoyed playing the organ. It was kind of like playing baseball in a way; I could hardly believe people were paying me to do it. And after Kristi's birth in September, the extra money sure came in handy.

When I went to spring training in 1966, I was in great shape. Sharyn made sure of that. It was an annual ritual. Each year before spring training I suffered through the "Sharyn McLain Total Fitness Program," and each year I wanted to die.

For 50 weeks of the year, Sharyn was the sweetest, kindest, most loving wife in the world. At 5-foot-1 and 105 pounds, she was about as imposing as Mister Rogers. But for the two weeks prior to spring training, Sharyn was more like an Army drill sergeant. Sweet little Sharyn became ruthless, heartless, unforgiving Sharyn, the nastiest dietitian and trainer on the face of the earth.

In early February, I weighed about 220 pounds, or about 18 over my playing weight back then. A lot of guys view spring training as the time to shed that extra flab, and that would have been fine with me. Not Sharyn. She was bound and determined that I would show up at Tigertown at 202. Two weeks before official workouts began, the four-course meals of steak, baked potatoes with butter and sour cream, milk and ice cream came to a grinding halt. From then on, it was grapefruit, boiled eggs, salad, spinach and grapefruit juice. Nothing else. Water was allowed, but I've never liked drinking water because fish make love in it. If I even glanced toward the refrigerator, where I knew I could find a quart of ice cream or a Pepsi, Sharyn would freeze me in my tracks with an icy stare. I didn't even bother trying to sneak out of bed in the middle of the night to raid the kitchen. Sharyn probably had the place rigged with alarms. So, it was more grapefruit juice, more boiled eggs and more salad, and I went to bed each night feeling like a cross between Peter Cottontail and Foghorn Leghorn.

When it came time to leave Detroit for the warm winds of Lakeland, I couldn't wait. Not only was the climate appealing, but so was the thought of dropping this diet nonsense. We packed the car and headed south. Somewhere down the road, I reached behind my seat to pull out a Pepsi and a Twinkie, which I had stocked up on for the trip. All I grabbed was air.

"Do you want grapefruit juice or water?" Sharyn asked.

My heart sank. She wasn't finished with me yet!

"Give me the damn grapefruit juice," I snarled. All I could think of was the long, hungry road ahead.

We spent the night in Dalton, Ga., before resuming our trip to Lakeland. I thought we'd never get there. When we checked into the hotel around 9:30 p.m., all I wanted was dinner. A real meal. After all, I was down to about 208, and I figured that once I arrived in Lakeland, it was the Tigers' job to train me. But Sharyn wasn't ready to let loose yet. She had one more night of torture left in her demented soul.

"OK, now I want you to run in place for 15 minutes," she said within moments of unpacking our bags, "and then I'll give you a grapefruit juice."

Fifteen minutes later, I was gulping grapefruit juice when she came up with another idea. She wanted me to sit in a hot, steamy shower and sweat off as much as I could.

"You have got to be kidding," I said. "I don't have sweat clothes."

Sharyn had something better. She handed me her girdle.

"How the hell am I going to get into that thing?" I asked. I outweighed her by more than 100 pounds, and forgetting the fact that wearing women's clothes was a bit kinky for me, I really didn't know how to put it on.

"Very carefully," she said, "and then put your vinyl warmup jacket on and sit in the shower for 30 minutes."

It took me that long to get into the thing. I pulled, tugged, squirmed on the floor and, in desperation, smeared Vaseline on my hips. I thought we'd fit the entire population of Lakeland into our bathroom before I could slip into that rubber band. When I finally sat down in the shower, I was too exhausted to complain—even when Sharyn said I'd be sleeping alone that night. No need to wear me out any more, I guess.

The next morning, I showed up for the first day of workouts and weighed in right at 202. After that, training camp was a breeze. Anything was easy compared to Sharyn's weight-loss program. Even prison! At least I could buy a Pepsi when I wanted one.

Sharyn's program must have helped because in 1966, I posted my first 20-victory season and was the starting pitcher for the American League in the All-Star Game. As a team, we took third place in the league, our best finish since I'd joined the club. Unfortunately, my most vivid memories of that season are unhappy ones. We had three managers that year, and two of them died.

Dressen was our manager when the season opened. He was 67 years old, and we all knew his health was not good. He was coughing all the time, and we were a little worried about the heart problem he had experienced in the spring of '65. Everything had seemed fine in '65 until one day he asked one of his coaches to drive him to the airport in Tampa, about 30 miles away. He said he had to fly home to California because his wife was sick. But the truth was that he was in terrible pain himself and he wanted to see his own doctor. It didn't matter to him that he'd have to suffer for a few hours before he got there. Charlie bought a ticket and flew to California, where his doctor quickly determined that he had suffered a heart attack. But even that didn't keep him down for long. By May 31, 1965, he was back in the Tigers' dugout. He managed the club the rest of that season and through the first 26 games of the '66 campaign before suffering another heart attack. That was it for Charlie's baseball career. He developed an acute kidney infection a few weeks later and died August 10.

The news of Charlie's death hit me hard. He had been a great friend and teacher, and I had a world of respect for the man. I wish he had lived to see me have my big years. But I'm glad he never saw me go to prison.

Dressen was replaced by Bob Swift, the coach who had filled in for him in 1965. Swift managed the club for only two months before he was hospitalized. At first the doctors thought he had food poisoning, but he later was diagnosed as having lung cancer. He was replaced by Frank Skaff, who finished the season. Swift, who was 51, died in October.

In 1967, the Tigers hired a new manager, Mayo Smith. Mayo was a great guy, a real players' manager. Everybody loved him. He was fun-loving, honest, direct and genuine. What you saw was what you got. Mayo loved his Scotch, and he'd get a little sloppy drunk once in a while, but he was a good man. Mayo was no great teacher or strategist, but he was a good judge of talent and character. He recognized that with the players he had, all he had to do was fill out the lineup card every night and we'd win more games than we lost. And we did.

More personally, Mayo liked me, believed in me and pretty much let me do my thing. That wasn't easy to do, either, because I was getting more and more rambunctious as my star grew steadily brighter in Detroit. My business interests outside baseball were expanding, which meant that I was finding more reasons to be away from the ball park. Mayo could have lowered the boom and said, "Denny, I want you to be here on time every day, no exceptions." But he didn't. He gave me the slack I needed and both of us were happy, especially since I generally produced what he wanted—victories. Being able to handle me effectively is proof that Mayo Smith was a talented manager.

And in 1967, Mayo's first season, we continued our steady climb. We won 91 games and missed out on the A.L. pennant by one game to the Boston Red Sox. My performance, however, was less impressive. I won 17 games, matching the number I wore on the back of my uniform, but I also lost 16. With 10 victories at the All-Star break, I had thought I might hit the 20 mark. That would've been nice because we had just bought a new house, and I figured a second consecutive 20-victory season would help my bargaining position. But I didn't win a game after August 29. I missed a couple of starts with an injury and never had my good stuff when the team needed me most.

On October 1, the last day of the season, we still weren't out of the pennant race. We had a doubleheader with the California Angels that day, and we won the first game to pull within half a game of the Red Sox. If we could win the nightcap, we would tie Boston and force a one-game playoff for the pennant. Mayo gave me a chance to make up for that bad month of September, but I just couldn't do the job. I started the second game, went less than three innings and gave up three runs. We lost the game and the pennant.

It was a season to forget—in more ways than one. I also had a business investment that went sour. In 1967, I became one of the few bookmakers in history to lose money, a fiasco that didn't become public knowledge for a couple of years. But by then it didn't matter. In the eyes of Detroit fans, I could have walked across Lake Michigan.

1968. What an unbelievable year that was in Detroit. The summer before, the city had been torn by race riots and people were crying out for something to pull them back together. That something turned out to be the Tigers. The one thing everybody could share was a rooting interest in the local baseball team.

And we gave them plenty to cheer about. We won the A.L. pennant for the first time in 23 years and went to the World Series, where the St. Louis Cardinals beat us in three of the first four games. But we bounced back to win three straight and become the world champions. For the first time in ages, everybody in Detroit had something to smile about.

Especially me. You couldn't have measured my grin with a yardstick. I had the kind of season that pitchers only dream about, and when I woke up, the people of Detroit had all but crowned me king. I owned that town.

Ironically, I was nobody's darling before that season. After my bad finish in 1967, a lot of folks were wondering what I would do in '68. Would I bounce back or was I just a flash in the pan? It was kind of funny. Sure, I had flopped down the stretch, but 17 victories was nothing to sneeze at. Only four other A.L. pitchers had more wins that year. Hell, 15- and 16-game winners are making millions of dollars today. The media monkeys were after my scalp.

But I had no doubt that 1968 would be a successful year. For one thing, I had a son, and that made me feel like I was 10 feet tall. Sharyn had lost a baby after Kristi was born, and we thought she'd never be able to have another one. So in January 1968, we adopted Denny, who had been born December 28, 1967. I was on cloud nine.

On top of that, I could see better and felt stronger. After wearing glasses since my junior year in high school, I had traded in my specs for contact lenses. All of a sudden, everything looked clearer to me—the batter, the catcher's glove, my fielders, even the pretty girls seated behind the dugout. The contact lenses helped me focus better and cut down on glare.

My strength improved dramatically because of bowling. I had rolled 60 or 70 lines a day during the winter and carried a 207, 208 average. It was amazing what that did for my arm and shoulder. I strongly believe that bowling was directly responsible for my ability to throw more than 300 innings. If I had continued to bowl the next off-season, my career might have taken a different course.

When the '68 season opened, I was lookin' good and blowin' smoke. So were the Tigers. After losing our season opener, we won nine straight games to move into first place. That ninth victory was my first, but I had pitched well in my other two starts, both of which we won after I had pitched seven innings. After notching my first victory, I really got on a roll. I won five games before losing one, and that fifth victory on May 10 put Detroit in first place to stay. At the All-Star break I had an incredible 16-2 mark and we were 9½ games in front of second-place Cleveland. I didn't start the All-Star Game—Luis Tiant did—but I pitched two scoreless innings in relief to go along with the three perfect innings I had tossed in '66. It was shaping up to be quite a year.

Johnny Sain was a big part of my success. Sain, the Tigers' pitching coach, had started working with me on a slider the year before. I think part of the problem I had in '67 was that I was using my changeup too much and forgetting about my fastball, plus I was throwing the slider too often before I could really control it. But the slider, which looks like a fastball but breaks at the last second, started working for me in '68. All my pitches became more effective, especially my fastball, and the results were obvious. I was killing everybody in the league.

Working with Sain was great. Most pitchers, me in particular, hate to run. But almost every manager and pitching coach in the major leagues believes that pitchers should run regularly to stay in shape. Not Johnny. He subscribed to the philosophy, "If running made you a good pitcher, Jesse Owens and Edwin Moses would have been 20-game winners." So Johnny, who had great success wherever he coached, didn't make his pitchers run. Thank God! Even after enduring Sharyn's starvation diet, my 6-foot frame still carried plenty of flesh—I had the build of a linebacker—and I could think of a lot better things to do with that bulk than running around the outfield track.

Sain's theory also kept me out of some hot water with my teammates. Even before 1968, I realized that Mayo Smith was not a clock watcher. If I arrived at the ball park late, he rarely said anything. He sometimes gave me permission to show up late. That could have caused some hard feelings among the other pitchers on the club, but as long as they were just sitting around the clubhouse themselves, no one got too upset. But if those pitchers had been out running wind sprints and I arrived late, you can bet that some guys would have raised hell. Maybe Mayo would put up with that from his ace hurler, but the other pitchers wouldn't. Thanks to Sain, that situation never arose.

So how did the guys react when I'd take advantage of Mayo's good nature? This happened in 1969, but the point is the same. Earlier that year, I had gotten my pilot's license and started flying my own plane whenever I could. One day in July, I had permission to be at a meeting in Chicago instead of traveling with the team to Cleveland, where I was scheduled to start that night. I was going to fly my plane over and meet the team there. The plan was simple: I would fly from Detroit to Chicago in the morning, take off from Chicago early in the afternoon, make the short hop to Cleveland and land at the downtown airport, which was near the ball park. Chances were I'd be sitting in the clubhouse, already in uniform, when the rest of the guys showed up.

Well, the meeting ran long and bad weather backed up the flights out of the airport. To make a long story short, I walked into the clubhouse about half an hour before game time.

I had made what I hoped was a nice, quiet entrance when Norm Cash grabbed my arm and pulled me into the visiting manager's office. Mayo looked up and Norm said, "Skipper, this is a young fellow named McLain who just dropped in and said he'd like to pitch for us tonight." Mayo thought that was pretty funny. He just laughed and didn't say a word about it. As for the other guys, they didn't have much time before the game to say anything, and after the game, what could they say? I pitched a shutout.

Winning atones for many transgressions.

I don't recall how much transgressing I did in 1968, but I sure as hell was busy. Pitching on only three days' rest for an entire summer probably would be enough for most guys, but most guys aren't Denny McLain. I've always preferred life in the fast lane, and in 1968 there weren't any speed limit signs in sight.

Airline pilots probably spent less time in planes than I did that summer. When I wasn't pitching, I was anywhere and everywhere. Go to a shopping center and you'd see me behind the keyboard of a Hammond organ, a company I represented. Go to a record store and you'd see the first of my two albums for Capitol Records, "Denny McLain at the Organ." Turn on the TV and you'd see me on everything from the "Today" show to "The Joey Bishop Show." Pick up a magazine and you'd see me playing catch with Steve Allen, rubbing elbows with Ed Sullivan and rehearsing a gig with the Smothers Brothers. And in between there were endless business meetings about investments, endorsements, organ tours and God knows what else. It was a blur. And I was floating through some kind of time warp.

The only thing I wasn't doing much was sleeping. Sometimes I'd work all night, sleep for an hour on a plane and then start another day all over again. I was working like a madman, yet somehow I managed to keep winning. It was like I was on a high-speed treadmill. As long as I kept moving, I was all right. The momentum I built up with my activities between starts seemed to carry over to the games I pitched. I wouldn't recommend that pace to anybody, but back then I thought it was the only way to go.

And who could argue with the results? By the middle of August, I was a 25-game winner and the club was eight games in front of the Baltimore Orioles, who had moved ahead of the fading Indians into second place.

The best inning I pitched that year—and possibly in my life—was in Boston when I won my 25th game. I had a 2-0 lead in the sixth inning when the Red Sox got men on second and third with nobody out. The next three hitters were Dalton Jones, Carl Yastrzemski and Hawk Harrelson, the heart of Boston's order. I struck out Jones and then got Yastrzemski to miss on two straight fastballs. The next five pitches I threw were strikes, and Yaz fouled off four before whiffing on the fifth. Two down, one to go.

At that point, Mayo Smith and Bill Freehan, my catcher, walked out to the mound.

"You gotta be careful with Harrelson now," Mayo said.

Harrelson was having the best year of his career, so Mayo's concern was understandable—except for the fact that Harrelson couldn't buy a hit off me, then or any other year.

"Mayo, please, there's two outs and I own this guy," I said. "I absolutely own him. He can't hit a foul ball off me."

"Well," Freehan said, "you gotta pitch him away, gotta pitch him away."

"Just get behind the plate," I said. "I'll get him."

Freehan went back behind the plate and set up on the outside corner, right on the black. I hit him with two straight sliders that were both bull's-eyes. Strike one and strike two. On the next pitch, Freehan moved about two feet outside and held out his glove. It was a ridiculous target, but I had a hunch it might work. In his last at-bat, Harrelson had complained about something to the plate umpire, Ed Runge, and Runge was the type who would get even when somebody got nasty. I threw that pitch two feet outside, and Runge barked, "Strike three!"

End of threat. We won, 4-0.

That was the way I pitched. When the best hitters were up with the game on the line, I was unbeatable. But when I was cruising along and got down to the bottom of the lineup, I had problems. The guys who really seemed to hit me consistently were the rinky-dink hitters like Eddie Brinkman, Mark Belanger and Joe Foy. Pitching is 90 percent concentration, and I guess I let up when I faced the little guys. I'd just throw the ball right down the middle, figuring they would take the pitch and hope to get a walk. But I didn't throw many balls, and these guys knew it, so they'd get nice pitches to hit. In fact, the reason I was in a bind when Jones, Yastrzemski and Harrelson came up was because I'd allowed Jim Lonborg, Boston's pitcher, to get a hit, one of two that day. That was par for the course.

It never mattered much. When push came to shove, I'd bear down and win the game. But it caused a few anxious moments for my teammates, not to mention Mayo.

I don't remember many other games I pitched in 1968, but I do remember my 27th victory. It wasn't one of my better efforts. When I went out to pitch in the top of the third inning at Tiger Stadium, I had a 4-2 lead over Baltimore. The Orioles promptly got their first two runners on base and I was looking shaky. The next batter was Boog Powell, a guy who owned me. And sure enough, he blasted a line drive up the middle that presented a serious threat to my manhood. Purely in self-defense, I threw my glove out and the ball landed in it. Lord knows, I could have been walking funny and talking with a high voice the rest of my life. Instead, I caught the ball, whirled around instinctively and threw to second base, where shortstop Tommy Matchick forced Curt Blefary and threw to first to nail Frank Robinson. Triple play! And it should have been a base hit. I went on to win, 7-3. That just goes to show how much luck can be involved in winning a baseball game.

I won my next two times out, too, so I was one away from victory No. 30. Talk about magic numbers. They can't get any more magical for major league pitchers. Dizzy Dean had won 30 games for the Cardinals in 1934, but after him, nobody. Not until I came along in '68.

The morning of Saturday, September 14, started nicely enough. I woke up around 10:30 and ate a nice breakfast that Sharyn prepared. I played the organ for a few minutes, made a few phone calls and met with a representative from the Hammond Organ Co. At about noon, my brother, who had come up from Chicago with my mother, drove me to the ball park. It was time to win my 30th game.

So much for peace and tranquillity. Tiger Stadium was a madhouse. It seemed as if every newspaper, magazine and TV and radio station in the country had sent its own reporter. Nobody knew if I would win, but everybody wanted to be there in case I did.

And the questions they asked! You wouldn't have believed it. When did you wake up this morning? What did you eat for breakfast? What kind of underwear are you wearing? What time did you last go to the bathroom? Following up on that last question, I guess, photographers in the clubhouse even trailed me into the urinals.

I tried to accommodate everyone, but I was damn glad when it came time to warm up. At least they couldn't follow me to the bullpen. And when I finally went out to the mound to pitch the first inning, I felt an enormous sense of relief. Finally, a little solitude.

I don't remember much of what happened in that game before the ninth inning. I know that I served up a couple of gopher balls to Reggie Jackson and that Norm Cash blasted a three-run home run for us. Campy Campaneris also knocked in a run for the A's, who took a 4-3 lead into the bottom of the ninth. I had been pitching fairly well—six hits, one walk, 10 strikeouts—so Mayo had stuck with me despite Reggie's moon shots. But with me scheduled to lead off the bottom of the ninth, Mayo decided he had to have some offense. He sent Al Kaline up to pinch hit for me.

Kaline was one of the greatest players in Tiger history. He usually played right field, but earlier that year, because of an injury, he had been switched to first base. By the end of the season, he wasn't playing all that much. But when Diego Segui walked Kaline to lead off the inning, I had a feeling that my teammates were going to win that game for me.

The next man up, second baseman Dick McAuliffe, fouled out while trying to bunt Kaline over. I still wasn't too worried, though, with our three outfielders—Mickey Stanley, Jim Northrup and Willie Horton—coming up next. Stanley singled, allowing Kaline to move to third. Then came the key play. Northrup hit a wimpy little ground ball to first baseman Danny Cater, who had Kaline dead as a doornail at home. But he threw wildly to the plate and Al scored, tying the game. I still think somebody must've bribed Cater. Or was it divine intervention?

Whatever, I started to smile. Victory No. 30 was all but gift-wrapped for me.

Stanley had run to third on Cater's error, so with one out, the A's had to bring in their outfielders. That's not a good situation with Willie Horton walking to the plate. True to form, Willie pounded a pitch from Segui over the left fielder's head. Stanley trotted home with the winning run and I waltzed into the record books.

Maybe "crashed" is a better word. As soon as I saw Willie smack that ball, I jumped in the dugout. So high, in fact, that I cracked my head on the dugout's concrete ceiling. You may have seen the picture taken of me and Kaline a moment or two later. I'm smiling, all right, but you'll notice that Al has both arms around me as we're coming up the dugout steps. That's because I probably couldn't have made it onto the field without his help.

It was almost a sense of deja vu. The last time I had whacked myself that bad was one of my first nights with Sharyn. After a particularly intense interlude, I got out of bed, walked toward the bathroom in the dark and bashed my head on the corner of the bathroom door. I fell right on my bare ass. Sharyn thought I had passed out because of her romantic abilities.

Thanks to Kaline, it didn't take long for the cobwebs to clear and I quickly joined my teammates in a big celebration. But I'll never forget that my initial reaction to becoming the major leagues' first 30-game winner in 34 years was to nearly knock myself dizzy.

Speaking of dizzy, Ol' Diz himself was there to see me win that game, and I really liked that. He didn't seem to mind at all that a cocky 24-year-old kid had matched his 30-victory performance. He was very friendly and gracious. He even called me "humble." Hey, when a great pitcher like Dizzy Dean is around, even I can be humble.

We clinched the pennant before it was my turn to pitch again. I was sitting on the bench September 17 when we played the New York Yankees. The score was tied, 1-1, in the bottom of the ninth, but by that time we were famous for our late-inning heroics. It was time for more. Don Wert singled to score Kaline with the run that won the game and the pennant. For the first time since 1945, the Tigers were going to the World Series.

Party time! The city of Detroit went wild. At Tiger Stadium, the fans celebrated by tearing down the left-field screen and storming the field. In the clubhouse, we celebrated by consuming and drenching each other with bottle after bottle of champagne. We stopped only to let the club owner, John Fetzer, say a few words.

"This bunch of kids has grown up into men," Fetzer said. The words were hardly out of his mouth before we displayed our maturity by dumping him into the whirlpool.

The pennant was ours, but we still had 10 games to play before the World Series. I was the starting pitcher September 19, our first game after the clincher. Such a game ordinarily would be meaningless, but this one was notable for a couple of reasons. It marked my 31st victory of the year as well as the next to last time Mickey Mantle ever hit a home run. There's a great story behind that homer. I was accused of deliberately letting him hit it.

This was the situation: Mickey was nearing the end of the line. He hadn't made any formal announcement, but everybody knew he might have to retire after the season. In fact, the fans in Detroit, realizing that this might be Mickey's last at-bat ever in Tiger Stadium, gave him a standing ovation. On top of that, Mickey was tied with Jimmie Foxx on the all-time home run list with 534, needing one more to move into sole possession of third place. All that has since changed, but at the time, Mickey was just one homer away from a rather lofty spot in baseball history.

I was aware of all this when Mantle came up to bat the last time that afternoon. And I felt for him. Mickey had been a hero of mine as I was growing up, and though we were never best pals or anything, I had come to know and like the guy. At that moment when Mantle walked to the plate, I decided to groove a pitch right into his wheelhouse.

That is not the same thing as "letting" him hit a home run. I could let him try, but I couldn't guarantee the result. If you've ever seen one of those home run-hitting contests at the ball park, then you know what I'm talking about. Even with the pitcher laying the ball in there nice and pretty and the batter giving it all he's got, the guy is lucky to hit three homers in 10 swings. That's why I didn't really "let" Mantle do anything. I just gave him the opportunity to try. I decided that Mickey wanted to hit that home run, and being the nice guy that I am, I wasn't going to be uncooperative. Besides, what's one more homer off a guy who gives up 35 or 40 every year anyway.

Before anybody starts complaining about how my grooving a pitch damaged the integrity of the game, understand that it was the eighth inning, the bases were empty and we had a big lead. There was no way I was going to blow it—not that year. Some people who remember that day seem to think that I had a shutout going, too, but you better believe that wasn't the case. Mantle was a friend, but I never had a friend I'd give up a shutout for. The score was 6-1.

When Mantle came to the plate with one out, I called Bill Freehan out to the mound.

"Tell Mickey it's coming right down the pipe," I said.

Freehan looked at me like I was nuts and said, "What do you mean?"

"Just what I said. Tell him he's going to get one right where he wants it."

Freehan seemed a bit confused and went back behind the plate. I saw him say something to Mantle, who spun his head around to look at Freehan and then looked back at me. He must have been confused, too. Mickey got ready for my pitch, which was right down the middle with nothing on it. He couldn't call room service and order a better pitch than that. But he never moved his bat. The umpire called strike one and I called Freehan back out to the mound.

"What the hell is wrong?" I asked. "Why didn't he swing?"

"I don't think he believes you," Freehan answered.

"Well, tell him again. I'm going to give him another one."

Freehan still looked bewildered, but he delivered my message again. I lobbed in another pitch that must have looked as big as a grapefruit, but Mickey took a rather tentative swing and fouled it off. Then he looked at me and grinned. At last. The message had gotten through. He finally believed me.

When I started my windup a third time, Mantle was ready. He swung so hard, he nearly popped his shoelaces. This time he made solid contact. The ball sailed far over the right-field fence, just inside the foul screen. With the crowd again on its feet cheering, Mickey began his home run trot. He rounded third and headed for home plate, where he looked right at me and tipped his cap.

I got the message—"Thanks, Denny"—and so did most everyone else in Tiger Stadium. But I didn't give a damn. I thought it was hilarious. Still, I could just see the stories in the papers and the questions from the Tigers and the commissioner about "the integrity of the game." The way some baseball people talk, you'd think "the integrity of the game" ranks right up there with "We the people" and "liberty and justice for all." Sure enough, the criticism and inquiries came, everything that I expected. But it was worth it to see Mickey reach that milestone.

An interesting footnote: The next batter was Joe Pepitone, who placed his hand over the plate and suggested that I lay one in there for him, too. My first pitch was a fastball behind his head, and all you could see was Joe's butt wiping the batter's box as he hit the dirt.

The Yankees were unable to get any more runs off me, so that victory was my 31st—and last—of the year. I had two more opportunities to increase my victory total, but we lost both games by 2-1 scores. I was charged with the first loss, against Baltimore, but the bullpen let me down the other time.

Or maybe it was Mayo Smith who let me down. On September 28, the day before the regular season ended, we were at home against last-place Washington, and it looked as if victory No. 32 was in the bag. I was winning, 1-0, after seven innings when Mayo decided to take me out. He thought it was a good idea to give me some rest before I pitched the World Series opener.

"What the hell do I need rest for?" I said. "I've pitched 336 innings this year, and you're worried about two more? Hell, Mayo, that's only 20 pitches!"

But Mayo prevailed, as managers usually do. When I realized I wasn't going to have my way—Don McMahon was already on the mound—I headed for the clubhouse. It wasn't long before the Senators had scored two runs in the top of the ninth to win the game. The whole episode left me a little teed off. It wasn't so much that I wanted to win my 32nd game. I was upset mainly because we lost. Winning a major league baseball game is one of the hardest things in the world to do, and I thought we could have won if Mayo had left me in there. Of all teams, the Senators!

That game closed the book on my 1968 regular season. I finished with a 31-6 record, a 1.96 ERA, 280 strikeouts, six shutouts and 28 complete games in 41 starts. I have to admit, I am rather proud of those numbers. After all, nobody has done anything like that since then. It still stands as the greatest single-season performance by a pitcher in more than half a century. Considering all the crap that's happened to me the last few years, I figure I'm entitled to take a few bows.

As for the Tigers, we won 103 games and finished 12 games ahead of the second-place Orioles. We drew more than 2 million fans to Tiger Stadium for the first time ever. The only challenge left for us was to beat St. Louis in the World Series.

I couldn't wait for the Series to start. The only way I could top off my incredible season was by leading my team to a world championship and beating the best the other league had to offer. The best pitcher in the National League that year was Bob Gibson, who had gone 22-9 with 28 complete games, 13 shutouts and an astounding ERA of 1.12. It figured that Gibson and I would be the Game 1 starters.

The scenario was perfect, but I wasn't. In the fourth inning, I walked Roger Maris and Tim McCarver, and Mike Shannon singled to left. Maris scored, and when Willie Horton fumbled the ball in the outfield, McCarver went to third and Shannon to second. They both scored on Julian Javier's single. I was removed for a pinch-hitter in the sixth. Gibson, meanwhile, was putting on a pitching clinic. All he did was shut us out on five hits and strike out a Series-record 17 batters. I felt bad about losing, but I realized that nobody was going to beat Gibson that day. My only consolation was that we'd meet again in Game 4 and I'd get a chance to make amends.

It never occurred to me that our next encounter would be even worse. It was. Gibson allowed only five hits again, although one of them was Jim Northrup's home run. One measly run, that's all we got. Hell, I had that much damage done to me by the time the second Cardinal came to the plate. The first batter, Lou Brock, hit a home run. That same inning, Maris reached base on my error and came around to score. In the third inning, rain stopped play for more than an hour. When the rain was gone, so was I. I had given up four runs in 2⅔ innings and we wound up on the wrong end of a 10-1 score. It was our third loss in four tries, and two of the losses had been charged to me.

After Mickey Lolich won for us in Game 5, I volunteered to pitch the sixth game. I had a sore right shoulder, which wasn't all that unusual because my shoulder had been hurting off and on since 1965, when I first injured it. But the pain was on more than it was off by that time, and I'd been getting cortisone shots all year. I wanted to contribute something to our effort against the Cardinals, though, so I took some more cortisone and went out there.

As much as I'd like to say that my gutsy performance was responsible for our victory that day, that's just not true. By the time I went out to pitch the third inning, my teammates had already staked me to a 12-0 lead. Stevie Wonder or Helen Keller could've made that lead stand up. I gave up a run in the ninth but won the game, 13-1.

The seventh game was a classic. The pitching matchup was Lolich vs. Gibson, both of whom had won twice in the Series already. Neither pitcher allowed a run until the top of the seventh, when singles by Cash and Horton, a triple by Northrup and a double by Freehan produced three runs. After both teams scored a single run in the ninth, the Tigers wound up on top, 4-1. We were world champions!

As happy as I was that we had won the World Series, I couldn't help but be a little disappointed in my own performance. I had been looking forward to a World Series that would be my personal showcase. It was a showcase all right, but not for me. The accolades I thought I would receive went to Mickey Lolich instead. Don't get me wrong, he deserved them. He pitched and won three complete games, allowed a total of five runs and, most importantly, beat Gibson in the final game. I always believed in sharing the glory with my teammates, so it probably wouldn't have bothered me if it had been anyone but Lolich. Anyone but him. Of all the guys I played with through the years, there was only one guy I simply did not get along with, and that was Mickey Lolich. I just didn't like the guy, and he didn't like me.

Lolich's success and my lack of it in the World Series didn't bother me too long. After the season, the awards started pouring in. To name a few, I was a unanimous selection as both the Most Valuable Player in the American League and the winner of the Cy Young Award, which goes to the league's best pitcher. The Sporting News named me its Man of the Year. The Detroit sportswriters even voted me Tiger of the Year. That may not sound like much, but I didn't always get along with those guys, so it was nice of them to give me that award. And the list goes on and on. It seemed as if everyone and his brother had some plaque to honor me. I was more than happy to accept them.

And it wasn't just awards. It was money, too, lots of money. My salary with the Tigers that year was only $30,000, but I earned several times that figure in the off-season. I had bookings to play the organ all over the place, and the money for that was pretty good. Less than a week after the World Series ended, I opened a two-week stand at the Riviera Hotel in Las Vegas. The Riviera is one of my all-time favorite places to visit, and I had a blast. I don't think I had Alan King or Shecky Greene worrying about being upstaged, but I did OK. I also spent hours at the craps tables, having a great time. Besides playing the organ, I hit the banquet circuit and did lots of endorsements, promotions and personal appearances. Everywhere I went, people seemed dedicated to the task of spoiling Denny McLain, and Denny McLain was dedicated to letting them do it.

As if all that wasn't enough, I became quite the business tycoon, too. A couple of years earlier, I had formed Denny McLain Enterprises Inc., but it didn't amount to much until 1969. By that time my company had several divisions, including one called Jetravel Inc., a passenger and freight air-charter service. But my biggest business was a distributorship for Dyco paint coatings. That business did very well. I had a small staff of five or six people and we had a good ol' time. It was a serious operation, but let's face it, by the time the 1969 season started, I wasn't around enough to be Mr. Businessman. I was too busy trying to win ball games. I just provided my name and money, dropped by the office now and then and left it up to my staff to run the show.

All of this was a mixed blessing for Sharyn. She was happy to see me succeed and make a lot of money, but she didn't like the constant demands on my time. I was always off somewhere doing something, leaving her and the kids at home alone. If she'd had her way, I'd have just stayed home and passed on a lot of the offers—especially the nightclub gigs. The bar atmosphere, with all the drinking and flirting that goes on, really bothered her. She could see me slipping away from her, and it would be quite a while before I reversed direction.

My first priority at this point in my life was raking in the bucks. Not surprisingly, my paychecks from the Tigers grew quite a bit in 1969. Jim Campbell, the club's general manager and a guy who really has been a good friend over the years, was no Ted Turner when it came to negotiating contracts, but he did more than double my salary to $65,000. After the season I had, I was thinking in terms of at least six figures, but Jim said no way. Only a handful of guys like Mickey Mantle and Willie Mays were making that kind of money, and they were all quite a bit older than me. I couldn't complain. The only guy on the club making more than me was Al Kaline, and he was 34 and a sure-bet Hall of Famer.

Did the Tigers get their money's worth in 1969? Damn right they did. I didn't come close to matching my 1968 numbers, but nobody really expected me to. In '69, I won seven fewer games and lost three more than the year before, my ERA rose nearly a point to 2.80, I struck out 99 fewer batters and I gave up more hits. But I still was good enough to share the Cy Young Award with Baltimore's Mike Cuellar. It just goes to show how remarkable my '68 performance had been.

The Tigers dropped off even more than I did. The '69 season was the first that the league was divided into two divisions and we finished second in the A.L. East, 19 games behind Baltimore. Lots of clubs have problems repeating as champions, and we were no exception.

First of all, we got off to a slow start. The fans in Detroit weren't too happy about it, and they seemed to take it all out on Willie Horton. The year before, when Willie belted 36 homers and was the team's hitting star, the fans loved him. But when he started poorly in '69, the fans began to boo. Hurt and confused, Willie just took off one day in May. A few days later, he came back. The club fined him $1,360, which was four days' pay. Nothing like a little turmoil to get the club back on its feet, right?

The pitching department also had its problems, starting at the top. Mayo Smith and Johnny Sain did not have a strong relationship. Sain knew his stuff and was an excellent teacher, but he had definite ideas about pitching and didn't like interference. From anybody. When he had run into problems with Twins Manager Sam Mele and coach Billy Martin while working in Minnesota, Sain had moved out of the coaches' dressing room and taken a locker with the players. He had similar problems with Mayo. The lines of communication between a manager and pitching coach should be strong, but Johnny and Mayo didn't speak for a couple of months. Johnny then made the mistake of taking his beef to the newspapers. That did it. With two months left in the season, Sain was fired. None of us benefited from that.

As if that wasn't enough, there was the ongoing saga of Denny McLain and Mickey Lolich. For the most part, we had a peaceful coexistence. We didn't like each other, but we didn't need a U.N. peacekeeping force between us, either. We just went our separate ways, did our separate things and went through the motions of sociability. Lolich had a great arm, probably the best I ever saw. But he also had a personality that rubbed people the wrong way, especially me. Lolich was the kind of guy who could say "good morning" and piss you off. What bothered me most was his petty jealousy. He couldn't stand to see other guys succeed. Amazingly, it seemed to me that Mickey sometimes pulled against the Tigers—and especially the other pitchers. I think he secretly wished that the Tigers would lose every game except the ones he pitched. You've probably heard it said that so-and-so has "a million-dollar arm and a 10-cent head." That was Lolich.

Why didn't Lolich like me? Beats me. I guess you'd have to ask him. I sure can't think of a reason.

Nobody knew about our mutual dislike until after the 1969 All-Star Game. We both were picked for the A.L. team, with yours truly designated as the starter. The game was scheduled for the night of July 22 in Washington, D.C. I was flying my new Cessna 337 Skymaster as often as possible that summer, so I planned to fly to Washington with Sharyn. Like I said, Lolich and I could generally occupy the same room without sparks flying, so when he asked if he and his wife, Joyce, could fly with us, I said OK. I could think of people I'd rather have taken as passengers, but nobody else asked. Only one of the Cessna's six seats was empty when the four of us and a co-pilot left for Washington.

That All-Star break was a busy one for me. The day after the game I had scheduled a dental appointment in Detroit in the morning and a business meeting in Lakeland in the afternoon. Lolich was well aware of my plans. I told him that we would have to fly back to Detroit immediately after the game so that I could make my dental appointment the next morning. That was fine with him. He was just happy to get a free ride.

The trip to Washington was uneventful, but pointless. The game was rained out. It was rescheduled for the next afternoon, but I still had that dental appointment. And it wasn't the type of appointment I could miss. I already had endured 32 grueling hours in the dental chair at Henry Ford Hospital while dentists pulled nine teeth, did the impressions and put temporary crowns in place, and this was to be the day my teeth-capping job would be completed. My teeth had been pretty lousy ever since I was a kid, and finally, at age 25, I was getting them fixed.

Mayo Smith was managing the A.L. All-Star team that year, so I went to him with my dilemma. As usual, he was understanding. Perhaps bearing in mind that I had been conscientious enough to schedule the appointment for what should have been a day off, Mayo gave me permission to fly back to Detroit immediately.

"Will you be back in time to start tomorrow?" he asked.

"I hope so," I answered, "but if not, go ahead and start without me." We laughed.

Lolich was just as understanding when I told him what was going on. I explained that I would be returning in time for the game but that afterward, I would be flying directly to Lakeland for my meeting. As a result, I wouldn't be able to fly him and Joyce back to Detroit. He said that he understood and everything was fine. The co-pilot decided to stay in Washington, so it was just Sharyn and me flying back to Detroit.

It was raining cats and dogs when Sharyn and I took off from Washington's National Airport around 11 p.m. We were expected to have rain for the first 200 miles or so, but no bumpy flying conditions. Sharyn, who thinks flying is great for birds but not for people, was a little nervous as we settled into our seats. We took off and climbed to 10,000 feet.

The Cessna was a "push-pull plane," meaning that it had one prop up front and another on the back. It was fully instrumented, the kind of plane that was safe for a guy like me who had been flying solo for only a few months. The plane did not have radar, so I had to depend on the air-traffic controllers on the ground. The guy watching me on radar was giving me headings—the direction to fly to miss the heavy thunderstorm areas. But with all the lightning, he lost us. We were out of touch for the next 15 minutes, one of the most terrifying times in my life.

Within 30 seconds of losing contact, I flew right into a massive thunderstorm. The plane was bouncing all over the sky, and my maps and charts were flying everywhere. I hit a switch on the instrument panel to turn on my ice lights and couldn't believe what I saw. The wings of my plane were caked with more ice than I have ever seen, before or since, on any plane. I almost fell out of my seat. Fortunately, I remembered the words of my flight instructor— "Airplanes don't panic, only pilots"—and tried to stay cool. But I wasn't having a hell of a lot of success.

The Cessna, which by that time was on autopilot, was being tossed around the sky like a salad. The manual said that in severe turbulence—and this sure qualified—you should turn off the altitude hold, so you can imagine the roller coaster we were on. I kept trying to get the air-traffic controller on the radio, but there was just silence. It occurred to me that the bouncing around might have snapped my radio antenna. I kept that thought to myself while de-icing the wings every two minutes and praying for the radio to start talking.

The only voice in the cockpit was mine as I tried again and again to reach the ATC. Sharyn was just sitting there with her eyes closed. I didn't want to know what she was thinking.

Suddenly, the front engine started sputtering. I applied more power, but after several seconds, it just plain quit. The Cessna is supposed to be able to fly easily on one engine. Well, I was about to find out if that was true.

The plane did fly, but not without problems. Like losing altitude. I was descending to 9,000 feet, 8,500, 8,000, and still no ATC on the radio. I finally got a break when the plane was able to hold altitude at 6,000 feet. There was still some turbulence, but the bounces weren't as big. And it was still raining, but no more ice. We were below the freezing level.

At this point, for the first time since we left Washington, Sharyn spoke. "It is time to consider giving up flying," she said.

With the plane finally under control, I tried to restart the front engine. After six or seven tries, it turned over. Just as it started, I heard the ATC on the radio. Thank God! He said he had lost me on radar and radio and feared the worst. For a while, so had I.

The ATC wanted to know why I was flying at 6,000 feet instead of where I was supposed to be. I told him about the storm, the engine failure and the severe turbulence. He told me that three jet airliners had been forced to fly around the storm I had just come through. Boy, I thought, those airline captains must be chickens. A little bump or two and they have to change course. I was just starting to get cocky again when the front engine sputtered briefly and brought me back to reality. We were damn lucky to make it through that storm alive.

The ATC gave me directions for the next leg of our trip and wished us well. About 10 minutes later we broke out of the storm and into a clear, lovely, moonlit night. Sharyn and I were both smiling, and I think the Cessna might have been grinning, too.

Sharyn is a good conversationalist, but she had only two more things to say to me the rest of that trip. First she informed me that she would not be returning to Washington for the All-Star Game. Then she said, "Dennis"—she always calls me Dennis, or worse, when she's mad at me—"you'd better get four engines on this plane because until you do, I'm not riding in it." She finally gave in on that ultimatum—about six months later.

We landed in Detroit and went home. I showed up for my dental appointment at 8 the next morning, and three hours later the two dentists still weren't through. Knowing that I'd be cutting it close anyway, I had arranged for a Learjet to fly me back to Washington. I invited the dentists to finish the work on the plane and then be my guests at the All-Star Game. They jumped at the chance. We took off around 11:30 a.m., and the final touches on my teeth were done in the air.

The trip itself took only an hour, so I figured we'd get to Washington around 12:30 p.m. That would give me about an hour to get to the ball park, find seats for the dentists, get dressed and warm up before the 1:45 p.m. start.

Tight, but possible. Except for one thing. Back then, Michigan didn't observe daylight-saving time like most of the rest of the country. I forgot to take that into account. So when we arrived at the airport 35 minutes after the hour, it was 1:35 p.m., not 12:35 p.m. Ten minutes before game time, and I was taxiing down a runway. No way I could make it.

When I finally arrived at the clubhouse of Robert F. Kennedy Memorial Stadium, the American League's substitute starting pitcher, Mel Stottlemyre of the Yankees, was already showering. He had been knocked out early. "Thanks a lot, Denny," he said when I walked in. "I really needed that start."

It was the second inning by the time I arrived in the dugout. Mayo called me over.

"Nice to see that you could make it," he said. "They wouldn't let me hold up the game until you got here. I'm sorry."

For a second I thought he was serious, but then he started laughing. He asked me if I'd pitch one inning, and I said sure. After giving me some time to warm up, Mayo let me pitch the fourth inning. Except for a ball that Willie McCovey placed in orbit, I did OK. The run was meaningless—it was the National League's last in a 9-3 victory—so I didn't worry about it as I went back to the clubhouse and quickly showered and dressed. As I was leaving, Lolich asked me if I was still going to Lakeland. I said yes. "OK," he said, "I'll see you tomorrow at the stadium." And that was that. Or so I thought.

I flew to Lakeland, ate dinner with a friend, confirmed my appointment for the next morning and went to bed. At 8 a.m. the next day, Sharyn called. She was holding the morning newspaper and thought I might be interested in one of the headlines: "McLain Strands Lolich and Wife in Washington," or something to that effect. The story quoted Lolich as saying that I had never told him I would be flying to Lakeland and that I had caused him and his wife a great inconvenience. What garbage.

I was livid. As soon as my meeting was over, I flew back to Detroit. By the time I got to the ball park around 5:15 p.m.—without going home first—my ears were smoking. Lolich was pitching against Kansas City that night, but he hadn't arrived yet. When he finally showed up, I was waiting for him at his locker. He wasted no time trying to tell me that he had been misunderstood. Not misquoted, mind you, but misunderstood. Quite a difference there.

We went back to the equipment room, where nobody could hear us, and I started to scream. After about two or three minutes, I did something I hadn't done since I was 12 years old. I challenged him to a fight. He declined, of course, which was good because I didn't really want to fight. I just wanted him to know that I was more than a little pissed.

Eventually, we shook hands. That's a typical gesture on my part. No matter what somebody does to me, I'm almost always ready to forgive and forget. Even if I spank my dog, five minutes later I've got him on my lap, petting him. That's an interesting analogy, considering the mentality of the man whose hand I was shaking.

Afterward, I just told the press that it was a matter of Lolich and me settling our differences. Officially, it was over. In truth, it was never really over. It was finished, but not forgotten.

When I was convicted in 1985, a reporter for the Detroit News asked some of my former teammates for their reactions. Lolich said that he wasn't sorry for me and that I had dug my own grave. I found that to be incredibly revealing. I didn't like him, but if he had been in my shoes, I think I would have felt sorry for him. Now, maybe not.

The season was only half over after that episode, but it didn't get any better. For one thing, the Tigers took away most of my flying privileges. And even though I threw nine shutouts, won 24 games and received another Cy Young Award, the team finished so far behind Baltimore that the year was kind of a bummer—especially when I thought about Johnny Sain being fired and the whole mess with Lolich. My shoulder was bothering me more, too. I was getting cortisone shots the morning before and the morning after almost every game I pitched. The pain just wouldn't go away. So, my attitude as I entered another off-season filled with organ bookings and business deals was a little less enthusiastic than it had been the year before.

I didn't know it then, but 1969 was the start of a long slide into oblivion.

C H A P T E R 4

Back to Earth

After the 1969 season, I went to war. Literally.

No, I wasn't drafted. And I sure as hell didn't enlist. In fact, I was very much opposed to the war in Vietnam. I couldn't figure out why we were over there. But I had great feelings for the guys who were being forced to fight. Guys my age, and younger, were doing what Uncle Sam had asked them to do, even if it was asinine. And they were coming home torn apart, both mentally and physically, if they came back at all. I had a ton of respect for these guys. They were patriots and they had guts.

Me? I had a good fastball. That didn't seem like much when I thought about American soldiers dying in Vietnam, but it must have counted for something. The USO was assembling a group of baseball people to make a three-week November tour of Vietnam and I was asked to go along. I was happy to oblige. If meeting baseball players lifted the morale of the troops, it was the least I could do.

The other guys in the group were White Sox third baseman Pete Ward, White Sox broadcaster Bob Elson and relief pitcher Tug McGraw, who had helped the Miracle Mets win the World Series that year. We visited guys in hospitals and actually went out to the fire bases where the soldiers were closest to the action. These fire bases were isolated, miles from the main camps. One night we got shelled, and all you could see were elbows and assholes trying to find holes in the ground. I was scared shitless. We were wearing badges that identified us as noncombatants, but I strongly doubted those shells would pay any attention to that.

After our second week in Vietnam, I got a message to call my wife at home. That was almost as scary as incoming enemy fire. I was sure that something terrible had happened to one of the kids. We now had three, having adopted our second son, Timmy, earlier that year.

Panicked, I called Sharyn. When she told me what she wanted, I was stunned—and mad.

"Where is our money?" Sharyn asked.

I couldn't believe it. Sharyn had tracked me down on the other side of the globe to ask me about our money. She knew perfectly well that I didn't have it. Ed May had it. And if she wanted to know where our money was, all she had to do was ask him.

Ed May was a Detroit lawyer. He represented Joe Sparma, a Detroit pitcher and a good friend of mine. Sparma had suggested that I talk to May about handling my finances. That seemed like a good idea. I had money coming in from all directions, but I wasn't sure what to do with it other than spend it. Seriously, what does a 25-year-old kid who went straight from high school to professional baseball know about financial planning? I also needed help paying my bills, many of which I had let slide for too long.

May looked like the answer. He said he would come in, square my accounts with all my creditors and keep track of my businesses. And that wasn't all. With his help, he said, I could expand. Instead of just being a distributor for Dyco paint, why not manufacture it? My profits would multiply, he said, and Denny McLain Paint, complete with my picture on the label, would keep me in business long after I retired from baseball. It was a free ticket to Easy Street. Well, not exactly free—I'd have to put up a lot of money at the start—but before long the cash would be pouring in like water through a floodgate.

Sounded good to me. All I had to do was play baseball. Ed May would handle everything else—the paint company, Jetravel, even paying the bill for the morning newspaper. Early in the summer of 1969, I gave May the go-ahead. After that, everything I earned went directly to him. He controlled my life. So when Sharyn called me in Vietnam to ask about our money, I was steamed.

"You know damn well where our money is," I told her. "With Ed May." I was relieved that our kids were OK, but I was really annoyed that she had gotten me all worried over nothing.

"You don't understand," she said. "Our house payments haven't been made in months and the electricity is going to be turned off. I keep calling Ed May, but he doesn't return my phone calls. What am I supposed to do about these bills?"

Now I *was* worried. Something was wrong. I immediately made arrangements to fly home. The trip took 20 hours, and I spent most of that time nervously trying to convince myself that it was all just a horrible mistake and that May would explain everything.

When I got back to Detroit, I went straight to May's office. No sign of him. Then I went to his home. Same thing. Then I went to Sparma's house, and he told me he was looking for May, too. Even Al Kaline, who had put some of his money in May's hands, was getting nervous.

A couple of days later, Sparma caught up with May at his office in Livonia, Mich. May had ripped us off, all right, and everything May had taken was gone. Joe reacted about the way you'd expect. He beat the hell out of the guy. When Joe was through with him, May looked like one big bruise. I know, because I got there about an hour later and saw the damage. I was tempted to rough him up some more, but I'm not the fighting type, so I just grabbed him by the lapels of his coat, said "I should kill you, you sonofabitch," and threw him back in his chair. Sparma had done enough damage already.

May, of course, was the one who really drew blood. Sparma was out a lot of money, Kaline somewhat less. For me, the tab was everything I had. All the money I had earned and everything I had invested in my paint company and other businesses was gone.

Where? I still don't know for sure, but Ed May does. The money probably wound up in the Orient, where, I was told, May and his secretary had taken a trip sometime before.

A few months later—in June 1970—I took a trip to bankruptcy court. My debts totaled more than $446,000, while my assets were more like $400. I owed everybody from the Water Department in Beverly Hills, Mich., the Detroit suburb where we rented a house, to the Detroit Tigers, who had advanced me part of my 1970 salary. You could say that I was down and out in Beverly Hills.

You might be wondering how anyone could be so stupid. Well, it came easy for me. Remember, I was only 25. Spending money came instinctively, but investing didn't. Financially—and probably in other ways as well—I was immature. When a straight-arrow-looking guy like Ed May came along and said he could keep me in line and make me rich, I believed him. Hell, Joe Sparma, one of my best friends, recommended him. Maybe I should have been more careful, but I just didn't give it much thought. Ed May had relieved me of that responsibility.

You have to realize that I was out of town playing ball half the summer. And when I wasn't playing ball, I was making appearances behind every organ and podium from Boston to Los Angeles. When was I supposed to be running my businesses? When I did drop by the office, it was a social call more than anything else. I was the boss, but what did I know? I went to the factory and saw the guys make paint. I saw them put labels on the cans. I saw them load the cans into boxes. That sure didn't make me an expert on the business. I was just the guy with the big name who put up the money. And Ed May took me for everything I had.

May later was disbarred for similar transgressions with other clients. That didn't do me any good. And while I got the worse end of the deal, my 86 creditors weren't far behind. The bankruptcy proceedings left them with no way to recover the money I owed them. All of us were left holding the bag. I was able to start over with a clean slate, but "clean slate" translated into "absolutely nothing." I was broke. And, to complicate matters, I had little means to support my family. That was because I had run into another of life's little hurdles. Here it was, the summer of 1970, and I wasn't even working. I was persona non grata in the baseball community.

The trouble started when I was featured on the cover of Sports Illustrated. Now, it might seem natural that a two-time Cy Young winner would be featured on the cover of a national sports magazine, but this cover story, dated February 23, 1970, was anything but ordinary. I was pictured, in uniform, from the chest up, and two headlines accompanied my photo. The biggest headline was in red letters that spelled out, "Baseball's Big Scandal." Above that in smaller, yellow letters were the words, "Denny McLain and the Mob." A third headline, "Downfall of a Hero," was above the story, which began on page 16. Obviously, this wasn't another star athlete-makes-good fluff story. No, Sports Illustrated was more interested in Denny McLain, gangster.

The story made for interesting reading, I must admit. And the gist of the story—that I had been involved in bookmaking activities in 1967—was correct. But the facts as presented by Sports Illustrated were so far out in left field that it was almost funny. Almost. I wasn't laughing.

The article was right about a couple of things. I was gambling, and for a while I considered myself a bookmaker. Other than that, the story could have been written by Hans Christian Andersen. It was a fairy tale.

Like Sports Illustrated reported, I was gambling in 1967. The number of my bets was fairly high, but the stakes weren't—usually only $50 on each football or basketball game. No baseball! I never bet on baseball. Even after leaving the game, I still haven't bet on it. Oh, I'd bet a candy bar or a Pepsi on a World Series game now and then, particularly when I was in prison and I *needed* that extra Pepsi, but nothing serious. Betting on baseball just didn't interest me.

Why? For one thing, I've always had too much respect for the game. That may sound stuffy coming from an ex-con, but it's true. Baseball is a great game, and I didn't want to compromise it in any way. Another good reason for steering clear of baseball bets was money. It's a cinch that if you bet on baseball, you won't have any. Betting baseball is a losing proposition, even if you're inside the game. I'm sure that fewer baseball players bet on their sport than athletes in any other sport. I know of football and basketball players who would make bets, usually through somebody else, on games in which they were not involved. But in all my years in baseball, I never knew of any player to bet on baseball. It's not that baseball players don't like to gamble. Lots of guys played the horses or bet on football and basketball. Hell, some guys would bet on a grasshopper race if the odds were right. But not baseball. It's too tough to handicap.

Bookmakers see it differently, of course. They'll take all the baseball bets they can get. To them, it's a sound business proposition. For one thing, rather than giving a point spread as in basketball or football, baseball bookies establish a "dollar line" that produces more vigorish—sometimes a great deal more —than betting on other sports. In addition, bookies have more confidence in baseball than any other sport. You'll hear about a point-shaving scandal in basketball now and then, but when was the last time anyone was accused of throwing a baseball game? 1919, the year of the Chicago Black Sox. As for football, just consider all the betting lines, injury updates and gambling tip services you see in different publications. Broadcasters and sportswriters mention point spreads all the time. Think gamblers don't use that information? Of course they do. But nobody ever talks about the dollar line on a baseball game. A betting atmosphere just doesn't surround baseball the way it does other sports. Don't get me wrong, I'm not saying that basketball, football, hockey, badminton or any other sport is dishonest. I'm just saying that bookies have great confidence in the honesty of professional baseball. It's ironic that baseball's integrity gets a resounding vote of confidence from bookmakers.

Anyway, Ed Schober and I were placing a lot of bets in 1967. Ed, the Pepsi-Cola guy who made sure my refrigerator was never empty, was a good friend. We played golf together, drank together, screwed around together, did everything together. Including gambling. Ed was a bigger player than I was. He had more money to burn, so he was betting $300 or $400 a game. That just meant he was losing more because neither of us was very successful.

Winning is great, but for me, the appeal of gambling was the excitement. I loved the action. Having a monetary interest, regardless of the amount, in the outcome of a game made it that much more exciting to watch. If I lost, well, at least I had fun in the process. And if I won, so much the better.

We played the horses sometimes, too, and of course I played cards with guys in the clubhouse. When I played poker with my teammates, I was easy prey. They even called me Dolphin because I was like a fish out of water. But gambling was a fun way to pass the time, so even if I dropped $100 or $200 in a particularly bad week, I didn't mind too much. I was just having a good time.

Schober and I were also betting with a guy named Clyde Roberts, who fared about as well as we did. Clyde ran the Shorthorn Steak House in Flint, a town located about 50 miles northwest of Detroit. I had been booked to play the organ at the Shorthorn, and I got to know Clyde pretty well. One day Clyde had an idea.

"You know, I think we're on the wrong end of this deal," he said. "We keep losing, and our bookie is making a lot of money off us. I know several guys who like to play. Maybe we should be taking *their* bets."

In other words, Roberts was saying that we should become bookmakers. I passed on the idea at first, but the more money I began to lose gambling, the more sense it seemed to make. You know, if you can't beat 'em, join 'em. Schober had the same thought. Dollar signs started to cloud our eyesight, so we said sure, we'd be bookies.

The deal was this: Roberts and a friend of his named Jiggs Gazell would run the operation out of the Shorthorn. Rumor had it that Gazell, whom I had seen around the Shorthorn a few times, was a small-time criminal, although I don't know if those rumors were true. Anyway, no bets were to exceed $100, and if Roberts and Gazell wanted to take a bigger bet, it would have to be approved by Schober. Ed and I didn't have to worry about the day-to-day operation of the handbook; we'd just come up with money to pay off winners when necessary, and the rest of the time we'd drop by to pick up our profits. Bearing in mind my lack of success as a gambler, I figured I'd have a healthy outside income for the next several months, thanks to guys who couldn't pick winners any better than I could.

A bookie needs a bankroll, so I had to borrow some money. I went to see a friend of mine. He was a banker by day, a gambler by night. He hung around the Shorthorn himself and knew precisely why I wanted the money. He loaned me about $4,500, as I recall, $500 of which I returned to him as a kickback. At my trial years later, I was accused—wrongly, I might add—of taking a kickback from a guy who had borrowed money from my employer. I didn't take kickbacks, but in 1967, I wasn't above paying one to get our bookmaking operation started.

We opened for business early in the '67 season. Understand up front that we didn't take any baseball bets—none that I knew of, anyway. We were taking bets on horses that ran at nearby racetracks. Gamblers could have placed bets on the horses legally at the track, but then they'd have to pay taxes on their winnings.

We got off to a bad start. Within a couple of weeks, I was back at the bank getting another loan, this time for about $3,000. A few more weeks went by, and still we were losing. Whenever I heard from Schober, he was telling me that Roberts and Gazell needed more money to pay off winners. In the eight or 10 weeks that I was involved in this operation, not once did we have a winning week. Not once. Bookies have a bad week now and then, but not all the time. Hell, bookmaking is one of the least risky businesses around. Somehow, I was losing money at it.

Something was fishy. It just took me awhile to figure out what.

We were getting hustled. Roberts and Gazell were taking Schober and me to the cleaners. You can't beat the horses. No one in the world can beat the horses consistently. That meant one of two things was happening: Either the gamblers playing with us lost just like everybody else and Roberts and Gazell were splitting the money we coughed up each week, or the whole bookmaking operation was a hoax. My guess is the latter explanation. I have no proof that anybody ever placed a bet with Roberts and Gazell, and the FBI reached the same conclusion when its agents investigated a few years later. Either way, Schober and I were getting screwed.

So, we thought we were bookmakers, but we weren't. We were chumps. Unfortunately, it cost me about $15,000 before I realized that. At that point, I told Ed sayonara. If he wanted to be a bookmaker, fine, but I was out. I'd lost enough money.

The Sports Illustrated article led off with a story about a guy named Ed Voshen. According to the magazine, this guy placed a bet with our book on a horse named Williamston Kid on August 4, 1967. The horse won the eighth race at Detroit Race Course and paid $21 to win, $9 to place and $6.20 to show. The magazine said that Voshen had bet $8,000 on the horse—$2,000 to win, $5,000 to place and $1,000 to show. Voshen's total winnings: $46,600.

Imagine my surprise when I got a call from Schober informing me that we'd been hit for 46 grand. My first reaction was "So what?" I didn't have anything to do with it because I'd dropped out of the operation several weeks before. And besides, Ed said he hadn't approved the bet, so I didn't see why he'd have to pay it off. Let Roberts and Gazell worry about it.

Well, Ed was upset and thought he had to pay off this guy. Roberts and Gazell apparently had convinced him that if he didn't, Voshen had friends who would change his mind. Schober was scared.

Ed asked me to loan him some money, which I did. It may seem stupid for me to put money back into an operation I had abandoned, but Ed was a good friend who needed help. I don't know if the money I loaned Schober—probably eight or 10 thousand bucks—ever got to Voshen, but that wasn't my concern. Ed needed the money, and I loaned it to him. It was that simple.

Schober kept getting threatening phone calls and letters—from whom, I haven't the foggiest—saying he had to pay off Voshen. Whoever it was, they sure had Ed worried about the safety of his family. Schober really thought he was in deep with the Mafia or something.

Sometime after the '67 season, Ed asked me if I would meet with Voshen and ask him to be patient. I wasn't crazy about the idea, but I said OK. I wanted to help Ed, plus I had my own reasons for wanting to talk to Voshen. Roberts and Gazell had been tossing my name around, and I wanted to let Voshen know in no uncertain terms that I had retired as a bookie and he wasn't going to get a dime from me.

One day when I was driving through Michigan, I dropped by the truck stop Voshen owned near Battle Creek. He wasn't there. Another time, Schober set up a meeting between me and Voshen at a restaurant at the intersection of 7 Mile and Telegraph roads in Detroit. Schober told me that Voshen would be there by 5 p.m. and that I should wait in my car in the parking lot. He didn't show up right away, and each time a car pulled into the parking lot and headed toward me, I almost lost my lunch. I had visions of a 1934 Packard screeching into the parking lot with gangsters hanging out both sides and emptying their machine guns into my white Corvette. It was really cloak and dagger.

But nothing happened. I sat in my car in rainy, nasty weather for more than three hours and Voshen never showed, despite Schober's assurances that he was on his way. That episode, as much as anything else, convinced me that the whole bet was a scam. If Voshen really wanted his money, he would've been there.

And that's where the story ends. Schober borrowed some more money from me, but when nobody ever came around to beat up Ed or threaten his wife and kids, he quit worrying about it. He'd lost a lot of money in the deal, much more than I had, but we never heard another word about it.

Until Sports Illustrated resurrected the issue—and completely rewrote history.

According to the magazine, Voshen went to Gazell to collect his money. Gazell, who was identified as "a member of a local Syrian mob loosely allied with Detroit's Cosa Nostra," scraped up $1,000 but said he couldn't get the rest. He told Voshen to see his partners—Schober and me.

The magazine said Voshen didn't do any better when he tried to get the money from Schober. Voshen then supposedly got a call from Lou Boudreau, who was calling on my behalf to let him know he'd get his money. My father-in-law then allegedly called him again, pleading for more time.

Bullshit. Lou Boudreau had no part in this mess. He never called anybody, never was called by anybody, never knew anything about it. If Voshen actually did place the bet with Roberts and Gazell—and I don't think he did—he may have been trying to collect his money. But my father-in-law had nothing to do with it.

Just wait. This fairy tale gets even better.

According to the magazine, Voshen grew impatient waiting for his bookies to pay up and went to Tony Giacalone for help. If that name rings a bell, it might be because the day Jimmy Hoffa disappeared in 1975, he was believed to be on his way to meet with Giacalone. Sports Illustrated identified Giacalone as an "enforcer for Joe Zerilli, the Detroit Cosa Nostra boss." The story was that Giacalone told Voshen to get lost, that it wasn't his problem. But he must have had a change of heart, the magazine said, which brings us to the Case of the Injured Toes.

The wounded toes were mine, and they constituted a big chunk of the Sports Illustrated article. On September 18, 1967, I lasted only two innings in a game we lost to the Red Sox. Shortly thereafter, I reported I had dislocated two toes on my left foot. As you'll recall, we were in the midst of a great pennant race, but I couldn't pitch again until the last day of the season. That was when I botched the second game of a doubleheader, costing us a tie for the flag.

Sports Illustrated said there were conflicting stories about how I hurt my toes. It had been the result of (a) stubbing my toes at home after my foot had fallen asleep; (b) banging into something while chasing raccoons that were raiding my garbage cans; (c) kicking a water cooler after being removed from a game, or (d) angrily kicking lockers in the clubhouse.

The truth? Probably a combination of all four stories. After that game against the Red Sox, I was mad. I hated losing, and I especially hated getting knocked around. So when I went back to the clubhouse after Mayo yanked me, I was destructive. I think I smashed every light bulb in the runway between the dugout and the clubhouse with my glove. Then I let loose on my locker. Just kicked the shit out of it. My toes were a little sore, but nothing serious. At least I could walk.

Later that night, I fell asleep on the couch at home while watching "The Untouchables" on TV. I was awakened by a noise in the garage. It sounded like an animal was knocking into the trash cans. When I got up to investigate, my foot was asleep and I sprained my toes. Now it hurt like hell. When I woke up the next morning, I could hardly walk.

Nobody was awake to vouch for what happened to me at home, but a few of my teammates—Joe Sparma and Mickey Lolich among them—later told reporters they'd seen me kicking things in the clubhouse after the game. So there you have it—the solution to the Case of the Injured Toes.

That explanation wasn't exciting enough for Sports Illustrated, so the writer offered another theory: "There is also a fifth version. McLain was ordered to report to Giacalone's boatwell; Tony wasn't as uninterested in the debt (to Voshen) as he had professed. Once McLain was there, Tony Giacalone and his brother Billy, another Mafioso, went into their 'angry act.' Giacalone is under the impression that he's a great psychologist, that he can outpsych anyone. He gave McLain the full act, including his famous stare. Then he brought his heel down on McLain's toes and told him to get the money up."

Pretty juicy story, huh? You can almost hear violins playing the theme from "The Godfather" in the background as the Mafia guy digs his heel into the pitcher's toes. Not as dramatic as finding a horse's head in my bed, maybe, but effective nonetheless. I hate to spoil a good story, but I must make one slight correction. It's bullshit. I never met Tony Giacalone in my life. I can't say I never heard of him because everybody in Detroit had heard of him. But I never met him. The closest I came was in prison. I heard Giacalone was released from Talladega about a month before I arrived. That was a shame because I would have liked to meet the guy. Maybe he could have told me where the story came from!

If you want to give a story pizzazz, just add a name that ends in a vowel. Sports Illustrated seemed to be following that strategy with Giacalone, and the U.S. government did the same thing 14 years later with a guy named Frank Cocchiaro. That was a guy I went to prison with.

In any event, I never was in any boatwell, never was threatened, never was asked by anybody but Schober to help pay off Voshen. Lies, lies, lies. The article also tried to connect me with a couple of criminals, a Mafia guy and a partner of Giacalone's, implying that I was in business with them or something. No sources were cited, and the alleged connection between me and them was never spelled out. Talk about bad reporting! I've been misrepresented by the media plenty of times, but this story takes the cake. To set the record straight, I had never met either of the guys mentioned, never owed them a nickel, never was their partner. Period.

Needless to say, I wasn't too impressed with Sports Illustrated's idea of investigative reporting. Before I drop it, let me quote from the first paragraph of the article, which started off talking about Williamston Kid's victory: ". . . the win set in motion forces that led to the violent death of one man; may have cost the Detroit Tigers the 1967 pennant; threaten the career of their star pitcher, Denny McLain; and test the integrity of major league baseball." Voshen did, in fact, die a violent death. The car he was driving one day in 1968 smashed into a tree. How that was connected to any bet he supposedly won, I'll never know. The Tigers certainly didn't lose the pennant because of that bet, either, because my foot injury was totally unrelated to the bookie business. I don't see how the integrity of major league baseball was involved because we never took any baseball bets (assuming Roberts and Gazell took any bets at all). Some people might think that any tie-in between a baseball player and gambling automatically places the integrity of the game in question, but I don't. Granted, the business was illegal, but it didn't compromise major league baseball one bit.

As for threatening my career, the victory by Williamston Kid certainly did that. Not immediately, of course—I won 55 games over the next two years—but thanks to all the publicity that resulted from Sports Illustrated's story, my career was temporarily put on hold in 1970. So, Sports Illustrated went one for four. I struck out.

One of the worst pieces of legal advice I ever got was when my attorney convinced me not to sue Sports Illustrated. I had every intention of nailing those bastards, but Mark McCormack, a fine lawyer who represented Arnold Palmer, talked me out of it. Bad move. The article was full of lies, and I could have made a fortune.

Before the story hit the newsstands, Bowie Kuhn, the new commissioner of baseball, got wind of it. He wasn't any happier about it than I was. On February 13, 1970, he summoned me to his office in New York. I'd already admitted to my attorneys and several FBI agents that I had been involved in a bookmaking operation, so when Kuhn asked me about it, I was honest with him. After less than an hour of playing Q&A, we were through. He gave the press a general idea of what our meeting was about and indicated that a decision on my future would be made soon.

I was scared. My whole world seemed to be falling apart. Word of my financial problems had become public knowledge. It seemed like everybody in Detroit was suing me for not paying some bill. FBI agents were calling me constantly to talk about a big gambling investigation they were conducting. And the commissioner of baseball was pondering what to do about me. Fires were starting all around me, and I was trapped with a dry hose.

On February 18, Schober and I testified before a federal grand jury in Detroit. The feds seemed to think I was involved with a nationwide sports gambling ring and organized crime, but they soon discovered otherwise. My testimony lasted about 45 minutes, just long enough for the feds to realize we were small potatoes, the victims of hustlers. I just hoped Bowie Kuhn got the same message.

The next day, Bowie again requested the pleasure of my company. For more than five hours, the commissioner talked with me, my attorney and some baseball administrators. There were a lot of private conversations and I was in on only a few of those. So I spent most of that time twiddling my thumbs and worrying.

And for good reason. When Bowie called me back into his office, he told me that I was suspended indefinitely. Until informed otherwise, I could not have anything to do with Organized Baseball.

When I heard that, my knees nearly buckled. I happened to be standing near a window, and I grabbed the sill for support. Sweating bullets and breathing rapidly, I looked down. It was a long way to the ground. For just a second, I considered jumping. I guess this sounds stupid, but with my financial bind courtesy of Ed May and now my livelihood in a state of limbo, it seemed like a good idea—for a moment. But I probably would have landed on a group of Boy Scouts and killed a couple. That was just the way things were going.

Kuhn told reporters that he was suspending me because of the things I had admitted to him, not the Sports Illustrated article. That pissed me off. I had come clean with the guy, and instead of cutting me some slack, he brought down the hammer. Does that make sense? Now if I had lied to him and he found out what I was doing anyway, that's one thing. But when somebody admits his guilt—and I don't think being taken in a scam made me guilty of anything but bad judgment—a little leniency should be in order. Did Kuhn really expect anybody else to come into his office and admit wrongdoing after what he did to me? If so, he was loonier than I thought.

I immediately headed for our home in Lakeland, where the Tigers were opening camp. It hurt like hell to be so close to the team, yet so far from the game. I couldn't even go to the ball park and talk to the guys. So, I spent most of my time playing golf. My golf game really improved over the following weeks, which is about the only positive thing I can say about my suspension.

My immediate concern was money. We didn't have any. Mark McCormack had come in to clean up Ed May's mess, but he couldn't manufacture an income for me. My $90,000 salary from the Tigers was cut off the minute Kuhn suspended me, and nobody wanted me to play the organ at their nightclub anymore. When you're hot, you're hot. When you're not, you're not. I wasn't.

To support my family, I did an exclusive TV interview with a Detroit station that paid a lot of bills, plus I made other personal appearances whenever a group would have me. The weeks dragged by while the commissioner blundered around, trying to figure out what to do with me. He certainly didn't seem to be in any hurry to let me know. When my 26th birthday came and went March 29, I still was in the dark. Our season opener, a game I still had hopes of starting, was only eight days away. I was playing 18 or 36 holes of golf every day and throwing a baseball three times a week, but whether or not that mattered was up to Bowie.

Kuhn was a rookie commissioner and I really didn't know what to expect from him. In the following years, it became apparent that he wasn't much of a commissioner. And I'm not just talking sour grapes. He was too much of a fan and not enough of an objective decision-maker. Why, for instance, did he let the designated hitter situation get out of hand? Either both leagues should have it or neither should. Plain and simple. But he wasn't strong enough to settle the issue and now we have two leagues operating with different rules.

But what really made me gag was Bowie's holier-than-thou attitude about "the integrity of the game." How could anyone in his right mind ban Mickey Mantle and Willie Mays, two of the greatest players in the history of the game, from any ties to Organized Baseball? What a joke. So they did public relations work for casinos in Atlantic City, where gambling is perfectly legal and aboveboard. How did that tarnish baseball's good name? Bowie's head must have been buried in someone's on-deck circle. Wake up and smell the pine tar, Bowie! Peter Ueberroth welcomed them back to baseball and the game seems to be doing just fine.

Finally, on April Fools' Day—believe me, the irony doesn't escape me—Kuhn announced his decision. I was out until July 1. He told reporters that the suspension wasn't longer because I hadn't actually been a bookmaker in 1967; I just thought I was. When some guy asked him to clarify that, he said "the difference is the same as between murder and attempted murder."

The media had a heyday with that one. Everybody considered that one of the most ridiculous lines of reasoning ever. A guy in Montreal wrote: "It follows, of course, that you and I may rob a bank today and if we discover later the loot was all non-negotiable bonds, we really didn't rob the bank. You're only guilty when the crime pays." Kuhn probably caught more flak for that remark than I did for trying to be a bookie.

Most sportswriters thought I got off easy. They said that a year's suspension, maybe more, fit my crime.

I disagree. Nobody had found me guilty of anything but stupidity and gullibility, so I figured I'd already been punished enough. On the other hand, I knew the commissioner was free to nail me to the wall. The press would have loved that. Still, when I got word that I'd be out for three more months, I was shocked. I never thought he'd do it.

During my suspension, I filled my days with golf, throwing baseballs and going to the movies twice a week with Sharyn. She and her family were very supportive. And it was nice having time to spend with Sharyn and the kids, but I really did miss playing ball. Mayo Smith had told me I'd be pitching against New York on July 1, so I just crossed the days off my calendar until then.

I don't know which was a bigger media circus: the coverage of my 30th victory in 1968 or my 1970 debut against the Yankees. More than 53,000 fans showed up, the biggest crowd at Tiger Stadium in almost a decade, and about six dozen writers covered the game. The fans were really behind me, cheering and clapping, and that was great. They just wanted to see ol' Denny start plowing through the American League again.

But that's not what happened. The Yankees blasted three home runs, took a 5-3 lead and sent me to the showers after 5⅓ innings. We wound up winning the game, but my season went downhill from there. In 14 games, I went 3-5 with a 4.65 ERA. I was terrible.

Most of my problem was concentration. I didn't have any. Before 1970, I didn't hear anything when I was pitching. I could tune out the crowd. But in 1970, with the suspension, the bankruptcy proceedings and all the resulting controversy swirling around me, I heard everything. And there's no way you can pitch when you're listening to the loudmouth in the second row. No way.

Another thing that people forget is that the mound was lowered five inches in 1969. I had a hell of a year in '69, but my strikeouts were down nearly 100 that season. That was a direct result of the mound being lowered. I'm not a tall guy, especially from the waist down, and I needed all the leverage I could get. The higher the mound, the more leverage you get, so when they dropped the mound five inches, my pitches lost a lot of their "oomph." Combine those factors with the increasing number of cortisone shots I was getting in my sore right shoulder, and I just wasn't the same pitcher who had won 108 games the previous five years.

Losing really got to me. I wasn't used to it and didn't know how to handle it. When my frustration reached the boiling point, I pulled off another of my dumb stunts. A stupid little practical joke to help relieve my tension.

One day in late August, I hid a bucket of warm whirlpool water in my locker and waited for a reporter to come by. Jim Hawkins, a young writer for the Detroit Free Press who was new to the beat, was my first visitor, and we chatted for a few minutes. When Jim started to leave, Joe Niekro, one of our pitchers, asked him to sit down. At that point, I dumped the bucket of water over his head. Just soaked him. Everybody in the clubhouse cracked up, and Jim even laughed. I'm sure he didn't appreciate the bath, but he took it very well. He got up and went somewhere to dry off.

That was fun. Not one to know when enough was enough, I decided to do it again. My next victim was Watson Spoelstra, an old-timer with the Detroit News. Maybe the fact that he wasn't a rookie reporter like Hawkins made him a little less tolerant, because after I soaked him with a bucket of water, he went to a phone and called Jim Campbell, the Tigers' general manager.

Campbell called me in the dugout in the first inning of our game that night. He obviously wasn't amused. After the game, he said, I was to haul my ass up to his office.

Mayo Smith went with me, which turned out to be wise. Campbell had always stood by me and given me more breaks than I deserved, and he still is a good friend. But this time I'd gone too far. I could almost see the steam coming out of his ears as we walked in the room. The real fireworks didn't start, however, until Campbell told me he was suspending me.

I went berserk. If Mayo hadn't been there, somebody might have gotten hurt. I started yelling and screaming, calling Jim every name in the book and telling him that I was sick of Detroit, sick of the Tigers, sick of the fans, sick of everybody. Ranting and raving like a lunatic, I got down on my hands and knees, right in front of his desk, and pleaded: "Get me the fuck out of here. Just get me out of here. Please, get me out of here!" Jim was still boiling, too, but neither of us took a swing. Actually, we both could've used a bucket of water over our heads.

A lot of the things that happened and were said that night made the papers, and I felt awful about it. What had started out as a harmless practical joke had become a catastrophe. I was fast becoming as popular in Detroit as a Volkswagen dealer.

Ironically, the guys who got doused seemed more understanding than anybody else. I'd picked sportswriters as my targets because they seemed to be all over my case while I was struggling that summer, but both guys were quick to accept my apologies the next day. They shrugged it off for what it was—a childish clubhouse prank.

Even after my explosive confrontation with Campbell, the Tigers might have been ready to shrug it off. But they never got the chance. My suspension was supposed to last a week, but before Campbell could reinstate me, the commissioner's office called, told him to hold off and summoned me to New York for another chat. Would you believe that I was suspended again? Sure you would.

This suspension didn't really have anything to do with the water-dumping incident. Somebody told the commissioner that I had been carrying a gun with me on road trips, which was a lie. The only time I had a gun with me was when I drove my car in Detroit, a city with a severe crime problem. I kept a small handgun under the front seat. Carrying a gun was a violation of the probationary status of my first suspension, and when Kuhn found out, he canned me for the rest of the season. From two-time Cy Young winner to three-time suspendee, all in less than 12 months.

I'd had enough meetings with the commissioner that year to last a lifetime. But he asked to see me one more time. Maybe he was lonely. Anyway, he suggested a trade. For once, I agreed with him.

Detroit was great and I loved playing for Mayo Smith, but I'd had it with just about everything else, from Tiger Stadium (heaven for hitters, hell for pitchers) to the media (just hell). Every time I blew my nose it was a front-page story in Detroit. My life was an open book. My main beef was that I knew some nasty stuff about the local sportswriters, yet they never saw their picture in the paper under some embarrassing headline. I know it goes with the territory of being a celebrity, but I just couldn't accept that. Fifteen years later, when I was on my way to prison because of a conspiracy that centered around my high profile, I couldn't accept that, either. I still can't.

Kuhn helped arrange the trade, but he had to weasel around the rules to do it. A suspended player can't be traded, and I still hadn't been reinstated when the season ended. But on October 9, 1970, the commissioner announced that he had secretly lifted my suspension October 1, the last day of the season, and that I was on my way to the Washington Senators.

Talk about the thrill of victory and the agony of defeat. I got both in one fell swoop. I was thrilled to be leaving Detroit, but I was about to find out that going to the Senators was worse than being sent to jail. I kid you not.

The manager in Washington was Ted Williams. Yeah, *that* Ted Williams. I figured he'd be a good guy to play for, and I had no doubt that I could win 20 games for the Senators in 1971. I figured I could win 20 for anybody. But I quickly learned that going from Mayo Smith to Ted Williams was like going from Gandhi to Godzilla. Instead of having a friend for a manager, I had a monster. Williams was a loudmouthed, egotistical, selfish sonofabitch. Before I met those rotten sleazeballs who perjured themselves to put me in jail, Ted Williams was guaranteed a top spot on my all-time "unfavorite people" list. He still makes my top 20.

Williams was a great hitter, no doubt about that. When I was a kid, I idolized the guy. But playing for Teddy Ballgame was a nightmare. He intimidated everybody. He seemed to thrive on towering over people and making them feel like shit. He berated players in the clubhouse and in the newspapers, and he was always bitching about how bad we were. He was right about that, but his constant insults certainly didn't help matters. I don't know what his problem was; maybe he just couldn't grasp the fact that most guys weren't as talented as he was. Whatever, Williams made life miserable in Washington.

Williams was no tougher on me than on anybody else. If nothing else, you can say he was consistent. He spread his hatefulness around pretty evenly. We clashed right off the bat when I told him I liked to pitch every fourth day and he said no, he'd be using a five-man rotation. What made Ted Williams such a pitching expert? I guess because he could hit it better than anybody. But take my word, as far as handling a pitching staff, he was no superstar. Even Williams had to admit that until 1970, I had done rather well on three days' rest. He didn't care. We had a couple of other run-ins that summer, but what I remember most is the day-to-day drudgery of being around the guy. My only relief was the three weeks in July I spent on the disabled list with a sore shoulder.

I had seriously hoped to turn things around in Washington, to get my career back on track. But in that atmosphere and with that team, it was hopeless. We were awful. Most teams measure their success by how many games they win in a season; we measured ours by how many we didn't lose. We were lacking in every phase of the game—pitching, hitting, fielding, baserunning, even standing at attention for the national anthem. Managing, too, but that's not why we finished 33 games under .500. We were just plain bad.

On the field, that is. Off the field was another story. Everyone is good at something, and this club excelled off the diamond. Some of the best times I had in baseball were with the Senators. We didn't know how to win, but we knew how to have a good time.

So how did I fare? I won 10 games, lost 22 and posted a 4.27 ERA. That's right, two years after leading the league in victories for the second straight season, I led the league in defeats. My pitching was nothing to brag about, but it would've been nice to get some runs. That's the only thing I missed about Detroit; the Tigers sure could score.

After that season, Washington lost the Senators for the second time. The original Senators had moved to Minnesota in 1961; now the second Senators club was on its way to Arlington, Tex., where it would become the Rangers.

I thought the move was terrific. I already had a radio/TV package lined up with a couple of Dallas stations, and I could foresee all kinds of business opportunities in a city that was getting its first major league baseball team. The folks in the Dallas-Fort Worth area were going bananas over getting the worst club in the league.

But I wasn't around long enough to share in that excitement. In spring training in 1972, I was traded to the Oakland A's.

Would you believe that I went from one manager named Williams to another? I was happy to be away from Ted, but Dick Williams wasn't any joyride, either. At least he was a good manager, and he has the World Series rings to prove it. But our relationship got off to a bad start when Dick all but told a reporter that the only reason the A's had made the deal was to put pressure on Vida Blue, who was a holdout at the time, and that when Blue returned, I'd be packing my gear. Nothing like a warm welcome.

At least I was forewarned. Blue came back, all right, and I was gone a few days later. The A's were a hell of a team—they had won the A.L. West crown the year before with guys like Joe Rudi, Reggie Jackson, Sal Bando, Catfish Hunter, Rollie Fingers and Blue—and I guess they thought their pitching staff was good enough without me. I pitched in only five games for Oakland, going 1-2 and not looking sharp at all. Then, on May 15, 1972, I was sent to the minor leagues for the first time since 1964.

I thought it was kind of funny that Oakland had acquired me in the first place. In 1969, I had cranked on Charlie Finley, the A's owner, about the guy he had playing the organ at the Oakland Coliseum. The organist really bugged me one day by playing while I was trying to pitch. He caused me to balk a run home, and I started hollering about it. I must have gotten a bit wordy because the umpire threw me out. First time in my life that had ever happened. Afterward, I told the press that Finley was running a circus and that he should do something about his organist. Not only was the guy lacking in class, but he wasn't that talented, either.

I didn't have to go to the minors. Retirement was a possibility. Just three years earlier I had won my second Cy Young Award, and now the A's wanted me to pitch in Birmingham in the Southern League, two notches below the majors. It was kind of tough to swallow. But my family was about to add one more member and I didn't have any other way of providing for it. No longer was I a hot commodity. The deals, the endorsements, the nightclub gigs—all were a thing of the past. All I had was my $75,000 baseball salary, which the A's had to keep paying if I went to the minors. That made my decision easy.

On top of that, I still loved to pitch. I'd been throwing a baseball about 20 years, and deep down I wasn't ready to call it quits. Countless cortisone shots and excessive use had left my shoulder pretty ragged, but I thought I still had a few good pitches left in me. I wanted another shot at the majors.

Still, it was a tough blow at an especially tough time. Sharyn was pregnant with Michelle, and it had not been an easy pregnancy. At one point she felt so sick that she had to go in the hospital. Sharyn's being pregnant had come as a big surprise anyway, and naturally, we were worried that she'd have another miscarriage. So I felt pretty bad when I went off to Birmingham and she stayed at our home in the Oakland suburbs with Kristi, Denny and Timmy. I didn't like being away, and when Sharyn delivered a month early, on May 27, I wasn't there for her. Kenny Holtzman, a good friend of mine who pitched for the A's, took Sharyn to the hospital and stayed with her until she went in the delivery room. We named Michelle after Kenny's wife.

Michelle, the baby of the family, is one of the greatest joys of my life, but it didn't look like she was going to make it right after she was born. She weighed only about five pounds at birth. Her liver wasn't functioning and she had jaundice. She didn't leave the hospital until she was about 3½ weeks old, so it was really touch and go there for a while. We've spent many sleepless nights worrying about her health, which hasn't been as good as our other kids' over the years, but she seems to be doing fine now. Michelle is a beautiful, healthy girl, quite a lady, and as far as we can tell, some loss of hearing is about the only lasting effect of her premature birth.

Michelle's condition definitely was on my mind that summer, although I don't think that was why I struggled on the mound. Dick Williams had said my fastball didn't have much zip, and when bush leaguers started launching my pitches over those Southern League fences, it occurred to me that maybe he was right. Physically, I just wasn't with it. I was a little overweight, and doctors had determined I had a potassium deficiency that was sapping my energy.

Once that problem was corrected, my strength started coming back. Meanwhile, that Alabama heat was loosening up my shoulder, which hadn't felt good for quite some time. Though I had a 3-3 record and a 6.32 ERA after six weeks at Birmingham, I thought the A's might be ready to give me another try.

Not hardly. The A's apparently were just biding time until they could find someone to take me off their hands. That someone was the Atlanta Braves, who acquired me in exchange for Orlando Cepeda on June 29, 1972.

Trivia question: What do Charlie Finley and the U.S. government have in common? They both sent Denny McLain to Atlanta.

That trade is a good example of how fleeting baseball fame can be. Orlando Cepeda was the National League's MVP in 1967, and I won the A.L. MVP the next year. Then in 1972 we were traded for each other, and it wasn't that big of a deal. I was several years younger than Cepeda, but we were both has-beens.

The Braves had so little pitching, though, that they were willing to give a has-been a try. The first time I pitched for the Braves was in the second game of a July 4 doubleheader in Atlanta. My name still meant a lot, I guess, because more than 50,000 people showed up. That was only about 40,000 more than the Braves usually drew. The fans greeted me with a standing ovation. Incredible. It was just like the game I pitched in Detroit after returning from my first suspension in 1970. There must be something special about making your debut in the middle of the season.

I'd had some memorable debuts in baseball, but this one was easily the weirdest. As a Little Leaguer, I had that 5-for-5 game my first time out. Then came that no-hitter in my professional debut. In my first major league game, I hit a home run. And now in my National League debut, I pitched a tie. Typical Denny McLain. Anything to be different.

My stuff wasn't too bad that afternoon. I had a 3-2 lead when Ron Santo, a hell of a hitter, led off the seventh inning. I jammed him with a fastball that he blooped about 30 feet beyond the first baseman. Wouldn't you know, it landed smack dab on the foul line and squirted away, and Santo had a triple. He scored on a sacrifice fly to tie the game. In the top of the next inning, rain started falling in sheets and the game was called. I had to settle for a 3-3 tie.

Lou Boudreau was in the broadcast booth calling that game for WGN radio in Chicago. He had to be encouraged to see his son-in-law pitching fairly well. And Sharyn was in the stands, hoping that this was a sign that the magic was coming back.

It wasn't. I pitched in 15 games for Atlanta, starting only eight, and went 3-5 with a 6.50 ERA. Those weren't the kind of numbers that made a club bend over backward to keep you around. Sure enough, at spring training in 1973, the Braves released me.

I don't remember much about the day I got canned. I know I'd pitched a couple of games that spring and done fairly well. Though my shoulder was sore and I came to camp with too much belly hanging over my belt, I thought my chances of making the club were pretty good. One night when I was scheduled to pitch in St. Petersburg, Braves Manager Eddie Mathews came up to me. I figured he was going to share a few words of encouragement before I started warming up.

A few words was all I got, but they weren't encouraging.

"Denny, I'm afraid we're going to have to release you," Mathews said.

And that was it. Five minutes later, my locker was empty and I was on my way out the door. Forever.

Denny McLain was washed up. I'd reached heights few pitchers even dreamed of, but on March 26, 1973, the Braves gave me my unconditional release. My major league career was over.

Three days later I turned 29.

CHAPTER 5

Wheeling
And Dealing

Here's another trivia question: Who is the only person whose father and husband both won MVP awards?

Answer: Sharyn Alice Boudreau McLain. Not surprisingly, my wife also is one of the greatest baseball fans I've ever seen.

Sharyn loves the game—the drama, the strategy, the physical performances. She knows as much about baseball as a lot of guys who played it. She was raised in a baseball family, and some of her fondest childhood memories are of getting all dressed up and going with her sister Barbara and her brother Lou to games her dad managed. And when I was playing, she attended just about every home game. It's just natural that she'd pick things up and become somewhat of an expert. She still watches the Cubs quite a bit, I guess because her dad was in the booth for so many years.

Sharyn loved to watch me pitch. She was always behind me 100 percent. She understood, and accepted, all my time away from home. It had been the same way with her dad. It just came with the territory. But when I hung up my glove, that changed. She expected me to be home more often. Not just in town, but at home.

That became a problem.

In the off-season before the Braves let me go, I had opened a couple of bars in Atlanta. For the first time, I was completely on my own. No partners. One of the joints, Gaffers, was more of a restaurant than a bar. It was a private little club for my pals that served about 30 to 40 people at a time. The other place, Denny McLain's Gaffers, served meals to local businessmen during the day but really was designed for the college crowd. It had pinball machines and live bands and was just a fun kind of place.

Fun for me, but not for Sharyn. I had been working my butt off to make these joints fly, and Sharyn was growing tired of my late hours. It was putting a strain on our marriage. She had been willing to accept my absence during my playing days, but she wasn't ready to play second fiddle to the bars. So, she left me.

Boy, did I ever get the message. After I left the house one day, she packed up everything we owned, loaded it into a U-Haul and drove back to Chicago with the kids. When I got home, the place was empty. She didn't even leave me a pillow.

I called her up, but she wouldn't come back. Not until I sold the bars. I played stubborn and told her I didn't want to sell. But when she filed for divorce, it dawned on me that she was serious. I finally put the bars up for sale and, fortunately, she came back.

While all this was going on, I got a call from Ray Johnston, who owned a Triple-A club in Des Moines called the Iowa Oaks. The Oaks had a working relationship with the White Sox.

"How would you like to come up here and pitch?" he asked. "If you can't pitch, you can do some other things for me."

That kind of offer appealed to Sharyn. She was all for my staying in baseball. And I still had the itch to pitch. So in April 1973, I was in Des Moines, back in uniform.

It was no use. The desire was there, but my shoulder wasn't. You just can't pitch with a bad shoulder, and my record (1-4 with a 7.55 ERA in eight games) proved it. Plus, I wasn't getting along with the Oaks' manager, Joe Sparks. To make things better for everyone, Johnston asked me to go pitch for his Double-A club in Shreveport. I went down there in July and finished the year. Though I did much better in the Texas League, winning six of 10 decisions and knocking more than three points off my ERA, my shoulder had had it. My pitching days were over—this time, for good.

Not yet 30 and with a family to support, I had to find a job. We moved back to Detroit, where I started doing radio and TV work that winter. Talking had always come easily to me, and Detroit was a good market. I hosted talk shows on Channel 20, a UHF TV station, and WEXL-AM radio. It was the toughest job I ever had in my life. My TV show, which started off live but then switched to tape, was on for an hour five nights a week, and my hourlong radio show was on six nights a week. It wasn't just sports talk, either. We talked about everything that was going on in Detroit. Unfortunately, there wasn't much happening there in the mid-1970s and it was tough getting guests every night. After a while, the everyday grind wore me down.

Probably because I was doing more than just broadcasting. In the summer of 1974, I played a little baseball on a semipro team in London, Ontario. It was just for fun, and I didn't even pitch much. I played catcher. I can't remember exactly what prompted me to play, but I think it had something to do with a restaurant or bar deal I was trying to work out with the owner of the team. That deal never panned out, but some others did.

Such as the one I got into with Paul Navarro, a Detroit physician. I bought into a shopping center called the Trading Post in Roseville, Mich., on the northeast side of Detroit. Actually, the building itself used to be a huge department store. It looked like a large K mart. We put up walls and leased space to more than two dozen small businesses.

Getting in was the hardest part. The previous owners, some evil-looking, motorcycle-type guys, refused to leave. Armed with a court order that evicted them, I went to the building one day to kick them out. Mike Schwartz, my attorney at the time and one of the dearest friends I've ever had, went with me. I knew these guys wouldn't leave quietly, so I'd already called the cops.

Wise move. I walked up a staircase to the office, where a guy came in behind me and put a shotgun to my head. He told me that he and his three buddies wanted me to leave.

"You're gonna have to blow my brains out," I said, "because I'm not leaving this building. You are."

"Like hell," the guy said. "Now I want you to walk down the stairs. Go very slow, or I'm gonna blow your fucking head off."

"You're not blowing anybody's head off," I said. "I want you out of my building."

We'd reached an impasse. Neither of us would budge. But with the shotgun still pointed at my head, I figured maybe the other guy had the edge. I walked out of the office to the stairs. These four lunatics followed me, but when they saw Schwartz at the bottom of the stairs, the chief wacko lowered the shotgun so that it was aimed at my back.

I was practically shitting in my pants as I walked down the stairs. I thought I was dead. God forbid that the guy would stumble because he'd have blown a hole in my back a foot wide. At the foot of the stairs, where Mike was watching all this, I told the lunatics one more time, "Get the hell out of my building."

The guy with the gun started to move toward me—I don't know what he had in mind, but I don't think he wanted my autograph—when suddenly, we heard loud banging on the back door. It was the cops. I was hoping they'd bust through and see the guy pointing the shotgun at me, but by the time they got in, the lunatics had run back up to the office and escaped.

I don't know how they got out or what they did with the shotgun because I never saw them again. Thank God. If this was what being a real estate mogul was all about, I thought maybe I should consider another line of work.

The International Mall, as we renamed the place, was designed to attract the young crowd. We had about 400 pinball machines, and on weekends we staged rock concerts. I brought in the groups Kiss and Rush long before they hit the big time. That's not to say I was out there boogeying with the kids, though. I probably didn't stay five minutes for any of those shows. They were so loud, I couldn't hear myself think. Getting my eardrums pierced by electric guitars never has been my idea of a good time. But the shows went over well with the kids.

Unfortunately, the pinball machines and rock concerts attracted too many of the wrong kind of customers. Kids would find these cubbyholes behind the pinball machines and hide out there, smoking marijuana and screwing around. Then they'd sneak behind the stage and play different kinds of games. I can't count the number of times I walked back there and found 15-, 16-year-old kids in compromising positions. There were a lot of fights, and the local cops eventually got tired of responding to all the calls. Eventually I cleaned up the place myself, but that just drove the kids away. Bye-bye, business.

The kids weren't our only problem. Our lessees didn't pay their rent. One guy was reliable, the guy who ran a smoke shop, where you could buy all kinds of accessories related to smoking—marijuana clips, hashish pipes and so on. It might not have been the most ethical business around, but it was legal, and the guy who ran it was the only one in the entire building who paid his rent on time. Most didn't pay at all. Combine that with the problems with the kids, and we were out of business in about a year.

In the meantime, I also was doing a lot of public relations, promotional and advertising work for Dino's Pizza, which sponsored my TV and radio shows. Some other deals were in the works, too, but when I got a call from Ray

Johnston sometime in early 1975, I was ready for a change.

Ray said he thought he could get me a job doing the color commentary on White Sox broadcasts. But his immediate offer was to come back to Des Moines and broadcast his club's games. That would give the White Sox a chance to evaluate me, he said. We moved to Des Moines, where I helped out with media sales and special promotions in addition to broadcasting the Oaks' 1975 games. The tough part was traveling again, which was hard on my family. Ray paid me well, but when no offer came from the White Sox, I decided I wasn't going to stick around.

Sometime before the end of that season, I got a call from Dr. Bernard Kraus, owner of the Triple-A Memphis Blues. Kraus had a problem. His International League club was struggling, and after suffering a massive heart attack a few months earlier, he wanted to unload the team. He said I was the kind of high-profile guy who could generate some excitement, and he wanted me to take over as general manager and to find a buyer who would keep the club in Memphis. It sounded like a good opportunity, so in September 1975, I took the job.

What I inherited in Memphis was a mess. The club had been completely mismanaged and was more than $300,000 in debt. Interest in the club was low, except among those who were waiting to be paid. I had to move quickly.

My first task was to find somebody with money to spend. Earlier that summer while working in Iowa, I had been asked by a Des Moines car dealer to speak at an AMC regional meeting in Kansas City. While I was there, I met up with Jerry Bilton, a high school friend of mine who said he had a car dealership in the Kansas City suburbs. After moving to Memphis, I called Bilton and asked if he would be interested in taking over the club. I told him that he'd have to put up about $100,000 over the next few months to make the club go, but by the end of the season we should be in the black. Bilton said he'd do it. When I brought Bilton in, Kraus stepped out of the picture.

As it turned out, the whole project was doomed from the beginning.

The agreement with Kraus was that Bilton wouldn't actually get Kraus' stock in the club until all the debts were repaid. Anybody who was willing to pay the bills and keep the club in Memphis could have taken over as "owner" of the Blues. Unfortunately, I don't believe Bilton was able to live up to his promise.

I worked my butt off to get that club back on its feet. My promotional efforts during the winter drummed up business and created excitement throughout Memphis. By the time the 1976 season started, I'd already whittled about $100,000 off the debt. I was selling billboards left and right and settling old debts by trading off season tickets, advertising spots and so on. The Blues were much better off already.

The first three months of the season went great. Attendance was up, and people seemed really happy with the way things were going. But about halfway through the season, the roof started caving in. First of all, we had problems with the weather. Many of the special promotions I had arranged were washed out by rain, and we ended up playing a lot of doubleheaders. That'll kill you in the minor leagues. On top of that, the team was lousy and fewer fans came to the ball park. Then the creditors, old and new, came calling for their money. The till was drying up.

As a result, the club was still up to its neck in debt when the season ended. In September, Kraus came back in, reassumed control of the club and fired me. Kraus didn't have a team for long, though. A few weeks later, the International League revoked the team's franchise. Minor league baseball returned to Memphis in 1978 after a one-year absence, but in a lower classification (Double A) and under new ownership.

In the weeks that followed, a lot of things were said and written about me ripping off the Blues. There was no money to pay the bills, so everybody was asking me questions. Bilton, the master of low profile, was never available to take any of the heat.

I am no thief. I was earning a salary, somewhere between $400 and $500 a week, and the rent on my house was paid. Nothing more. I felt bad that the team had died under my management, but it really wasn't my fault. The franchise needed a big infusion of money and it never arrived. The Blues couldn't be saved. Hell, if not for me coming in a year earlier, they wouldn't have had baseball in Memphis in 1976—not one bat, not one base, not one pitch. And they were saying I'd killed the Blues.

You know how well I came out of that deal? Less than a year later, I had to file for bankruptcy again.

In the fall of 1976, I went to work as a salesman. My product was radio and TV advertising time for the William B. Tanner Co., a big ad agency in Memphis. How big? Well, Tanner sold out to a conglomerate in 1982 for something like $36 million, and in 1985 he was sentenced to four years in federal prison for mail fraud and income tax violations. Funny how a guy could reach such a lofty perch and then wind up in federal prison, isn't it? Not really. When it happened to me, I didn't find it funny at all.

Creditors were breathing down my neck while I was working at Tanner. Early in 1977, I was awarded a $31,500 workmen's compensation settlement from the Tigers and several other clubs because of the damage that all those cortisone shots had done to my arm, but that just postponed the inevitable. My salary at Tanner wasn't enough to get me out of hock, and by July I was back in bankruptcy court, listing debts of more than $1 million and assets of less than $1,000. To put it bluntly, I was broke. Again.

I left Tanner in October 1977, long before the boss' legal problems developed, because I was offered an opportunity to move back to Florida and start out in a new business. Merle Dixon, a retired friend from Lakeland who had become a millionaire in the insurance business, called me up one day and told me about these giant-screen TV systems he was all excited about selling across the country. He wanted me to be vice president in charge of marketing for his company, Viewpoint.

Marketing is right up my alley. If there's one thing I do well, it's command attention. And once I get to know a product, its weaknesses and especially its strengths, I can sell it. This product intrigued me.

The Viewpoint was a projection system that you hooked up to whatever TV set you already had. It included a cone-shaped lens that projected and enlarged the TV picture onto a separate screen that was anywhere from four to seven feet wide. It gave you a hell of a picture—unless you turned on the lights. The projection system was like those used in a movie theater, so the room had to be pretty dark when the TV was on, just like in a theater. Keep the drapes closed during daylight hours and the lights off at night and you were fine. If you think about it, you don't usually have that many lights on at home when you watch TV anyway, so that wasn't much of a drawback.

The Viewpoint's appearance was. It was ugly. Great picture, but with that cone sticking out front, it was an ugly piece of furniture. And you had to place either the unit or the screen in the middle of the room because the picture was projected across eight or 10 feet of space. It wasn't like you could just pick a spot on the wall and set it there.

I had serious doubts about whether the units would sell, but I traveled coast to coast pushing them. I'd fly around the country, meeting with distributors and major retailers, but as I had suspected, sales weren't great. Cosmetically, the Viewpoint just couldn't cut it.

When Dixon hired me, he said he was committed to losing as much as half a million dollars before giving up. Well, when the losses reached about $60,000, he bailed out. When he sold the business to an insurance company, the end was in sight. The insurance company put a couple of guys in charge who didn't know what they were doing. Viewpoint started going downhill fast and I decided I'd had enough. I liked the product's potential, but not the people I was working for. So I started out on my own.

You might wonder how a former baseball player could possibly start his own big-screen TV business. Good point. I didn't know squat about how to make these units attractive as well as functional, but I had come across a guy from Denver who did. Jack Swallow.

Jack was one interesting character. He was about my age, and he looked like a country bumpkin—old Levi's, ratty tennis shoes, torn T-shirts, the whole bit. He looked like he'd have a tough time just turning a TV set on and off. But the fact was that he was a genius, or damn close to it. I called him the Mad Scientist because he could do anything. Whether it was a new screwdriver or a new mousetrap, Jack came up with something every day.

Jack also knew everything about television, including how to project a big image without having that cone sticking out the front. Sometime in the early spring of 1978, Jack and I became partners.

Jack designed a unit that we called Projector Beam. It went through a few variations, but by the time he was through, it was beautiful. The first improvement was the cone. We got rid of it. That was a big step right there. Then we worked on making the unit self-contained. Instead of selling a projection system that you added to your TV, we sold the TV and big screen all in one unit, like a console. No more hassles with the TV sitting in the middle of the room and a separate screen a few feet away. And you could even watch the set in broad daylight.

The TVs we used were Bohseis, a pretty decent set that we got from Korea for about $139 each. We also added a power unit that juiced up the back of the set. It absolutely voided the TV's guarantee, but it gave a much brighter picture. What Jack came up with was a big-screen TV that looked a lot like the ones that have become so popular today.

Now we had a product that would sell. It was just a matter of building them.

That required money—for both inventory and the salaries of the people working for us—and until the orders started coming in, neither Jack nor I had any. So, while Jack was refining the Projector Beam, it was my job to come up with cash.

The one place I knew I could make money was the golf course, so that's where I went. I'd been a scratch golfer for several years, and by that time my handicap actually was somewhere on the minus side. My qualifications as a golfer were solid. And there were plenty of guys around who enjoyed hitting the links with a retired baseball star.

If I was such a good golfer, you ask, why didn't I just join the pro tour? Simple. The pros are great golfers. I was a good golf gambler. When a pro approaches the 18th tee, you know he won't choke. But when the average guy tees up that same hole, there's a hell of a chance that he'll gag it. I was somewhere in between, probably because of my experience as a professional athlete. Pitching to Harmon Killebrew with the score tied in the bottom of the ninth can teach you how to handle pressure. I used that to my advantage.

The average good golfer, the guy who thinks he's good enough to put up big money, also lets his ego get in the way. When we made a match and he told me his handicap was six, I could be pretty sure it was 10 or 11. I used that. It's just human nature to puff yourself up, and I knew it.

The golf game I usually played was anywhere from $20 to $50 a hole, one down. That meant that when a guy was one hole down, he could start a new bet. For example, you and I are playing $20 a hole, and I win the first hole. You owe me $20, but you still have that bet on the first hole as well as a new bet when we get to the second hole. If you win the second hole, you win those bets, putting you one up, or $20 ahead ($40 on the second hole minus the $20 you lost on the first). But if I win the second hole, you're down $60. You can win that back on the third hole, though, because then you still have the bets on the first two holes as well as a new bet on No. 3 (a total of $60 riding on that hole). As you go on, the stakes keep getting bigger and bigger.

Confused? Don't feel bad. Even for the veterans, the toughest thing was keeping score. Sometimes I actually carried a legal pad out there, and even then I needed a CPA more than I needed a caddie. But it was a great way to make money. I played 27 or 36 holes of golf every day, and usually won. If I had a really bad day, I lost $100, tops, and then I was really ticked off. Most days, though, I came home with a few hundred dollars—and sometimes a lot more.

Winning at golf was crucial. That's why I'd work in the office or meet with people every morning, and then no matter what I was doing at 12:15, I was out the front door and on my way to the golf course. I knew how valuable that money was to our operation.

On top of that, I'd spend a lot of evenings playing gin rummy against the same guys I'd beaten in golf earlier that day. We'd put the clubs away and head inside, and then I'd beat their brains out playing cards for an hour or two. I might have been the Dolphin in Detroit, but I was a shark in Florida. I guess it makes a big difference whether you're playing to kill time or to make a payroll and pay the rent.

One golf outing in particular sticks in my mind. Jack Swallow had sold one of our big-screen TVs to a guy from Denver, and while they were talking, the subject came around to golf. Swallow mentioned that I like to play, and the guy's eyes lit up like a Christmas tree.

"The baseball player?" he said. "I'd like to play against him."

"Well," Jack said, "let me get you a game with him next time he's in town."

"Boy, I'd look forward to that. Does he gamble?"

Does a Twinkie have calories? Jack had to keep himself from laughing. "Yeah, he'll play for something," he said.

It just so happened that I was going to Denver a few days later. I had to take delivery of a bunch of TV cabinets that were coming in from the West Coast. There was one problem: The cabinets were arriving COD. That was a major problem because the bill was something like $7,000 and we didn't have it. But we had to have those cabinets. They were gorgeous. A guy out west had built them with real wood, not pressboard, and they were a great selling point. The question was whether we were going to rob a bank or write a bad check.

The cabinets were due to arrive at the end of the week, and on Wednesday morning I was teeing it up at Cherry Hills Country Club with this guy Jack had met. He was your typical good golfer. He could hit the ball, but he wasn't nearly as good as he thought. He was going on and on about how far the ball flies in the thin Colorado air. Well, some of us can hit the ball pretty far at sea level, and when we get up in the mountains it really takes off. I was already one up on the guy.

We agreed to make it a full day, which meant 36 holes. After the first 18, I already was ahead $2,800. I hadn't had a round that profitable in two or three years. As far as paying off that COD, I was almost halfway home.

Then this guy started getting cocky.

"There's no way you could play that well again," he said. "Now let's play for some real money."

This guy was incredible. Just because I had never played Cherry Hills, he figured my beating him was beginner's luck. I've learned that the name of the game is to hit the ball on the green, two-putt and go to the next hole. If you can hit the ball straight and putt worth a damn, you can play anywhere. But if he wanted to believe that his knowledge of the course made him a better player, that was fine with me.

As it turned out, "real money" meant quite a bit more than $100 a hole, one down, which was our bet for the first round. It doesn't take long for a bet like that to get out of hand. Not only that, but he said he wanted a medal-play bet, too. I hadn't played medal (fewest strokes wins) in years, and I wound up giving him a stroke.

Bad decision. He played the round of his life, and as we approached the 18th hole, he had a two-stroke lead in the medal play, although he was losing in the match play.

This guy couldn't get over how well he was playing. On the 18th tee, which was separated from the 18th fairway by a big lake, he figured he could do no wrong. "I'll play you one hole for $2,500," he said.

I didn't have $25 in my pocket, but I said, "Fine, OK, I'll take it."

What happened next was unbelievable. He was sure he could bust that ball over the lake, but a breeze was coming in and he hooked his tee shot into the water. After I hit a beautiful tee shot straight onto the fairway, an easy six- or seven-iron from the green, this guy teed it up again and put another ball in the lake, a real duck hook.

"OK," he said, "I'll concede the match-play bet."

We were even on the medal play then, but he still thought he could bust one over the lake and beat me. "I'll play another ball against the one you have out there," he said, "for another $2,500."

Beautiful. This guy was gagging so bad, he couldn't have hit Pikes Peak without hooking it to one side. When all was said and done, this guy lost, in addition to the $2,800 on the first 18 holes, another $14,000 on the last 18—and most of that on one hole. He gave me two checks, one for $8,000 and the rest on a check he asked me to hold for a couple of days. Both checks were good, and the COD for the TV cabinets got paid.

Hustling golf was a way of life for me while I was trying to get the Projector Beam business rolling. Even when I was out of town, I'd leave the afternoon open and make sure I had a match set up wherever I was visiting. I played less when I traveled, but that was OK. More travel meant more business, and that, of course, meant more money.

My source of transportation at that time was a Swearingen Merlin IIB, a twin-engine prop jet. Nice airplane. I needed the plane because on most of my trips, I'd visit three or four cities a day. It was a great way to cover a lot of territory in a short time. I might start the day in Texas, then fly to Memphis and have lunch there. After seeing a couple of dealers, I'd fly somewhere else for dinner and meet with more dealers. A plane doesn't do you any good when it's sitting on the ground, so I used the Merlin as much as possible. It was great for moving equipment from one city to another, too.

I don't know which was more fun, playing golf or flying a plane. Probably flying. In fact, I once told a reporter that I'd rather fly than make love. In retrospect, that's a real close call.

I've loved aviation ever since I started flying a lot with the Tigers. Captain Bud—I can't remember his last name—was our pilot for those charter flights, and he'd let me sit in the cockpit and watch. I got a big kick out of that. Learned a lot, too.

In 1968, when I was making tons of appearances all over the place, I started chartering some smaller airplanes. It was better than flying commercially, but it sure got expensive. When the big bucks came rolling in after that season, I decided it made a lot more sense to buy my own plane. I bought that Cessna 337 Skymaster in 1969, and the love affair blossomed from there.

Like pitching and golf, it's that individual confrontation about flying that appeals to me. It's just me and the plane against the elements. Just to get the plane up in the air and put it back on the ground requires a thorough under-standing of the plane and all its precision instrumentation, not to mention the weather and many other factors. And there's no better test of your mental capabilities than the decisions you make when you're in the air and something goes wrong. That's one way to find out if you've got your act together.

I'm comfortable flying any type of airplane. Just give me the manual and I can fly it. Over the years I've flown everything from a single-engine prop plane to a Learjet, and I'm still alive to talk about it.

Don't get me wrong, I'm no Chuck Yeager. And I've had a few close calls. One night when I was flying a Rockwell Commander 520 out of the airport in St. Petersburg, I lost an engine. When you lose an engine in a 520 with two people on board, it's nothing short of miraculous to make it back to the airport. I managed to get the plane over Tampa Bay, and utilizing all the skill and determination I could muster, I was able to turn the plane around and get it back to the airport. One time when I was playing ball, I skidded off the end of the runway with Sharyn, Kristi, Denny and Timmy on board. The plane had blown a tire and we barely missed crashing into other planes that were parked along the runway.

Those incidents were scary, but I've probably had more close calls in cars than in planes. The freedom and sense of control I experience while flying make the risks worthwhile. Sometimes, it really is better than sex.

In the late afternoon of August 27, 1979, I had just taken off for a trip to Memphis when the phone in my plane rang. Our house was on fire. The caller told me that everybody had gotten out safely and no one was hurt, but I'd better come home. I did a 180, landed back in Lakeland and grabbed a cab. The cab ran out of gas on the way there, and I wound up hitching a ride the rest of the way. By the time I got home, there wasn't much left. Three cement walls and not much else.

Even though I wasn't home at the time, the fire was partly my fault. I had left an emergency flare in our house, which was a very nice single-story home in a fashionable part of Lakeland. The flare was for use in case I had to make an emergency landing and bail out at sea, but since my flight route to Memphis would not take me over much water and the flare was heavy, I didn't take it with me. My son Denny, who was 11 at the time, found the flare inside a bag in a linen closet, took it into his room and started messing with it. He pulled the cord and it flared, just like flares are supposed to. The poor kid got scared and started to throw water on it. How was he supposed to know that these flares are designed so that water won't put them out?

Naturally, he panicked. Hoping that he could put it out before anyone noticed, Denny locked his door and threw the flare in a toy box in his closet. Before long he had a full-scale fire. Fortunately, my daughter Kristi saw smoke coming from under Denny's door and alerted her mother. Sharyn got Denny to open the door and get the hell out of there. A girlfriend of Sharyn's and several other kids were there, too, but everybody got out with no problem. While a neighbor called the Fire Department, Kristi's boyfriend and Sharyn tried to douse the flames with a garden hose. That was a futile effort, so all they could do was stand outside and watch the place burn.

Most of the walls in that house were done in oak, and as dry as it was, it burned quickly. By the time the firemen arrived, the house was engulfed in flames. There wasn't much they could do to save it. When I arrived, the flames were gone but what was left of the house was still smoldering.

My first reaction was relief. Sharyn and all four kids were standing outside, safe and unharmed. Thank God. Losing your house and the stuff inside is tough, but I tell you, you don't even think about that when your family is involved. All you care about is their safety.

Then you think about your valuables. It occurred to me that I had left

$1,000 in cash under the mattress of our bed. I had won the money the day before and just stuck it there. Sharyn knew about it, so I asked her if she happened to retrieve the money before getting out.

"Oh my God!" she cried. "I didn't even think about it."

"Damn!" I said. "The house is bad enough, but not the cash, too!"

I went running into what was left of the house, much to the dismay of the firemen. I went into our bedroom, which happened to be the only room that wasn't totally destroyed, and I flipped up the mattress. Staring up at me were portraits of Benjamin Franklin and several of his friends. At least we got one break that day.

That was about it, though. Only a few odds and ends survived. The house itself, which we were leasing from Merle Dixon, was insured, but the contents were not. I had failed to make the most recent payment on the policy.

Among our losses were a 1927 Bugatti car that was worth about $12,000 and about 80 Bohsei TV sets that we had stored in the garage alongside the Bugatti. They'd just been delivered a day or two before, and I hadn't gotten around to taking them to the manufacturing center. But losing those things didn't bother me nearly as much as losing the scrapbooks that Sharyn had kept since we were married. Different mementos of my personal and professional life were destroyed, including my MVP plaque and both Cy Young Awards.

As it turned out, that was a blessing in disguise. Several years later, when I was on trial, a key government witness was discredited because, on a date in question, I was in Detroit, in front of a big Tiger Stadium crowd, being presented with replacements for those awards.

We had lost everything we owned, and that seemed like a fitting conclusion to what was really a depressing period for my family. My big-screen TV business, so promising only a short time earlier, was already burning out of control when Denny set off that flare.

We had been building a great business. We were moving lots of sets, and orders were coming in for more. We had offices in Tampa and Seattle, a manufacturing facility in Tampa and a big warehouse in Denver from which we shipped the finished products. We opened nine or 10 of our own stores in Tampa, Denver, Birmingham, Atlanta, West Palm Beach and even Yakima, Wash., plus we sold them to a bunch of Curtis Mathes dealers. The business was on a roll. All that time I'd spent hustling golf to make Projector Beam go was starting to pay off.

And then we hit a snag. The first person to tell me about it was Jack Swallow. He had a high-pitched voice, and when he called sometime in the summer of 1979, he was about 12 octaves higher than the best sopranos.

"Denny, Denny, Denny, Denny!" he squeaked.

"Jack?"

"Denny, Denny!"

"Jack, is that you? What's the matter, Jack?"

"Denny, the screens are going bad! I don't know what to do! I can't get them to stay!"

"Jack, calm down. What's the matter?"

"The screens, dammit! The fucking screens are rolling!"

"What do you mean, rolling?"

"Denny, go take one out of the box. You'll see!"

I went out to the garage, and just like Jack had said, the screens were rolling. The stuff that coated the glass was bubbling and peeling right off. Not just on a TV set here and there, but on every damn one. It was like each screen knew what the others were doing.

As they say, you get what you pay for. We had bought these screens from a vendor in St. Petersburg because they were the cheapest ones available. It was the only way we could beat the price of our main competition. Still, we didn't expect them to be defective. I went everywhere to find someone who could make us a deal on some decent screens, but no luck. When the screens went south, Projector Beam went with them.

We owed a lot of people a lot of money, but we didn't have it. We expected to have it when the sets were sold, but now they weren't going to sell. The TVs we'd been shipping out as fast as we could make them were coming back even faster. Shortly after our house burned down, Projector Beam went out of business because of the damn screens.

I wanted to go to court and sue the company that sold us those screens, but was advised to forget it. The company probably didn't have enough insurance to make it worth my while anyway.

And by that time, I was bushed. A growing business with a million-dollar future that I had created and nurtured had just collapsed and died before my eyes. I didn't have any other bright ideas brewing, so I told Sharyn, "I've had enough." I needed a break. For a while, I didn't even try to find a new business.

We were leasing a house on the south side of Lakeland at that time, and then we moved to St. Petersburg. The teachers at Denny's school thought it was a good idea that he be removed from the scene of the crime, so to speak. The fire had left Denny and the rest of us terribly depressed. Lakeland was wonderful, perhaps the greatest city we'd ever lived in, but I think it did us some good to start over again a little farther down the road.

Meanwhile, I was making a living back on the golf course. That suited Sharyn just fine. She didn't know the stakes involved in some of my higher-priced outings, but she knew I could make enough to take care of her and the kids. That's what concerned her.

Over the next several months, all I did was hustle golf. It wasn't the most stable form of employment, but I was having a good time. I'd golf around town or I'd drive down to Miami, where there were lots of guys with money, and I'd bring home about $1,000 a week. Looking back, that was one of the happiest times in my life.

It was the calm before the storm.

CHAPTER 6

Shifting Into Overdrive

One day in late summer of 1980, I came home from an afternoon of golf and found a telephone message. If I'd known then what I know now, I would've just wadded up that message and tossed it in the trash. But I read it, picked up the receiver and dialed the phone, thus taking my first step on the road to prison.

"Hi Barry, this is Denny McLain. What's going on?"

The voice on the other end of the line belonged to Barry Nelson, and something was always going on with him. Once in a while, it was even legal. But all I knew about Barry at this time was that he was a wheeler-dealer with a knack for making money.

I had met Barry about two years earlier when I was trying to get Projector Beam off the ground. I had done business with him and his partner, Stanley Seligman. They had helped me by factoring some of my accounts receivable. Factoring is a great way for a young business to get operating capital. If Projector Beam was owed $10,000, say, I could sell that debt to a factor for 80 percent, or $8,000. That would give me an immediate cash flow rather than having to wait on my debtors. They had a small firm, but it was quick and reliable. You can't expect more from factors.

Now Nelson had a new business down in Hollywood, Fla., and he wanted to talk to me about it. He said he was going to be in the Tampa area soon, and he wondered if we could get together. I said sure. When Barry came up, I gave him a ride to an apartment complex he owned. While we were looking around the place, he sprang an idea on me.

"Stanley and I have opened up a mortgage company," he said. "We've been operating in South Florida for about a year and a half, business is dynamite and there's all kinds of money to be made. We need somebody to run a new operation in Tampa because boy, there's a ton of money here."

Music to my ears. If there was lots of money to be made, I was interested. I'd been doing well enough on the golf course, but I was ready for a new challenge. I always listen when somebody suggests a new deal, and this one really got my adrenaline pumping. I was about to become a mortgage broker.

Nelson and Seligman owned First Fidelity Financial Services Inc., which was based in Hollywood. They had three or four offices in South Florida, and they later opened another in Sarasota. I agreed to become part owner and office manager of Tampa Equities Corp., a branch of First Fidelity. All it cost me was a $15,000 investment. The original plan was for a golfing buddy of mine named Ken Keller to be an equal partner, but he ran into financial problems and eventually bowed out. So, I owned half of the Tampa office, and Nelson and Seligman owned the other half. We opened up for business in the early fall of 1980.

Here's how the business worked. Almost all of the loans we made were for second mortgages that had to be paid off in no more than five years. But before we could loan anybody a dime, we had to have some cash. That money came from investors. We'd look for people who wanted to invest several thousand dollars and then pay them, say, 18 percent a year on their money. When somebody wanted to borrow that money, the investors would have the opportunity to approve or reject the loan. The money would be secured by the property involved because the borrower always had to have equity. In theory, it was a risk-free proposition for investors. If a borrower defaulted, all we had to do was foreclose on the mortgage and sell the property. The investors' money was safe.

Or so I thought. It was safe from everything except internal theft, a major problem that would crop up later. But for would-be investors, this really appeared to be a sweet deal. Where else could a guy get an 18 percent return on his money? If an investor put up $100,000, he'd get back $1,500 a month in interest. And with the sky-high interest rates of the early '80s, he'd sometimes get more than 18 percent. How could we afford to pay that much? Simple. We charged the borrower a lot more.

Let's say you wanted to borrow $50,000 for a second mortgage. Up front you had to pay about 20 percent of the loan amount, or $10,000, to get the money. It might have been a little more or a little less, depending on the market at that time, but 20 percent is a round figure that's also pretty accurate. Half of that initial outlay, $5,000, was the brokerage fee (or points), 70 percent ($3,500) of which was kept by the home office in Hollywood and 30 percent ($1,500) of which was mine. That was our agreement. The other half of that 10 grand covered legal fees, title searches, other incidental fees and whatever it took to pay off the borrower's other debts—with Sears, Mobil and so on—so that we'd have a secure position on the property. Then you'd get your loan at an annual interest rate of, say, 19 or 20 percent—something that was a little higher than what we were paying our investors and that reflected the going market rate.

Sound expensive? Well, it was. It cost a fortune to borrow money back then, so the smart people were the ones loaning or investing it. But there still were lots of people who needed loans. And even though we were charging quite a bit more than the banks, we had people lining up outside our door. These were people who already had been turned down by the banks. Desperate people. They needed a second mortgage to keep their house or business, but they were bad credit risks and couldn't get a loan.

They could from First Fidelity. You might say we specialized in "St. Jude loans." St. Jude is the patron saint of lost causes, and we helped out our share of those. They were risky loans, no doubt about it, so we charged a lot for them. We were happy to loan money to people with good credit records, too, but when they found out what it would cost, they took their business elsewhere. But the guy with bad credit didn't have much choice. And at that point, he didn't give a damn what he had to pay for the money if it meant he could keep his property. A desperate borrower will sign anything today and have borrower's remorse tomorrow.

I know what you're thinking. It sounds like First Fidelity took advantage of people. Not really. The rates we charged were perfectly legal. High, but legal. And we didn't force anybody to borrow a plug nickel. We provided a service. First Fidelity was a last-resort lender. If we didn't loan these people money, they could kiss their houses and stores goodbye. They were hanging on by their fingertips, and we gave them one last shot. Some made a go of it. Others didn't.

A good example of First Fidelity clientele was Robert W. Merkle, an assistant state attorney for Pinellas County at that time. Merkle's wife, Angela, came into our office in September 1980. The Merkles already had been turned down for a loan by everybody in town because of bad credit. Every credit card they had was overdrawn, and they were behind in their mortgage payments. They had five kids at the time, and at least twice as many problems. Angela Merkle was hoping that First Fidelity could help.

She came to the right guy. I'm probably the worst guy in the world to be approving loans. Anybody who has ever met me will tell you that I'm a sucker for a sob story. I'm gullible. The child is dying, the father is leaving, the mother is sick, the car is wrecked, the dog needs an operation—whatever the story, I'll buy it. And I always believe that the guy I'm loaning money to will pay it back. So when Angela Merkle came to me shortly after we opened the Tampa office of First Fidelity, I was more than happy to do what I could to help. When she left my office that day, she was so happy, tears were in her eyes.

Angela returned to my office with her husband on a Saturday morning a couple of days later. Ordinarily, wild horses couldn't drag me in to work on a Saturday, but I honestly felt sorry for these people and wanted to help.

Bob Merkle, who was about 36 years old back then, was one big guy. He was about 6-2, 230 pounds, and looked like a football player, which he was in college. But like me, much of his weight had gravitated down to his midsection.

While we were going over the loan application, Bob Merkle really got teed off at his wife. He acted like he didn't know about all their debts and that everything was her fault. He really chewed her out good. He screamed and yelled and called her all kinds of nasty things that you just don't say to your wife, especially in front of somebody else. It was an ugly scene.

The Merkles also argued about how much money they needed to borrow. Angela originally had asked for $15,000, but Bob said they could get by with about $7,000, just enough to put out the biggest fires. I suggested they take something in between because they needed it. But Bob said no, they could get by with the lesser amount. So, I agreed to recommend that First Fidelity loan the Merkles $7,000.

Before they left, Merkle mentioned that he loved to play golf. I offered to take him up to Avila Golf and Country Club, an exclusive club north of town where I was a member. He thought that was a great idea, and we played golf together several times after that. I often wound up on the golf course with First Fidelity's borrowers and investors, so Merkle was just one of many. We always wagered, of course, because that's the only way I know how to play golf. If I bend over to stick a tee in the ground, I expect some money to be riding on the outcome. We played as partners, and he always shared in our winnings.

Despite picking up a few extra bucks on the golf course, Merkle had problems repaying his First Fidelity loan. He sent checks down to Hollywood, where the money actually changed hands, but a couple of them bounced. I covered for him, getting his wife to send a new check down to Hollywood. And they never finished paying off the loan. More than two years after the initial loan, the investor who bought Merkle's second mortgage filed a foreclosure suit. The suit eventually was dismissed, but only after the Merkles had settled with the investor by refinancing the mortgage.

That was in May 1983. About a month later, I got a letter informing me that a grand jury was investigating me. The author of that letter was none other than Robert W. Merkle, who by that time had become U.S. attorney for the Middle District of Florida. It was his office that ultimately prosecuted me and sent me to the slammer.

You think there might have been a little conflict of interest there? I mean, a guy who had defaulted on a loan I approved, who had played golf with me, drank with me, gambled with me, even traveled to Fort Lauderdale once with me, was given the opportunity to nail me in court. Even more unbelievable was the fact that when we tried to get Merkle removed from the case, the judge said no. She said she didn't see any reason why a guy who had written bad checks to pay off a loan I recommended shouldn't be allowed to prosecute me. To top it off, she wouldn't let me subpoena Merkle or his wife. I'd already made several statements about Merkle's bad financial dealings, and I guess the judge didn't want me to embarrass him any more.

Amazing but true. These were just a couple of many outrageous things the government did in order to send me to jail, and it all started because of a small loan I made to a couple who needed help.

Back when I first met Merkle in 1980, though, I was excited about my new job as a mortgage broker. My only problem then was a guy named George Lerner. I had known George from my big-screen TV days, when he had raised a small amount of money for me. George had a mortgage broker's license. I didn't. To open Tampa Equities, someone in the office had to be a licensed mortgage broker. I asked George to join us, with the understanding that he had to drop all of his own business deals and work full-time for us. He was doing mortgage brokering, factoring, leasing, all kinds of stuff, but he wasn't very successful at any of it, so he agreed to wind it all up in 90 days.

Well, it got to be December, and Lerner still was wheeling and dealing with his own schemes. That wouldn't have been so bad if not for the fact that he was doing it with my telephones, my typewriters, my paper, my copy machines and my secretaries. Basically, I was funding his personal business and getting no return whatsoever.

George had to go. I had passed the broker's test and become licensed myself by that time, so George was expendable as well as expensive. I fired him.

With Lerner gone, I was running the Tampa office myself. It didn't take a Rhodes scholar, but it was more time consuming than I had imagined. George had been letting the office girls do a lot of things that, according to Florida law, they needed a license to do. I had to take up that slack. That meant earlier mornings and later evenings, especially after I got involved in finding investors sometime in the spring of 1981. But that was OK. I loved working there.

Why? For one thing, the work wasn't that hard. The office ran itself for the most part, and reviewing loan applications became easy. I also met a lot of people and made a lot of friends.

Best of all, I still got to play golf every day. Not as much as when I was hustling for a living, but every afternoon I made sure my calendar was clear so I could play about 18 holes. That was all right with Nelson and Seligman because they knew the people with money—the guys we needed as investors—were out there golfing, too. A lot of First Fidelity's business came straight from those afternoon golf outings.

So, I had the best of both worlds. I had an income from First Fidelity that was straight commission. For every investor I brought in and every loan I made, I earned a percentage that at that time was working out to about $5,000 or $6,000 a month. Plus, I was bringing home some good money playing golf. I was having the time of my life.

First Fidelity was going great, too. Johnny Unitas, the great quarterback for the Baltimore Colts, was our spokesman. He had nothing to do with the company itself, but he appeared in several newspaper ads and TV and radio commercials that brought us a ton of business. Like Nelson had said, there was lots of money to be made, and we were raking it in.

One thing bothered me. It was taking forever to get money from the home office to the borrowers. Money my customers needed was coming in 30, 45, 60 days late. Sometimes the checks they sent me would bounce. We didn't lose many loans because remember, these were people who needed money desperately. They were waiting on their money as patiently as somebody with a fire can wait on a fire wagon. They'd be on the phone with me every day asking: "Where's my money? I'll pay more if I can get it now." But the problem wasn't in Tampa. The problem was in Hollywood, where there was a huge backlog of loans waiting to be serviced.

By the spring of 1981, I was fed up. I went straight to the boss.

"Why is it taking so long to get the money?" I asked Barry Nelson.

"We have so many loans to do," he said, "so much volume, we just can't get to it all."

The answer to that seemed obvious. "Hire more people! If we're doing that well, you can sure afford to put on a couple of more girls at $180 a week."

"Oh, no," he said, "we run a tight ship."

I didn't find out until many months later what Nelson's idea of a tight ship really was. Tighten your belt buckle and ship me your money. It seems Barry was turning into quite the world traveler, courtesy of First Fidelity's investors. They had the money to fund the loans all right; they just preferred to spend it on themselves. Barry Nelson was going to Europe, Barry Nelson was going to Africa, Barry Nelson was going to the Mideast. Stanley Seligman was racking up some mileage of his own. They weren't doing anything for the company on these trips. They were just taking vacations. And you can bet that neither of them was going coach. They went first class, from airplane seats to hotels to restaurants.

Especially restaurants. Every 10 days or so, I'd go down to Hollywood to do my paperwork and check on my loans, and Nelson and Seligman would be out every night having dinner at the best places in town. You'd never catch these two under the golden arches. It was nothing for them to go to dinner—the two of them, mind you, no guests—and have a $250 dinner tab. They ate every meal like it was their last. Barry Nelson was famous for ordering a six- or seven-pound lobster and devouring it in minutes. He literally attacked the lobster, leaving nothing but the shell, and then he'd sit back and wipe lemon juice and butter off his chin and shirt. If you lit a match, he'd go up in flames. Not a pretty sight.

Besides ripping off investors, these guys also took kickbacks. If somebody came to Nelson needing to borrow $50,000, Barry would say: "You need 50 grand? OK, I'll give you the money." That was fine and dandy, but then he'd say: "When you get your money, I'm going to give you two checks. One will be for $5,000, the other for $45,000. You will give me the $5,000 check, and the 45 thousand is yours—less all the costs of the loan." These people paid, too. It was that or forget about getting a loan.

But they weren't the only First Fidelity people taking kickbacks. A number of others were, too. Not me. Hundreds of loans I made, and not once did I take a kickback. It would've been easy, but hell, I was doing fine with my commissions and golf winnings. Why jeopardize the greatest job I'd ever had?

I was aware of people taking kickbacks at First Fidelity, but I had no idea that Nelson and Seligman were robbing the investors blind. Sure, they were taking some expensive vacations, but I didn't know who was footing the bill. They had all kinds of ways of laundering the money. Nelson set up a phony insurance company, PMI Ltd., in the Bahamas and sent much of it there. This ripoff went on for quite some time, and when the State of Florida shut down First Fidelity on April 1, 1982, about $9 million was missing. This was no hot-dog stand theft; it was a major league scam.

Stanley Seligman had dropped out of the ownership picture long before First Fidelity went kaput. In July 1981, he sold his interest in the company to his nephew, Guy Seligman, and Seymour Sher. Stanley stayed on as First Fidelity's attorney, but he no longer was an owner. My guess is that he got word the state was investigating the company and he decided to take his money and run. Guy must have found out, too, because he sold out to Sher about three months before the doors were closed. That left Nelson and Sher as the two primary partners.

Sy Sher originally came into First Fidelity as an investor. I first met him in 1980, shortly after Tampa Equities had opened. He was a little guy, about 5-8 or 5-9, with a round belly and light-colored skin. If he was out in the sun too much, he looked almost like an albino. And when you talked to him, there was no question that he was from New York. You could easily picture Sy working in a deli. When someone first told me in the middle of 1981 that Sy was tied to organized crime, I couldn't believe it. Sy didn't look like he'd hurt a flea. I never would've guessed that we'd wind up going to prison together.

We did have something in common back in 1980. Both of us were bookmakers. That's right, 10 years after I'd been suspended from baseball for my unsuccessful attempt to become a bookie, I was doing it for real. And making a bundle.

Here's how that came about. I was spending a lot of time at the dog track, either in Tampa or St. Petersburg. I like betting on the dogs. It's a hopeless wager, but I get a kick out of it. I'd go to the track three or four times a week, and more often than that if it was too cold to play golf. I hung around with a group of guys who liked to gamble as much as I do. We were all professionals —stockbrokers, pilots and so on—with money to blow. I guess there were about half a dozen of us, and we'd bet on sports as well as the dogs.

One night in 1980 we were at the dog track feeling a little depressed. Our bookie had gotten busted. It was a Monday night, which meant we were stuck without anybody to take our action on the Monday Night Football game. That's when I had an idea.

"I'll take the action," I said.

Just like that, I was a bookmaker. All I asked was that they not all load me up on one side. In other words, I didn't want them all betting on the same team because if they won, that would've been a disaster for me. They split about $15,000 in bets pretty evenly down the middle, so I was sitting pretty. With me getting the "juice" from the losing bets, I knew I'd wind up making about $1,500 on one game, which was about what I figured to lose on the dogs that night. Couldn't complain about that.

Word got around that I paid off my winners, so a few more guys started to play with me. Reliability is a bookie's most important trait. A bookie can be as irritating as fingernails on a chalkboard, but as long as he pays off, he'll have people lining up to give him their action. By the same token, a bookie with the charm of Cary Grant will be out of business in a week if he doesn't pay off.

I was taking action from guys who came and went, but I don't think I ever dealt with more than nine or 10 at a time. It wasn't any big-time operation; just a small group of friends who liked to gamble. And these guys were players. The minimum bet was $1,000. Why such high stakes? It made sense for a couple of reasons. For one, I didn't want some guy who ran the desk at the Holiday Inn or flipped hamburgers at Burger King having to pay me $50 a week to settle a $200 bet. More importantly, I didn't want to take bets from guys who were going to hurt their families if they lost a few thousand dollars. I didn't want anybody's grocery money. That wasn't good for them and it wasn't good for me. Gambling was fun, and I didn't want to piddle around with guys whose lives were going to get messed up if they lost.

There was no maximum bet because I could lay off. In other words, if I had more action than I thought it was safe to handle, I could get somebody else to take it. Laying off is a form of reinsurance, a way to protect yourself. My layoff guy was Sy Sher. Whenever I felt loaded up on one side, I called Sy and he covered whatever I gave him. He did this for lots of bookmakers, not just me.

I knew bookmaking was illegal, of course, but it didn't really bother me. I didn't advertise or anything, but I didn't live in fear that I'd be discovered, either. To me, it was just a little game among friends. I certainly didn't see any harm in that.

One night at the dog track I met a stockbroker who gave new meaning to my "little" game. I ran into him again at the track a short while later, and he said he'd like to bet with me. He said he spread his action around with other bookies, too, which was fine with me. I'm not the possessive type anyway, and when I discovered how much money he was betting, a little piece of his action was all I needed.

I'd been around gamblers as long as I could remember, but this guy was the highest roller I'd ever seen. I called him the Maniac. He always bet big and lost big. One week he lost $92,000 to me. Remember, I wasn't the only bookie he was using. I could only imagine how much he lost to other guys.

Surprisingly, the Maniac didn't run and hide. He came to me and gave me four or five checks that were postdated over the next 10 days or so. He asked me to cash them as they were dated. I said OK, and I'll be damned if not one of them bounced.

When he gave me the checks, he told me he wasn't playing anymore. That sounded like a wise move, although I hated to lose a regular paying customer. But then he completed his sentence.

"I'm not playing anymore," he said, "until I pay off the 92 grand."

Sure enough, the Maniac was betting with me again two weeks later. And losing, too. I handled just a portion of his action for about a year, and in that time he had only one winning week. But he always paid off. I don't know where he got his money, but he never stiffed me.

Somewhere along the line you probably heard Garrett Morris do his "baseball has been bery, bery good to me" skit on TV. Well, to paraphrase, bookmaking has been bery, bery good to me. During the 1981 football season, I made about $150,000 as a bookie. That's clear profit, after paying for dinners, lunches, golf outings, drinks and whatnot. And then I had my First Fidelity and golf income. I was having a ball.

And then I had a heart attack. In December 1981, I was batting around a new deal with Dr. John Greene, a Tampa physician who had borrowed about $140,000 from First Fidelity as a second mortgage on a farm he had in Plant City. After getting the loan, John became my doctor and we played a lot of golf together. One day he told me about a new type of medicine that was about to hit the Tampa Bay market. Walk-in emergency clinics. These clinics are all over the place now, but it was a new concept back then. John thought I might want to get in on them.

Anyway, John and I were sitting in my First Fidelity office after playing golf one day. We'd had a considerable amount to drink in the hot sun that afternoon, and both of us were sauced. I wasn't feeling good, had bad stomach pains, and I was sitting in my chair when all of a sudden I felt like someone had jumped on top of my chest. John probably saved my life because he took me to the hospital, where they told me I'd suffered a mild heart attack.

For the next five or six weeks, I took it very easy. The doctors put me on some medication and changed my diet. I started walking for exercise and eventually lost a lot of weight, getting as low as 202. I looked bad at 202. The best pitching I did was at about 210 or 212 pounds, so you can imagine how gaunt I looked.

Really, the heart attack was no big deal. It slowed me down for a couple of months, but before long I was back to normal. I regained the weight I'd lost and jumped back into my business activities with both feet. The only change was that I gave up drinking. I'd never been much of a drinker anyway, but after that scare, I decided to stay away from booze completely.

The spring of 1982 was a busy time. I still was running my bookmaking operation, although now I had a partner named Felix Bertucci. I had met Felix at a golf tournament in Tampa two or three years earlier. I'd see him at Avila now and then, but it wasn't until the middle of 1981 that we started to become friends. Felix was in the real estate business, and he called me about doing some creative financing with interest rates. Though nothing ever came of that proposal, we became golfing friends. He was a lefthanded golfer, and we played in some lefty-righty tournaments.

After the Super Bowl in 1982, Sy Sher shut down his bookmaking operation. I no longer could lay off bets with Sy, so Felix became a 50 percent partner in my book. We continued taking bets through the end of the 1982 NCAA basketball tournament, at which time we closed down, too. Bookies love college basketball—it's a guaranteed moneymaker—but pro hoops is a different story. If guys are smart, they can pick pro basketball winners fairly well. We didn't want to get into that, so we just quit taking bets.

Business at Tampa Equities that spring was great. I brought in more than $1 million in investments for First Fidelity, the majority of that between June 1981 and March 1982. The funding of loans still was slow, which really bothered me, but since our borrowers weren't going anywhere, I could live with it.

I also had heard rumors about the state investigating criminal activities at First Fidelity. Actually, I'd been hearing rumors to that effect almost since day one. Within about three months after we opened Tampa Equities, I first heard that the state was investigating First Fidelity. I guess I should have been worried, but Nelson told me it was just a minor bookkeeping matter. Well, Nelson was the kind of guy who could tell you dogs had wings and you'd believe him, and I took him at his word. Shortly thereafter, the state gave First Fidelity a clean bill of health. It appeared that Nelson was right. But as I later found out, the guy who did the audit was paid to overlook some big holes in the books.

In the summer of 1981, rumors about a state investigation popped up again. Stanley Seligman had sold out by that time, which was a pretty good clue that the heat was getting intense. But I didn't notice. Even when Sy Sher told me there was a $400,000 hole in the books, it didn't seem like that big of a deal. We were raising that much from investors every week, so it seemed logical that the hole was just somebody's accounting goof. Meanwhile, Nelson again was putting on a pretty good song and dance about how there was nothing to worry about.

Which was just what I wanted to hear. I was making lots of money, so why would I want to rock the boat? I could've pursued the matter and tried to find out if the state was looking into serious criminal activities, but I didn't. I was comfortable, and I really didn't feel like nosing around and stirring up trouble. And if something criminal was going on, I figured that as long as I wasn't part of it, my hands wouldn't get dirty.

Boy, was I wrong. By rubbing elbows with Barry Nelson, Stanley Seligman and other scumbags, I got plenty dirty. And I couldn't wash it off.

All this time, I had no idea that Nelson was ripping off investors. Sy Sher might have been in on the scam, too, although I kind of doubt it. As Barry's partner, he went on a number of those overseas vacations, plus they split kickbacks from loans with each other and Guy Seligman. But when First

Fidelity was closed down, Sy and some of his relatives lost about $150,000 that they had invested. I think Guy Seligman never let Sy know how bad the situation was. If Sy was profiting from the First Fidelity scam, I think he was doing so indirectly. Nelson was the chief ripoff artist.

In any event, I didn't catch on until it was too late. Even then, I didn't know the extent of it. When the State of Florida locked the doors of First Fidelity's offices on April Fools' Day—again, the irony doesn't escape me—I was devastated. I really had no warning. All of a sudden, a business that I had thought could go on forever was closed.

Worst of all, they shut the doors with Barry Nelson owing me $95,000 in commissions. Now that made me mad. It was one thing if Nelson stole from investors, but ripping me off was quite another. I knew it would be a cold day in Tahiti before I'd get that money.

The Final Four had ended three days earlier, on my 38th birthday, so two of my primary sources of income—bookmaking and First Fidelity—had dried up. But I wasn't ready to give up my lucrative career as a mortgage broker yet. It was at this time that I got more deeply involved with Felix Bertucci, one of many guys who would later come back to haunt me.

Felix had a real estate business in Tampa called Executive Realty Group. He had plenty of extra space there, so he let me have an office at Executive Realty even before First Fidelity was closed. That was the base for our short-lived joint bookmaking operation. I also made a couple of small loans of my own from that office. While I was at First Fidelity, I loaned small amounts of money—$5,000 or less—to a guy here and a guy there. First Fidelity wasn't interested in loans that small, so if a guy came in needing a couple thousand dollars and I had it to spare, I'd just do the loan myself. These guys got better deals from me than they did from First Fidelity because I wouldn't charge a brokerage fee or make them buy insurance and I'd give them a better interest rate. These loans were no big deal. Guys would get the money they needed and I'd make a few bucks.

But when First Fidelity closed, the state took away my mortgage broker's license. I think anybody who ever worked for First Fidelity lost his license. I couldn't do loans anymore. But a guy named Augie Paniello helped me get back in the business. Augie's main business was an airline delivery service. If an airline lost your luggage, somebody from Augie's company delivered it to you when they found it. Augie also was a mortgage broker in Tampa whom I'd met at First Fidelity because he had worked with us on occasion. Augie moved into an office at Executive Realty in April or May of 1982, and we started Southland Mortgage Co. Augie was the licensed mortgage broker and I was the guy in charge.

We were hoping it would be another First Fidelity, but we just couldn't find enough investors to keep it going. We made a few loans and even expanded to another office in Clearwater, but by the end of the summer that business was pretty much over.

The summer of '82. God, what a time that was. Airplanes, drug deals, exotic islands—I saw it all that summer. "Life in the fast lane" doesn't even begin to describe it. I was in overdrive and still accelerating.

Everything I did that summer was centered around my newest business venture—walk-in medical clinics. I don't think I had ever been as excited about a new business as I was about the clinics. They were just a dynamite idea.

John Greene, the doctor who was with me when I had my heart attack, had introduced the clinics idea to me late in 1981. I mentioned them to Sy Sher and Barry Nelson, but they weren't interested. So, Greene and I worked on the clinics ourselves. John started working at a couple of clinics in Tampa so that he could get firsthand experience in the business, and he brought me some of their financial statements. Those really caught my eye. These clinics were serving about 80 or 90 patients a day at an average of about $50 a patient. Even before expenses, four grand a day is pretty impressive.

Here's how the clinics worked. They normally were open from 8 a.m. to 8 p.m. seven days a week, and you didn't need an appointment. If something was wrong, you just walked in. The doctors there treated your normal, everyday illnesses—strep throat, earaches, stomach flu—and injuries like broken arms and cut foreheads. They operated full-service emergency rooms, although they didn't handle too many life-and-death situations. They would if they had to, like any doctor would, but if somebody was that bad off, they'd try to get the guy to a regular hospital. The point of these clinics was to provide the services you'd ordinarily get from your family doctor, but with less hassle. A tremendous concept.

The clinics were different from First Fidelity in at least one big way. At First Fidelity, all we inventoried was money. There was virtually no overhead. At the clinics, we had lots of material inventory—all the equipment doctors need to do their job, from Band-Aids to stethoscopes to X-ray machines. Obviously, the start-up cost for a clinic was steep—about $200,000.

I had a good chunk of money, mostly what I had earned as a bookie, to sink into this venture. But I still needed partners. John Greene was a natural since he was a doctor. I'd be a good administrator, but I certainly was no M.D. John could help staff the clinics with qualified doctors. And Felix Bertucci was interested. He said he'd put up some money, as would some friends of his.

Well, this marriage was not made in heaven. Greene had an aversion to work and Bertucci had a fondness for the funny stuff—cocaine. He was a serious addict.

And neither one of them did his job. Neither Greene nor Bertucci put a dime into the clinics. Fortunately, I got some other investors who made it possible to open our first clinic in September 1982. That was in Plant City, about 25 miles east of Tampa. Greene was supposed to be the doctor running that facility, but after the opening, he never came up there to work. Plant City wasn't a good location anyway—a big day there was 10 patients, and we needed 20 just to break even—so I shut it down after about a month. At that point, I told Greene to take a hike.

I got rid of Bertucci, too, but that took a little longer. After First Fidelity closed, I had given Felix about $40,000 to bail out Executive Realty. He had been nice enough to give me an office there, so I returned the favor by giving his business a boost when it needed it. I considered him a friend, and I figured he'd do the same for me someday if I needed help. For the next few months, I gave Felix a chance to work out his problems and pay me back.

We also got into a few other deals together, including a restaurant. Felix was sitting in his office at Executive Realty one day when he saw an ad in the Wall Street Journal. He read the Journal every day because he thought he was Mr. High Finance. Anyway, he showed me an ad about a restaurant in Pensacola that was for sale with no down payment. That's my kind of deal. We went up to take a look at the place, and people were everywhere. The cash register was really ringing that night. So, we talked to the owners and told them to draw up the papers. We'd buy it.

I thought that was a great way to get Felix out of my life. By sending him to Pensacola, he could golf during the day, run the restaurant at night and, with any luck, start earning some money. He wasn't making any headway with Executive Realty, and he still owed me at least 40 grand. That's not to mention the clinics, which he hadn't put up any money for at all. Felix was really becoming dead weight.

His drug problem also was getting out of hand. He was acting goofy all the time. I guess he was high; his behavior became very erratic. I'd even caught him "doing a line," as druggies say, on more than one occasion. Finally, I told him I'd had it with him and drugs. I didn't give a damn about the restaurant, the clinics or Executive Realty; if I caught him snorting coke one more time, he was out the door.

Surprise, surprise. I caught him again. I was at the restaurant one night when Felix excused himself to go to the bathroom. I went in a minute or two later and saw him wiping something off his nose. That white powder again.

"Hey, I can't carry you anymore," I said. "I can't support your wife, I can't support your cars, I can't support your golfing and I sure as hell won't support your drug habit. I'm through with you."

That's how I got rid of Felix Bertucci. The restaurant wasn't doing well anyway, so I just walked away from it. Without my money, Felix had to shut down the restaurant and Executive Realty a month or two later. I was out thousands of dollars, but I didn't want to deal with Felix anymore. The guy was bad news.

Before I'd booted Bertucci and Greene, we still needed additional investors to make the walk-in clinics fly. In the summer of '82, I spent most of my time looking for them. And it was for that reason that the three of us decided to buy a Piper Cheyenne II, the most beautiful plane I've ever owned in my life.

What a plane. The Cheyenne, a twin-engine prop jet, cost $1.2 million and was worth every penny. The terms were so great, I couldn't pass it up. I paid something like $45,000 down and $11,000 a month. Greene and Bertucci were supposed to buy into it, too, but they never did, so I considered it my plane. We got it on a lease-purchase agreement.

The Cheyenne was brown and white, and the interior was done in autumn colors. It sat eight people, including the crew, and had all the modern electrical equipment you could imagine. It had leather seats, a full bar and a couple of telephones, too. Very sleek. I loved that plane.

So, what did a glamorous airplane have to do with walk-in medical clinics? Everything. We had big plans for the clinics, and that Cheyenne was going to be one of our biggest sales tools.

We had gotten a guy from Mississippi named Jerry Lampley interested in the clinics. Lampley, a friend of Felix's from Gulfport, Miss., was in the oil business. He thought the clinics were a great idea. In fact, he thought we should put them all across the country, franchise them. We're talking about a multimillion-dollar project.

To bring this off, we had to find a lot more investors and get them just as fired up about the clinics as we were. That's where the Cheyenne came in. After we opened our first clinic, we would use the plane to bring people to Florida and show them what we could do. The plane was a big part of our sales package. They would travel to Florida in style and then see the building, the equipment, the nurses in their little white uniforms and the doctors with their stethoscopes. It was a great dog-and-pony show, complete with beautiful brochures, three-piece suits and high-tech aviation. We had a hell of a product to show off, and we wanted to do it right.

We did use the Cheyenne to fly in potential investors, but it never worked out the way we had hoped. Everybody seemed impressed enough with the plane, but nobody bought into the medical clinics. So much for best-laid plans. We did find some investors, but through other sources.

Still, that plane was my pride and joy. Unfortunately, it also was the reason for my downfall. When my Cheyenne got tied in with cocaine that summer, I became a tasty target for a certain U.S. attorney who couldn't pay his bills.

My problem was that I was too generous. If the plane wasn't being used by me, Greene or Bertucci, I was happy to let somebody else use it. We had two pilots, and all we asked of the person who borrowed the plane was that he pay for the fuel and a little extra to cover the pilots' salaries and basic operating costs. If it had been just me using the plane, I never would've gotten into trouble. But I just didn't have enough sense to say no.

Even to Barry Nelson. The guy owed me $95,000 in commissions from First Fidelity, yet what did I do when he asked if he could borrow the Cheyenne? I let him. I didn't trust Nelson any farther than I could throw him, but I still let him use the plane. He was working on a business deal and I still had a silly notion that I might get some of my money.

Nelson said he needed the plane for a dog-and-pony show of his own. That was no big surprise. Nelson was the king of dog-and-pony shows. He was so slick, he could sell ice to an Eskimo. Barry is a chunky guy—about 5-10 and 220 pounds with a build like the Pillsbury Doughboy—but he dressed impeccably. The finest clothes, and everything coordinated. He also wore 10 pounds of gold everywhere, carried a little purse with him and drove a new Mercedes with a telephone in it. A real Dapper Dan. And his personality would just sweep you off your feet. He could be lying through his teeth, but words would come out of his mouth sounding like the gospel truth. When it came to deals, Barry made Monty Hall look like an amateur.

Nelson and two of his friends, Stan Myatt and Mel Kaplan, supposedly wanted to buy a refinery in New Jersey. They were going to use it to smelt gold and silver ore and then sell the pure metal, or something like that. I wasn't clear on all the details. Anyway, Barry told me that the owners of the refinery knew his reputation and weren't about to come to Florida to see him. That much was easy to believe. But Barry thought that if one of his partners showed up in New Jersey on a fancy plane like the Cheyenne, the owners would be impressed. It sounded reasonable to me, so I told Barry that if he paid for the fuel and paid me an additional $1,000, he could use the Cheyenne.

On the evening of June 27, 1982, just a couple of weeks after we had gotten the Cheyenne, I flew down to Fort Lauderdale with Felix Bertucci. We had plans to play golf, plus I had some work to do for an elderly friend named Benny Milton. Benny was a retired bookmaker who had invested about $3 million in First Fidelity, including about half a million that I personally raised. Most of that money went out the window when First Fidelity went under. I was doing everything I could to help recover the money invested by guys I'd brought in—guys like Benny. I felt responsible, and I believe that I eventually took care of every one of them. It took me a while, but I got the job done. I'd find out exactly whose mortgages their money was tied up in and then work out some way for the investors to get paid.

I spent the morning and early afternoon of June 28 working on Benny's investments and playing golf with him and Felix. I also met with Barry Nelson to spell out the ground rules regarding his use of the Cheyenne. No. 1 was that he had to pay me up front. I absolutely did not want to be in a position of Nelson owing me money again. He said he'd get the money and then meet me later.

Well, Nelson was nowhere to be found that day. I borrowed Benny Milton's car and drove all over the place looking for him, but no luck. He obviously was avoiding me.

When I got to Fort Lauderdale-Hollywood International Airport, Nelson still wasn't there. I was pissed. I thought seriously about not letting the plane leave because if it took off without Nelson paying me, I knew I was lunch meat. No way he'd pay me after services already had been rendered. But Stan Myatt intervened on Nelson's behalf and said he'd make sure I got paid.

Let me tell you about Stan Myatt. What a character. Myatt supposedly was a former CIA agent. The story was that Myatt was the last American to leave Chile after the overthrow of President Salvador Allende in 1973. If you can believe what I heard, Myatt got out of there by the skin of his teeth and even had to leave behind a suitcase with $1 million in it because it was too heavy to carry. When Nelson introduced us in May 1982, Myatt was presented as Mr. Covert Operations.

And Myatt played that role to the hilt. He was a big guy, about 6-3 and 240 pounds, had black hair and was very gruff looking. He always carried a gun, the biggest handgun I'd ever seen. I don't know much about guns, but this thing looked like it could make Clint Eastwood's day. And Myatt kept an even bigger weapon, a submachine gun like an Uzi or something, in his car, which had tinted glass so nobody could see in. This guy was right out of "Miami Vice."

To top it off, Myatt was a perfect gentleman. That just made him even more fascinating and enhanced the mystique surrounding him. So, when Myatt assured me that I'd get my money from him if Nelson didn't show up, I cooled off and let them load the plane.

Huge mistake. If I had grounded that plane, told all those people to get lost and then flown home, I probably never would've been indicted. But that would have been too sensible. God forbid that I would be sensible.

Nelson had told me that two other passengers would be joining Mel Kaplan and the two pilots on the flight to New Jersey. One was a guy named Todd Siegmeister, whom I'd met briefly just a couple of weeks before, and Todd's girlfriend, Carol Jankola. It was my understanding that Siegmeister, a lifelong friend of Nelson's, and Jankola were just catching a ride back home. I had no problem with that.

I took my golf clubs out of Benny's car and Kaplan put them on the plane for me. These were some nice clubs with fancy head covers, and I figured that if I left them in the car or the hotel, they might get ripped off. And I didn't intend to play any more golf in Fort Lauderdale since I would be going home the next day. After everything was loaded up, the Cheyenne took off about 2 or 3 p.m.

Nelson had assured me the plane would be back in Fort Lauderdale by 3 p.m. the next day. Well, a promise from Barry Nelson is about as solid as an elephant in quicksand. So, I guess it didn't come as a complete surprise when the plane didn't show up the next afternoon. When the Cheyenne hadn't shown up by 5 p.m., I went looking for Nelson.

After checking his office, his home and other places, I finally caught up with Nelson around 8:30. He was down in Miami at his favorite restaurant, the New York Steak House. This was a great restaurant, very expensive, and I knew that Nelson had devoured many a seven-pound lobster there. Sure enough, there he was at a table with Stan Myatt, eating lobster.

"Where's my plane?" I snapped.

"It's been delayed," Nelson said, not looking the least bit concerned. "It'll be back either tomorrow night or the next day, at the latest."

"No way, Jose," I yelled, getting louder with each word. "I'm not waiting a day and a half to get my plane back. I've got work to do in Tampa and I need to get back now. And by the way, I want my money, and it's going to cost you guys another grand for the delay."

"OK," Nelson and Myatt said in unison. "And," Barry added, "we'll give you a bonus."

What? Barry Nelson offering somebody a bonus is like Bob Feller throwing a knuckleball. It just didn't seem right. He wouldn't give a crippled kid the time of day. This whole thing was starting to smell fishier than the lobster carcass on his plate.

"Keep the damn bonus," I yelled. "What the fuck is going on?"

Like two schoolgirls, Nelson and Myatt looked at each other and started giggling. They had a secret they just had to share.

"Sit down and listen," Myatt said. "We're doing a dope deal, and we used the Cheyenne to transport the seller and the cocaine to New Jersey."

My eyes nearly popped out of their sockets. I couldn't believe it. Nothing Nelson did surprised me, but I was very disappointed in Myatt. I didn't think he'd do that to me.

"I'm calling Kaplan right now and telling him to get his ass back here," I said. "Give me his phone number."

"Give us one more day," Nelson said.

"Go fuck yourselves!" I was getting louder by the second.

"C'mon, Denny, have a heart," Nelson pleaded. "We need the money. The guy I got the coke from is breathing down my neck, and if I can't pay him, I'm in deep shit. Denny, this guy scares the shit out of me."

"Is Mel involved in this?" I asked. Kaplan was a good friend of Barry's, but I really had trouble seeing him participating in a drug deal.

"Yes and no," Nelson replied. "He doesn't know there's cocaine on the plane. He's going to see the owners of the refinery and take care of some personal business. Before he comes back, he's going to pick up some money from Todd Siegmeister and bring it back to me. He doesn't know what the money is from. He's just bringing it back."

So, Todd Siegmeister was a dope dealer. And he wasn't just hitching a ride on my plane. He was going to New Jersey to sell cocaine. Terrific.

Nelson gave me the number of the hotel where Kaplan was staying, but Mel didn't answer. After trying several times, I went back to my hotel and tried some more. I finally reached him around midnight, sometime after I had talked to the pilots.

"Mel, the plane is leaving at 8 a.m. tomorrow morning," I told him. "If you want a ride back, be at the plane at 8. I want it back here before noon." Mel said OK, and when I asked him if he knew about anything funny going on up there, he said no. I believed him.

I showed up at Fort Lauderdale-Hollywood International right on time the morning of June 30, 1982. Unfortunately, the plane wasn't so punctual. I spent another hour or two waiting on the Cheyenne with Felix.

It was a windy, hot summer day, and we relaxed by a pool at Walker's Cay Air Terminal. This area on the north side of the airport had an aviation service where private planes like mine would park and refuel. Most airports had places like this, but Walker's Cay was exceptional. It had girls, and I mean good-looking girls, who worked as ramp people and hung around the pool. These girls wore tight white shorts and little T-shirts that were cut off about midway between their belly buttons and breasts. All foxes. The pilots of these private planes would lie around the pool, swim a little and look at the girls while their bosses took care of their corporate business.

I was enjoying the sights when Larry Knott tapped me on the shoulder.

Talk about a rude awakening. My attention was diverted from bathing beauties to a certified psycho. I'd known Knott for only three months or so, but that was long enough to figure out that he was not a good person to be around.

Knott was about 46 years old, maybe 6-foot and 210 pounds, with long hair, a mustache and a crater face—very gruff looking. He was from Georgia, and his gruffness was tempered somewhat by a thick Southern drawl. He was a street-smart hoodlum dedicated to a life of crime. He was the type who would wake up in the morning and say, "Gee, what illegal activities should I pursue today?" And he pursued plenty.

I had met Knott at First Fidelity. After being referred to me by Augie Paniello, Knott had come into my office one day to see if I'd help him finance a big ship he wanted to buy. I told him that First Fidelity didn't finance anything that flies, floats or rolls. We didn't need any of our investments moving. I couldn't help him.

But somehow, Knott and Felix Bertucci became buddies. Cocaine pals. They became so close that Felix even worked out a deal for Knott to get a beach-front condominium at a fancy resort community north of St. Petersburg. Felix also let Knott use the Cheyenne on occasion. These two losers really hit it off.

One night, I joined them for dinner. They weren't exactly my idea of desirable dinner companions, but Felix was my business associate and we did share some meals. And at that point, I didn't know the extent of Felix's cocaine problem. But while we were eating, Felix asked Knott if he could connect him with some coke. Great dinner conversation. Even worse, Knott asked me if I knew someone who could sell $15 million in stolen cashier's checks and bonds. I told him he was as crazy as Charles Manson. I was starting to like Larry Knott less by the minute.

That dinner took place just a couple of weeks before Knott showed up at Walker's Cay. I had seen him a couple of times the day before while I was looking for Barry Nelson, but I didn't expect to see him at the airport. It shouldn't have surprised me. Knott was a central character in the drama that was unfolding around me. And of all the guys who wore black hats in this mess, his was the darkest.

"Denny, I've got a serious problem with Barry Nelson," Knott said. "I fronted him three kilos of coke, and that bastard better have the money for it when I find him."

Another piece in the puzzle. Knott was supplying the dope. He was the guy who had Nelson praying that this deal came off. Also in on the deal, Knott said, were Myatt and a guy named Bill Johnson, who was supposed to be another former CIA agent like Myatt. Siegmeister was the salesman hired by Nelson.

And Knott was starting to get nervous about the whole deal. Anybody who has ever been waiting on money from Barry Nelson knows the feeling. Knott talked to me for a minute or so and then went back inside the airport.

Felix Bertucci and I were waiting with our luggage when the Cheyenne finally landed around 2 p.m. Kaplan and the two pilots were the only people expected on that flight, so I was surprised when Todd Siegmeister stepped off the plane carrying a brown shoulder bag. Kaplan was supposed to bring Nelson's money back, so I couldn't imagine what Siegmeister was doing back in Florida.

That, of course, wasn't my problem. As I was loading my bags onto the Cheyenne, Knott showed up and a heated exchange took place between him and Siegmeister. I couldn't hear what they were saying because of all the airplane noise, but it was clear they weren't exchanging recipes.

After a minute or two, Knott called Felix and me over. He was hopping mad about something. Frankly, I could see why Nelson was worried. Knott looked homicidal.

"I've got a problem," he said as coolly as he could. "Would you guys go over with me to see Barry Nelson?"

Felix said he couldn't go because his wife was expecting a baby any day and he had to get back to Tampa. But Knott was insistent that he wanted a mediator and I said I'd go along. After I took my bags off the plane, Felix and the two pilots took off.

I should've gone with them. I really should've. My life would've been a whole lot simpler if I'd just gone home and left Knott, Nelson and Siegmeister in Fort Lauderdale to work out their own problems.

But I couldn't do that. Knott was going to kill Barry Nelson. There was no doubt in my mind. And while a lot of people probably would've cheered him on, I felt like I had to do what I could to stop it. Maybe the world would be a better place without Barry Nelson, but I couldn't just stand by and let a lunatic like Larry Knott commit murder. Both Nelson and Knott had asked me to mediate this conflict, and I figured my presence would help to calm them down.

Besides, Nelson owed me $2,000.

The first order of business was to find Nelson. Knott wanted Siegmeister to come along, too, so the three of us piled into a black, four-door Chevy—Knott behind the wheel, me shotgun and Siegmeister in the back seat.

Siegmeister needed the whole back seat. I was a little on the heavy side myself, but Todd Siegmeister made me look good. He was a greasy, dirty, slimy kid of about 23 with a heavy New York accent. He was about 6 feet tall, had at least a 38-inch belly and wore pants that were four sizes too small. A real slob. He could have the back seat.

I asked where we were going, and Knott said we'd try Stan Myatt's office first. It took about 15 minutes to get there, and for the first 10 there wasn't much conversation. All of a sudden, Knott started yelling at Siegmeister. Really blistered him. If there was a cuss word he left out, I sure wasn't aware of it.

Siegmeister obviously had messed up, but I still didn't know how. Had he lost the money? Had somebody gotten busted? What?

Finally, I asked.

"This fat asshole," Knott replied, gesturing toward Siegmeister, "didn't sell the cocaine! Can you believe that? Hell, this dumb bastard couldn't sell women to a Navy crew that was out at sea for a year!"

Knott was irate. He yelled at Siegmeister some more and told him that he'd pay for his incompetence with a broken arm or leg. Then he asked Todd where the coke was now.

"I've got it right here," Todd said. "In my bag."

Well, I thought Knott would go through the roof. He veered over to the side of the road, stopped the car and really gave Siegmeister a verbal lashing. Drill sergeants probably could've learned a thing or two.

Personally, I didn't know whether to laugh or cry. I was horrified that I was riding in the same car with two fighting lunatics and a bag containing three kilos of cocaine. On the other hand, the whole scene, in retrospect, was pretty funny. These guys looked like the Keystone Kops. I even said something to Todd about how I thought dope was supposed to move from south to north, not north to south. And there was Siegmeister, transporting cocaine from New Jersey to Florida!

Nelson wasn't at Myatt's office, but Knott reached him on the phone. Nelson said he'd meet us at the Turnberry Isle Yacht and Country Club.

Turnberry is an incredible place in North Miami Beach. Plush with a capital P. Elegant rooms, valet parking, beautiful golf courses, tight security, the whole bit. In fact, Gary Hart's well-publicized excursion to the Bimini islands with model Donna Rice in March 1987 began at Turnberry, where the yacht "Monkey Business" was moored.

When we pulled up to the gate, Knott had to get clearance from the security guard, who checked with someone on the phone and then pressed a button to open the gate. Knott pulled into a circular drive by the main entrance, and after a valet parked the car, Siegmeister checked into a first-floor room that Nelson already had reserved. All three of us walked into the room.

"Denny," Knott said, "why don't you wait for Nelson in the lobby. I'd like to talk to my fat friend here."

"OK," I said, "but don't do anything stupid."

I left the room, and about 10 minutes later Nelson walked in. He owed me $2,000, but the guy actually was glad to see me. He didn't have to face Knott alone.

Nelson and I walked down the hallway to the room. I had taken the key, so I opened the door and we stepped inside.

The drapes had been closed, so the room was kind of dark. But about 20 feet in front of us we could see Siegmeister down on his knees, with his back to us, and Knott standing right in front of him. Todd had something in his mouth and I really wasn't anxious to turn on the light and see what.

I almost wished my first impression had been true. As we walked into the room and Nelson locked the door behind us, we could see that Todd was sucking the business end of Knott's .45-caliber automatic.

I don't know how Todd felt at that moment, but I was as scared as I've ever been in my life. And Nelson looked as if he'd just found a corpse.

Siegmeister was on the verge of becoming one.

"What the fuck are you doing?" Nelson shrieked.

"I'm going to blow his damn head off his shoulders," Knott responded.

"You goofy bastard!" Nelson screamed. "What is killing that kid going to accomplish?"

"If I kill him, he'll never dilute someone else's cocaine again, that's what."

Siegmeister *was* a dumb bastard. He had told Knott that he had taken out about eight ounces of cocaine for his own use and replaced it with lidocaine, which is hard to distinguish from coke and costs a hell of a lot less. Siegmeister was ripping off his own partners.

Knott pulled the hammer back on the gun.

"Larry, don't!" I yelled. "Don't be crazy! Take your cocaine and make this punk kid pay for what he stole, but don't shoot him!"

Knott kept the gun in Siegmeister's mouth and looked straight in the kid's eyes.

"Start praying," he said, "because by the time I count to five, you will be one dead, ex-dope-dealing bastard."

Knott started counting—one, two, three—and I kept screaming and pleading for him to cut it out. Then I noticed that the way the gun was pointed, the bullet would come out the back of Siegmeister's skull and head straight for my groin. I stepped to the side.

"Four, five!" Knott pulled the trigger.

Click!

No bullet! The gun wasn't loaded. And Knott was in hysterics.

"I've scared people like this before," he gasped, struggling for words between laughs, "but I've never seen anybody pee all over themselves before."

Sure enough, Siegmeister was slumped on the floor, the leg of his pants soaking wet. It was one of the sickest sights I've ever seen.

Nelson was white as a ghost. I thought he was going to die. As for me, my heart must've been a lot stronger than I thought because it didn't give out. After what I'd seen, it should have.

"Knott, you're crazy," I said. "I'm getting out of here. I've had enough of this madness."

Just then, Knott asked Siegmeister who had told him to mess with the cocaine.

"No one," Todd said, still sitting in his own mess.

"Who told you to bring the coke back to Florida?"

"Barry," he replied. "He told me to bring it back if I couldn't sell it."

"You two rotten cocksuckers!" Knott screamed. "You owe me! I will give you one day to pay me $16,000 for the dope that asshole stole. Get the money or else, Barry. You asked me for this coke; now pay for it!"

Nelson just wanted to forget the deal and get the hell out of there.

"Go to hell," he said, "and take your shit with you. I'm out. And no one in the world will know if there's eight ounces of lidocaine in the shit."

Strong words to a guy who still had a cannon in his hand. Knott reached into a briefcase on the bed, pulled out a clip and loaded it into the .45.

"Larry, what are you doing now?" I yelled.

Knott headed toward Nelson. It was rather obvious what he was doing.

"I'm gonna kill that fat sonofabitch."

"That's enough, Larry," I begged. "Please, Larry, you asked me to come over here and help you, not witness a double murder."

That shows you just how smart I was. I figured that if Knott killed Nelson, he'd go ahead and kill Siegmeister, too. It hadn't occurred to me that I also was a witness. A triple murder, perhaps?

I guess the words "double murder" got Knott's attention because he seemed to settle down for a minute. Everybody breathed a little easier. I turned to Nelson.

"You owe him $16,000 for that scum on the floor stealing the coke," I said. "And don't forget, you owe me $2,000 for the use of my plane. Go to Myatt and get the money."

"Myatt left at noon today for Vegas," Nelson said. "He won't be back for a week."

"Call him," I said, "and tell him to wire you the money."

Knott thought that was a good idea. "Call that cocksucker right now," he said, "and tell him he has until 6 p.m. tomorrow. After that, I'd better not be able to find you."

Nelson tried to reach Myatt several times, but no luck. That just gave Knott time to get mad all over again.

"You fat fuck," he said to Nelson, "I didn't like you when I met you and I sure hate your fucking guts now. Why would you hook up with someone who doesn't know what the fuck he's doing?"

"You heard what this dumbshit said a week ago. He said he has a lot of customers."

And he did. Siegmeister, as I later learned, had been dealing coke successfully for several years. But on that particular deal, he came up dry.

"He had a week to line up the sale of three lousy kilos and failed," Knott growled, "and then he stole eight ounces. I don't believe it."

Knott was furious. With the gun in his left hand, he shoved his right index finger into Nelson's chest, called him something obscene and pushed him back just a little. Nelson pushed Knott's finger aside and tried to move away. But Knott socked him in the gut, doubling Nelson over. I had sat down on the bed, and Nelson fell right next to me. I grabbed Knott's right arm and he stopped. He then kicked Nelson once for good measure and said to me, "Let's get out of here."

My sentiments exactly. We started for the door, me in front of Knott, when the lunatic turned around and said: "Fuck it! I'm going to blow his head off."

Knott pulled the trigger. Click! Click!

No bang. Knott had done it again. The clip was empty. Nelson was so scared, he almost vomited. And Knott was laughing his head off. He put the gun back in his briefcase, which, I noticed, also contained handcuffs and a rope.

By that time, I had decided Larry Knott was not going to be my friend. I like almost everybody, but I couldn't tolerate someone who gets his jollies by scaring the hell—and everything else—out of people. He was crazy, stupid, weird and sinister. I wanted no part of him.

So what did I do? I agreed to hang around another day.

It wasn't my idea. Knott and I left the room and Nelson came out to the lobby about five minutes later. Nelson asked me to stick around until his 6 p.m. deadline the next day to make sure Knott didn't get crazy on him again. Knott wanted me to stay, too. Both of them seemed to think I had some influence over the other. As much as I wanted to go home and leave these idiots behind, I figured I'd better play peacemaker awhile longer.

And I wanted my $2,000 from Nelson. If I went home, I knew I'd never see that money. By keeping him in sight, at least I had a chance.

Maybe you're wondering whether it bothered me to be hanging around with all these dope dealers. It did, but not enough to make me run away. I thought my being there would prevent a murder or two, plus I wanted my money. I didn't have any part in their sordid dealings. I just loaned a guy an airplane. If he uses it to do something goofy, that's not my fault. All I wanted was my money. I am not a drug dealer, never have been and never will be.

Things were pretty quiet for me the rest of that day. I got up the next morning and went down to Turnberry's restaurant for breakfast. I was sitting by a window overlooking the pool around 11 a.m. when Barry Nelson joined me at my table. I asked him if he had come up with the $18,000. It took him a while to answer me, so I knew the answer was no.

"I talked to Myatt last night," Nelson explained, "and he said he wouldn't cover the coke Siegmeister stole. He'll try to sell the rest of it, but the $16,000 is my problem. And he said I'd better take care of it because he's dealt with Knott before, and he's definitely a crazy weirdo."

Nelson had already figured that out and he was worried.

"Will you loan me $16,000?"

If it were anybody but Nelson, I would've asked him to repeat that. Only Barry Nelson could be 95 grand in debt to somebody—not to mention the two grand he owed me for the Cheyenne—and ask for 16 more. The guy was unbelievable. But he said he had some bank accounts in Europe, which was news to me, and he said he'd be able to pay me back after he got the money in a couple of days.

For once, I didn't reach into my wallet or pick up the phone. I told Nelson he'd have to borrow the money from someone else. Like Mel Kaplan. Nelson said he'd try.

We finished breakfast and went to Knott's suite, which was fabulous. It had two adjoining bedrooms, a bathtub big enough for eight people and surrounded by mirrors, and a huge living room with a wet bar. It looked like a battlefield. Knott had had a party the night before, and towels, clothes, glasses and dishes were everywhere. It must've been a good party because no one could make a mess like that and not have fun.

"Did anyone die in here last night?" I asked.

Knott looked at me coldly and said no. Then, seeing Nelson behind me, he added, "But that doesn't mean it couldn't happen today." Here we go again!

I suggested to Knott that he give Nelson a day or two to come up with the cash. For some reason, he was willing to extend the deadline. He said he'd take half of the money that night and the other half the next day. Nelson said he'd call Kaplan to see if he could get $8,000.

While Nelson went to use the phone, I took some clothes off one of the stools by the wet bar and sat down. A few minutes later, Nelson came back and announced that he would have $5,000 by 6 p.m.

"Find the other $3,000, Barry," Knott said. "I'm not kidding."

Just then, the phone rang. Knott asked me to answer it. I said hello, and to my surprise, Felix Bertucci asked to speak to Knott.

How did Felix know we were here? I had registered under a false name, Dennis Hogan, because I was concerned about people knowing I was around while this Keystone Kops caper took place. Knott also had used an alias. Knott took the call in the other room, and when he came back, I asked him if Felix was involved.

"Yeah," Knott said. "He has a guy in California who will help sell the rest of this stuff."

"Larry," I said, "Felix will use more than he'll sell."

"Felix won't screw me," Knott replied. "He knows I'm not playing games."

So, Felix was a dealer, too. I knew he snorted the stuff now and then, but I didn't know he'd sell it. I was learning a lot.

Knott figured he had his problem solved, so he told Nelson to get Siegmeister over there on the double. I don't know what Knott had in mind, but when Siegmeister showed up, Todd surprised everybody by announcing that he had found a doctor in New York who would buy the three kilos.

"Are you sure you've got it sold?" Knott asked.

"I sure am," Todd bragged, "and for $65,000 per kilo."

Knott's eyes lit up. He supposedly was paying $50,000 per kilo, so he saw a nice $45,000 profit in the making. Bertucci, I learned later, had promised only $58,000 per kilo.

After thinking awhile, Knott said, "I must be crazy to trust you again."

Hear, hear. I couldn't believe that Knott would give a second chance to a guy who had stolen eight ounces of coke and failed to sell a gram. But greed distorts the brain. Once again, Siegmeister was the man on the spot.

And Nelson had a reprieve.

"I expect $5,000 by 6 p.m.," Knott told Nelson after Siegmeister had left, "and the other 11 in seven days. Maybe this kid will bail your ass out of a real jam."

"If I pay you this money," Nelson said, "I'm off the hook, right?" Nelson just wanted out.

Knott nodded his head. For the moment, he was content to let Siegmeister do his thing.

And I was free to leave. Only one problem. When I called Felix about the Cheyenne, he said he had given the pilots the day off. They couldn't come get me until the next day. Sharyn wasn't too pleased when I called and told her it would be one more night before I came home.

At 6 p.m., I was in my room when the phone rang. It was Nelson, calling from the phone in his Mercedes. He said he'd be there in 30 minutes—half an hour after his deadline. Knott showed up at my door after I hung up, and we went to the lobby to wait for Nelson.

At 7 p.m., Nelson finally arrived. He gave Knott $3,000.

"You absolutely promised me $5,000," Knott said.

"Well, this is all my partner had today," Nelson said. "Maybe more tomorrow."

Knott must not have felt like killing anybody that night because he took the $3,000 and didn't say much more. Three grand is better than nothing, I guess.

"Do you guys want to go to dinner?" Nelson asked.

The nerve of the guy! He owed me $2,000 right then and $95,000 somewhere down the line, and he owed Knott $13,000. And he wants to take us to dinner! That's Barry Nelson for you.

"Barry," Knott said, "if I went to dinner with you, that would mean we're friends, and then very soon you'd stick it in my ass again. Since I don't consider you a friend, I'll pass on dinner and I'll expect to see you tomorrow before 6 p.m. with the other $2,000. Then I want the rest within seven days. Is that understood? Please don't make me come looking for you."

"I'll be here," Nelson said.

"I'm hungry," I said. "Let's go to dinner."

We went to the New York Steak House, where the hostesses and waiters knew Nelson by name. After we were seated, the hostess asked if we'd like to see a wine list. Of course Nelson wanted a wine list. Doesn't everyone order wine with their seven-pound lobsters?

Barry had the usual, and since Barry was buying, I had a big ol' lobster, too. But before we ordered, we were joined by Mel Kaplan.

I liked Mel. He was a nice guy, very pleasant company, and he always treated me well. Back then he was about 50 years old, 5-10 and 165 pounds, and handsome. Mel's only problem was Nelson. For some reason, they'd been friends for about 25 years, and the only times Mel got into trouble were when he did business with Nelson.

After we ordered our meals, Nelson got up to use the phone. Mel then asked me if Barry had paid Knott.

"Yeah, Barry gave that lunatic $3,000," I said.

Mel was stunned. "Denny," he said, "I gave him $6,000. Five for Knott and one for you for the airplane."

Nelson was at it again. He'd taken $6,000 from perhaps his only friend in the world and kept three grand for himself. I had half a mind to call Knott and tell him to get his gun ready. When Nelson returned to the table, I was furious.

"Barry, you asshole, what did you do with the other $3,000 that Mel gave you?"

"I've still got it," he replied nonchalantly, "and I'm going to use it to pay off my credit cards."

"Some of that money is mine," I snapped, "and I'll take it now. How are you going to give Knott some more money tomorrow? You're really crazy. Mel here loans you the dough to get that lunatic off your case, and you steal the money. What the hell is wrong with you?"

"Well," Nelson said, "today is today and tomorrow is tomorrow. I'll cross that bridge when I get to it. Right now, I'm going to eat this lobster, drink my wine and forget about that moronic idiot."

I couldn't believe it. Barry Nelson had to be nuts. I couldn't make him give me my money in a public restaurant, so I had to sit there and eat my meal without speaking to Nelson.

My adventure at Turnberry was about over. I got up the next morning, July 2, and was eating breakfast with Knott when Felix Bertucci arrived around 10 a.m. A couple of hours early, but that was fine with me. They discussed Felix's offer of selling the cocaine to a guy in California, and when I got up to leave, Knott still hadn't decided whether to let Felix or Siegmeister sell the dope.

I couldn't have cared less. I just wanted to go home. By the time we took off in the Cheyenne around noon, I felt like I'd been away from home for ages.

We based the Cheyenne at St. Petersburg-Clearwater International Airport. It was a longer drive from my home in north Tampa to the St. Pete airport, but it cost quite a bit less than basing the plane in Tampa. So, we landed in St. Pete and taxied up to Interair Jet Service, a huge facility with lots of hangar space, a nice lobby area and friendly people. One of these nice people directed us to our parking spot.

We were in the back cabin getting ready to open the door when Felix spotted two policemen. They were standing about 50 feet away on the bottom step of the entrance to Interair. I looked up, and one of them was pointing at the Cheyenne. As they started walking toward us, Felix whispered to me, "I've got a pound of coke in my briefcase."

"What the hell are you talking about?" I hissed.

"Just what I said. There's a pound of coke in this case."

"Let me out of here," I said, reaching for the door. I opened the door, and lo and behold, two of Pinellas County's finest were standing right below me. Felix was sweating, and my heart was pounding like a drum.

"Hi," I said as casually as I could. "How're you doing today?"

"Fine," one of the cops answered. "Is Denny McLain on this plane?"

"I'm Denny McLain."

"We were out here on business," the cop said, "and we were told when you called in on the radio that the call letters 806CA were your letters and your plane. Can we take a look inside at the cockpit?"

Apparently these guys just liked planes. I said sure, they could look around. Then they offered to help us with our luggage. Nervously, I handed down four bags, including Felix's briefcase. We got off the plane, and while Felix went to get his car, I stood around with the cops until the pilots shut the engines down.

While we were waiting, one of the cops took a step backward and accidentally knocked over Felix's briefcase. I thought I was going to have the big one. My heart went right into my shoes. I just knew the case was going to fly open.

It almost did. One of the latches on the case popped open while the other stayed shut. "I'm sorry," the cop said as he picked up the briefcase and tried to close the latch. It wouldn't lock.

I figured this was it. The cop would open the case, see the cocaine and arrest me on the spot. I was dead meat.

"Just leave it," I said. "I'll have Felix fix it. After all, it belongs to him, so he knows how it works."

The cop apologized again and put the briefcase down. To my relief, Felix pulled up next to the plane in his Pontiac just then and opened the trunk. The pilots invited the cops up to the cockpit, so while they went up and talked about the plane, we threw the bags in the trunk and slammed the door shut.

It took all the self-control I had to keep from screaming at Felix. He offered to give me a ride, but I said no way. I wasn't about to ride in his car with drugs in it. I'd had my fill of that.

"Listen, this won't be the first time you'll be in my car with drugs," Felix said. "This is just the first time I've told you about it."

"Get my bags out," I seethed. "I'm calling Sharyn."

I got my luggage and sent Felix on his way. I called Sharyn, and while I was waiting for a ride, the cops stopped by and asked me why I didn't catch a ride with Felix.

"Oh, my wife and I have a dinner date in Bradenton," I said, "and we'll be heading down there straight from the airport when she gets here."

When Kristi pulled up to Interair instead of Sharyn about 45 minutes later, I was damn glad the cops had left. I would've had a tough time making them believe that my 16-year-old daughter was my wife.

CHAPTER 7

The Road
To Court

If you get the chance to fly on the night of July 4, do it. It's an incredible experience. If the night is clear, the whole sky is one big panorama of color. All those fireworks shows are spread out below, and you just fly from one to another.

But beware of your traveling companions. I wasn't too choosy on July 4, 1982, and it came back to haunt me.

The day before, while I was still recovering from that crazy episode at Turnberry, I had gotten a call from Felix Bertucci. He wanted to know if I'd like an all-expenses-paid trip to Atlantic City.

Is the Pope Catholic? All Felix asked was that I fly him and Larry Knott up there on the 4th and back home the next day.

There were three good reasons I should have said no. First, Sharyn wouldn't like me going out of town on a holiday that I could spend with her and the kids. Second, this was the same Larry Knott who had gone bananas three days earlier. Third, if Knott and Bertucci were involved, it was a good bet that drugs were, too.

Felix said not to worry, there would be no drugs on the Cheyenne this time. Knott was going up to New Jersey to meet with Todd Siegmeister, but it was just to collect the profits from the cocaine deal. I could live with that. If Knott was picking up money, then the deal was over and I wasn't involved. No problem.

As for Sharyn, Felix suggested that I tell her I had to leave on business. That was partially true. I had been planning to investigate Atlantic City for potential sites of future walk-in medical clinics. It didn't have to be that week, but it would happen sometime. As expected, Sharyn wasn't too thrilled with that explanation. But she didn't try to stop me from going.

I wish she had. But I was a free spirit who took orders from no one and I wasn't about to let wisdom prevail over my pursuit of a good time. So I said yes. What was so attractive about Atlantic City that I'd agree to spend two more days with Larry Knott? Simple. I'd never been there before. I'd been to Las Vegas lots of times and had a blast, but I'd never seen the Boardwalk and the bright lights of the Atlantic City casinos. It sounded like fun.

More importantly, it didn't take much to get me in the cockpit of that beautiful Cheyenne. Just give me a destination, pay for the fuel and I was on my way.

I'd flown the Cheyenne myself for the first time the day before when John Greene wanted a lift to West Palm Beach. This plane was considerably differ-

ent from the smaller ones I was used to. I just dropped Greene off and flew
right back, under the watchful eye of one of my hired pilots, Cary McCord.
The trip was perfect. When Felix called me about going to Atlantic City, I
couldn't wait to fly that baby again.

And Felix was well aware of my weaknesses. He could have just asked me to
let Cary fly them up to New Jersey, but he hadn't put a dime into that plane
and he knew I could keep the Cheyenne grounded if he didn't make it worth
my while to operate it. Until he made a payment on the Cheyenne, I called the
shots. That's why he was willing to pay for the fuel, the pilots, the operating
costs, my hotel and food, anything I needed. All I had to bring was gambling
money.

As it turned out, Felix didn't make the trip. He and Knott arrived at the St.
Pete airport at 6 p.m., only to hear his name being paged. When he got word
that his pregnant wife was having contractions about 15 minutes apart, he
decided he couldn't go. It would be just me, Knott and Cary McCord. Felix had
paid for the fuel before he left, so I was feeling good as we took off.

The flight was gorgeous. As darkness began to fall, the fireworks began.
Pushed by a strong tailwind, we cruised along at about 320 miles per hour and
just absorbed the view from 24,000 feet. Most spectacular was our approach to
Atlantic City as we saw the displays in Philadelphia, Baltimore and other cities
on the Eastern Seaboard. It was breathtaking.

A little less than three hours after leaving St. Pete, we landed in Atlantic
City. We parked the plane, grabbed a cab and went to the Dunes Hotel, where
Felix had made reservations. Sort of. I wasn't surprised to learn that Felix had
failed to guarantee the reservations with a credit card, so they had been can-
celed at 6 p.m. We were told that the hotel was booked solid, as was every
other hotel in town because of the holiday. But a couple of minutes later, after
I had greased the front-desk clerk's palm with a crisp $20 bill, we were headed
to our room. It had two double beds and a rollaway for Cary.

After Knott bought us dinner, I hit the casinos. My game is baccarat, a
sophisticated European card game that James Bond played in the movies. It's
similar to blackjack in that you usually get only two or three cards, but it
moves a lot quicker. That's why I like it.

I found a table where no one was smoking and sat down. I had brought
$6,000 for gambling and bought $1,000 worth of chips. I started out betting $20
a hand, but when I fell behind, I raised the bet to $50. In 15 minutes, my $1,000
was gone.

That's the way it usually happens. People fall behind, then raise the ante and
try to catch up. It doesn't work that way too often.

But this was my lucky night—at least in the casino. I reached into my
pocket, pulled out another grand and kept playing. An hour later, I had won
back not only my original grand, but also another $27,000! I left the table and
got one of the guards to help me with my chips and cashed them in. They gave
me nothing but 50- and 100-dollar bills. I couldn't believe I'd won that much
money in just an hour!

I called Sharyn from the hotel lobby to share my good news, then went up
to our room. Knott and Cary seemed genuinely happy for me and suggested
that we celebrate. When I look back on that celebration, I have to laugh. Here

we were, Denny McLain, former baseball star and high roller, and Larry Knott, drug dealer and all-round bad dude, pigging out with Cary at 3 a.m. in our hotel room on humongous banana splits we had ordered from room service.

The next day, while Knott was out doing his business, I checked out the city, trying to figure out if there was a market for walk-in clinics. Eventually I made it back to the casino. My luck had changed, though, and I lost a few thousand dollars. Thanks only to a winning streak at the craps table was I able to recoup my losses and check out of the Dunes $27,000 ahead.

About 3 p.m., Knott returned and said he had to go up to Newark. His meeting had been fouled up, and the people he needed to see wouldn't be able to get to Atlantic City until late that night. He didn't want to wait. I would have preferred to stay and gamble, but Cary asked me to come along and help fly the plane. He had only 10 hours of flying time in the Cheyenne himself, and he wanted a co-pilot when he flew into such a congested area.

The flight to Newark was quick and Knott said he wouldn't be long, so we just waited for him at the airport. Then we'd head back to St. Pete.

Wrong. Knott called and said he'd hit another snag. Could we stay in Newark overnight? The thought was a lot less appealing than a night in Atlantic City, but what choice did I have? It was Knott's show. I was just along for the ride.

Cary and I caught a cab to a Holiday Inn where Knott already had checked us in. Cary had his own room, while I was sharing mine with Knott.

As I opened my door, I was hit by a sensation of deja vu. Todd Siegmeister was in there, and once again he was being ripped apart by Knott. It was Turnberry all over again.

I don't think Knott had a gun, but if yelling could kill, Siegmeister would have been dead. Knott was threatening him with every punishment imaginable if he didn't come up with at least $20,000 by the next morning. One caught my attention. He told Todd that he was going to put him in a bathtub full of water and electrocute him with a cattle prod that he just happened to be carrying in his briefcase.

The problem this time? Oh, nothing much. Siegmeister had lost half of the cocaine, that's all. Honest. Siegmeister told Knott that he and another guy had taken a train from Fort Lauderdale to Newark with the three kilos of cocaine. It was a 24-hour ride, and Todd said he and his friend took turns watching the cocaine when one of them had to leave their compartment. Somehow, 1½ kilos got stolen on the train.

The Keystone Kops revisited? When I heard that, it was impossible to keep a straight face. Needless to say, Siegmeister didn't think it was funny at all. He knew firsthand that it was not healthy to be on Larry Knott's bad side. And I knew firsthand that these two characters had bumbled and stumbled their way through what has to rank as one of the most poorly executed crimes in the history of bad men.

Siegmeister insisted he hadn't stolen the cocaine, but Knott wasn't interested in excuses. He just wanted $75,000 to cover the cost of the lost coke, plus another $75,000 when Todd sold what was left. By that time, Knott was just trying to break even in this fiasco.

"Add whatever you want to it," yelled Knott, who was holding up Siegmeister by his shirt collar and spitting invectives two inches away from the kid's acne-covered face. "Add however much stuff you want. I just want my money. I've got people to answer to myself, you scumbag. And quit using the stuff because if I catch you, I'll break your snorting nose!"

Siegmeister just stood there and took the abuse. Finally, when Knott paused for a minute, Todd said he had a friend who could bring Knott $20,000 the next morning. Knott wanted to hear that from the guy himself, so Siegmeister called his friend.

About an hour and a half later, in walked a guy named Jerry Mendelson, who looked even more disgusting than Siegmeister. Mendelson, I later found out, took cocaine like a diabetic takes insulin. At least daily.

Mendelson told Knott not to worry, he knew what was going on and he didn't want Todd to get hurt. He said he'd personally deliver $20,000 to Knott the next morning. Knott said that was all he needed to cool down.

I was hoping Mendelson would come through because I wanted to go home. The next day, I went down to the hotel restaurant for breakfast around 10 a.m. and found Knott and Siegmeister at a table. I told Knott I wanted to be in the air by noon, and he said he should be ready because Mendelson was due any minute.

About an hour later, Siegmeister was paged. When he returned, he was white as a sheet.

"Uh," Todd stammered, "guess what? Jerry changed his mind. He's not giving you the money. I don't know why."

Knott didn't say much. He just grabbed Siegmeister by the arm, took the check to the cashier and hauled Todd away. About 25 minutes later, Knott came back and said he was ready to go.

As we were leaving, I saw Todd crying and holding his ribs tightly.

"Any rough stuff?" I asked Knott.

"Of course not," he said sarcastically. "He just tripped over a chair in the room."

It had not been a fun trip for Knott. Half of his coke was gone, the other half was in the hands of an incompetent slimeball, and he hadn't collected a dime from anybody. In fact, he'd spent two or three grand on the Cheyenne and hotels and meals for me and Cary, and it didn't look as if he'd ever get much for his efforts. Too bad, tough guy!

I came out quite well—on the surface. I got a free vacation, $27,000 in gambling profit and a lot of laughs from watching the Keystone Kops in action. Unfortunately, I also paid a stiff price years later when the jurors at my trial thought that I was an active participant in Knott's drug dealings. As it turned out, for each grand I won at baccarat, it cost me a month in prison, and then some.

As if watching the Keystone Kops, pushing the medical clinics, operating Southland Mortgage, trying to clear up the First Fidelity mess for investors and playing a lot of golf wasn't enough to keep me busy in the summer of '82, I also was getting involved in some deals with Stan Myatt. That led to another profitable adventure a couple of days after my trip to Atlantic City.

Myatt and I had been trying to sell each other on deals all summer. I wanted to get him involved in the clinics, and he wanted me to help bring people with money to this island in the Bahamas that he claimed to own. He didn't bite on the clinics, but that island fascinated the hell out of me. So much so that I allowed Myatt to place the corporate logo of the island on the cabin door of the Cheyenne.

The island was called Great Harbour Cay. It was a tiny little thing, about three miles wide and half a mile long, just a speck on the map. But it was gorgeous. I mean, if heaven is this peaceful, no one should be afraid to die. Myatt flew me down there one day, and I fell in love with the place. There wasn't much there besides an airport landing strip, a restaurant, sand, trees, water and a few beautiful condos. The nicest one of all belonged to Myatt, who had knocked out the walls in about three smaller buildings and put it back together into one gigantic palace. He had at least 5,000 square feet of the most beautifully furnished beach-front property you've ever seen.

Myatt said he wanted to sell the island. Maybe develop it, maybe just sell it outright for a profit. He had a big dog-and-pony show in mind. Well, I don't know if he really did *own* the island, but he was pretty convincing. I guess the idea of a former CIA operative having a secluded island getaway made sense to me.

So, Myatt asked me to talk to people about the island. That was easy enough. When I saw people with money, and I saw quite a few, I'd tell them about this terrific little island in the Bahamas they might want to look into.

Larry Knott was the one who inadvertently got me into this new adventure. He had asked me if I could help out a friend of his who had a problem. Knott said his friend was "hot with the cops" and needed to get out of the country. There could be some money in it for me.

Immediately I thought of Myatt. In addition to having this island about 150 miles off the coast of Florida, he also claimed to have a U.S. Customs Service guy on his payroll. He had a Customs guy in the Bahamas working for him, too. If anybody I knew could sneak someone out of the country, it was Stan Myatt.

The guy who needed help was named Jim Pritchett. He was a wealthy real estate agent who moonlighted as a drug dealer. Knott told me at the time that he thought Pritchett might be tied in with drugs, but he wasn't sure. Knott knew damn well that was what Pritchett did for a living, but he was trying not to scare me off.

I didn't scare that easily. I probably should have, but until I found out exactly why Pritchett was hot and exactly what he wanted, I wasn't worried. I could always back away if the guy was poison.

He was a felon, but I didn't know it yet. In 1980, he had been convicted of manslaughter. In fact, Pritchett was the first person in U.S. history to be convicted of committing manslaughter while flying an airplane. A landmark case, as they say.

One day in 1978, Pritchett took his girlfriend up for a ride around the Florida Keys in his Cessna 337 Skymaster. While in the air, Pritchett decided to snort some cocaine. Not only that, but they also got romantic. Now, flying a plane is enough to keep you occupied. Sure, planes have autopilot, but that's for high altitudes. Pritchett was flying about 30 feet above the water and nearly clipping the masts off sailboats. When you're making circles that low, it's a good idea to check your controls and look out the window occasionally. Well, Pritchett was doubly distracted. He had a head full of coke and his girlfriend was performing oral sex. Pritchett was having such a wonderful time that he let his right wing dip in the water. The plane cartwheeled and caught fire, his girlfriend was killed on impact and Pritchett was convicted of manslaughter.

Pritchett appealed, but in April 1982 the appeals court turned him down. In a letter dated July 12, 1982, he was mailed a notice to report within 15 days to begin serving his five-year sentence in a Florida state prison. When he didn't show up, he officially became a fugitive July 27.

Pritchett didn't show up because I had taken him out of the country a couple of weeks earlier. But I had no idea at that time what I was doing.

After Knott told me about his pal's predicament, I called Myatt. The first thing I wanted to know was how hot Pritchett actually was. Myatt checked with his federal government sources, then returned with some interesting news.

"The guy's not hot," he said.

"What do you mean he's 'not hot'?" I asked.

"I mean there are no warrants out for his arrest. I guess he's a coke dealer, all right, but the guy isn't hot."

Technically, Myatt was correct. At that time Pritchett wasn't a fugitive. The letter ordering him to surrender hadn't even been mailed yet. If Myatt knew that Pritchett was fleeing an impending prison sentence, he didn't tell me. Since Myatt had called people in the federal system, not the state, maybe he wasn't told about Pritchett's state conviction. But if he was, then Myatt kept it to himself. Had I known that Pritchett actually was a fugitive-to-be, I would have dropped the matter right there. But according to Myatt, we had the opportunity to earn some money by hiding a guy who wasn't wanted by the cops. It sounded like a perfect no-risk deal.

"What do you want to do?" Myatt asked.

"Well, I don't want any part of the cocaine business, but we can help the guy out if he wants to hide. Especially if he's not hot, right?"

"He's not hot. Let's do it."

Knott had said Pritchett would call me, which he did at Myatt's office. He wanted to meet me, but he wouldn't tell me where he was. All I knew was that it was somewhere north of Fort Lauderdale. Pritchett gave me instructions: Drive to a certain intersection, park my car and wait on the corner. His people would pick me up and bring me to him. I did what he said, and sure enough, three guys pulled up in a car.

When I got in the back seat, these guys told me to lie on the floor, face down. Then they put a smelly green Army blanket over my head, just like in the spy movies. My first thought was that this car was not air-conditioned. My second was that I was being kidnaped. It was my understanding that the cops weren't after Pritchett, so I really didn't understand the need for this cloak-and-dagger charade. But I went along with it, partly because I could smell a payoff and mostly because it was exciting.

Twenty minutes later we pulled into the garage of a house. They took the blanket off my head and let me out of the car. I was soaked with sweat. I looked around but had no idea where I was. Still don't.

We walked into a beautiful house. It was big and fancy, but virtually empty. Except for a couch and a TV, the living room was bare. I saw a telephone with some equipment on it. I guess that was to make sure the phone wasn't bugged. This clearly wasn't the Beaver Cleaver residence.

One of my chauffeurs introduced me to Pritchett, who was there with his wife, a man of about 20 whom Pritchett said was his son, and another young couple. We exchanged pleasantries, then Pritchett got to the point.

"Can you get me a place to hide?"

I said yes, but that I needed to confer with my partner. Myatt and I hadn't discussed specifics yet. But I didn't want to call Myatt from Pritchett's house. Something about the device on the phone made me leery.

That meant another sweaty trip on the floor of the car with a blanket over my head. Pritchett's men drove me back to my car and said they'd return in half an hour. I watched them leave, then went to a phone booth and called Myatt.

"Are you ready to set this guy up in your place in the Bahamas?" I asked.

"Sure," Myatt said. "How do we get him out there?"

"We'll use my plane."

"How much are you going to charge him?"

I didn't know. I was thinking along the lines of $10,000 or $15,000. It was only a 29-minute flight from Fort Lauderdale to Great Harbour Cay in my Cheyenne, so my expenses were minimal. But this guy supposedly had money, and I figured I'd aim high.

Myatt aimed even higher. He suggested $25,000. I said I'd see what I could do.

Right on time, my chauffeurs returned to pick me up. By then I knew the procedure, so I just crawled on the floor and grabbed the blanket. When we got back to Pritchett's, I told him that everything was set for him to leave that day.

"What time do we have to be at the airport?" he asked.

"If someone will drive me to my car," I said, "I'll come back here, pick you up and take you to the airport myself."

"Oh, no, no, no, we can't do that."

I'd forgotten the ground rules. It was OK for me to know where Pritchett was going, but not where he'd been.

"I'll get to the airport," he said, "but I've got a problem about going out of the country."

"Don't worry about it. We've got Customs covered."

Which was true. Myatt had it set up on Great Harbour Cay so that he could come and go as he pleased, as could the people with him. And if he wasn't going to be there himself, all he had to do was call ahead. I don't think his contacts for returning to the United States were that strong, but at that point, Pritchett just wanted out.

We decided that we would meet at the airport at 4 p.m., about 90 minutes from then. I told him my pilots would be ready with the engines running, and his group could just step on the plane and go.

After being returned to my car again, I went over to Myatt's office. Around 3:15, Pritchett called. He said something was wrong and I had to get back over to his house on the double. Another trip on the floor of the car and I was back at Pritchett's.

"I've got a problem," he said. "My brother's been busted. I need to leave enough money here to get him out on bond. Can you arrange it?"

"No problem," I said. "How much do you think the bond will be?"

"About $250,000."

"And you're going to put up cash?"

"Yeah. Can you get it done somehow?"

"Sure, but that's a lot of money. Where do we have to go to get it?"

"We don't have to go anywhere."

With that, Pritchett took me into a back bedroom and opened up a suitcase. In it were stacks of money, $5,000 in a stack. I was no stranger to large amounts of money, but I'd never seen anything like that before. Right in front of me was $335,000. I couldn't take my eyes off that cash. When Pritchett asked me a question, I didn't even hear him. He had to repeat it.

"How much am I going to have to pay you guys to put up the bond?"

As soon as I saw that suitcase, the price tag on Pritchett jumped. "You've got to figure $35,000 for us," I said.

"That's $285,000."

"And you've got to figure another $35,000 to take you to the island."

"That's a little expensive."

"But that's what it costs."

Pritchett agreed to the price and handed me the suitcase with $320,000 in it. All he had left was $15,000. But then he pulled out another suitcase and opened it. There must have been another $150,000 in there. He tossed in the three stacks of bills from the other suitcase, closed it and said: "I'm taking this with me. I need some pocket money."

It was time to leave, and for the last time I was told to lie on the floor of the car and cover my head with a blanket. It was hard to fathom. I'd just left the guy's house with $320,000 of his money, knowing full well where he'd be hiding out for the next few weeks. But he didn't want me to know where he'd be living for the next 30 minutes.

When I got back to the corner and opened my car door, I was shaking. I had $320,000, and I was scared that the police might pull me over. What would you tell a cop who found that kind of money in your possession? You'd won it at bingo? I didn't have an answer, so I started the car and drove straight to the first gas station I could find. I filled up the tank and, more importantly, checked my brake lights and turn signals. I drove back to Myatt's office, not once exceeding the speed limit, rolling through a stop sign or trying to sneak through a yellow light. If anything, the cops were going to pull me over to give me a citation for safe driving.

When I got back, Myatt asked if Pritchett had squawked at paying us $25,000.

"I've got that covered," I said.

When I told him about Pritchett's brother and the $250,000 bond, Myatt said we'd have to get 15 percent for handling that. I said I had that covered, too. We drove off to see a bondsman, who said he'd be glad to handle the bond. After dropping off Myatt at his office so he could arrange the release of Pritchett's brother, I drove to the airport.

Pritchett, his wife, son and the other young couple showed up shortly after I did and got right on the plane. About that time, Myatt arrived, too. He already had cleared Customs for Pritchett's group in Great Harbour Cay, so they just waved bye-bye and took off.

As the plane climbed into the sky, Myatt and I were leaning against the fender of a truck.

"Well, Denny," Myatt said, "Pritchett can forget about his brother getting out of jail anytime soon. I've got a guy who can handle these things, and he says it would take an act of Congress to spring this bum. He's bad news. He's got a long string of cocaine convictions, and they caught him this time with enough to cover a ski slope. He doesn't have a prayer."

So, Pritchett's brother would have to sit in jail. That was fine with me. Apparently, he deserved to be there. In the meantime, I had the $250,000 that was supposed to be his bond money, plus the $70,000 that we were to get for handling his bond and taking Pritchett to the Bahamas. But Myatt didn't know that yet. For whatever reason, I hadn't told him.

"Denny, you never mentioned where Pritchett was keeping all that damn bond money," he said. "Did he just take it with him?"

"No."

"Where is it?"

"In my car."

"In your car? How much did he give you?"

"$320,000."

Myatt was silent. He just stared at me for several seconds, then broke into a silly grin.

"Guess how much we're going to charge him to stay on the island?" he said.

"How much?"

"$320,000."

I loved it. The excitement was spine-tingling.

The Cheyenne flew to Great Harbour Cay, dropped off the Pritchetts and came right back. The next day, Myatt and I were going to fly there ourselves. We had to tell Pritchett about his brother and discuss his rent to stay on the island.

The first part didn't figure to be too risky. Pritchett had to know that springing his brother would be a problem. As for his rent, neither of us wanted to be the one to break the news. We'd heard the guy could be mean.

"Stanley, it's your island," I said. "You tell him."

"Everything's gone just fine with you doing the talking so far," he said. "You're the spokesman. And if he doesn't like it, tell him he can swim back. All I have to do is call Customs and Pritchett's ass is grass."

Myatt had a point. A dope dealer on the lam could spend a long time rotting in a Bahamian jail.

The next morning, Myatt and I flew to Great Harbour Cay. Pritchett was staying in Myatt's condo, so he couldn't complain about his accommodations. We just hoped he didn't complain about the rent.

That afternoon, Pritchett and I took a walk along the beach. Pritchett didn't look that mean, but he spooked me. He was about 45 years old, maybe 6-3 and 230 pounds, with short, light-colored hair, big ears, almost no neck and a deep tan. He was wearing Levi's, a T-shirt and shower shoes. You could tell by the way he talked that he had very little regard for human life and was not the kind of guy you'd want to hang around. Hell, he told me about the manslaughter conviction and even laughed about how that girl in the plane had died while giving him a blow job. He was an arrogant, selfish sonofabitch. I didn't like him.

And I was about to tell this guy that the total cost of his stay on Great Harbour Cay was the slightly exorbitant rate of $320,000. A guy like him might not take too kindly to extortion, which is basically what we were doing. But I had no qualms whatsoever with extorting money from that kind of filth. It occurred to me that if he didn't like the terms, he might just beat me senseless and toss my body in the waves. Needless to say, I was shaking in my shoes as we sloshed through the surf.

It didn't make me feel any better to know that Myatt was walking about 50 feet behind us, packing that big .45 in the back of his pants. On the one hand, if Pritchett tried anything funny, Myatt could come to my rescue. On the other hand, Myatt also could shoot both of us and keep all the money himself. Myatt was no stranger to ripping off drug dealers, and there was no reason to think he wouldn't rip off a former baseball player, too. I'd made it easy for him to do just that by letting him hide all the cash at his house. Not too bright.

So, I was with two guys, neither of whom I trusted and both of whom had reason to kill me. I made sure that I wasn't in Myatt's line of fire. I didn't want a bullet leaving Pritchett's body and burrowing into mine.

First I told Pritchett that we couldn't get his brother out of jail, even with Myatt's connections. Fortunately, he said he understood.

"It's probably just as well for you," I said, "because you couldn't afford to spring him and still pay for this place. Myatt's going to see that you get all the protection and food you need, but it's going to cost you."

"How much?"

Time to put up or shut up. It was a good thing the sun was making both of us sweat because there was no way I could look cool in that situation. I was scared shitless.

"For everything—the plane, Myatt's pad, protection, food—we need $320,000."

Pritchett's jaw almost hit the sand. I thought he was going to kill me on the spot. He yelled, screamed, swore, kicked the sand, pushed at me and called Myatt and me a couple of thieves and much worse. He wasn't the least bit happy.

But he eventually calmed down. I guess he realized there wasn't much he could do about it, so he might as well kick back and enjoy his tropical hideout for the next few weeks. He even admitted later that the money didn't matter much to him. He could always get money. The important thing for him was freedom, and if that cost $320,000, then so be it.

Myatt and I hung around for a few hours and then flew back to Fort Lauderdale. I picked up my half of the loot and continued on to St. Pete, where Sharyn and my son Timmy picked me up at the airport. I should point out here that Sharyn had no idea what I'd been doing. Oh, she knew I gambled and had made book, but I kept all these episodes to myself. I figured that what she didn't know wouldn't hurt her. Well, she found out a lot when I went on trial, and it hurt her plenty when I went to prison for 29½ months.

I got off the plane carrying a bag with $160,000. Not stock certificates, not bonds, not checks, not IOUs. Just cold, hard cash. So when Timmy said, "I'll carry your bag, Dad," I told him no. But he really wanted to be helpful, and I finally relented.

"OK, Timmy, but be sure you don't set it down anywhere," I said. "You might forget it."

I never took my eyes off Timmy while he was carrying my bag. It was only when we walked by a soda machine and Timmy put down the bag to buy a Pepsi that I stopped watching him. I watched the bag.

I didn't say much in the car as we drove home. I was too tired. It had been a busy couple of days, and I just wanted to relax. When we got home, I went right inside and took a shower. After showering, I opened the suitcase and dumped the money on the bed. I wanted Sharyn to see it.

A minute later, Sharyn came in to bring me a sandwich. She glanced at the bed, but the bedspread was a greenish color and she didn't notice anything right away. Then she spotted it. Her mouth dropped open, and I could hear her catch her breath. "Oh, my God," she said.

Then she flashed a stern look at me. "Dennis, did this have anything to do with drugs?" she asked coldly.

"I didn't buy any drugs, I didn't sell any drugs, I didn't transport any drugs," I said. "But I'm pretty sure the guy who used to have this money was a drug dealer."

Sharyn didn't say anything for a minute. Finally, she smiled and said, "Well, better we get to spend it than him."

I like the way that girl thinks.

That 160 grand went into a pool of money from which I was paying for any number of things—the Cheyenne, equipment for the clinics, Southland Mortgage, you name it. But scores like Pritchett don't happen every day, and I had to keep the money pumping. That was why I got hooked up with Earl Hunt.

Stan Myatt introduced me to Hunt. According to Myatt, Hunt knew everything there is to know about airplanes. He flew them, fixed them, sold them, serviced them—if it was connected to flying, he could do it. Myatt thought maybe I could give Hunt a job. Hunt was having some financial problems at the time, Myatt said, but given a chance, he could bring in some serious money.

I couldn't help but believe that after meeting Hunt. This guy had a personality like Barry Nelson's, and he was just as crooked. He said all the right things at the right time. He convinced me that he was Mr. Aviation. Wilbur and Orville would never have had a chance with this guy around. That's how good Earl Hunt was.

Hunt supposedly had a little operation at an airport in a small Ohio town outside Cleveland. It was a fixed-base operation, or an FBO, which meant he handled ground work. Starting sometime in August 1982, we had a number of discussions about what it would take to really get his FBO cooking. He said that with a few more fuel tanks and some other equipment, he could make some big profits.

Hunt said a plane would be handy, too. He could do some charter business and bring in $5,000 a month in addition to what he made pumping gas and servicing aircraft.

It wasn't McDonnell Douglas, but it looked like a nice little sideline. I could dabble in aviation and bring in a few extra bucks at the same time. I agreed to buy into Hunt's FBO, sight unseen, and try to find a plane he could fly.

Hunt did some looking, too, and came up with a Cessna 402 owned by a doctor in Mississippi who agreed to lease me the plane for $3,000 a month. In turn, I told Earl that after the first payment, he'd have to make the payments to me because I expected him to put some money up for this deal, too. I was just getting him started. We got the plane in September.

Well, this deal didn't work out well at all. First of all, after getting a $5,000 loan from me and getting all the documents prepared by his attorney, Hunt failed to sign the agreement on his FBO. I sent him a check for $7,500 to put fuel tanks in the ground, but when I found out that we didn't have an agreement in writing, I told him to hold the check. Once the agreement was signed, I said, he could cash it. He tried to cash the check anyway and it bounced. Nothing ever came of all of Hunt's big talk about his wonderful FBO, which I've still never seen and now doubt ever existed.

But that's another story. The real problems centered on the Cessna 402. Hunt not only failed to make the payments, but also decided the best way to make a profit with an airplane was to import drugs.

Hunt started talking to me about drug deals almost immediately after we got the Cessna. I told him I wasn't interested. Not in the slightest. And I told him he'd damn well better not use the Cessna for any drug deals. "If you do," I said, "I'm gonna come and slap the shit out of you. Don't put me in any drug deals and I won't have to hurt you. I mean it, Earl. Don't screw with my life and my future."

Now, I'd never hurt anybody in my life. I was just trying to show Hunt I was serious. Granted, it was foolish to let Hunt go ahead and use the plane, but I really thought our little chat would keep him in line. Besides, I didn't see any way Hunt could use the Cessna to import drugs. He'd need a long-range plane to move drugs from South America or wherever to the United States, and the Cessna didn't have that kind of range. The Cessna would make it halfway across the Gulf of Mexico and quit. Hardly the ideal plane for a drug dealer.

Well, Hunt decided he'd do it anyway. Without telling me, he took out some of the seats and put in a bladder tank. That extra tank enabled the Cessna to fly a lot farther than it could before. Now he could do his drug deals.

And he might have gotten away with it if not for a guy named Brad Jeffords, who worked for Hunt. In fact, Hunt had taught Jeffords everything he knew about airplanes and considered him his best friend. They were like brothers.

But Jeffords didn't have the same taste for guns that Hunt had. A few weeks after Hunt got the Cessna, Jeffords noticed a change in Hunt's personality. He said Hunt developed a "John Wayne" attitude and was packing an automatic pistol. Hunt apparently thought he could pull off any deal he tried, and if anybody tried to stop him, he'd just shoot his way out.

Jeffords got scared and went to the cops. Before long he was working as a confidential informer for the Florida Department of Law Enforcement. Everything Hunt told Jeffords was then reported to the FDLE. Unfortunately, one of the things Hunt told Jeffords was that I was involved in Hunt's drug deals. It wasn't true, but you can imagine how the FDLE agents' ears perked up when they heard that.

One of Hunt's first plans for the Cessna was to import a big load of marijuana into Louisiana. Federal authorities installed a bug called a transponder on the Cessna. This gadget allowed them to follow Hunt's flight on radar from start to finish. They just had to wait for Hunt to get his dope and nab him when he came back.

A few days before the flight, Hunt found the transponder. He was going over the plane with a debugging device and there it was. Now, that should've been a pretty good clue that somebody was watching him, right? Well, that didn't stop Hunt. He disconnected the transponder and went ahead with his deal anyway. He really thought he was John Wayne—you know, "Here I am, pilgrim, now try and stop me."

The October day when Hunt flew out of Louisiana to get the marijuana, agents for the Drug Enforcement Administration, U.S. Customs and the Louisiana State Police were sitting right there with cameras rolling, watching him leave. They were still sitting there when Hunt came back from Belize, a small country in Central America, with 1,188 pounds of marijuana. Hunt landed the Cessna, shut down one of the two engines and was pulling up to the hangar when all these guys came flying out of barns, cars, trees and everything else yelling: "Don't move! Don't move! You're under arrest!"

Hunt still thought he was John Wayne. He started the other engine and took off down the runway. The cops were shooting at him, and Hunt leaned out the cockpit window and shot back while trying to run over these agents with the plane. They finally got him to stop, but not before putting a few holes in the Cessna.

Hunt immediately started singing. Within minutes of his arrest he told the feds, "You've got me, but I'll give you somebody so big that you'll have to let me go." And he did. He gave the feds Denny McLain, and a few weeks later, Earl Hunt was out of prison on bond.

Hunt admitted up front that I had nothing to do with his marijuana deal. He said it was McLain's plane, but McLain wasn't involved. So far, so good. But Hunt told the feds that I had masterminded a 400-kilo cocaine transaction that went sour. And that, my friends, is how Denny McLain became the target of a federal investigation of drug trafficking. Because Brad Jeffords turned in Earl Hunt, who lied to save his fat ass.

Even before Hunt took off on his suicide mission, I had been trying to find him. He hadn't made his first payment on the plane, and when I couldn't reach him on the phone, I started to worry about what he might be doing. I sent letters and telegrams to Hunt and his attorney demanding that he return the Cessna. A lot of good that did. The next thing I knew, Hunt was arrested and the Cessna had been confiscated by the authorities.

For the next couple of months, I had no idea what was going on with Hunt.

Then he called me one day in late December and said he'd been released from jail on bond. The fact that his bond had been pretty stiff—he told me it was $2.5 million—indicated that he probably was cooperating with the cops. Where else would he have gotten that kind of money? But I told Hunt that maybe we should get together anyway. I'd heard all kinds of rumors about the shootout when he was arrested, and I just wanted some firsthand information about what had happened. After all, I was on the hook for the plane.

A few days later, Hunt called me again and told me he was in Tampa. Could I come over to his hotel? I said I'd try, but by that time I was very suspicious that he was trying to set me up for something. I never went to see him, and Hunt went on his way.

Smart move. As I found out later, the cops had a stakeout set up at Hunt's hotel room. About a dozen federal and state agents were waiting with their cameras and mikes to take pictures of me talking with Earl Hunt. I don't know what they expected me to say, but it probably wasn't my thoughts on the Super Bowl. They waited several hours before packing up and going home. So much for their damned stakeout.

In January 1983, I was subpoenaed by the State of Florida. Considering the people I'd been associating with, you'd think maybe I'd be worried. But I wasn't. It was my understanding that the state attorney just wanted to talk about First Fidelity. Hey, that was fine with me. I had nothing to hide, and I was happy to do what I could to make Barry Nelson, Stanley Seligman and those other thieves pay for their scams and kickbacks.

But when I arrived to give my deposition, the first thing the guy did was Mirandize me. That's the legal term for reading me my rights. You know, "you have the right to remain silent, you have the right to an attorney," all that good stuff you've heard on TV a million times. Well, that startled me. I asked why he was reading me my rights, and the guy said it was because the information in my deposition would be passed along to the authorities regarding a criminal investigation of several people, including me.

That was a different ball game. I thought maybe the state knew about my bookmaking. Without my attorney present, I wasn't about to give a deposition.

"Gentlemen," I said, "this deposition is over. If you want my cooperation, give me immunity. Otherwise, forget it."

I got up and left. I figured they'd be back in touch anyway, so the deposition could wait. In the meantime, I asked my attorney to find out what was going on. But no one told him anything. After a while, I just forgot about it.

I was too busy to get bent out of shape about a state investigation. Except for bookmaking, I hadn't done anything wrong. I'd been around a lot of people who had broken the law and I figured they were the ones who needed to worry, not me. If the state or the feds or anybody else wanted to talk about those people, they knew where to find me. But while they were screwing around, I had a business to run.

The walk-in medical clinic in Plant City had been a disaster, but in November 1982 I opened another in Lakeland. By the beginning of 1983, that clinic was posting some impressive numbers.

The Walk-in and Emergency Clinic in Lakeland brought in about $15,000 in

November 1982. The next month it did about $44,000, and in January 1983 it did about $96,000. Those are gross estimates, meaning that salaries, operating costs and so on had to be taken out before determining the net profit. For the first few months, that profit went toward paying off all the equipment I'd bought. But that debt was being reduced quickly, and with business booming, I was planning to open clinics in Bradenton, Sarasota and any number of cities. Franchising the clinics still was a possibility, although I gave some thought to starting two or three clinics, selling them for a million bucks each and moving to Hawaii. If the money ever ran out, I knew how to start some more.

The key was marketing. A medical clinic was just like any other product. It had to be presented to the public and sold, just like a Sears Roebuck store or Pizza Hut. I was good at that, and I marketed the hell out of the clinic. I took out big ads in the local newspaper and ran a few radio spots. I also had a girl who went out to local businesses and solicited workman's compensation claims. She'd drop by, explain how we operated and leave a coupon they could use if they ever had a problem. We generated a lot of business that way.

There were a couple of other marketing secrets to making a clinic successful, but I'm keeping them to myself. Who knows, maybe I'll get back in the business someday. I really enjoyed the clinics. They combined just about everything that makes a job fun—meeting with the public, helping people, offering personal challenges and, above all, making lots of money.

But I made a big mistake. Early in 1983, I let some partners join me in the Lakeland clinic. One was a Lakeland attorney, another was a local business-man and there also were a couple of doctors. These guys had money to invest, which appealed to me because their money was traceable. I had money avail-able, but a lot of it was cash from bookmaking and the Pritchett deal, which isn't the kind of money you can declare on a financial statement. With my partners' legitimate money out front, I could add in my money and it wouldn't be so noticeable.

The main reason for taking on partners, though, was to get doctors actively involved. The toughest part of the clinics business is hiring doctors. Working at a clinic had its advantages; doctors had regular hours and didn't have to deal with patients calling them about sore throats in the middle of the night. But most doctors can make more money with their own practice, so it's a chore finding good physicians who will work on salary. I had been killing myself, working 12 hours a day to run the clinic, and most of that time was spent worrying about doctors. I figured that if I had a couple of doctors putting money into the clinic, they'd make sure the place was properly staffed. Their interests would be protected, and so, in turn, would mine.

Unfortunately, it didn't work out that way. First of all, these guys wanted to give Plant City another whirl. I told them that was crazy. The population of that town just couldn't support a walk-in business that needed at least 20 patients a day just to break even. But I had made the mistake of selling 70 percent of the business to my partners, so when they said we're opening Plant City, that's what they did. It was a guaranteed failure, and that clinic ultimate-ly bit the dust.

I also didn't like the way my partners were tinkering with the day-to-day operation of the clinics. They were big on board meetings where they felt like they had to discuss the daily problems and this and that. There were no prob-lems—not in Lakeland anyway. The thing was doing nearly $100,000 a month. Leave it alone and everyone will be able to pay for their kids' college educa-tion. If it ain't broke, don't fix it. And they wanted to fix something that was doing nothing but making $20 bills every couple of minutes.

Well, the Lakeland clinic survived, but I didn't. The partners forced me out.

I couldn't believe it. I'd worked my butt off for months and built that business to the point where it was bringing in $100,000 a month. I'd done everything that was humanly possible to do, and I was out? "That's right," they said. "You're out."

What had happened to bring about this sudden change in events? A bomb-shell had dropped, that's what. And once again, it was my buddies in the media who lit the fuse.

Rob North, a reporter for WXFL-TV in Tampa, led the bomb squad. In May 1983, he did a weeklong series on Channel 8 in which he reported that a federal grand jury was investigating my alleged involvement in a conspiracy to import cocaine. He also reported that I was being investigated for loan-shark-ing, that I had impersonated a physician at the Lakeland clinic and that "uni-dentified sources" had linked me with a guy named Santo Trafficante, who was reputed to be the big Mafia leader in Florida. It was quite a series of reports.

Bullshit, too. If a federal grand jury was investigating me, that was news to me. And the actual charges of criminal misconduct were outrageous.

Especially the accusations that I was a loan shark and a drug dealer. Those are serious crimes, and I wasn't guilty. North was doing some heavy damage to my reputation. Granted, my reputation wasn't exactly pure. I never claimed to be a saint. But I sure as hell wasn't a dope dealer or an extortionist.

That stuff about me impersonating a physician made me mad. Two of the girls who had worked at the clinic told North that in December 1982, I had put on a white jacket like a doctor wears, examined a patient and ordered that a shot be administered. As far as I'm concerned, that was just sour grapes on the part of two girls who had lost their jobs. I had a white jacket that the girls had given me, but I never tried to pass myself off as a doctor. I seldom wore the thing. And even if I had, I was back in my office and most patients never even saw me. There's a lot of things I'll try, but practicing medicine isn't one of them.

Equally ridiculous was North's contention that I was connected with Santo Trafficante. I've never met the man in my life. What would the Mafia want with my high profile? That's one club in which anonymity is desirable, and I'm anything but anonymous. The only remote tie-in between me and Traffi-cante was Augie Paniello, the mortgage broker who had helped out with Southland Mortgage. Augie was Trafficante's son-in-law. But I seriously doubt that Augie had anything to do with the Mafia. With all due respect, Augie isn't the brightest guy in the world, and if he's an organized crime figure, then the Mafia is in trouble.

As you can imagine, this series by Rob North came as quite a surprise. The first thing I wanted to know was where he had gotten all this garbage. I didn't think North would just make it up, so he had to get his information from someone.

Who? I still don't know. All I know is that people not only in the Tampa Bay area, but also around the country, were being told that Denny McLain was Public Enemy No. 1. And that bothered the hell out of me.

It bothered my partners in the clinics, too. They said I had to go because the stories about me were hurting the clinics' business. I don't believe that. Business might have suffered briefly, but the Lakeland clinic went right back to pumping out cash pretty quickly.

I was, in effect, banished to Bradenton. The partners gave me enough cash and equipment to open my own clinic and that was it. They knew I wasn't going to fight them. The last place I wanted to go at that time was a courtroom. That was because in June 1983, I had received official word from the U.S. attorney's office that a federal grand jury was investigating me. Until I knew what that grand jury was after, I wasn't about to rock any boats.

Ever since Channel 8 had run its expose, I had been trying to find out if I was the target of a federal investigation. I tried to reach U.S. Attorney Robert Merkle countless times, but he never returned my calls. It wasn't until I sent Merkle a telegram that I finally got a written response. He informed me that I was, indeed, being investigated.

And that was it. Merkle didn't tell me why I was being investigated or where the government was getting its information. He said I'd be invited to appear before a grand jury, but he didn't say when. It was all very mysterious. I could only assume that the investigation had something to do with Rob North's series, but that didn't make sense. I wasn't guilty of anything North had alleged, so I couldn't imagine why the government would be pursuing it. I hired a prominent criminal attorney named Ron Cacciatore, but even he was stonewalled.

I certainly didn't think the feds believed I had anything to do with cocaine. Marijuana, perhaps, since Earl Hunt had been busted carrying all that pot in my Cessna. But cocaine? The only time I'd even been around a cocaine deal was when all that craziness was going on at Turnberry and Newark the previous summer. And that deal wasn't mine; I was just watching from the sideline. So the more I thought about it, the more convinced I became that the focus of the investigation was First Fidelity. And since I hadn't done anything wrong at First Fidelity, it was difficult to imagine why I should be concerned. As the weeks and months went by with still no word, I just chalked it all up as an idle threat.

I had bigger problems to worry about. In August 1983, Sharyn filed for divorce. That came on the heels of Sharyn filing for bankruptcy.

I should've seen it coming. For several years, I'd been so wrapped up in all my business deals that I didn't have time for Sharyn and the kids. I'm not ashamed of working hard to provide for my family, but I realize now that I should've slowed down. Anyone who has been locked away in prison knows one thing above all else: Time, especially that spent with loved ones, is far more precious than money.

When Sharyn filed for divorce, she was trying to get my attention. She wanted to remind me that she and the kids were still there and that maybe I should spend some more time at home. Well, she succeeded. I knew I'd messed up. Sharyn got her point across and gave me until sometime around Thanksgiving to get my priorities straight. When she let me move back in, it was with the understanding that I would become your typical devoted family man. I don't know about typical, but the rest I've lived up to.

Sharyn's bankruptcy was my fault, too. I had put too many financial obligations in her name and when several went belly-up—such as the hundreds of Bohsei TVs that were ruined when the screens rolled—Sharyn officially became a debtor. It was my mistake, sheer stupidity, and I felt terrible that Sharyn got tied up in the legal end of it. Without question, that financial mess contributed to her decision to file for divorce.

By the time I moved back in, my new medical clinic in Bradenton was turning in some dynamite numbers. The Physician's Care and Emergency Clinic was just as profitable as the clinic in Lakeland, only this time I was on my own. No partners to push me out. I worked full-time on the Bradenton clinic while also exploring the possibility of opening clinics from Boston to San Antonio.

And then I got one of the biggest shocks of my life. I received a letter from Merkle's office informing me that I was invited to appear before a federal grand jury on March 12, 1984, to defend myself against charges that I was involved in racketeering, narcotics, extortion and a bunch of other nasty things.

What the hell was going on? For nine months I'd been trying to find out why I was under a microscope, and all of a sudden I'm the guest of honor before a federal grand jury? It was crazy. Where were the investigators for those previous nine months? All that time I'd been expecting somebody to come to my door and say, "Mr. McLain, let's sit down and talk about these allegations." And I would've been happy to do that. You want to talk about Barry Nelson? I'll tell you about Barry Nelson. Want to talk about Stanley Seligman? I'll tell you about Stanley Seligman. Larry Knott? Todd Siegmeister? Earl Hunt? Felix Bertucci? Sure, I'll tell you what I know. Just give me a chance.

The U.S. government never gave me that chance. By the time I was invited to appear before the grand jury, the feds already had their case against me ready to go. That invitation to testify was just a courtesy before they signed the papers and took me to court.

That letter really threw me for a loop. The grand jury thought I was involved in some serious crimes, and in less than a week I had to talk about it. I called Ron Cacciatore, and he requested an extension. I was given until March 16, but those four extra days didn't help at all. I chose not to testify, simply because I didn't have enough time to prepare to defend myself against charges that the government had spent months investigating.

The grand jury no-show was on a Friday and the following Monday, March 19, 1984, I was driving home from my attorney's office in Bartow, where a civil suit against me had been dismissed that day. I was in a good mood, cruising along on Highway 92, when I heard the radio crackle with a major news bulletin. The U.S. attorney had held a big press conference in Tampa to announce that Dennis McLain had been named in a federal grand jury indictment on charges involving racketeering, extortion and narcotics.

When I heard that, I hit my brakes and turned around. I floored the accelerator and boogied right back to my attorney's office in Bartow.

"Wait'll you hear what I just heard," I blurted. "I've been indicted. What do I do now?"

This guy wasn't a criminal lawyer, so he said I should talk to Cacciatore immediately. Cacciatore got in touch with an assistant U.S. attorney named Lynn Cole, who had handled the federal grand jury and the preliminary investigation for the government. She said that I didn't have to do anything right away. I had until Thursday to get enough money together to post bond. There wasn't any big arrest or anything.

I wasn't the only person listed in the grand jury's indictment. Also named were Sy Sher, Barry Nelson, Larry Knott, Mel Kaplan and two guys I barely knew, Frank Cocchiaro and Jose Rodriguez. It struck me as odd that several names seemed to be missing—Stanley Seligman, Guy Seligman, Felix Bertucci, Earl Hunt and Todd Siegmeister, to name a few. These guys were up to their necks in illegal activity, but their names were nowhere to be found. That gave me a pretty good clue as to who was supplying the government with erroneous information about me.

The grand jury charged various individuals with five counts of criminal wrongdoing. Each of the seven people listed in the indictment was named on at least one count, but only one person was listed on all five: Dennis Dale McLain. The grand jury obviously had me confused with Al Capone.

Let me try to explain the indictment. It was packed with lawyer language, but here's the meat of it: I was accused of racketeering, conspiracy, extortion, possession of cocaine with the intent to distribute and conspiracy to import cocaine. If convicted on all five counts, I was facing up to 90 years in prison and a $90,000 fine.

Count One charged me, Sher, Nelson and Cocchiaro with racketeering and the collection of unlawful debts. Racketeering is a rather vague term that refers to the illegal collection of money. A lot of things fall under that umbrella, including fraud, extortion, bookmaking and drug dealing. The collection of unlawful debts means loan-sharking. If you loan somebody money at an interest rate higher than that allowed by law, it's a usurious loan. Most people call it loan-sharking.

Count One also mentioned something else that was important. According to the government, Sher, Nelson, Cocchiaro and I were part of an enterprise that conducted these illegal activities. In other words, we were working together. If we had committed these crimes independently, then we couldn't be found guilty on that count.

The same four people were charged in Count Two with conspiracy. What that meant was that we had secretly plotted all these illegal activities together as a normal part of our business.

Nelson dropped out of Count Three. In this count, Sher, Cocchiaro and I were charged with extortion. They supposedly had threatened a man from Sebring, Fla., with bodily harm if he didn't pay off a loan with which I was remotely connected.

The last two counts were particularly nasty. In Count Four, the grand jury charged me, Nelson, Knott and Kaplan with possession of cocaine with intent to distribute. And in Count Five, Rodriguez and I were charged with conspiring to import cocaine.

The indictment went on to list several events that detailed the extent of this so-called conspiracy. The indictment filled 22 pages, and the name at the bottom was Robert W. Merkle, U.S. attorney for the Middle District of Florida.

My old golfing buddy. My old gambling buddy. My old drinking buddy. The guy who had browbeat his wife when they came to First Fidelity for a loan. The guy who had defaulted on the loan and then told the investor to stick it up his ass after First Fidelity was shut down. The guy who never paid off the loan until the investor sued him. Bob Merkle ordered the indictment that brought me to trial in U.S. District Court.

I was confused. The charges in that indictment simply were not true. I couldn't believe that I was really going to be tried for them and that Bob Merkle was the man pushing the buttons. I'd known for several months that Merkle wasn't my pal anymore, but it still came as a shock to see my former friend calling the shots for the opposition.

Think about it. Merkle and I had been pretty close. Even when he wrote a couple of bad checks to First Fidelity, I tried to cover for him. I did everything I could to help keep him above water. When Merkle was struggling, I called him several times and told him to get with it or First Fidelity would have to foreclose on him. I didn't have to do that; it was somebody else's job. I never did that for anybody else. But I cared for Merkle, his wife and that slew of kids they have, so I went out of my way to help him.

And how did Merkle repay my friendship? He went out of his way to nail me. He had to know I was innocent. No matter what those other scumbags were saying, he knew me well enough to know that I wasn't an extortionist or dope dealer. But he went after me like a hungry shark.

Why? I still don't know the answer to that. My guess, though, is that Merkle went after me because he knew it would generate publicity. Even though I'd been retired for years, people still remembered baseball's last 30-game winner. By taking me to court, Merkle knew he'd get his picture on TV. And that's important to him. He loves to be in the public eye. He even jumped at the chance to announce my indictment at a big press conference before I'd heard about it. I guess he looked at it as a kind of surprise party with me being his present to the voters.

If you check Merkle's record, you'll find that most of his cases are high-publicity affairs. He had told me several times that his goal in life was to become U.S. attorney general. Well, bagging Denny McLain was a big step in that direction. I was a prize for his trophy case. And even if he didn't get a conviction, he'd still get plenty of publicity.

I realize these are serious charges. I'm saying that Merkle abused the power of his office for personal gain. And it might worry me a little to make such charges if I was alone in my beliefs. But when it comes to distrusting Merkle, I'm in good company.

On February 21, 1986, the St. Petersburg Times ran an editorial headlined "Merkle's McCarthyism." It said, in part: "Twice now, U.S. Attorney Robert Merkle has used the power of his office to smear defenseless people in court.

. . . The late Sen. Joseph McCarthy treated people the same way. He said what he pleased about them, knowing that their denials could never quite overcome the impression left by his casual accusations. The Senate eventually censured McCarthy for his tactics, which disgraced the Senate as an institution. Merkle's tactics have become a disgrace to the U.S. Justice Department, which needs urgently to restrain him."

That wasn't a convicted criminal with a chip on his shoulder talking. That was a major newspaper. And another major newspaper, the Tampa Tribune, published its views on Merkle a month later. On March 23, 1986, the Tribune ran a full-page editorial titled "U.S. Attorney Merkle Must Go."

In the editorial, the Tribune outlined several instances in which Merkle had gone overboard in his attempts to seek out and destroy corruption. In one case, the Tribune wanted to know why Merkle had allowed allegations of criminal misconduct on the part of two Tampa officials to become public and then failed to charge them with any crime. "The answer," the paper said, "must be that there was an absence of corroboration. Merkle didn't have the goods. His well-meaning intolerance of corruption has turned this man of zeal into a man without any understanding of fair play."

Basically, the editorial said Merkle pursued his job with no regard for the rights of individuals, who are presumed innocent until proven guilty. In conclusion, the paper asked the Department of Justice "to solemnly review the evidence, to see for itself how its top man in these parts has disgraced his profession and damaged the lives of innocent people. We urge the Justice Department, respectfully but urgently, to get Merkle out of here. We further urge that he be replaced by the most vigorous prosecutor available—but one with a sense of fairness and a decent regard for the tenets of American justice."

When I was indicted in 1984, Merkle was just warming up his mudslinging crusade. Four years later, his unethical tactics were drawing national attention. In a January 10, 1988, installment of "60 Minutes" titled "Mad Dog Merkle," Morley Safer talked to several attorneys and law enforcement officials who had nothing good to say about the man.

"Every time I hear the word 'government' from him, I'm beginning to think government is a dirty word," attorney F. Lee Bailey said.

Lee County Sheriff Frank Wanicka and his chief deputy, Dave Wilson, have firsthand knowledge of Merkle's tactics. They have been accused of drug involvement by several grand juries, but Merkle failed to get a single conviction.

"Our reputations are tarnished forever because of Mr. Merkle, and he's done it to many people, not just us," Wanicka said.

"He has turned an awful lot of policemen against the system," Wilson added.

Kevin Kalwary, a Tampa reporter, also was dragged before a grand jury, and he doesn't even know why.

"The method of operation seems to be, throw out a net, bring in 20 fish, hopefully the five fish that you're looking for are in there, you get them and you throw the other 15 back out," Kalwary said. "Maybe the fish can swim when they're thrown back out, maybe they just flop around for a while. Is it fair to those people?"

The only people interviewed by "60 Minutes" who support Merkle, who was shown strumming a guitar and singing before a group of lawyers, were your average folks on the street. They love him, but as the Lee County chief deputy reminded Morley Safer, "Hitler was popular with the public."

That just goes to show why a grand jury indictment is so powerful. When John Doe picks up his morning newspaper and reads that the U.S. attorney has indicted seven people on drug charges, he just assumes they're guilty and that the U.S. attorney has done his job. No subsequent exoneration or acquittal will change that first impression. But the people who work inside the judicial system and the people who are unwittingly drawn into it know the tremendous potential for its abuse. Just pray that you're never caught in a misguided net thrown by a dangerous zealot like Merkle.

The system definitely is being abused in the Middle District of Florida. Merkle thinks he's Eliot Ness, but he has no regard for truth and justice. He's relentless, reckless and ruthless. And in 1984, he was out to get me.

Now I'm a pretty optimistic guy, but after the indictment I became terribly depressed. My first inclination was to concede victory to Merkle and just end it all. I felt sorry for myself and I felt awful about the shame I was bringing on my family. I figured it would be better to spare them the humiliation of seeing me stand trial.

I wasn't contemplating anything painful, like slitting my wrists or hanging myself, but a bullet to the brain was a distinct possibility. Messy, but quick. I had a snub-nosed .38 that I kept in the house for protection, and I picked it up and looked at it. I even looked around for the bullets, but when I couldn't find them, I put the gun away.

Sharyn had hidden the bullets. She told me later that she was worried about me because she'd never seen me so depressed. I don't know if I ever would've loaded the gun and pulled the trigger, but she saved me from having to make that awful decision.

After overcoming the initial shock, I decided that I wasn't going to let Merkle win that easily. He'd have to beat me on his own turf. In court.

Earlier that day, March 22, I had surrendered to the authorities at my scheduled bond hearing before U.S. Magistrate Paul Game. Cacciatore had been told by Lynn Cole that my bond would be $200,000, so we were shocked when Cole yelled and screamed and demanded a $500,000 bond. Merkle was playing hardball. Why else would Cole have told Cacciatore one thing and done another? It was looking grim already.

After Sharyn and a few other people testified, Game agreed to reduce the bond to $200,000. He knew I was no threat to flee. I had to post $10,000 in cash and sign a note for the $200,000 bond. After that was done, I was fingerprinted by an FBI agent and my picture was taken. The dehumanizing process had begun.

After the bond hearing, Cacciatore wasn't my lawyer anymore. We didn't seem to be in synch on my legal strategy, so we decided to part ways.

I had the distinct impression that Cacciatore thought our best move would be a plea bargain. Plead guilty, that is, in exchange for a shorter sentence. The way I understood it, I might get off with as little as six months or a year for pleading guilty to racketeering, which sometimes brings a 20-year sentence.

The thing is, I hadn't done any racketeering. Bookmaking, yes, but not racketeering. I didn't like the notion of saying I'd done something that I hadn't, but I felt Cacciatore was leaning that way.

If I was going to be called out, I at least wanted to go down swinging. I wanted my day in court. And I wanted to be represented by an attorney who felt the same as I did.

In retrospect, I might have been a lot smarter to cop a plea rather than make a stand. Six months or a year in camp, which is a lot more like home than a full-fledged prison situation, would've been a lot better than the sentence I wound up with. But at the time, I simply couldn't plead guilty to crimes I hadn't committed. It just wasn't right. I believed in our judicial system, which is designed to seek the truth and protect individual rights. I figured the only way to win was to play ball. Unfortunately, I struck out.

I'm not so sure the U.S. attorney's office would have worked with me on a plea bargain anyway. Like I said, a lot of names were missing from that indictment, so it looked as if the government had made quite a few deals already. If I got a special deal, too, the case would lose its high profile and there would be almost no one left to prosecute. Merkle wouldn't want that. This was one battle I'd have to fight.

My first task was to find a new attorney. That was easier said than done. My arraignment was scheduled for March 29, my 40th birthday, but that had to be postponed because I still had no one to represent me. After another postponement, I finally was arraigned April 11, by which time I had a lawyer. I pleaded not guilty to all five counts, and a May 2 trial date was set.

I had gotten several recommendations for good criminal trial lawyers and I went straight down the list, calling each one. But everybody was either too busy or too expensive to take my case. We never even got to the details of why I'd been indicted.

The fourth name on my list was Arnold D. Levine of Tampa. I went to Levine, hat in hand, and explained that Sharyn and I didn't have $100,000 to pay him up front and we didn't know how much we'd have down the road. Our only source of income was the Bradenton clinic, and business there had dropped quite a bit after the indictment.

But Levine listened. He and Rick Levinson, a partner in his firm, sat down with me for about two hours and listened to the facts in my case. They really seemed to care. That impressed me. Levine said he wanted $35,000 up front to handle everything from that day until the date the trial started, and then it would be $2,500 a day during the trial. I came up with $35,000 and said, "Arnie, you're my man."

Arnie was involved in another major criminal trial, so the May 2 trial date had to be postponed until September 10. His first goal in my case was to get Merkle completely removed. Everybody concerned believed it would be impossible to get a fair trial with Merkle's office prosecuting me. Merkle had gotten his pound of flesh with the indictment; now it was imperative that someone else handle the prosecution. Considering that we could prove there was a conflict of interest between Merkle and me, we made a great case for getting him booted.

At a pretrial hearing May 15, we went before U.S. District Judge Elizabeth A. Kovachevich, a respected member of the Florida judicial community. We asked her to remove Merkle's office from my case. The Justice Department could assign any prosecutor in the country to handle it. Our only request was that it be anyone but Merkle. With Merkle at the helm, the potential for prosecutorial vindictiveness was too great.

The hearing lasted seven hours, and it got pretty nasty. We exposed all of Merkle's credit problems, the bad checks he had written, his argument with his wife in front of me and the foreclosure suit on his second mortgage. I talked about all the times that we had golfed, gambled and drunk together. Everything came out in that hearing.

When Merkle testified, he tried to downplay our relationship. He said that we had played golf, but only twice, and that we didn't gamble. Get serious! I never played without having a money bet. Merkle also testified that we had never taken a weekend trip to Fort Lauderdale together in April 1981. He said it was purely coincidental that we happened to be flying on the same plane. I guess it also was a coincidence that we were sitting right next to each other and that later we had drinks together at the hotel. Of course, he said he never saw me after leaving the airport. I guess the guy I was drinking with was just someone who looked like him.

Despite Merkle's denials, our case was overwhelming. I don't care how little you knew about the law, it was plain as day to everyone in the courtroom that there was enough of a conflict of interest that it might prevent me from getting a fair trial.

Plain to everyone, that is, except the judge. She heard all this evidence and said that she did not find enough prejudice to warrant Merkle's removal. The case would stay in Merkle's hands.

We were stunned. We couldn't believe that any judge could hear such overwhelming evidence and then make that decision. It was one of the most shocking things I've ever heard. She couldn't see any possible prejudice in this situation? She had to be either blind or biased.

The trial hadn't even begun and we already were getting the message: This judge wasn't going to cut me a break. I think Kovachevich had it in for me from the start because she and Merkle were pals. Back when Merkle was an assistant state attorney in Pinellas County, Kovachevich was a circuit judge over there. She presided over many of the cases Merkle prosecuted. They shared many of the same conservative ideals and developed a close professional relationship. As a result, Merkle became her "golden boy." It's no surprise that when we were fighting Merkle, we were fighting Kovachevich, too.

Over the summer, the government beefed up its case against me by handing out special deals left and right. Barry Nelson pleaded guilty to one count of racketeering and agreed to testify for the government. The conspiracy and cocaine charges were dropped. Then Larry Knott and Mel Kaplan, who had been named on only one count, pleaded guilty to cocaine possession with intent to distribute and agreed to testify. Their plea agreements were kept secret, but it was obvious that all three were going to get favorable treatment by cooperating with Merkle.

Merkle never asked me to cooperate. No one ever came to Levine and said, "If Denny tells us what he knows about these other six guys, we'll go easy on him." Not one person. Instead, Merkle went easy on Nelson, who had stolen millions of dollars from investors and borrowers in Florida, and Knott, a cocaine dealer who had been in trouble with the law for more than 30 years. Kaplan wasn't a big-time criminal like these other two guys, so his getting favorable treatment didn't really bother me. Kaplan and I were in roughly the same boat. But seeing Nelson and Knott get deals really burned me up. And I could only imagine what lies they would come up with.

In August, Levine still was wrapped up in that other trial. He wanted to be fully prepared for my case, so he tried to get another postponement. Kovachevich said no. And when she discovered that Arnie wouldn't be available until after my case was scheduled to start, she got so uptight about her docket being delayed that she assigned me a public defender. That was on August 20, three weeks before my September 10 court date.

What a farce. This guy, H. Jay Stevens of Orlando, was supposed to investigate the cast of characters in the government's arsenal. For almost two months he had all of the evidence the government had furnished us, but all he did was read it. He didn't try to interview or investigate a single witness. My defense was going nowhere fast.

I can't really blame Stevens. My case was terribly complex, and it required a lot of time and effort to sort things out. Like most public defenders, he meant well, but these attorneys just aren't paid enough to give cases like mine the attention they deserve, especially when they have so many other clients to represent. Stevens knew my case was too much of a burden, and he wanted out. I just wanted Levine back.

I blame Kovachevich for putting both of us in that situation. I've asked around, and I've yet to find anyone who has heard of a federal judge appointing a public defender for someone who already had secured his own counsel. Arnie told me that kind of judicial behavior is unheard of. It just doesn't happen. But it happened to me. Kovachevich was telling me that even though I already had paid Arnie 35 grand, I had to use her choice of lawyers. It was outrageous.

Stevens eventually told Kovachevich that he wouldn't be ready in time for the trial, so it was postponed again, this time until October 29. If the judge was upset that her docket was getting backed up even more, I was furious that she had stuck me with a public defender. I persisted in trying to get Arnie back and finally, on October 15, she granted my request. But she wouldn't grant Arnie's motion for another postponement, leaving him only two more weeks to prepare my defense. When you're faced with the onslaught of five or six dozen government witnesses, that's not much time.

Meanwhile, the government was stacking the deck against me even more. On October 16, the government revealed that Stanley Seligman had agreed in April to plead guilty to racketeering in exchange for his testimony. His indictment had been sealed, and when he agreed to become a government witness, his identity was concealed for his protection. At that time, the government expected Seligman to testify against me and Nelson. But with Nelson no longer a defendant in the case, that just left me to crucify. And another crook was off the hook.

By that time, we were aware of several other five-star government witnesses. Todd Siegmeister and Felix Bertucci had both been granted immunity against prosecution for their testimony, and Earl Hunt, who was in federal prison after being convicted in 1983 for his birdbrained marijuana deal, was expected to testify, too. The U.S. government was assembling quite a collection of up-standing citizens to lead its pursuit of truth and justice.

I just hoped that somebody at the courthouse was on call with air freshener to clean up the stench left by those scumbags.

In the arms of my mother, Betty McLain.

A moment in the sun with my dad, Tom McLain, outside our Markham home.

Second row, far left—that's me with my Markham team. My dad was coach.

I have never claimed to be an altar boy, but this photo proves otherwise. I'm the obedient lad on the right.

All spruced up with my brother, Timmy. I still don't like wearing ties.

A budding major leaguer.

At my high school graduation in 1962 with my grandmother, Rose McLain.

Standing proudly with a car I bought after signing my first pro contract.

Baseball wasn't always a piece of cake.

As a member of the White Sox organization.

Sharyn and I with her parents, Lou and Della Boudreau, at our wedding reception in October 1963. We were on cloud nine.

Kristi, Sharyn and Denny enjoying a sunny day.

Charging from the dugout, with a boost from Al Kaline, to celebrate win No. 30.

Dizzy Dean was among my well-wishers after my 30th victory in 1968.

The pitching form of a 30-game winner.

The license plate on this new Thunderbird tells the story of my '68 season.

Strutting my musical stuff at the Riviera Hotel in Las Vegas, six days after the 1968 World Series ended.

Me and Denny at the Tigers' annual father-son game in 1969.

Propped against the nose of my first plane—a Cessna 337 Skymaster.

I was the center of attention after Bowie Kuhn suspended me in 1970.

Preparing for my first start after sitting out three months of the '70 season.

Ted Williams, me and Curt Flood at spring training with the Senators in 1971.

A year later, I was training with Reggie Jackson and the Oakland A's.

Bill Knight

The glory years were behind me by the time I got to Atlanta in 1972 (left) and to Des Moines with the Iowa Oaks the next season.

Pitching for my last professional team—the Shreveport Captains in 1973.

Chuckling at a listener's remark while hosting a Detroit radio show in 1973.

As host of ''The Denny McLain Show'' on WXON - TV in Detroit.

With Sharyn at Tiger Stadium in 1982, receiving replicas of my baseball awards.

Sharyn and I entering the courthouse to hear the verdict on March 16, 1985.

After the verdict—probably the lowest point in my life.

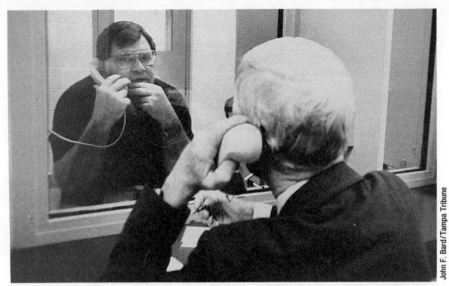

Talking with the Tampa Tribune's Tom McEwen at the county jail in Sanford, Fla.

Lt. Don McCullough was a real pal during the two months I spent in Sanford.

I seconded the sentiments of the Rail Gang at Cincinnati's Riverfront Stadium.

Jim Smothers/Talladega (Ala.) Daily Home

September 4, 1987: My first step as a free man after 2½ years.

Discussing my ride to the airport with Eric Kinkopf of the Detroit Free Press.

A happy reunion at the Talladega airport with Michelle (hugging me) and Kristi.

Sharyn and I enjoying a walk along a country road in Roanoke, Ind.

Michelle, Tim, Sharyn and me before Christmas 1987.

As close as I ever get to ice skating.

Me, Sharyn and Judge Mike Schwartz. No, it's not my tux.

Relaxing with Michelle and Sharyn.

Me with the four most wonderful kids in the world. Going clockwise, that's Denny towering over me, followed by Michelle, Tim and Kristi.

The Trial

There's an old saying that loose lips sink ships. Well, loose lips certainly sank the USS Denny McLain on its maiden voyage to U.S. District Court.

The joint trial of me, Sy Sher, Frank Cocchiaro and Jose Rodriguez began October 29. After a jury of five men and seven women was selected the first day, Judge Kovachevich listened to several minor defense motions on day two. Opening arguments were made on Halloween, which was a fitting way to begin what eventually would become a masquerade of justice. Over the next few days, the jury listened to testimony from four government witnesses, including Alton Dale Sparks, the Sebring man who supposedly was a victim of loan-sharking and extortion.

And then it was over. On November 8, the judge declared a mistrial. Just like that, the jurors were sent home and we had to start over again from scratch.

Get this: The mistrial was declared because the judge found out one of the jurors had indicated he thought I was innocent.

Jurors aren't allowed to talk to anybody about the trial until it's over. Not their wives, their kids, their friends, and especially not other jurors. They're supposed to keep their thoughts to themselves until all the evidence has been presented and it's time to render a verdict. Well, one of the jurors was talking to his boss one day and happened to mention that he thought "the baseball player's gonna win this one," or something like that. The boss called his attorney to report what he'd heard, and the attorney called Kovachevich. After a closed-door hearing in her chambers with all the attorneys, she declared a mistrial.

Granted, the juror had violated an important instruction. He had not only formed a conclusion before all the evidence was in, but also shared that conclusion with someone else. The guy's boss had nothing to do with the case, but in the court's eyes, the jury was tainted. I don't understand that. If he did not influence another juror, what harm did he do?

That decision sure as hell made me wonder about a couple of things. One, was Kovachevich trying to keep me from catching a break? Two, what would've happened if that jury had remained intact? I already had one juror in my corner, and he had sided with me while the government was presenting its case. He hadn't even heard my side of the story! Levine had been great with his cross-examination; when the trial was halted, he was tearing Sparks to pieces. Were other jurors leaning toward an acquittal? We'll never know.

We were back to square one. Then to complicate things further, Paul Johnson, Sy Sher's attorney, lost his voice for several days and the trial was delayed again. It was November 19 before we got back to business. A new jury was selected, this time consisting of nine women and three men.

I didn't like those odds. Quite frankly, I felt better about having men decide my fate than women. I believed that men could identify more with me. The more men on the jury, the better chance I had of being acquitted.

This new jury worried me for other reasons, too. As I recall, three jurors had been members of previous juries that had returned guilty verdicts. In other words, 25 percent of the jury was experienced in sending people to jail. A couple of jurors were retired government employees. It sure made me nervous to know that they were drawing retirement benefits from the side that was prosecuting me. Doesn't that sound like a conflict of interest?

Worst of all, not one member of the jury was self-employed. The judge excused every potential juror who worked for himself because she thought their businesses would suffer during a long trial. I can understand that, but wouldn't it have been fair to include just one juror who was self-employed like me? Someone who couldn't depend on a regular salary and had to hustle for every buck? I didn't think that was asking too much, but Kovachevich apparently did.

When I looked at that group of 12 people, I did not see a jury of my peers. "Peers" means equals. Aside from a common nationality, what did one juror have in common with me? How were we in any way equal? I could only hope and pray that these 12 decent people would examine the evidence and see the truth. They might not comprehend my way of life, but as long as they could apply logic and really look for the truth, I still could get a fair shake.

After breaking for Thanksgiving, the trial began in earnest November 26. It was expected to last six weeks, but it would be nearly four months before the jury returned with a verdict. They were four of the most tiring months of my life.

When the trial started, our hours were 9:30 a.m. to 5 p.m., Monday through Thursday. We had Fridays off. But after just one week of testimony, Kovachevich decided to speed up the pace. She changed each day's starting time to 7:30 a.m.

That was awful. The pace was grueling. Working from 7:30 to 5 may not sound too bad, but our days didn't end at 5 p.m. Each evening we ordered a copy of that day's testimony so we could examine it and prepare for the next day. I'm talking about hundreds of pages of testimony daily. The transcript didn't even arrive at Levine's office until 9 or 10 p.m., and it would be midnight or later before we'd go home. We wouldn't get to sleep until 1 or 2 a.m. Then we'd have to get up three or four hours later to be ready for the next day's 7:30 a.m. start.

No human being can take that pace for long. After the first week, everyone was beat. One night Arnie was so tired he didn't even recognize his own son's voice when he called to wish Arnie a happy birthday. Me, Arnie, the other attorneys, the judge, the jurors—everyone was exhausted.

Especially the jurors. They had trouble staying awake. One juror in particular slept through a large portion of the trial, and several others nodded off occasionally. It was unnerving to look over at the jury box and see the people who would determine my future sitting there with their eyes closed and mouths open.

Kovachevich recognized the problem but took a ridiculous approach to correcting it. Instead of moving the starting time back to 9:30, she told the jurors that they could stand up, stretch and walk around while witnesses were testifying. In fact, she let witnesses, attorneys and the court reporter exercise at will. She would even stand up herself. I'm surprised she didn't bring in a television, a VCR and a Jane Fonda workout tape.

The judge also let the jurors drink coffee and eat during the trial. I'd look up while someone was testifying, and the jurors would be filling their coffee cups or picking out doughnuts. The jury box looked like a buffet line.

This is justice? Using artificial stimulants to keep the jury awake? The judge did everything but hand out NoDoz. I wouldn't have believed it if I hadn't seen it. It was bizarre.

Kovachevich insisted her remedies were effective. She always referred to the jurors as her "troops" and complimented them on how well they were holding up.

But Levine introduced evidence to the contrary. On December 12, he brought in a clinical psychologist to observe the proceedings. The psychologist, Dr. Sidney J. Merin, wrote a report in which he detailed the inattentiveness of the jury. Merin made it clear that there was no way the jury could do its job effectively under those conditions. At best, the exercise, food and drink were a distraction. At worst, they provided only a brief stimulation that left the jurors more numb than they were before.

Arnie showed Merin's report to Kovachevich and asked for a mistrial. Barring that, he at least wanted a return to normal hours. But the judge denied the motion. She even refused to hold an evidentiary hearing to look into the problem. By law, a judge must at least inquire into whether a defendant's rights to a fair trial are being prejudiced when confronted with substantial evidence of juror misconduct, which is what falling asleep amounts to, even if it isn't their fault. But she wouldn't do it.

Kovachevich had dismissed the first jury when she heard one juror was leaning toward an acquittal. But when presented with an expert's opinion that the second jury was not functioning at full speed, she let the trial proceed. Was she really interested in my getting a fair trial? Of course not. All she cared about was her precious docket and how many hours we were behind schedule. To hell with my rights.

In fact, Kovachevich regularly made a point of mentioning how much time the trial had consumed. She repeatedly told the attorneys to pick up the pace and reminded them that they were being timed by the courtroom deputy clerk. The woman was obsessed with the clock. An ultimatum she delivered to the attorneys typifies her fixation on haste. "This case better go to the jury the week of March 12," she said. "I'm telling you all that right now or you are really going to see a show in here the week of March 18 like they haven't seen around this building."

We maintained that grueling 7:30-to-5 schedule for almost two months. Finally, on January 30, 1985, we went to a 9 a.m. start. But that was too little too late. By then everybody was dead, and we just dragged through the rest of the trial.

Besides being exhausted, the participants in my trial also had to put up with numerous distractions. Construction in other parts of the courthouse was sometimes deafening. And the temperature in the courtroom jumped around more than Michael Jordan in a new pair of Nikes. One day it would be so cold you had to wear a coat, and the next it was so hot you'd be ripping off your tie. Sometimes the temperature would change from minute to minute or vary depending on which part of the courtroom you were sitting in. Even Kovachevich admitted the conditions were lousy.

The result was a situation in which the jurors had difficulty concentrating. They were sleeping, stretching, walking, eating, drinking, shivering, sweating, rocking, yawning—everything but listening to testimony. One time they even asked the judge if the curtains could be opened so they could watch a parade go by. She said no, but the fact that they asked showed they really weren't in the ball game.

A judge is supposed to provide an atmosphere in which the facts of the case can be presented, heard and pondered without the participants being distracted. That's known as courtroom decorum. But my trial was a three-ring circus. If you were bored by the testimony, you could always find something else to occupy your attention for a minute or two.

Despite all the courtroom theatrics, my trial could not be classified as exciting. Everyone was too tired. Nor was it well attended. You might envision a packed courtroom with hundreds of baseball fans listening breathlessly to the testimony against the former pitching star. Well, the courtroom wasn't big enough to hold hundreds of people, and we still had plenty of empty seats most of the time. Between the opening and closing arguments, the only people in the courtroom were those who had to be there—the judge, jury, court reporter, bailiff, defendants, attorneys, witnesses and a journalist or two. I drew a good crowd when I testified, but that was an exception. For the most part, we did our business in private.

Inside the courtroom, that is. Outside, my life was anything but private. The trial was a daily news story in the Tampa area, and that made life difficult for my family.

It was toughest on the kids. You know how cruel youngsters can be; my kids heard all the wisecracks and insults you'd expect. Tim, Denny and Kristi, who at that time ranged in age from 15 to 19, didn't have it too bad. Their friends were mature enough to give them support, and the other kids their age were more curious than mean. But Michelle had a rough time. She was only 12, and she took a lot of abuse. It tore me up to hear Sharyn talk about how my baby had come home from school crying again.

Actually, we had one more child to worry about. A few years earlier, we had taken in a friend of Kristi's who needed a home. She wasn't ours legally, but we considered her a part of our family.

Dale DeVita and her mother moved into the house next door to our Tampa home. Dale's parents were divorced, and her mother, a nurse, worked all day and traveled quite a bit. Dale, who is a year younger than Kristi, started spending a lot of time at our house. She and her mother had some sort of falling out, and before long Dale moved in with us. We were happy to have her. She's a terrific girl who just needed a normal, loving family environment and a chance to work out a few problems. Dale got her life back together, and she moved back in with her mother after graduating from high school. But we still think of Dale as our fifth child.

As the trial plodded on, Sharyn and I tried to pretend as if nothing was wrong. The kids knew I was charged with some serious crimes, but we always maintained an optimistic outlook. We never talked about the possibility that I might be found guilty and have to go to prison. Sharyn and I discussed it privately, but not in front of the kids. They were worried enough already.

When the McLains celebrated Christmas in 1984, you never would've known that I was in the middle of a trial. We had a few days off and tried to enjoy every moment, so nobody talked about it. There were fewer presents than normal under the tree, but that was the only indication that all was not well.

Money was starting to get tight. Very tight. I had been forced to sell the Bradenton walk-in clinic shortly before Christmas, and I didn't get a very good price. With that gone, I was unemployed.

I really messed up in Bradenton. Before I was indicted, a group of doctors had offered me a new condo and about $150,000 in cash, spread over several years, to buy the clinic. The whole package was worth about $250,000, which was a good deal. But I didn't want a condo and delayed payments. I wanted cash.

"Keep the condo," I said. "Cash me out. I don't want to carry paper. Cash me out and you've got a deal."

When the doctors said they didn't have that much cash, I said thanks, but no thanks. Bradenton was doing 100 grand in business every month, so I figured I could wait until someone was willing to deal on my terms.

In retrospect, I should have accepted their offer. A condo that was paid for and a regular income easily would have carried Sharyn and the kids through my 2½ years in prison. But I got greedy and my family paid the price.

Before the trial, the clinic got some bad publicity. One of my doctors was accused of fondling female patients. When it rains it pours. We had affidavits from patients and nurses who swore that he had done it several times. As soon as I found out, I fired the guy. But when the story made the papers, it hurt business like you might expect. Combine that with the fact that other clinics were opening in Bradenton, and my clinic's value plummeted.

Desperately in need of cash to take care of my family, I had to sell. I went back to the same doctors who had offered to buy it before and asked if they were still interested. They were, but they got the clinic at some fire-sale price.

The clinic wasn't the only thing we sold during the trial. We also sold the replicas of the Cy Young and MVP awards that the Tigers had given me a couple of years earlier. They brought only $6,500, but we had to scrape up every dollar we could. We also sold one of our cars and just about everything else of value. And Kristi had to drop out of Hillsborough Community College after one year because we couldn't afford her tuition.

Sharyn even sold her diamond engagement ring. I had paid $950 for it 21 years before, and she got $200 from a pawn shop. I felt terrible about that. I'd gotten us in that jam, and there she was selling her ring. She has made more sacrifices for me and the kids than I'll ever be able to repay.

Sharyn knew we had to eat and we had to pay Levine, although keeping my family fed was my top priority. Fortunately, Arnie wasn't breathing down our necks for the money; in fact, it was quite the opposite. He told us not to worry. He wanted his money, but if we didn't have it, well, he could wait until we did. And when I went to jail still owing Arnie thousands of dollars, he stuck with me and helped me through my appeal. Now that I'm free and earning money again, I can start repaying my debt to this tremendous attorney and friend.

Arnie earned every one of the 2,500 dollars he charged for each day of the trial. The government presented dozens of witnesses who said awful things about me, but Arnie did a brilliant job of cross-examining each one and revealing the flaws and inconsistencies in their testimony. He also showed that the witnesses weren't always the fine, upstanding citizens the government would have the jury believe. He outlined their criminal backgrounds and discussed the reasons each one had to cooperate with the government.

Surprisingly, two of the biggest criminals who got the sweetest deals—Barry Nelson and Stanley Seligman—never testified. Ernst Mueller, an assistant U.S. attorney who took over the case for Merkle after Lynn Cole resigned to enter private practice, had told the jury in his opening statement that both men would testify. But about midway through the trial, Mueller changed his mind. Nelson and Seligman got favorable treatment without ever taking the witness stand.

Why? Two reasons. One was because Mueller couldn't afford to put them on after hearing what other government witnesses were saying about them. Their credibility already had been destroyed. And the two people who damaged their credibility the most were their own nephews.

Gordon Douglas is Nelson's nephew. At one time, he was a part-owner of the First Fidelity office in Miami. Douglas had wonderful things to say about his uncle. He told the court that he didn't think Nelson had "ever even endeavored to make an honest living" and that his reputation for honesty was "on a par with Attila the Hun." He said that he wouldn't let Seligman help his mother across the street and that both Nelson and Seligman were "world-class liars." Guy Seligman, Stanley's nephew, seconded that opinion. Another government witness said Nelson was "not honorable or honest as far as truthfulness."

One of the funnier lines from the trial came from Douglas, who was just as repulsive as the people he was blasting. After saying that Nelson must be in the Guinness Book of World Records for the number of businessmen he had buried, Douglas said Barry and Stanley were "certainly a marriage made in heaven." When the attorney cross-examining him asked if that meant Stanley also belonged in the Guinness book, Douglas replied, "Yes, but you see, he is an attorney, so that, you know, takes away his amateur status."

With character references like these, Mueller would have been a fool to put Nelson and Seligman on the stand. But the real killer was the "Nelson/Kaplan tapes."

These cassette tapes caused a bit of a furor. In mid-January, Mel Kaplan testified that he had secretly taped some conversations between himself and Todd Siegmeister on his home phone in New Jersey. Levine requested that the tapes be brought to Tampa and admitted as evidence. The judge told Arnie that he could listen to the tapes when they arrived. A few days later, Levine sent his secretary to the airport to pick them up. The package, which was ripped when she found it, was marked "To be opened by Judge Kovachevich only." The secretary brought the package to Arnie, who did just what the judge had told him he could do: Play them. He poured the tapes out through the rip and listened to them.

Arnie loved it. He expected to find only two tapes, but Kaplan's attorney had sent eight. And they were loaded with material that would help me. Most of the tapes were of conversations between Kaplan and Barry Nelson in which they discussed how they would testify. They were getting their stories straight. The tapes of Kaplan and Siegmeister provided more of the same. In short, the tapes were strong evidence that government witnesses were giving perjured testimony against me.

Here's a sample: "Remember everything we do," Nelson told Kaplan on one of the tapes. "Just try to remember all the details and put them together in your mind, and by the time I talk to you, we'll put together a package." And I'm sure they did.

The judge and other attorneys were outraged that Arnie had listened to the tapes without permission. But Arnie argued that if there was anything in those tapes that would help me, he wasn't going to ignore them. Besides, the judge had indicated that he could listen to them when they arrived. After a week of argument among the attorneys, Kovachevich decided to let everybody listen to the tapes, which were edited in part before the jury could hear them.

As soon as those tapes were revealed, Mueller announced that Seligman would not be testifying. A few days later he made the same announcement about Nelson.

Now it was our turn to be outraged. From day one, Mueller had been saying that Nelson and Seligman had pleaded guilty and would testify that I was involved in a number of specific criminal acts. The prosecution then introduced a lot of evidence in the form of hearsay attributed to Nelson and Seligman. This hearsay touched on virtually every count in the indictment. But when they didn't appear on the stand, Arnie had no chance to cross-examine them.

That was a joke. A key principle guaranteed by the Sixth Amendment is that a defendant is entitled to confront his accusers. But the jury at my trial heard evidence attributed to Nelson and Seligman without ever seeing them take the stand. Kovachevich kept asking Mueller if all this hearsay evidence was going to be tied up and he kept saying yes. But then it wasn't. What it amounted to was that Nelson and Seligman were testifying by proxy without having to face cross-examination. We could have called them to the stand ourselves, but we figured that would just hurt my case. They'd probably tell more lies. The point was that the judge had admitted hearsay from two "world-class liars" based on the belief that they would testify, and then they didn't.

Mueller did bring in plenty of other witnesses who more than made up for the lies that Nelson and Seligman never got a chance to tell. What follows is a brief rundown of the key government witnesses.

• Alton Dale Sparks.

Sparks, who goes by his middle name, was the key to the first three counts of the indictment. He also was the most unbelievable witness the government put on the stand. His testimony was a complete farce, and I still got convicted.

In January 1981, Sparks obtained a second mortgage of $145,000 from the Sarasota office of First Fidelity. To get that loan, he presented Dick Schwartz, the office manager in Sarasota, a financial statement showing his net worth to be more than $1.25 million. Sparks told Schwartz he was making about $20,000 a month from two discos he owned and operated, one in Sebring and the other in DeLand, Fla. He said he needed the $145,000 to renovate and improve all of his properties.

One more thing about that loan: To make sure he got it, Sparks gave Schwartz a $10,000 kickback.

A couple of months later, I got a call from Schwartz. He said Sparks needed another $40,000 to continue his renovation work. First Fidelity didn't make third mortgages, but he had heard me mention that I knew of someone who might. Could I help out Sparks?

The guy I had referred to was Sy Sher. Barry Nelson had told me that Sy made a number of personal notes. I had never dealt with Sy on that basis, but when Schwartz called on Sparks' behalf, I thought Sy might be interested. I asked Schwartz if Sparks was a good risk, and he told me about Sparks' discos, house, income and that net worth of more than $1 million. He assured me that it would be a very secure loan. I figured that since Schwartz had just done all the paper work on the First Fidelity loan, he must know what he was talking about. I trusted his judgment.

On my recommendation, Sy Sher loaned Sparks $40,000. Other than introducing Sparks to Sy, I had nothing to do with the loan. I didn't provide any of the money or receive a commission, and I didn't even know the terms of the loan until later. As it turned out, Sy was charging 2½ percent a week, or 130 percent annually. Definitely loan-sharking. But remember, it wasn't my loan. All I did was introduce them. If Sparks wanted to pay Sy $1,000 a week in interest alone, that was his business.

Around the first of May, it came to my attention that Sparks had only one disco in operation. DeLand wasn't open. That worried me because if he had only one business operating, he had only half the earning power he had claimed. The less earning power, the less likely he was to pay back his loans. The loan that worried me was Sy's. Sparks was the first borrower I'd ever referred to Sy, and I felt responsible.

So, I went down to Sebring and talked to Sparks, who admitted that the DeLand disco was closed. He said he had run out of money before the place was ready to open.

I was mad. He had lied about his income, net worth and business operations, putting me on the hook with Sy for that 40 grand. I told Sparks that we had to start a weekly payment program. Either Basil Caruso, my assistant at First Fidelity, or I would go to Sebring every week and pick up a minimum of $1,000, which then would be sent to Sy. Sparks agreed to that plan.

That went on for a few weeks, but Sparks was sinking deeper and deeper into debt. He was paying Sy his weekly interest plus a little more that went toward reducing the principal, but he didn't make a single payment on his $145,000 loan from First Fidelity. This self-proclaimed millionaire was turning out to be a stiff.

Finally, in mid-July, Sparks agreed to sign a quitclaim deed for the Sebring disco over to Barry Nelson's wife. Nothing, not even his family, was sacred to Barry. In effect, First Fidelity assumed control. Sparks would still run the club and keep all the receipts from his pinball machines, but after his employees had been paid, all other profits would be applied toward reducing his First Fidelity debt. In the meantime, we would try to sell the disco and satisfy the existing mortgages. If any profit was left after that, Sparks could have it.

Sparks Bottle Club, as his disco was called, was a real redneck joint. It was open from 1 a.m. to 5 a.m., Tuesday through Saturday. With those hours, this obviously wasn't the spot for a church social. But if you were riding a motorcycle, wearing a cowboy hat or driving a pickup truck and wanted some late-night action, this was the place to be. In the one or two times I visited there, I saw several fights. It was a tough place.

That would've been OK if the disco had been out in the middle of nowhere. But it was located downtown. Some nearby residents got upset and eventually the Sebring police got tired of answering complaints about noise and fights. In August 1981, the City of Sebring passed an ordinance that forced the club to close by 2 a.m. For all intents and purposes, that put Sparks Bottle Club out of business.

Dick Schwartz and I did what we could to get the place back on its feet. I even paid Sparks' legal fees so that he could file a lawsuit against the city. But Sparks Bottle Club remained closed, and First Fidelity and Sy Sher were out a lot of money because neither Sparks nor his properties were worth what he had claimed.

That's the condensed version of the Dale Sparks story. Three years later, I was accused of loan-sharking and extortion in connection with that deal. To explain that radical turn in events, let's look at Sparks' testimony.

Sparks told the court that on May 20, 1981, he was threatened by me, Sy Sher and a third man regarding the $40,000 loan. According to Sparks, the four of us met at a Steak and Ale Restaurant across the street from First Fidelity in Hollywood, where this third man, whom Sparks called "The General," threatened to cut off his ears and hand them to him if he failed to pay Sy his money. The implication was that I was in on this extortion.

If Sparks was threatened, I never knew about it. At the trial, we produced receipts from Avila that proved I was golfing in Tampa that day. I couldn't have been in both places at once. That was strike one against Sparks' extortion fairy tale.

Strike two was his identification of The General. The government contended that Frank Cocchiaro, one of my co-defendants, was The General. But when it came time for Sparks to identify The General, he couldn't do it. He walked right by Cocchiaro twice in court—once in the proceeding that ended in a mistrial and again in the second trial—and failed to make a positive ID both times. He testified that The General had a mole on his cheek, but Cocchiaro didn't. The government alleged that Cocchiaro had a mole removed, but Mafalda Kline, Cocchiaro's live-in girlfriend for many years, testified that he never had a mole on his cheek. Considering that Sparks said he listened to The General threaten him for an hour, you'd think he'd remember the guy's face.

Strike three was Sparks' contention that The General scared him so badly he went into hiding for more than a year. He said that even as he spoke, he was "still trying to conceal" himself because of the threat. Well, Rob North certainly had no trouble finding Sparks when he went to Sebring to interview him for that 1983 series on Channel 8. We also produced a videotape showing Sparks in front of his father's disco, standing and smiling in the middle of downtown Sebring. Sparks even announced his address at a public trial in Sebring during the time he supposedly was so worried about his safety. For a guy in hiding, Sparks sure was easy to find.

Sparks also testified that his mother knew about the threats and that when he was arrested one day for passing bad checks, she got worried about him and called the FBI. Funny thing was, the FBI had no records of Sparks' mother reporting any threats made against her son. And the government did not produce his mother to corroborate his story. If Sparks' mother knew about threats to her son, why didn't she testify? Because it probably never happened. Like I said, I wasn't there.

The craziest story Sparks came up with was about a trip he supposedly made to Ohio. Sparks claimed that I told him to rustle up some money by selling marijuana. In the first trial, Sparks testified that he got a grocery sack full of marijuana from a friend and drove north to sell it. But before reaching Ohio, Sparks said, his car broke down. He said he gave the mechanic some of the marijuana as payment and then returned to Sebring.

Then in the second trial, Sparks changed his story. He said he didn't drive to Ohio; he took a train! The government even produced a document that it claimed was Sparks' train ticket. But we hired a private investigator who was able to show that the government's document was not a ticket; it was only a reservation. On top of that, the reservation would have gotten him only as far as Washington. There was nothing to prove he ever made it to Ohio. Sparks also testified that he sold some marijuana for $3,000, left the remainder in the basement of his brother's house and then flew back to Florida. But the government couldn't produce a ticket to prove that, either. Finally, Sparks said he later drove back to Ohio to retrieve the marijuana and had car problems on the way back, which was when he traded some of the drugs for car repairs. His testimony was so screwy, it's not surprising the government failed to produce a witness who could corroborate it.

What prompted Sparks to change his mind about his travel arrangements? A dream. The greatest line from the whole trial was when Dale Sparks said, "I had a dream." He testified that sometime between his two trial appearances, he had had a nightmare that jogged his memory about what really happened. Sparks had a dream and the government said, "Convict Denny McLain." Incredible.

Sparks also changed his testimony about a guy from Sebring known only as Blue. At one point, Sparks testified that he had gotten the marijuana from Blue. He said he'd known the guy for years but didn't know his name. Everyone just called him Blue. Sparks later testified that there was no Blue. Still later he testified that there were two Blues, nicknamed the Blues Brothers. It sounded like a John Belushi and Dan Aykroyd routine.

Three different stories, all from the same mouth. If you were a juror, wouldn't that make you question the guy's credibility? Arnie had a field day.

Tearing Sparks apart was easier than taking candy from a baby. And Mueller even got frustrated with his star witness, who ignored, sidestepped or simply didn't understand many of his questions. That drove Mueller crazy. "Mr. Sparks, would you please answer the question?" he'd say. "Mr. Sparks, do you understand what I'm saying?" He was badgering his own witness. Even the judge got on Sparks' case.

Nevertheless, the government also did everything it could to make Sparks look good. Mueller introduced as evidence a letter from a Sebring minister who said nice things about Sparks. Mueller neglected to mention that this same minister had been kicked out of the church after being arrested and charged with fondling Boy Scouts. How's that for a sparkling character witness?

There were numerous other flaws in Sparks' testimony. For instance, he said the City of DeLand refused to let him operate the club after hearing about a wet T-shirt contest I had suggested for his Sebring disco. Yeah, that was my idea. I figured that would go over big with his cowboy clientele, and it did. Sparks had one of his best nights ever. But that wasn't what turned DeLand against Sparks. We produced a letter from the Sebring police chief to his counterpart in DeLand that described all the violence and other incidents at the Sebring disco. Largely because of that letter, the City of DeLand refused to grant Sparks a liquor license. That was what kept him out of business. Sparks also said we met several times between June 30 and July 10, 1981. We presented credit card and telephone records that proved I was on a family trip to Chicago during that time.

So what did Dale Sparks leave us with? A mass of contradictions. You could've driven a truck through the holes we shot in Sparks' testimony. We also destroyed his credibility. We showed that the financial statement he submitted to get the $145,000 loan was fraudulent. In so doing, we proved that when he testified to the veracity of that statement before the grand jury, he committed perjury. He lied about his employment. He wrote numerous bad checks and twice was convicted for it. He filed false tax returns. He failed to report income from the operation of his pinball arcades. He paid a man a $1,000 kickback to get a phony appraisal of his DeLand property. If you can believe his own testimony, he also possessed and sold marijuana. All this and more, yet Dale Sparks was given immunity to testify against Denny McLain.

Sparks was the most incredible "victim" I've ever seen. Mueller portrayed him as a poor, unfortunate soul who had lost his house, car and two discos. Well, it was a shame that Sparks lost his discos. If he'd been able to control the violence, maybe he could've made a go of it. But that wasn't my fault or Sy Sher's fault. And it certainly wasn't our fault that Dale Sparks borrowed all that money and couldn't pay it back. If Sparks had been honest about his financial situation, Sy wouldn't have loaned him a nickel in the first place.

And what ever became of that money? Nobody knows. He obviously didn't spend it on renovations of his house and discos. He failed to produce a single receipt showing that he had used the money for the reasons he had represented on the loan application. Sparks admitted on the stand that he owed money to this mysterious drug supplier called Blue, so it's a good bet that he grabbed the cash and took it straight to Blue to avoid a good beating.

Here's what we do know about the money: Of the $185,000 he borrowed, he repaid only $17,500, and 10 grand of that was interest. He didn't pay First Fidelity a cent. Subtract from that the $10,000 kickback he paid to Dick Schwartz, and he made a pretty hefty profit—more than $155,000. And the government called him a victim! In fact, the government asked that Sparks receive some benefits through the Victims' Compensation and Assistance program. It was one of the craziest things I'd ever heard. But that explained why Sparks would make a fool of himself on the stand. By sending me to jail, he stood to make a lot of money.

According to a report from a private investigator, Sparks hasn't changed much since the trial. When my appeal was upheld in 1987 and it appeared that I might have to go to trial again, Arnie sent an investigator down to Sebring, where he interviewed several people who had dealt with Sparks. One man called Sparks a "pathological liar. . . . I wouldn't believe him if he said his name is Dale Sparks." Another man said that "until I got involved with one of their (the government's) good witnesses, I didn't know what to think about McLain. But now I know they put the wrong man in jail." This same man called Sparks a "professional liar and con man." According to another couple, Sparks is the type of person who would lie even when the truth would suffice.

Some things never change.

● John Paul Higgins.

Higgins, the government's No. 2 witness against me, had a lot in common with witness No. 1. Like Sparks, he went by his middle name, got a loan from Sy Sher and lied through his teeth.

But you wouldn't confuse the two by looking at them. Sparks was a little guy, about 5-9 and 160 pounds, with red hair, a red beard and a red face. He reminded me of a strawberry. Higgins was about 5-10 and 225 pounds with a big belly, long black hair, a mustache and effeminate mannerisms. But they dressed similarly. Both Sparks and Higgins wore three-piece suits that either didn't fit or didn't match—a striped tie with a checked jacket, brown pants with black shoes, that kind of thing. The government was trying to pass these guys off as innocent little country bumpkins who had been victimized. Sparks, who ordinarily speaks very fast, sounded like a 45-rpm record being played at 33. Every word was spoken slowly and carefully. It was all part of the government's grand scheme to elicit sympathy from the jury.

I met Higgins shortly after we opened the Tampa office of First Fidelity. We sent out letters to mortgage brokers throughout the Tampa area, inviting them to do business with us. Higgins responded to that offer, and he spent a lot of time in our office. Paul and I became pretty good friends.

When Higgins asked me if First Fidelity would loan him $35,000 for a second mortgage, I was glad to help. I ordered an appraisal of his house, which got a glowing report. It appraised for about $97,000. The loan was approved in early fall of 1980, and since Higgins was a fellow broker, I didn't charge him a brokerage fee.

A few months later, Higgins told me he was expanding his business and needed some quick cash. If I could arrange for him to get $15,000, he said, he'd pay off the loan in a month or so. Just like with Dale Sparks, I told him to talk to Sy Sher. Sy agreed to loan him the money, which Higgins repaid in no more than four weeks.

Presto! Just like that, Higgins had tremendous credit. About a week after paying off his first loan from Sy, he was back asking for another $100,000. He was all gung-ho about Diversified Assets, this new business he said he had going with a guy named Timothy Johnston, and he wanted the money to keep his budding conglomerate in high gear. J. Paul Higgins thought he was J. Paul Getty. And his partner seemed just as ambitious. Johnston said he wanted to be President of the United States.

Well, 100 grand was out of the question, but Higgins was willing to take less. Since Higgins and Johnston both seemed like good guys, I decided to talk to Sy, whose main concern was Higgins' collateral. All Higgins had was his house, which I figured still had another $40,000 in equity, based on that dynamite appraisal. Sy said he'd go 30. In August 1981, Higgins signed a note and mortgage for $30,000, with interest and principal due in 30 days. The interest rate on the note was 18 percent a year. And that was accurate. What it didn't reflect was that Higgins would pay Sy 3 percent a week for the money. Higgins needed the money for a month, so he'd pay just 12 percent for it if he met his 30-day deadline. That was a hell of a good deal. But if he took longer to repay the loan, the 3 percent interest would stop after the sixth week, and the annual interest rate would be 18 percent.

Again, I had nothing to do with the terms. Higgins and Sher worked those out.

About a week or 10 days later, Higgins came to my office with an incredible sob story.

"Tim Johnston has ripped me off," he said.

"You've got to be kidding," I replied. "You thought he was going to be the next President."

"Well, the next President has ripped me off. He wrote a bunch of checks at the bank and took off with about $30,000. Denny, there's just no way I'm going to be able to pay Sy Sher when that loan comes due in September."

"That's not good."

After talking to me, Higgins went to the Hillsborough County Sheriff's Office and filed a complaint against Johnston. Then we tried to decide what to do. If worse came to worst, I figured he could sell his house, pay off all his loans and start over.

And then I saw the house.

The first thing that hit me was the stench. You could cut it with a knife. Dog crap was all over the house. Water at least an inch deep was standing in the utility room. Cockroaches and other insects were everywhere. It was absolutely disgusting. I couldn't imagine how anyone could live there. Hell, if I'd been one of the dogs, I'd have moved out. But Higgins and his wife were living there, right in the middle of all that excrement.

The shame of it was that the house could have been gorgeous. It was beautiful on the outside, with a big yard and trees, but the spacious interior was a pit. For some reason, Higgins had let that house deteriorate after the appraiser went through.

The house would never sell for anything close to the amount Higgins owed. Maybe if he cleaned it up it would, but he didn't hang around long enough to do that. Higgins quitclaimed the house to me and then disappeared a couple of weeks later. Three lenders had about $96,000 wrapped up in the house, but I was lucky to sell it for $65,000. That just about covered the first two mortgages, but Sy Sher never got back a penny of the money he had loaned. I found out that Higgins was filing for bankruptcy, so there wasn't any point in pursuing him. I never saw him again until he showed up at my trial.

Higgins was more impressive on the stand than Dale Sparks. He answered all of Ernst Mueller's questions and kept his story straight. But when Arnie sank his teeth into Higgins, the jury saw his true colors.

Higgins told both the grand jury and the jury at my trial that he had never signed a promissory note and mortgage for $30,000 from Sy Sher. That was important because the government alleged that he was being charged 3 percent a week interest. That rate computes to 156 percent a year, which, of course, is illegal. Well, Sy was charging 3 percent a week all right, but the note indicated that the obligation would be repaid in 30 days and that the annual rate would not exceed 18 percent. That is legal. Think about it: Would I have prepared paper work for an illegal loan? Of course not. And Higgins evidently figured we'd be unable to produce this paper work.

Higgins swore up and down that he never signed either the note or the mortgage. Well, Arnie knew Higgins was lying. He had the original note and mortgage, showing an interest rate of only 18 percent a year, right there at the defense table. He showed the documents to Higgins, who was speechless. Higgins didn't know what to say. Arnie really shook him up. And he didn't stop there.

Higgins also told the court the same story he had told me about Timothy Johnston ripping him off. He testified that Johnston had signed and cashed two checks totaling $24,000 that bounced. Arnie pressed Higgins on this, and Higgins insisted that Johnston had signed the checks. The next day, Higgins kept looking at his watch and telling the judge that he was in a hurry to get back to Ocala, where he worked. With Higgins just minutes away from leaving the stand, in walked a private investigator Arnie had hired to get the checks from the bank. It was just like a scene from "Perry Mason." Arnie picked them up and showed them to Higgins. Right there, plain as day, was Higgins' signature at the bottom of each check.

Higgins almost had a stroke. He gasped for breath, and the judge had to ask him if he could continue. It probably was the most dramatic moment in the trial.

Higgins was never ripped off by Timothy Johnston. They were in a scam together. And so was Johnston's girlfriend, who worked at the bank and approved the checks. Higgins tried to tell the court that he wasn't in on this check-kiting scheme, but we proved otherwise.

The scam worked like this: Higgins wrote the bad checks so that he would have the money to pay back Sy Sher's $15,000. With his "good credit" firmly established, he was able to get another 30 grand from Sy. He was defrauding the bank so he could get even more money from Sy. And when he started feeling some heat from the FBI about his bank account, he used the $30,000 to cover his tracks.

Isn't it amazing that the FBI didn't pursue this character? Instead, I was accused of loan-sharking and extortion. If anyone was a victim here, it was me. Sy made it clear that while it wasn't my fault these guys were stiffs, he still expected to be paid. If Sparks and Higgins didn't come up with the $70,000 they owed Sy, I'd better. I had personally vouched for the loans, and Sy was calling me on it. By the time we went to prison, I had reduced the debt to about $30,000.

The government alleged that I had committed extortion by threatening Higgins and his family with bodily harm. Higgins testified that he ran into me at Diamond Hill Golf-Country Club one day in September 1981 and that I got mean. According to Higgins, I said something like: "No one, no one in your family is safe, including Notre Dame. I want that money now." Higgins had a son attending Notre Dame.

To disprove that absurd accusation, my love for golf came in handy. The courses where I played kept meticulous records, and there is no record of me playing golf at Diamond Hill anytime near the date Higgins claimed I threatened him. It couldn't have happened.

Higgins said I threatened him on other occasions, too. He even wore a bug and tried to coerce me into threatening him. The government introduced the tapes of our conversations, which I had no idea were being recorded, and not one threat can be found on them. Higgins also testified that I told him to sell marijuana to make a few bucks, but the tapes revealed nothing incriminating regarding drugs. That was because I never told Higgins to do anything but pay his damn bills.

I saved the best for last. We put on the stand an elderly man named John Ambler who had been ripped off by Higgins for everything he and his wife had. Ambler was still recuperating from a triple heart bypass operation when Higgins waltzed in and gave him the big sell on Diversified Assets. In his most disgusting moment, Higgins conned this 70-year-old man into selling his mortgage company for 50,000 shares of stock in Diversified Assets. He charged the couple a dollar a share, but the stock certificate he gave them reflected a value of only a penny a share. It didn't really matter what the certificate said because Higgins' company was a fraud anyway. When Ambler finally realized that he had put their life savings and everything they owned into a worthless stock certificate, he was lucky his heart didn't fail completely.

This is documented! All these facts and pieces of evidence were brought out during the trial. We proved beyond a shadow of a doubt that Paul Higgins was a perjurer, a thief and a lowly piece of scum. Why the jury didn't pick up on that, I'll never know. And why a judge would allow documented perjury as trial testimony is just beyond imagination.

Arnie tried to get Higgins' testimony thrown out. Sparks', too, for that matter. But Kovachevich, in her divine wisdom, let their testimony stand. When I say that she protected her friend Bob Merkle by doing everything she could to help his case and hurt me, this is precisely what I'm talking about.

Like with Sparks, the government portrayed Higgins as a victim. The government wanted the taxpayers of the United States to dig into their pockets and find some way to repay him for the losses he had incurred. Losses? You mean that pigsty he lived in and mortgaged to the hilt? You mean that $30,000 he failed to repay Sy Sher?

Here's the real Paul Higgins: He falsified a credit application. He falsified a tax return, showing twice as much income as he had. He filed a false police report. He lied to the grand jury and he lied at my trial. He wrote bad checks. He ripped off a bank for thousands of dollars. He borrowed $30,000 from Sy Sher and didn't pay back a nickel. And he conned an elderly couple out of almost their entire life savings. Doesn't your heart just bleed for him?

I think Arnie said it best. In his closing remarks to the jury, he said "that the stench given off by Mr. Higgins and his testimony and his appearance and his demeanor permeates this whole case."

By comparison, his house smelled like a rose.

• Dick Schwartz.

In a way, Dick was a victim, just like me. When First Fidelity was shut down, Dick also was owed a lot of money by Barry Nelson. We both were had. But the similarity of our situations didn't stop Dick from joining the government's team of lying witnesses.

Shortly after First Fidelity's demise, Dick loaned me $15,000. I had lost some money in the stock market, and his loan helped me cover some checks I had written.

Several weeks later, he asked me to repay the loan. "Like hell," I said. "I'm still on the hook for your pal over in Sebring." I was stuck owing Sy Sher $30,000 because of Dale Sparks, and since Dick had gotten me mixed up with Sparks in the first place, I figured that 15 grand made us even.

Dick didn't see it that way. Maybe that was why he told the court that I borrowed the $15,000 to buy cocaine.

No kidding. That's what he said. He testified that I borrowed the 15 grand, cashed his check and bought cocaine. But we produced the check, which clearly indicated that it was deposited into the Tampa Equities account. And the bank statements show that there were no $15,000 withdrawals, either. No cashed check plus no $15,000 withdrawals equals no cocaine purchase. Simple arithmetic.

Dick testified that in June or July of 1982, he visited me at the Lakeland clinic in an effort to get his $15,000. Guess what? The clinic didn't even open until November 1982. Dick visited me, all right, but he was wrong about the timing. In fact, the Christmas lights at the clinic clicked on while we were talking outside. This was a small discrepancy, true, but also another example of government witnesses misrepresenting the facts.

Dick's testimony contradicted Dale Sparks' on a couple of topics. Dick testified that he was present at a meeting in Fort Lauderdale where The General threatened to cut off Sparks' ears. But the date of this meeting was several days off the date given by Sparks, who testified that Dick wasn't even there. Sounds like a couple of government witnesses who failed to get their stories to jive. That's not surprising, though. Sparks couldn't even get his own testimony to jive from one day to the next.

A funny footnote to that story: Schwartz testified that when Sparks was threatened, his face became flushed. But as everyone in the courtroom could see, Sparks' natural color is red. How a guy with a strawberry-red face could become flushed is beyond me.

Dick admitted on the stand that he took the $10,000 kickback from Sparks for the $145,000 First Fidelity loan. He testified that he split the kickback with Barry Nelson and Stanley Seligman. Sparks said the kickback was split among Schwartz, Nelson and Denny McLain. Hey, if I was in on that kickback, don't you think Dick would have said so? But he said I had nothing to do with it. Sparks was lying, and once again government witnesses were contradicting each other.

Dick was a saint compared to Sparks and Higgins. But he did take a kickback, which is a criminal offense, and he filed a tax return that failed to reflect that income. The government gave him immunity to testify, but the least he could have done was tell the truth and return the $3,400 he got from Sparks' kickback. The government didn't even ask for it.

● Danny Cowart.

I was accused of taking a $7,000 kickback from Danny Cowart on a $205,000 loan he got from First Fidelity in 1980. Cowart, a real estate developer, all but told the jury that I didn't get the kickback, but I still got convicted.

The loan was all set up when I called Stanley Seligman to ask when Cowart could get his money. Seligman said he could get the money immediately if Cowart would pay a $12,000 kickback—$4,000 for him, four for Nelson and four for me. I told Seligman he was crazy. I wanted no part of any kickbacks. My $6,000 commission was enough.

But Seligman insisted. I relayed that message to Cowart, telling him that I didn't want anything. If he wanted to give Seligman a kickback, that was his business. Cowart agreed to give Seligman $7,000.

A couple of days later, I met Cowart in Hollywood. Seligman had arranged for him to get $90,000 of his money right away—one check for 80 grand, the other for 10. Cowart cashed the check for $10,000 on the spot. As we were driving back from the bank to First Fidelity's offices, Cowart handed me $7,000 and asked me to give it to Seligman. He said he could do it himself, but since I was going inside anyway and he had to get somewhere, he'd appreciate it if I'd turn over the money. I did just that, giving Seligman every single dollar.

Cowart never said I kept the kickback. He testified that he handed me the $7,000, but he had no idea what happened to it after that. The gist of his testimony was that Seligman was scum. He said he had never had any unpleasant business dealings with me. If anything, he was grateful to me for getting the kickback reduced $5,000.

The government said that made me guilty of extortion. I just don't see how my carrying $7,000 from Cowart's car to Seligman's office made me guilty of anything. The government never produced a shred of proof that I kept the money. In fact, the government later required Seligman, not me, to repay Cowart for the kickback. The government also never proved that the kickback was "induced by the wrongful use of fear of economic loss," the words used in the indictment to describe the alleged act of extortion. Cowart said he was so happy to get the loan, "I'd (have) paid more if I had to." Does that sound like an extortion victim?

I don't think Cowart's testimony hurt me. But the jury did. Isn't it strange that I was accused of taking only one kickback? I must have handled 150 loans at First Fidelity, and the government tried to tie me in to just that one payoff.

And the key government witness never said I kept the money. Somehow, the jury decided I did. I guess the jurors must have been stretching or sweetening their coffee when Cowart was testifying.

• Gordon Douglas.

Douglas, Barry Nelson's nephew, was presented as a victim of Sy Sher's loan-sharking activities. But the government used Douglas to get at me in a different way. Mueller maneuvered Douglas to testify, or lie, about my involvement in crimes I wasn't even charged with. Uncle Barry may be the Attila the Hun of liars, but Douglas wasn't exactly an amateur.

Douglas testified that we had discussed the possibility of doing a big marijuana deal while he was working undercover for the cops. He said I wanted him to fly about 50,000 pounds of marijuana into the country. That was bullshit. I never talked to Douglas about any such thing. And we subpoenaed the FBI, the DEA and damn near every law enforcement agency in the country, and no one had any record of Gordon Douglas ever working as an informer on a marijuana deal. Nobody corroborated his story.

Douglas also testified that Stanley Seligman had gotten me a hooker once. I almost fell out of my chair when he said that. Stanley Seligman reminded me of the old movie villain with the black cape and stovepipe hat who tied the heroine to the railroad tracks. He was very evil looking. And he never gave anybody anything. In fact, if you took the word "I" out of Seligman's vocabulary, he would be absolutely speechless. I didn't need the likes of Stanley Seligman to get a woman, especially in Fort Lauderdale. The government was really reaching to make me look bad to the jurors.

That was improper strategy. The government couldn't convict me on the evidence, so it played games with the jury by badgering me with a lot of irrelevant testimony. Now I'm not saying that I was Mr. Perfect. I was guilty of some things—the bookmaking fiasco in 1967, writing bad checks and not filing income tax returns. But I was innocent of most, including Gordon Douglas' testimony about drugs and hookers. Arnie kept telling the judge: "If he's going to be accused of these things, indict him. If not, don't admit the testimony. Prosecute him for what's in the indictment, not this other stuff." But whenever this happened, the judge denied Arnie's motions for a mistrial and allowed the jury to consider the evidence. Oh, she'd tell the jury to disregard things occasionally, but if you really believe that jurors can completely erase their memories, then you're a bigger sucker than I am. The government beat me to death with a bunch of allegations that never should have been put before the jury.

Douglas was just another shining example of how bad the government wanted Denny McLain. He received numerous kickbacks as a mortgage broker, laundered dirty money, committed perjury in other trials and smoked marijuana. He also had been sued for stealing money from a trust fund belonging to his girlfriend's kids. This guy wasn't much better than his Uncle Barry.

But the most telling example of Douglas' character came from the testimony of a man who had testified against Douglas in a previous trial involving kickbacks. This man said that after the trial, he was approached by Douglas outside the courtroom. Douglas asked very nicely, "Is your daughter still alive?" and the man replied, "Yes, she is." Douglas said, "I'm sorry to hear that. I was hoping she would have died of cancer by now."

That's Gordon Douglas. Always the gentleman.

● Guy Seligman.

Seligman was another witness who didn't hurt me much. But his testimony is memorable for the crimes he admitted on the stand, knowing that he was free to talk because he had been given immunity.

Guy Seligman admitted to smoking marijuana with Gordon Douglas, selling cocaine, taking Quaaludes and distributing Valium. He had lied to the grand jury. He had been involved in numerous kickbacks. He had laundered money in the Bahamas. He had defrauded at least one investor out of $400,000 and countless more out of God knows how much money. And on and on and on.

The man who got ripped off for the 400 grand testified that Seligman "has no credibility whatsoever" and "is not considered to be an honest person." But the best line came from Seligman's pot-smoking pal, Gordon Douglas. He said that while their uncles Barry and Stanley set the standards, Guy was notable in his own right as an "apprentice" liar.

Guy Seligman's criminal activities were laid bare for all to see. Yet the government gave him immunity. Amazingly, the last I heard, Guy was attending law school. Someday he could be practicing in the same office with Mad Dog Merkle.

● Felix Bertucci.

The above-mentioned witnesses focused on the first three counts of the indictment—racketeering, conspiracy and extortion. Good old Felix managed to leave them all in the dust, telling lies that pertained to the first, second, fourth and fifth counts. Felix spared us his insight into Count Three because he had no knowledge of the alleged extortion of Dale Sparks.

You remember Felix—the cocaine-snorting bastard who let me bail him out at Executive Realty and then stiffed me when it came to the walk-in clinics. Well, Felix showed up at my trial with stories to tell on everything from bookmaking to drug dealing. And they were just that—stories.

Three of the crimes referred to specifically in the racketeering and conspiracy charges were separate three-kilo, 10-kilo and 400-kilo cocaine deals. Felix provided testimony about all three.

He testified that I tried to arrange the sale of 10 kilos of cocaine in July 1982. He said that on my instructions, he flew to Fort Lauderdale and then drove a rental car to West Palm Beach, where he stayed in a hotel for two days until two men contacted him. He said the men loaded a duffle bag containing the cocaine and another bag containing an Uzi machine gun into the rental car, which he drove back to the Tampa area with the two men. Felix said he called me upon his return and that I met with the men, but the deal fell through when the prospective buyers from Texas got nervous and went home.

There were a couple of problems with Felix's story, besides the fact it never happened. Felix testified that he put the alleged cocaine suppliers up in a hotel in Brandon, but there is no hotel receipt to verify that. Felix also gave a specific time that he supposedly called me collect, but the phone records showed no such thing. Other than his testimony, the government had little by way of hard evidence.

On the three-kilo deal, Felix said that he was present at Turnberry sometime between June 30 and July 2 to witness some of the events down there. Well, Arnie introduced flight logs from the Cheyenne that showed Felix had flown from Fort Lauderdale to St. Petersburg on June 30 and didn't return until July 2. The logs were quite clear. Felix said no, that's not right, I flew down there commercially, and I can get the airline ticket to prove it. The judge said fine, bring it to me. He never did. Another lie that was admitted into testimony.

In his grand jury testimony, Felix also tried to place me in the middle of an ill-fated 400-kilo deal. He testified that I was in Fort Lauderdale for a meeting to run this deal September 17, 1982. For once, the media came to my rescue. We presented a newspaper article proving that I couldn't have been in Fort Lauderdale planning a cocaine deal. I was at Tiger Stadium in Detroit, accepting replacements for the Cy Young and MVP awards that had been destroyed in the Lakeland fire. I couldn't have asked for a better alibi.

And the government knew it. After Arnie revealed this fact in his opening remarks, Felix changed his tune. He said he wasn't sure where I was that day. The government tried to emphasize that I didn't have to be in Florida to orchestrate the deal, but we still pointed out this beautiful alibi. And the fact that Felix altered his grand jury testimony was proof that he was lying.

Felix went on and on about me coordinating these drug deals. He made a lot of claims for which I was unable to provide an answer. But think about it: If somebody asked you where you were on a certain date three or four years ago, would you remember? Even if you remembered, could you prove it? I thought we were doing pretty damn good to blast as many holes in the government witnesses' testimony as we did. When we couldn't, it was my word against theirs. And Arnie did a hell of a job showing the jurors why they shouldn't believe the government witnesses.

Arnie did a good job of portraying Felix as the liar he was. Phil Dann, an attorney from St. Pete who knew Felix and me from our days with the restaurant in Pensacola, testified that Felix habitually "manipulated facts in a way which caused a result or precipitated a result he wanted." On a scale of zero to 10, with zero being a pathological liar and 10 being a man who only told the truth, Dann said Felix was about a three or four. And on cross-examination, Felix could not explain to Arnie the difference between telling the truth and telling a lie. That came up after Arnie had proved that Felix had lied in the past, including to the grand jury. When Arnie pressed him on the difference between telling the truth and telling a lie, Felix responded, "Not much." And yet I can only presume that the jury accepted this man as a credible witness.

Felix even lied about things that didn't matter. For instance, he told the jury that the minimum bet in our bookmaking operation was $100. Hey, I didn't take any bets under a grand. There is no plausible explanation of why he'd lie about that. I guess it's just his nature.

Felix's track record was enough to make any jury sit up and take notice. He had filed false tax returns, submitted false financial statements and written bad checks. He even forged my signature on a $1,000 check that was written on a closed account. According to his own testimony, Felix also was involved in several cocaine deals. Amazingly, he sat on the stand and swore he never used the stuff himself. I knew differently because I had caught him doing cocaine on several occasions. And Todd Siegmeister even testified that he had attended a big cocaine party at Felix's house. This was yet another example of government witnesses contradicting each other. It was incredible how many times the jury was asked to believe two government witnesses who told strikingly different stories. And believe it they did.

Felix even contradicted himself. In order to get a guilty verdict, the government had to prove that the crimes listed in the indictment were committed by members of an organization working together. If we were working separately, there was no racketeering, no conspiracy. Felix testified that our bookmaking operation was not separate from Sy Sher's. He said Sy was the boss and we answered to him. Well, that wasn't true. They were completely separate operations. I laid off a lot of bets with Sy, but I didn't answer to anybody except the bettors who had to be paid. And Felix even indicated as much when he said: "I was acting under the guidance and instructions of Dennis McLain's bookmaking operation. Under no circumstances would I consider anyone other than Dennis McLain the head of the operation in Tampa." Does that sound like the description of someone who merely reported to someone else?

As you might expect by now, Felix got total immunity. He admits on the stand that he was involved in several cocaine deals, yet the government manufactures a case against me and lets a piece of scum go free.

• Todd Siegmeister.

That same fat, filthy slob who had botched up Larry Knott's drug deals appeared at my trial in all his splendor. Judging by the results, he might be a better government witness than a dope dealer. He couldn't sell three kilos of cocaine, but I got convicted.

There's no question that Siegmeister was the incompetent salesman in the three-kilo cocaine deal. He admitted that on the stand. There's also no question that I was present while much of that fiasco was taking place. I admitted that on the stand. But Siegmeister testified that I was a participant in the deal, not an observer.

Once again, it was my word against his. The jury had to decide whom to believe, and Arnie made a good case for me.

Siegmeister's recollection of the facts was ridiculous. For instance, he testified that the travel bag in which he carried the cocaine was almost new. His girlfriend, Carol Jankola, testified that he had bought it months before. Todd said that he had never used the bag before. Carol said he had used it many times to carry narcotics and drug paraphernalia with him on trips. Todd said he had never snorted cocaine in his parents' house. Carol said he had. It was one discrepancy after another. And they were both government witnesses.

The biggest contradictions focused on the Cheyenne flight from Fort Lauderdale to New Jersey. The three passengers—Siegmeister, Jankola and Mel Kaplan—and two pilots weren't even close to corroborating each other on details of that trip. Kaplan said Carol was zonked out the whole time and had to be carried off the plane, while Carol said her eyes closed now and then but she remembered participating in conversations. Todd said yeah, she did talk from time to time. They also couldn't agree on who sat in which seat and where some of the luggage was placed, including my golf bags, where the government claimed the cocaine was stashed. Arnie even brought chairs in the courtroom and tried to arrange them according to their testimony. It looked as if everybody was sitting in the same seat.

I'm not trying to pick on Siegmeister. The guy's memory probably was scrambled by cocaine abuse. Or maybe he was right and the other witnesses were wrong. Granted, these were minor details, but the point is somebody's testimony was flawed, and that should have made the jury wonder.

Our biggest shot at Siegmeister was provided by a cop. We brought down a policeman from Livingston, N.J., who had known Siegmeister for about nine years. Sgt. Phil Falzo said that he and his fellow cops all shared the same opinion of Siegmeister—that he "is untruthful." How's that for irony. A cop saying that about a government witness.

Mueller tried to win that point back on cross-examination. He asked Falzo, "To your knowledge, has Mr. Siegmeister ever lied under oath?" Falzo said no, and Mueller left it at that. It wasn't until Arnie delved a little deeper that the truth was revealed. "Do you know of any incident where he has ever testified under oath?" Arnie asked. Falzo replied, "Not to my recollection, sir." Arnie was like Paul Harvey the whole trial. He'd take the government's side of something and then provide "the rest of the story."

What did Siegmeister get for his trouble? Immunity, of course. The guy admitted on the stand that he had been dealing drugs for at least five years, making as much as half a million bucks annually and not reporting the income, and the government said: "Thanks for everything, Todd. Have a nice life. We'll try not to bother you."

• Mel Kaplan.

Judge Kovachevich committed a major blunder on Kaplan's testimony, a blunder that eventually helped me with my appeal.

Before Kaplan pleaded guilty to the one count on which he was indicted— the three-kilo cocaine deal—a plea agreement prepared by Bob Merkle's office was shoved in his face. Sign it or go to jail, Mel was told, and he obviously didn't want to go to jail. Mel testified during my trial that only parts of the plea agreement he had been forced to sign were true.

The facts stipulated in the plea agreement were that Kaplan, Barry Nelson, Todd Siegmeister, Larry Knott and myself were principal participants in a conspiracy to sell three kilos of cocaine. The agreement detailed Siegmeister's futile attempt to sell the cocaine in New Jersey, his return with the drugs to Fort Lauderdale, a meeting at Turnberry, Siegmeister's return to New Jersey by train and his meeting with Knott at the Holiday Inn in Newark. In many ways, it was an accurate representation of what happened. But according to this agreement, I was no innocent bystander; I was a co-conspirator. Mel Kaplan put his stamp of approval on the plea agreement, but only because he was afraid of going to jail.

When Mel testified, he said up front that he didn't vouch for everything in the plea agreement. He said he had no idea that cocaine was on the plane until Nelson told him so after he was indicted. In other words, Mel was proclaiming his innocence even after pleading guilty. He testified that he had signed the plea agreement only because his attorney had urged him to do so and that he had no knowledge of many of the stipulated facts in the agreement.

That was all fine and good. Mel was cross-examined on the basis of his testimony, not the information in the plea agreement. But later in the trial, the government introduced as evidence Mel's plea agreement *without omitting its stipulated statements of fact.* Levine screamed till he was blue in the face, but Kovachevich allowed it. That meant the jury was allowed to read the government's prepared version of the facts, not the facts Mel had presented. Mel's "confession" was being waved in the jury's face even after he had disavowed any knowledge of the "facts" it contained.

It was like the government was telling each juror: "Forget what Kaplan said on the stand. Here's what really happened. Kaplan signed it, his attorney signed it, Ernst Mueller signed it, so it must be true. Trust us." I couldn't defend myself against the plea agreement because you can't cross-examine a piece of paper. It was a clear violation of my Sixth Amendment rights.

I believe that the judge's flagrant error of allowing that document to be admitted in evidence was a major reason why I was found guilty of the drug deal. Arnie was masterful at discrediting the witnesses against me, but he couldn't discredit the document, which directly implicated me in the drug deal. It was highly prejudicial and there was nothing I could do about it.

Compared with Siegmeister, Bertucci, Knott, Sparks, Higgins and many of the other government witnesses, Kaplan looked like a Boy Scout. He had been convicted of income tax evasion and had bribed a federal official, but it seemed that most of his problems could be traced directly to Barry Nelson. During the trial, he even said something to the effect that every time he did business with Nelson, he inevitably wound up behind a microphone in a courtroom.

On the other hand, Mel might have been dirtier than he looked. It came out in the Nelson/Kaplan tapes that he and Barry had close ties to Stan Myatt and Bill Johnson, the former CIA guys who were always conning somebody. The tapes imply that Nelson and Kaplan probably participated in some of their scams, which may explain why Mel was willing to sign a "confession" to a crime he says he didn't commit.

What did Kaplan get in exchange for cooperating with the government? Like Nelson, Knott and Stanley Seligman, he'd have to wait till the trial was over to find out.

• Larry Knott.

Knott did the same song and dance about me being in on the three-kilo deal. But we located a key flaw in his testimony that should have taken me out of the deal entirely.

Knott testified that Jim Pritchett, the guy I met for the first and last time when I flew him to the Bahamas in July 1982, was my source for the cocaine. Knott also testified that Pritchett and I made arrangements for the drug deal while playing golf with Pritchett's son and Felix Bertucci. He swore that this golf outing took place June 27, 1982, at Inverrary Country Club. Inverrary is an exclusive club outside Fort Lauderdale where Jackie Gleason used to sponsor a tournament on the PGA Tour. I've played there before, but we proved I wasn't there on the date given by Knott.

Fancy clubs like Inverrary keep strict records, and the only way you could play there and not have your name recorded is if you're a guest sponsored by a member and you pay in cash. The member's name would be recorded, but not yours. For any match, somebody's name has to be written down somewhere.

We brought up Inverrary's accountant, who testified that she had no record of any golf game on that date in which I or any of those people were involved. Our names don't show up anywhere. Other than the testimony of Knott and Felix Bertucci, who corroborated Knott's story, the government had no solid evidence to place me at Inverrary when drugs were discussed.

That wasn't all. Knott testified that he, Bertucci, another passenger and the two pilots of the Cheyenne flew from the Bahamas to Fort Lauderdale the night of June 26—the night before this alleged golf game. But the Cheyenne's flight logs proved different. And both pilots testified that the plane was in the Tampa area on June 26 and that it flew to Fort Lauderdale and on to the Bahamas the next day, then back to Fort Lauderdale on June 28. That being the case, there couldn't have been any golf game at Inverrary on the 27th. And if there wasn't, why should the jury believe anything else Knott said?

Knott had more reason to lie than any other government witness. The better his performance in court and the worse he made me look, the better deal he stood to get when it came time to be sentenced for pleading guilty to Count Four. And this was one guy who needed a sweet deal.

Before being indicted in this case, Knott already had a list of about 16 arrests dating back to 1952. The charges included passing worthless checks, robbery, impersonating a police officer, counterfeiting, carrying a concealed weapon and various drug violations. Even before pleading guilty he had four felony convictions. In fact, he was in federal prison serving five years for possession of marijuana with intent to distribute when my trial came up. If he didn't cooperate with the government, he was looking at spending the rest of his life behind bars. By cooperating, he was hoping that any prison sentence he received would run concurrently with the one he already was serving. His motivation for lying was strong.

● Earl Hunt.

Remember Jose Rodriguez, the defendant who was named with me on Count Five? Poor Joe, as he was called, had to sit there through weeks of testimony twiddling his thumbs and waiting for somebody to talk about him. But when it finally began raining on him, it poured. Rodriguez was drenched by Earl Hunt accusations.

Earl was in fine form. It wasn't his first gig as a government witness and his experience showed. After his kamikaze attempt to smuggle 1,188 pounds of marijuana into Louisiana in October 1982, he pleaded guilty and testified against his five co-defendants. Hunt was sentenced to three years, but his future brightened considerably when he emerged as a potential high-powered witness in the case of United States of America vs. Dennis McLain. Several government agencies, such as the U.S. attorney's office and the Florida Department of Law Enforcement, really went to bat for him. After making all kinds of appeals on his behalf, they got Earl out of jail after about six months. All he had to do in return was mention me and Rodriguez as often as possible when talking about that 400-kilo cocaine deal.

I won't go into detail on this because it was the only count in the indictment that I beat. Fortunately, if I had to pick one charge to be acquitted of, this was it. The loan-sharking and extortion charges were bad, but I've never had much use for drugs. I hate them and I hate the thought of people thinking of Denny

McLain as a drug dealer. And the 400-kilo charge was the biggest of the two drug counts.

Briefly, this was the government's case: I was supposed to be involved with a group of guys who tried to import 400 kilos of cocaine from Colombia on my Cheyenne in August 1982. Rodriguez, a native of Honduras who ran a luxury car dealership in Miami, was supposed to be the guy who acquired the cocaine in South America and had it waiting for Hunt at a remote landing strip protected by several armed guards. Stan Myatt and his buddy Bill Johnson were the alleged ringleaders of this project. Hunt testified that after Johnson called off the deal for some reason, I took over and rescheduled it for September, this time in the Cessna 402. Hunt said my plan was for Hunt to drop the cocaine from the plane into the ocean, where it would be picked up in an 80-foot yacht sailing near the Bahamas. That deal never came off, either, but the government said that since I tried, the jury should find me guilty of attempting to import cocaine.

The government was wrong. I have never been involved with drugs. And you know what? I don't think there ever was a 400-kilo cocaine deal, except in the mind of Joe Rodriguez. From what I could tell, it was a big scam to rip him off.

It appears as if Myatt and Johnson got Rodriguez to put up $92,000 for this project and then skedaddled with the dough. Myatt and Johnson made a living off conning drug dealers. In fact, they once conned the DEA by becoming government informers, getting fronted about 50 grand to set up a drug deal and then taking off with the money. These two guys, who got a mere five years' probation each on some drug charge during my trial, even ripped off the feds.

Hunt apparently had gotten into the Rodriguez act, too. About a week after returning from that 1982 Tiger Stadium ceremony in my honor, Rodriguez came to Tampa and asked me, "Where's my 32 grand?" I didn't know who he was or what he was talking about. Rodriguez said that he had given Hunt $32,000 to give to me so that I could arrange everything for the 400-kilo deal. When the deal sputtered out, Rodriguez wanted his money back. I told him that I was sorry, but Hunt never gave me a dime and I had nothing to do with his deal. Hunt and the Myatt/Johnson tandem had taken Rodriguez for more than $120,000, and all he got in return was a court date.

I don't think Hunt, Myatt or Johnson ever had any intention of importing 400 kilos of cocaine. Rodriguez apparently did, but he just got conned. And that's why we both were acquitted on that count. It takes more than one person for a conspiracy, and Rodriguez was in this one alone. The Nelson/Kaplan tapes showed that Nelson and Kaplan were somehow connected with Myatt and Johnson. If there were any conspiracies, they involved those guys, not me or Rodriguez.

Of course, the fact that I was in Detroit when this deal supposedly was being orchestrated didn't hurt, either.

Even though the jury didn't buy Hunt's testimony, it's worth noting the deal the government gave this admitted drug smuggler. When he testified, he was on parole from his 1983 marijuana possession conviction. He had been convicted of drug charges in 1980, too, and admitted being involved in other drug deals. He had been found guilty of fraud and criminal conduct in other cases.

We produced witnesses who testified that Hunt had scammed them out of money and that he was a liar and a fraud. Hunt was just as much of a con artist as Myatt and Johnson.

Hunt's deal? Well, he didn't have a formal grant of immunity, but he did have an understanding. If his performance was good enough, he wouldn't be prosecuted for a single thing he said. And he wasn't. Of course, his 1983 sentence was drastically reduced, too, and the government even tried to help him get started in business again. It's amazing that the government could protect and even help a miserable, sorry bastard like Earl Hunt.

There you have the main government witnesses against Denny McLain. George Lerner, Brad Jeffords, Carol Jankola and Jerry Mendelson were there, too, along with more than four dozen other solid citizens. There were so many scumbags running around the federal courthouse that they should have rented a hall and held a convention.

But the story of my Barnum-and-Bailey trial would not be complete without mentioning two of the government's more dramatic performers. Meet FDLE agents Tom Beach and Ken Sanz.

Beach and Sanz were assigned to my case. The state was called into the case because Bob Merkle is big on joint federal-state task forces, especially on drug investigations. Merkle had to love these guys.

Beach and Sanz are perfect examples of how law enforcement agents can endanger the American justice system. Showing no regard for people's rights, these agents just find a target and aim to kill. They're like 30-game winners. They set their sights and then do whatever it takes to win. The end justifies the means. Only they're not operating in the world of fun and games. They hand out immunity guarantees and plea bargains left and right, they influence witnesses' testimony and they even threaten defense witnesses. How's that for abuse of power? All of the above happened after Beach and Sanz decided to make a career out of convicting Denny McLain.

I've detailed the special deals obtained by many of the government witnesses. Here's how Felix Bertucci got his.

Remember that $1,000 check Felix forged my name on? After Felix ran off with the money, the bank filed criminal charges against him. A warrant was put out for his arrest in Tampa, so he went back to Mississippi to hide out. Sometime later, Beach and Sanz found out where he was living and called him. They told Felix that if he repaid the $1,000 and cooperated in their investigation of me, they would take care of that arrest warrant and see what else they could do for him. Felix eventually got immunity.

From that point on, Felix cooperated. And how! When Beach and Sanz said jump, he said, "How high?" And when they said, "Tell me about Denny McLain," he told them anything they wanted to hear. You can see that by looking at the transcripts of Felix's testimony before the grand jury and then at my trial. His story kept getting better and better. That's what happens when Tom Beach and Ken Sanz are put in charge of a criminal investigation.

Beach and Sanz were there when Dale Sparks needed help tying Frank Cocchiaro into the government's make-believe conspiracy. Remember, if you want to create an organized crime racket, you have to have an Italian. But Sparks had a hell of a time trying to identify Cocchiaro as The General. Long before the trial, Sparks examined a mug book and identified a guy named Murray Stein as The General. Murray Stein wasn't The General, assuming such a person ever existed. Stein was a retired postal worker who had never heard of Dale Sparks. He didn't even resemble Cocchiaro very much. But that's who Sparks picked out as The General.

But about five months later, Sparks was sitting in a room alone with Beach and Sanz, looking through a mug book. Suddenly, Sparks declared that he knew who The General was and pointed to a picture of Cocchiaro. Well, I'll be! Sparks suddenly had seen the light and Frick and Frack had their eyewitness identification. It was all very impressive. But I still have to wonder how he was able to change his photo ID, yet he couldn't identify Cocchiaro when he walked right in front of him at the trial.

My first impression of Frick and Frack was that Sanz was the more evil of the two. He just looked sinister. Beach, on the other hand, looked like Tom Sawyer. He had a natural magnetism that made people say, "Gee, what a nice guy." But Tom Beach is the most devious man I've ever met, and I *have* met some doozies.

Here's an example: Beach threatened one of our witnesses. A man named Ted Bonard was going to testify against Earl Hunt, who had ripped him off. His testimony would help show the jury what a con artist Hunt was. But Bonard had some legal problems of his own, and Beach made it clear to Bonard's attorney, Richard Sparkman, that if his client testified, he'd make life hell for Bonard. Sparkman finally got tired of the threats and testified about what Beach was doing. He said on the stand that Beach had threatened his client.

Did Beach deny it? Nope. Ernst Mueller had a chance to put Beach on the stand to deny Sparkman's allegation, but he didn't do it. Sometimes silence speaks louder than words.

These FDLE agents were dangerous. They were able to take witnesses and evidence and reshape them to fit the case. That's a clear and dangerous abuse of power.

And it could happen to anybody—even you.

I will say this about Frick and Frack: They took their jobs seriously. They didn't miss a trick and even played games with the jurors. They would smile at them, nod to them and play eyesies with them, saying, "Hi, how are you doing today?" The judge even reprimanded them a couple of times.

We made Beach look bad once. When Inverrary's accountant came to testify, she brought the June 27, 1982, receipts with her. Arnie looked over at Beach and there he was, going through them. When Arnie saw that, he called the accountant out of order and put her on the stand. Arnie asked her where the records were and she indicated that Beach had them. He'd been investigating the case for about two years and he was looking through the records for the first time at the trial. Brilliant detective work.

One of my favorites from the Nelson/Kaplan tapes was this little quote from Mel Kaplan: "Beach just writes down whatever people tell him. Right, wrong, he writes." And it doesn't matter, as long as he wins.

Characters like these were only half of my problem. My case also was sabotaged by a judge who seemed to be part of the same personal vendetta and a prosecutor who seemed to care more about a guilty verdict than justice.

Sy Sher, Frank Cocchiaro, Joe Rodriguez and I never should have been tried together. Joint trials are great when all the defendants are charged with the same crime. They save the taxpayers' time and money. But in our case, the joint trial made it impossible for any of us to get a fair shake.

I was on trial for all five counts in the indictment. I don't think Arnie got too bored with the proceedings because my name came up a lot. But Rodriguez was on trial for just one count, and it was weeks before anybody even mentioned him. He and his attorney just sat and listened. Sher and Cocchiaro were charged in the first three counts, but when the conversation turned to drugs, their attorneys were pretty quiet.

Even before the trial, everybody's attorney was screaming for severance. That meant split us up and try us separately. And for good reason: With the jury looking at a group of defendants, it was inevitable that some of the dirt attributed to one defendant would smear the others. There had to be some carry-over. I was thrown in the same crowd as Cocchiaro, who already was serving a 10-year federal prison sentence for mail fraud. When the organized crime backgrounds of both Cocchiaro and Sher were discussed, my name became a natural association.

A joint trial also made it difficult for one guy to conduct his defense without unfairly influencing the jury against the other defendants. Here's an example. In the first three counts of the indictment, Sy Sher and I both were accused of loan-sharking and extortion in connection with the $40,000 loan to Dale Sparks. You'd think we were in this thing together, right? Wrong. When Sy's attorney was cross-examining Sparks, he introduced in evidence lawsuit papers that had been filed by Sparks and his wife against First Fidelity and me regarding the loan. Sy wasn't named in the suit. Now, it made perfect sense for Sy's attorney to do that. If Sparks didn't name Sy in the suit a couple of years before, why was he naming him in our trial? Good point. But the introduction of those papers could only hurt me. Arnie objected, saying that the papers would prejudice the jury against me. The judge overruled Arnie's objection. Arnie then moved to sever. Had I been on trial by myself, that evidence never would have been admitted. But if Kovachevich insisted upon allowing it, then it was only fair that I be granted a severance.

She denied Arnie's motion, just like every other motion to sever. Are you kidding? Kovachevich was obsessed with not wasting a minute of the court's precious time. Do you think she'd grant a severance, which would render worthless all the time already invested in the trial? No way. She wasn't about to back up her docket any more, even if it meant denying everybody a fair trial.

Ernst Mueller wasn't exactly your straight-arrow, justice-seeking prosecutor, either. He wasn't a bad lawyer. He just went too far a few times. And I don't blame Mueller for that. He seemed to be a pretty decent guy. But remember, he was the puppet on Mad Dog Merkle's string and he had to do whatever it took to win this case.

Mueller insulted Arnie many times. Some of the words he used to describe Arnie's statements, questions and objections were "ridiculous," "frivolous," "silly," "baloney," "nonsense," "outrageous," "disgusting," "unethical," "trite," "tricky" and "insulting and obnoxious." Mueller also accused Levine of lying and intentionally misleading the jury several times, and his apologies were always made out of the presence of the jury. Meanwhile, the government was "not trying to hide anything," Mueller said.

That's bush league. Cases are meant to be won or lost on the basis of the evidence, not the attorneys' opinions of each other. Mueller's conduct was clearly out of order. And because the jury heard all these remarks, Mueller's misconduct should have caused a mistrial. There was no way the jury could look at the evidence fairly after being told that my attorney was a liar. But Kovachevich refused.

She also refused to let us call Merkle to the stand. Mueller was talking about all these bad loans I supposedly handled, so we wanted to question some borrowers who didn't complain about their loans. We wanted to call Merkle and ask him: "Was there anything wrong with your loan, Mr. Merkle, other than the fact you didn't pay it? Did Mr. McLain ever lean on you? Did he ever charge an exorbitant interest rate? Did he ever get on the phone and scream at you?" Of course not. But the judge wouldn't let us do it. Our relationship wasn't too prejudicial for him to prosecute me, but I wasn't allowed to question him in return.

We did call many other witnesses, most of whom provided discrediting information about government witnesses. Sharyn even took the stand to identify pictures of Michelle's room, where Earl Hunt and Todd Siegmeister had testified that they had spent the night. Michelle's room was filled with so many stuffed animals, the place looked like Disney World. Neither Hunt nor Siegmeister ever stayed at our house, and it's interesting that neither one mentioned the dolls when describing the room. It was a minor point, but one worth making.

Sharyn's February 27, 1985, appearance on the stand marked the first time that any member of my family attended the trial. Witnesses are not allowed to hear other witnesses' testimony, so she couldn't come until after she had testified. In the meantime, she had avoided newspaper, TV and radio reports like the plague. She never even picked up a sports page because she was afraid she'd come across something about the trial. It was easier for her to hear it from me than from the newspaper or TV. She and the kids all believed I would be acquitted, but everybody felt better when we acted like nothing was wrong. Hearing my name on the radio was a reminder that everything wasn't OK.

After Sharyn testified, she attended the trial regularly. At different times, Kristi, Denny, Tim and Dale came with her. Michelle never came; she was just too young to understand what was going on. But it was reassuring to look back and see Sharyn and four of the greatest kids in the world sitting in the courtroom giving me support for the last couple of weeks of the trial.

I testified after Sharyn. I was the only one of the four defendants who took the stand. The attorneys for Sher, Cocchiaro and Rodriguez apparently thought the government's case wasn't strong enough for a conviction and didn't see any reason for their clients to testify. But Arnie and I thought that since I was implicated in so many crimes, it would be a good idea to dispute each one.

The only thing I didn't dispute was the bookmaking charge. I admitted up front that I've always been a gambler and that I had taken bets. But everything else was trash.

After my two days of testimony, a number of people came up to me and said: "Boy, they never touched you. You were great." I must admit, I was feeling pretty good when I stepped off the stand March 6 and Arnie rested his case a short while later. With the jury instructions that the judge had approved the day before, I figured my chances of acquittal were excellent.

Each of the attorneys had submitted proposals for jury instructions. Kovachevich granted some and denied others, but she approved two critical ones proposed by Paul Johnson, Sher's attorney: In order to find anyone guilty of racketeering or conspiracy, the jury had to decide that the defendant was a member of a criminal enterprise and that he knew *all* the goals of the alleged conspiracy.

For Sher and Cocchiaro, that was beautiful. One of the goals of this alleged racket was cocaine importation, and Mueller had told the jury that Sy and Frank had nothing to do with that. According to the jury instructions, they had to be acquitted.

And it would be much tougher to convict me. If the jury decided I had nothing to do with cocaine importation or any single one of the other charges, I had to be acquitted.

But then the judge shocked everybody. She changed her mind. Mueller started screaming after Kovachevich approved Johnson's jury instructions, and two days later she approved Mueller's instructions instead. The jury still had to decide the defendant was a member of a criminal enterprise, but now he only had to be found guilty of two separate acts of racketeering. All of a sudden, Sy and Frank were back in the ball game and the odds against my acquittal were jacked up.

They say it's a woman's prerogative to change her mind, but this judge was very selective about whom she listened to. She had finally made a decision that would benefit me, so she decided it was all right to change her mind. And I have no doubt that her decision directly resulted in my conviction.

Even with the new jury instructions, I thought all the time that I would be acquitted on all five counts. In fact, I thought everybody would be acquitted. Not one person positively identified Cocchiaro, so I figured his was an easy acquittal. Dale Sparks was the only guy who even remotely tied Frank to any alleged conspiracy, and Sparks' testimony was so screwed up the jury would be foolish not to dismiss it entirely. Without that ID, which was tentative at best, Cocchiaro couldn't even be brought into the case. Rodriguez was the victim of a con, so I couldn't see him being convicted, either. Sher was a little tougher because it was clear that he had given usurious loans and made book, but the government still had failed to prove an overall conspiracy. I figured Sy would be acquitted, too.

Me? I was guilty of bookmaking, that's all. And that's not what I was charged with. I was accused of racketeering and conspiracy, with bookmaking just one example of a racketeering act. I wasn't guilty of anything else. I didn't make any usurious loans, extort any money, make any threats or earn an illegal buck from any of the loans mentioned in the indictment. I figured I had some exposure on the three-kilo cocaine deal, but that was just circumstantial.

If trying to keep the peace at Turnberry and giving Larry Knott a ride to Atlantic City and Newark made me guilty of aiding and abetting a drug deal, then I guess I have to live with that. But I still don't buy that line of reasoning. I didn't buy any drugs, sell any drugs, transport any drugs or make a penny off any drugs. Ever. How could I be a drug dealer?

The key to this whole case was the word "RICO." You won't find this word in the dictionary, but it means a lot in a racketeering trial. RICO is an acronym for "racketeering influenced corrupt organization." That's the criminal enterprise that Sy, Frank and I were charged with being members of in the first two counts of the indictment. We weren't charged with bookmaking. We weren't charged with making usurious loans. We weren't charged with extortion, except in Count Three, which was the Sparks loan. We weren't charged with taking kickbacks. We weren't charged with any drug transactions, except where I was charged in the fourth and fifth counts. All of these crimes were listed in the first two counts of the indictment, but that wasn't the charge. The charge was being a member of a single RICO. And if the jury decided we were members of a RICO *and* we were guilty of at least two separate acts of racketeering, then we could be found guilty. But if no single RICO existed, we had to be acquitted.

I figured I was in good shape for two reasons. One, the only crime I was guilty of was bookmaking, and the jury would have to find me guilty of two to convict me—*if* there was a RICO. But more importantly, there was no RICO. Maybe Sy and Frank did work together. They were friends, no question about that, and there was good reason to believe they were tied to organized crime. But the government had to prove that each defendant was a member of the same RICO, and since I didn't work with them, that theory was shot to hell. My bookmaking operation was completely separate from Sy's. As for the loans, all I did was introduce Sparks and Higgins to Sy. They took it from there. Some crimes besides bookmaking may have been committed, but not by me. And in any event, there was no pattern of racketeering that connected the three of us in a RICO. The government had to prove a lot, and I don't think it came anywhere close.

Arnie's closing statement to the jury was tremendous. He reminded the jury over and over that to find me guilty, the evidence had to prove that I was guilty "beyond a reasonable doubt." It was spelled out in the jury instructions that proof beyond a reasonable doubt is "proof of such a convincing character that you would be willing to rely and act upon it without hesitation in the most important of your own affairs."

That's heavy stuff. In other words, when each juror was considering a witness' testimony, he had to decide whether the witness' word was so convincing that he would act upon it in a matter of life and death. If Dale Sparks was a doctor and he said your leg had to be amputated, would you let him do it? Substitute the name of Paul Higgins, Earl Hunt, Felix Bertucci, Todd Siegmeister, Larry Knott and the other government witnesses and ask yourself the same question. Would you trust them so completely that you would act "without hesitation in the most important of your own affairs"? Arnie did a terrific job of showing why you would be a fool to trust any of these degenerates any farther than you could throw them.

Arnie pointed out another jury instruction that should have gotten me off Count Four, the three-kilo drug deal. The "mere presence" instruction said that "mere presence at the scene of a transaction or event or the mere fact that certain persons may have associated with each other and have assembled together and discussed common names and interests does not necessarily establish proof of the existence of the conspiracy." So, contrary to Ernst Mueller's arguments, my admitting that I had given Knott a ride to Atlantic City and Newark did not necessarily make me guilty of conspiracy in the drug deal. I may not have shown good judgment, but that didn't make me guilty. The government had to prove that I was in on the deal itself.

I didn't think the government could do that. For starters, I was innocent. And the government's case was based on the word of so many proven perjurers that I thought the jury would see it for what it was—a fabricated lie.

On March 13, 1985—my son Tim's 16th birthday and three days after Sharyn's birthday—the case went to the jury. Remember the judge's ultimatum about the week of March 12? Ironically, the 12 people entrusted with determining my fate were not the same 12 we expected. Just before sequestering the jury for its deliberations, the judge sent home the juror who had slept the most during the trial. She was replaced by an alternate juror who had stretched, eaten and drank through the four months of testimony with everyone else. Just my luck, the alternate also was a woman.

The shouting was over. All we could do was wait.

CHAPTER 9

Welcome to My Nightmare

A pitcher protecting a one-run lead with the bases loaded in the bottom of the ninth toes the rubber before delivering a 3-2 pitch to the opposing team's slugger. A placekicker awaits the snap before attempting a 45-yard field goal with one tick on the clock and his team down by two. A guard nervously dribbles the basketball before launching the front end of a one-and-one free-throw attempt that would tie the score with no time remaining.

You call those pressure situations? Well, multiply that anxiety level by about 100 and you'll have some idea of how we felt while waiting for a verdict.

For three days, Sharyn and I sat in a hotel room near the courthouse with Sy Sher and his wife, Jessie. We were too nervous to wait at home; for some reason, being at home made us more restless. So, we sat, talked, played cards, chewed our fingernails—anything to pass the time while waiting for the phone to ring. Sy and I must have played a thousand hands of gin rummy in those three days. I'd passed countless hours in baseball clubhouses that way, but I was fighting boredom then. Now I was fighting panic.

At about 3:30 p.m. on Saturday, March 16, I was picking up one of Sy's discards when the phone rang. Jessie answered.

"Jessie, this is Sheri." Sheri Levinson was Arnie's secretary. "The jury is back. Everyone is supposed to go to the courthouse immediately. Good luck."

I felt relief and anxiety simultaneously. I was relieved that this nightmare of a trial was about to end. I was worried about what my future might hold in store. The tension had been building for three days. We went back home, gathered up all five kids and headed for the courthouse. It was about 4:15 before everyone was assembled to hear the decision.

As soon as the jury walked into its box, I knew I was dead. Not one juror looked at me, any of the other defendants or our attorneys. They kept their eyes down until the judge spoke, at which time they looked straight at her.

The jury forewoman handed a manila envelope containing the verdicts to the deputy clerk, who carried it to Kovachevich. She opened the envelope, glanced at the verdict forms and then handed them back to the deputy clerk, who read each one. I was first.

"Ladies and gentlemen of the jury, please harken to your verdicts," the clerk read. "We, the jury, find the defendant Dennis McLain guilty of the offense as charged in Count One, guilty of the offense as charged in Count Two, guilty of the offense as charged in Count Three, guilty of the offense as charged in Count Four, not guilty of the offense charged in Count Five of the indictment. So say we all."

Sharyn cried out, "Oh, no!" and buried her face in her hands, but I didn't flinch. I was stunned. I just froze in my chair as the clerk read the other verdicts.

Next came Sy Sher. He just looked down at the table while the clerk announced that he was found guilty on all three counts. So was Frank Cocchiaro, who looked straight ahead without blinking. The only happy defendant was Joe Rodriguez, who jumped to his feet, pumped his fists in triumph and started crying when the clerk revealed that the jury had found him not guilty.

The worst was yet to come. Frank already was serving time and knew he wasn't going anywhere that afternoon, but Sy and I figured we'd be allowed to post bond and remain free until sentencing. Ernst Mueller had other ideas.

"It is my view that the defendant should be detained, that he represents a danger to the community," he said. "... I cannot think of any appropriate reason why Mr. McLain should not be detained after a four-month trial when the jury has diligently appeared and now made these findings. I think it would be tantamount to ... giving the appearance of a mockery if the defendant were simply to walk right out of here with the jury after that work."

Arnie argued that the idea of me being "a danger to the community" was ludicrous. But he might as well have saved his breath.

"This court determines that the detention that is required in these circumstances is immediate," Kovachevich proclaimed, "and thereby, this court orders that Mr. McLain be taken into the custody of the U.S. marshal at this time."

When I heard that, the reality of the situation finally hit me. Denny McLain, a danger to the community? Convicted murderers and rapists are freed on bond all the time. Even Barry Nelson, Stanley Seligman and the other scumbag government witnesses had been allowed to remain free on bond. If the worst the government said about me was true—and it wasn't—I never did anything more violent than yell at a guy. What the hell was Kovachevich thinking? That I would run outside and kill somebody after being a bookmaker? Hell, if I was that kind of person, I'd have knocked off guys like Felix Bertucci and Larry Knott before they ever had a chance to testify. But I was respectful of the judge, prosecutors and everybody else during every hour of that damn trial. Nobody worried about me doing anything crazy then. Had I somehow become a vicious animal in the last five minutes? Locking me up made no sense at all, but then neither did anything else that had happened in the last four months. It was obvious that the federal government, led by the Hanging Judge and Mad Dog Merkle, still was coming after me with both guns blazing.

A bond hearing was set for the next morning and sentencing was set for April 19. While all this was going on, I noticed the narrow windows that sat two floors above the ground outside. I thought about pushing away the table, rushing for a window and leaping out. But I weighed about 300 pounds and the windows were only about three feet wide. That might have been embarrassing.

The judge also ordered that Sy be taken into custody immediately. Sy, Frank and I then were led from the courtroom to the U.S. Marshals Service office for processing. On the way out, I hugged Sharyn. She and the kids were all crying.

My mind was such a mess that I can't remember if I said anything to them or not. What do you say in that situation? "I'm sorry" just doesn't cut it.

After spending about an hour in the marshals office completing paper work, we were split up. Frank was taken to Hillsborough County Jail, where he had resided during the trial, while Sy and I were taken to Manatee County Jail in Bradenton. Most of the TV crews and reporters were staked out by the Hillsborough jail a couple of blocks away, so the marshals figured it would cause less of a stir if they took me somewhere else. The marshals were super nice, and I appreciated that. When they first handcuffed me, they made the cuffs so loose that I could actually slip my hands through them. If not for a requirement that all federal prisoners be transported to jail in handcuffs, I don't think they would have made me wear them at all. I'd gotten to know these guys pretty well during the trial, and they couldn't believe that the judge was locking me up, either.

The marshals led Sy and me from the courthouse to their car outside, where a big pack of journalists was waiting. They wanted me to comment, but for one of the few times in my life I didn't feel much like talking. Being paraded in front of the media in handcuffs was just too humiliating.

We arrived in Bradenton around 6:30 and were taken into a big room where we were photographed, fingerprinted and relieved of all our possessions. In my case, that amounted to a necklace and 65 cents.

So far, so good. Everybody was nice, and a few people even asked for autographs. To them, I wasn't prisoner No. 04000-018. I was Denny McLain, former baseball hero. Those who didn't ask for autographs just smiled, said hi and went about their business. The guards let me make several phone calls, too. Except for the fact that I couldn't leave, I felt like I was at a Holiday Inn.

That was because I hadn't been locked up yet. Around 8:30, reality slapped me in the face.

I figured Sy and I would be placed in the same cell, or at least in an area with several other people. But when the guard led me down a long corridor to a cell at the end of the hallway, there wasn't anyone else around. I was completely isolated. And when the solid steel door slammed shut behind me, it was the most sickening and chilling sound I'd ever heard. For the first time in my life, I was in jail.

"Denny," the guard said, "this is as bad as it can get; you'll be OK." He obviously had never seen the Atlanta pen.

My room was grim—just a plastic mattress with no blanket or pillow, a sink, a toilet and a ceiling light that never went off. It was 8 by 10 feet wide with brick walls. The guards would not let me have anything to read, so I counted the bricks and paced back and forth all night long. I never slept a wink.

The first five minutes were the worst. I was breathing so fast that I almost started hyperventilating. After calming down a little, I started walking—and contemplating suicide.

Killing myself had crossed my mind a few times when things had gone wrong before, but the consuming desire to end it all never really possessed me like it did that first night in jail. If I'd had a razor blade, you wouldn't be reading this book. I looked all over that cell for something sharp but found nothing. Jailers don't take too kindly to their guests checking out early, so they do whatever it takes to make the cells suicide-proof. They took my belt, of course, which was just as well. Even if I could have reached the ceiling, which was impossible, I was too fat to hang myself. The belt would just break and I'd wind up with a broken back when I hit the concrete floor. Being in the can was bad enough, but being crippled and imprisoned would be even worse.

I know suicide is a cop-out. When the going gets tough, the tough get going and all that. But that first night, I couldn't shake the idea that if being in prison meant day after day of isolation and loneliness, I couldn't hack it. That's not me. I can't stand being alone. I thrive on people. If jail was going to be like this, being alive just wasn't worth it.

I also figured that I was worth more to my family dead than alive. With me in jail, Sharyn and the kids would have a hell of a time surviving. My legal fees had wiped us out. But if I were dead, my life insurance would pay them a big chunk of dough. I'd had the policy for years and it even covered suicide. That night seemed like a perfect time.

The night passed slowly. Not once did a guard drop by to check on me, so I was alone with my self-destructive thoughts until morning. A guard finally showed up to bring me what he called breakfast, but it looked like slop. I drank the milk, which was warm, and left the rest.

The federal marshals arrived from Tampa promptly at 8:30 Sunday morning to take us back to the courthouse for our bond hearing. They brought coffee for Sy and Pepsi for me, and once again they fastened our handcuffs loosely. They seemed confident that we would be free within a couple of hours. Kovachevich had surprised them by locking us up the night before, but they didn't see any reason why we shouldn't be free until our sentencing.

We were locked up in a holding cell until our 11 a.m. bond hearing. As we were escorted into the courtroom, I saw several friends who were there to testify on my behalf—Tigers General Manager Jim Campbell, attorneys Mike Schwartz, Mike Martin and Phil Dann, sportscaster Pete Sark of Michigan, golf pro M.G. Orender of Diamond Hill, Sharyn and Dale. Arnie and I also took the stand.

Everybody who came to help said the same thing: Denny McLain poses no threat to society. If you release him on bail, he'll be back for sentencing. He's no risk to flee.

But Mueller was really an ass. He called me "a second-degree sociopath" and said "there is no way we can keep McLain from committing crimes unless we have a 24-hour surveillance on him." He even suggested that since I knew how to fly, I might take off for a foreign country.

That was ridiculous. I had a wife and five kids to support. I wouldn't just leave them. As for me being a sociopath, Mueller was crazy. I'd been free on bond for a year and never hurt a flea. Why would I start now?

We put nine character witnesses on the stand besides myself. The government had none. The only person who said I shouldn't be granted bond was Mueller. He told the court that I had no respect for the law.

Well, as of the moment Kovachevich sided with Mueller and denied me bond, that statement was absolutely right. My faith in the U.S. judicial system was shot. Justice had not been served. All the crooks had received immunity and I was going to jail. The system had failed.

If I had any respect left for Elizabeth Kovachevich, that disappeared when she locked me up. She had a good public image, but I discovered firsthand that she was willing and able to abuse her power as a federal judge—and there aren't many positions in the country more powerful. Not one shred of evidence had been produced to show that I was a danger to the community, yet she put me in jail. What she was doing was vengeance, plain and simple. She never had any intention of setting me free. The bond hearing was just a formality at which time she could humiliate me in public again. And Sy got nailed just as bad. He was denied bond, too. The Hanging Judge had a rope for every occasion.

My kids were outside the courtroom as I was led to the marshals office after the hearing. "Where are they taking you, Daddy?" they asked.

I couldn't answer them. I was so ashamed, I couldn't even force out a word. I just kept walking and started crying.

Sy and I were led to a holding cell. Arnie came by and saw the two of us fighting back tears, and he could hardly keep his composure. He felt terrible about what was happening. "Don't give up," he said. "I'll get you out somehow. We'll fire off an appeal the first of the week."

Before being taken back to jail in Bradenton, Sharyn and I embraced outside the marshals office. We were both in tears, and neither of us knew what to say. We were too shocked to speak.

The marshals were shocked, too. "I can't believe they locked you up," said one on the way to Bradenton. "The worst thing about it," said the other, "is that it's not in her character to do that. She must have a vendetta against you."

We asked the marshals to see if they could get us placed in the same cell. Another night like the previous night and I might go crazy. They did, and we were placed in a cell with three other guys.

This cell was about 30 feet by 40 feet and had eight cement beds. We were each given a bedroll to place on the cement slab, but no sheet or pillow. We were in this jail's best suite, but it wasn't at all like the Hilton. At least we knew this would be our last night in Bradenton. The next morning we were scheduled to be taken to Seminole County Correctional Facility in Sanford, Fla., where we would await sentencing.

We talked briefly with our three cellmates and then played cards for two or three hours. Our game was interrupted briefly by dinner—a chicken patty, gravy, corn and bread. But none of it looked very appetizing, so we just drank our milk and kept playing.

After our cellmates finished eating, they tried to make small talk. One of them asked why we were in jail.

"RICO," we said.

"Who's that?" he replied.

Sy and I started laughing, but only on the outside.

Later that evening we took showers. We had been wearing the same clothes for about 36 hours, and even though we had to put them back on, it felt good to wash off. We were starting to smell and were afraid that our cellmates might ask us to leave.

Before going to bed, I called Sharyn and Arnie. Arnie was very upbeat and told me not to worry. Sharyn was still in shock, but otherwise OK. I felt the same.

The guards never turned the lights off in that jail, I guess because there weren't any windows and they didn't want total darkness. It was cold, too, and my only cover was my suit coat. Needless to say, I didn't get much sleep that night.

Breakfast was served bright and early the next morning at 6. Don't ask me why. The marshals weren't coming to pick us up until 10, so we didn't need a wake-up call. And I can't imagine anyone getting out of bed to eat watered-down eggs, grits and sausage links that looked like rabbit turds. But my cell-mates were happy to take everything off my hands. Again I drank only milk.

Milk served as my lunch, too, when the marshals failed to arrive on time and the previous night's dinner was recycled as lunch. We passed the time playing cards until about 2:30, when the marshals finally showed up in a van. We were handcuffed to a chain around the waist before stepping into the van.

Seven other passengers were making the trip to Sanford with us, including Frank Cocchiaro. Frank was every bit as bitter about the convictions as we were, and we bitched about the trial for almost the entire 2½-hour ride.

The Seminole County Correctional Facility is located right off a major divided highway about 20 miles north of Orlando, and if you were driving by you'd think it was a YMCA or something. It doesn't look like a prison. There are no armed guards, trained dogs, gun turrets or spotlights. It's just a regular building. The only thing out of the ordinary were the fences topped with barbed wire that surrounded the facility.

The van pulled into a driveway, through a gate and into a garage, where we were told to get out. I was the first prisoner led into the booking room, and the first thing I heard was a guard asking someone: "Is McLain here? I'd like to get his autograph." Even in prison I was famous. A VIP in handcuffs.

I already liked this place better than the Bradenton jail. It was much bigger and cleaner. There was room for 236 prisoners, and I actually felt like I could breathe. The guards were just as polite as the ones in Bradenton, and I had that eerie feeling again that I was checking into a hotel.

After being fingerprinted and photographed again, I called Sharyn and Arnie to let them know where I was. A guard then placed me in a dark, damp, 6-by-8 holding cell. I wasn't there long, thank God, because it was more suffocating than my first night in Bradenton. It felt like a dungeon. I was rescued by a guard who took me to get a prison uniform. After wearing the same clothes for three days, I was ready for a change of wardrobe, even if it meant donning prison garb.

Don't go picturing Denny McLain in prison stripes. That must be a myth because everything I wore in prison was a solid color—in this case, blue. I was given two two-piece jump suits and two pairs of white shower shoes. The jump suit may not have been too stylish, but it sure was comfortable. If it had had a fly, it would have been perfect. But the zipper area was sewn shut. I could understand inmates not being allowed to have a lot of things in jail, but a zipper? I thought a guy's right to a zipper was protected by the Constitution. Has anybody really ever tried to commit suicide by zippering himself to death?

Sy was just like an old woman trying on clothes. He tried on four or five different sets. Who was he trying to impress? But that's just Sy. He likes good-fitting clothes. The jump suits came in only four sizes—small, medium, large and extra large. Guess which size I picked?

We then were given bedding. The plastic mattresses they gave us felt like bags of cement. They must have weighed eight or nine pounds. We also got two sheets, towels and a pillow made out of the same heavy material as the mattress.

Sy, Frank and I were led down a long hallway to a heavy pair of bulletproof glass doors. A guard in a small area enclosed by glass pushed a button that opened the doors, allowing us to walk into cellblock B. I noticed a camera on the ceiling that tracked our every move. After going through another set of glass doors, we were in cellblock B-1—our home until sentencing.

Frank got a warm welcome. About 18 guys already were in our cellblock, and many came up to greet him. A few also said hello to me and Sy, but most remained in front of the TV—a beautiful color set. There hadn't been any TV in Bradenton.

Frank immediately took charge. He found a room for Sy and me on the upper level of the cellblock. We put down our gear and inspected our surroundings. Cell No. 11 was about 7 by 10 feet with a solid steel door. The only opening on the door was a window about 6 by 18 inches that had steel wire in it. This window allowed the guards to take head counts in the middle of the night. Our cell also had a sink, a toilet and a concrete slab for one person's mattress about two feet above the floor. In one wall there was a narrow slit of a window about four inches high and three feet long. At least some sunlight would brighten up our cell.

Frank also gave us some toiletries and a couple of pieces of advice about prison: No. 1, don't be intimidated. If you don't stand up for yourself, nobody else will. No. 2, be careful who you talk to. Everybody wants out of jail, and a lot of guys become snitches to try to get on the cops' good side.

I passed on the macaroni and cheese dinner that night. I could afford to lose weight, and I just didn't have any appetite for prison slop. Besides real food, what I really had a taste for was a Pepsi, and there were none to be had. The withdrawal was painful. Going from 20 Pepsis a day to none left me with such a sugar and caffeine deficiency that I got some ferocious headaches. Those headaches were punishment enough for my particular crime.

The rest of that first night was spent playing cards and getting acquainted with the routine. Meals were served at 6 a.m., 11 a.m. and 5 p.m. The only other food came from the commissary, where we could buy candy bars, potato chips, Twinkies and other snacks. Unfortunately, there were no Big Macs or Chicken McNuggets. We were allowed to buy up to 40 candy bars a week, and I ate as many as I could bum off Frank since I didn't have any money yet. I had to get my sugar fix somewhere, so I turned to chocolate.

Prisoners like me who required medication got that at 5:10 a.m. and again at 8 p.m. It was ridiculous to get up and take medicine that early, but I did it every day.

Before going to bed, I called Sharyn and completely lost it on the phone. I was crying like a baby. Not loud, but tears were streaming down my face. I don't think I ever cried the whole time I knew Sharyn until I went to prison. The last time I could remember crying was when my dad died. But losing my freedom and being separated from my family left me as lonely and afraid as I've ever been.

Sharyn, on the other hand, was terrific. She told me to stop crying and pull myself together. I couldn't believe what I was hearing. Was this the same girl I had married 21½ years before? Never in my wildest dreams would I have expected Sharyn to be that strong. But she was. When I was feeling as low and worthless as a man can feel, she lifted me and gave me hope.

At 11 p.m., the lights dimmed to half-power and Sy and I returned to our cell. Sy, who was 59 years old, got to put his mattress on the concrete shelf by virtue of his seniority. I stretched out my mattress on the cold floor. The room was laid out in such a way that I had to sleep with my head under the sink, only about a foot from the toilet. I had two fears as I sacked out that first night. No. 1, if I were to have a nightmare, I could knock myself silly on the sink. No. 2, Sy might get up in the middle of the night to take a leak. I asked him to please wake me up first.

I had just started to doze when a guard walked into our room and took a head count. On the way out, he closed the door behind him. We were locked in. The sound of that door clanking shut and locking was awful. It was like the lid of a coffin being closed with me inside. More than anything else, that sound drove home the fact that I was an inmate. Freedom was a thing of the past.

I finally fell asleep, but three or four hours later the guard was back, shining a light in my face for another head count. Where in the hell could I have gone? Out the little steel trap in the door? Through the four-inch-high window? Hell, I couldn't even fit my arm through that. We were trapped in an automated fortress of cement and bulletproof glass. Unless Airwolf flew in and blasted a hole in the side of the building, we weren't going anywhere.

The door to our cell was opened electronically at 5:10 a.m. Sy and I got up and walked down the steps to the main room of the cellblock, where a nurse was standing behind a glassed-in area. She dispensed the medicine through a small opening in the glass box. Our meals were delivered on trays the same way. I took my pills for high blood pressure and sinusitis and then read the Orlando newspaper until breakfast was served. I gave everything away but my milk. It was about a week before I could force myself to eat any prison food. I survived on milk and whatever I could get from the commissary.

The next few days were pretty much the same. I spent most of my time playing three-handed gin with Frank and Sy and pinochle with a guy named Little Frankie who had been caught robbing a bank. I took a shower and called Sharyn and Arnie every day, but those were about my only breaks from cards.

Frank Cocchiaro taught me a few tricks that made life easier. Every joint has its little secrets. In Sanford, you could make your room darker by covering the light with a newspaper. Frank showed me how to put pieces of playing cards in the light fixture and then prop up a folded newspaper with the card pieces. That made it possible to sleep without the light shining in your face. He also showed me how to place a matchbook in the door latch so it can't lock on you accidentally during the day.

I don't drink coffee, but the guys who did had an ingenious way of warming it up. A big pot of coffee was brought into the cellblock each morning. The coffee drinkers would take empty milk cartons and put extra coffee in them for later in the day. When they wanted a cup, they would take an aluminum ashtray and bend it around the bottom of the milk carton. Then they would tie a string to the milk carton and suspend this contraption in the air. Heat was provided by burning toilet paper. In a couple of minutes, they had hot coffee! They said it tasted a little waxy, but as long as the guards didn't find out, they were happy.

Almost everybody liked reading the newspaper. Surprisingly, the most popular section was not the sports or comics. Most guys reached first for the section on local and state news. They wanted to keep up to date on the world of crime and justice, particularly justice. Any story that pertained to a trial was big news because everybody wanted to know what kind of sentences were being handed out for what crimes by what judges. The point was to see if justice was being applied evenly.

I must confess, I started looking for that same news myself. I was looking at anywhere up to 75 years in jail and a $75,000 fine, and I wanted some idea of what to expect when Kovachevich got her chance to whack me. I figured that whatever sentence was standard, I'd get twice that.

Our laundry was washed twice a week. Each inmate placed his dirty clothes and sheets in a bag with lots of holes in it and gave the bag to the trusties. Without even taking the laundry out of the bags, the trusties threw all the bags in a washing machine and then a dryer. The laundry never left the bags. It always came back wet, so we had to hang everything over the balcony post to dry out.

Sy and I cleaned our room every day. We mopped the floor with detergent and water. I figured that if I had to sleep on the floor, at least it would be clean. Sy took care of the toilet. He was fanatical about it. He'd spend 20 minutes with a brush in one hand, Comet in the other, scrubbing like a madman. The one-piece toilet, which had no lid and was solid steel aluminum, shined like new when Sy was through. I could see my reflection in it. Sy was so proud of his work that he would get upset every time I used the toilet. Gee, I didn't even know we were having company.

Actually, the jail overall was clean and the temperature was comfortable. The employees there were pleasant and took a lot of pride in their work. Their attitude certainly was a reflection of the man in charge, Lt. Don McCullough, one of the nicest people I met during my 2½ years in the can.

I met Lt. McCullough my second day in Sanford. He brought me a telephone message and we had a long conversation. I told him a little about my case, and he was very sympathetic and understanding. We spent hours talking about anything and everything over the next several weeks.

Lt. McCullough was the boss, but he also was my personal answering service. I got dozens of calls from newspaper and TV people who wanted an interview, and he brought each message to me himself. I think I heard from representatives of every news organization in the world except Tass. But the only call I returned in my first few days in Sanford was from Tom McEwen, sports editor of the Tampa Tribune. Tom is one of the few media people I've come across who reports what you say, not what he wants to hear. He is not a sensationalist, so I knew he'd give me a fair shake. I agreed to an interview at the jail, but we still had to talk on the phone. We were separated by a pane of bulletproof glass.

The first time I really felt optimistic about my future was March 21, my sixth day in jail. That was when Arnie filed my bond appeal to get me released until sentencing. As long as the Court of Appeals in Atlanta showed some common sense, I figured I could be back home with my family in less than a week.

The next day I was visited by a woman who identified herself as my pre-sentencing officer. My first impression of Beverly Webster was positive, simply because she was a woman and I hadn't seen many lately. She was a little on the heavy side, but at least she was female and smelled good.

It didn't take long, though, to figure out that this was a woman to be feared. It was her job to go over the case with me, learn something about my background and current family situation and then prepare a report. That report was important because the information it contained would not only affect my sentence, but also accompany me throughout the prison system. Wherever I went, that report would help determine whether I was a high- or low-risk prisoner, my eligibility for parole and several other things. It was critical that the report be objective and complete.

But Webster showed me right off the bat that she wasn't thorough. We had a four-month trial and my whole life to talk about, and she spent only an hour with me. That was it. As she was leaving, she said to call her any time if I wanted to talk. Well, I tried calling her a few days later and guess what? The switchboard at her office did not accept collect calls. Inmates can't call any other way. How was I supposed to reach her? Mental telepathy? It scared me to death to think how that report might turn out.

The weekend provided a little change from the daily routine. The first Saturday morning I was in Sanford, the cell doors opened at 5:15 and I went down for my medicine. The nurse wasn't there yet, so I sat downstairs and waited. And waited. And waited. Finally, at 8:10, the nurse showed up. She told me that medication was not available until after 8 a.m. on Saturdays and Sundays. Now she tells me! I felt like a putz for sitting around for three hours. The only other person awake in the whole cellblock was a guy called Rock, who spread out his mattress in front of the TV and watched cartoons. All this guy ever did was watch TV, spend hours on the phone and treat everybody like dirt. He never even got dressed. He just walked around in his underwear all day. He'd been in jail for three years. I hoped that I never turned into a vegetable like him.

Everybody was sleeping late that morning because lights out wasn't until 2:30 a.m. on Friday and Saturday nights. I'm not sure what they expected us to do with that curfew extension, but most guys stayed up late anyway, watching TV and playing cards.

The most popular show in cellblock B-1 was "Miami Vice." Along with "Crime Story," which stars Dennis Farina, a real-life former cop from Chicago whom I knew from back when my uncles were on the force, "Miami Vice" was my favorite. Most of the guys liked it because of the rock music. Personally, I preferred the oldies on "Crime Story," but the show was still good. It was funny to hear everybody cheer the bad guys and boo Crockett and Tubbs.

If the TV-watching habits of inmates were any indication, there wasn't much rehabilitating going on in Sanford.

One of the funniest things I ever saw in prison was when everybody "got down" with "Friday Night Videos." Black men, white men, big men, little men, old men, young men—everybody was dancing. They weren't touching each other, bumping and grinding or doing anything sexual. Just dancing. It was bizarre. You'd have to see it to believe it.

Sunday was the big day for me that weekend. I was expecting two visitors— Sharyn and Arnie. Sharyn wanted to bring the kids, but I asked her not to. I just couldn't stand the thought of my children seeing me that way. Even more, I was afraid that I'd break down in front of them. You have to understand, my kids have always idolized me. To them, I was a rock of strength and courage. If I couldn't be strong, how could I expect them to be?

I slept until lunch time Sunday morning and then got ready for Sharyn's visit. I showered, shaved, put on a clean jump suit and then read the paper while nervously watching the clock. I was really uptight. How would she react? How would I react? But I was excited, too, just to touch her and hold her.

At 1:15, I was notified that I had a visitor. A few minutes later I was escorted to the visiting room. Waiting for me were Sharyn and all five kids—on the other side of a glass partition. I wouldn't even get to touch them.

That did it. I just went to pieces. I told everybody I loved them and then started crying so hard that Sharyn had to chase the kids away.

"I knew that would happen if the kids came," I said, wiping away tears. "Why did you bring them?"

"They couldn't be stopped," Sharyn replied. "They demanded it. They wanted to see you."

What kids! I was so proud of them I almost burst out crying again. I finally settled down and we talked mostly about the appeal. We figured that with any luck, I would be free in a few days. Sharyn was in full control the whole visit, which really impressed me. She didn't shed a tear. For the first time I realized that the kids could get strength from their mom as well as their dad. Thank God for that, because I was feeling pretty fragile.

Half an hour after the visit began, it was over. My family had driven 2½ hours one way to see me for 30 minutes. It hardly seemed fair. I started crying again as we waved goodbye through the glass, but by that time I wasn't ashamed anymore. A dozen other guys had visitors in the room, and at least half of them were crying. I had stored up a lot of tears in the years since my dad died, and this was as good an occasion to shed them as any.

As I was walking back to my cell, I spotted Arnie waiting for me. Wow, back-to-back visitors! And Arnie could stay as long as he wanted since he was my attorney. We spent two hours together talking about the bond appeal.

I had asked Arnie to bring Frank Cocchiaro some cigars, and he came through with 50 of the disgusting things. Cigar smoke makes me want to puke, and it always seemed to drift in my face when we were playing cards. But Frank had been a big help to me ever since we arrived in Sanford, and it was my way of saying thanks—with some assistance from Arnie.

The hard part was getting the cigars into the cellblock. If the guards saw them, they'd take them away. So, I had dressed for the occasion by putting on socks, which I had not worn before that day. I stuffed about 30 cigars in my socks and underwear and smuggled them inside. I got the rest in later the same way. The cigars were individually wrapped, so Frank didn't have anything to worry about. Frank looked like a kid at Christmas when I gave him his present.

It struck me as funny that somebody might consider what I was doing a conspiracy. Did smuggling cigars into jail make me guilty of another RICO? At least this conspiracy really happened.

I earned my first buck in prison the following Monday morning. Rod Luck, the sports anchor for Channel 6 in Orlando, had called and offered me $5,000 to do an exclusive interview. We later came up with a different arrangement— $3,500 up front and 25 percent of any income from the sale of the tape to other stations. In return I would answer his questions and refuse all other requests for TV interviews until after my sentencing. Knowing how badly Sharyn needed the money, I jumped at the offer.

Lt. McCullough called me to his office about 9 a.m. and we chatted for about 45 minutes until Luck arrived with two cameramen. After they set up their equipment in the visiting room, we spent about two hours filling 40 minutes of tape. Luck did a job and a half. He was courteous and professional, and above all, he let me answer his questions completely. He tried to finish with a dramatic touch by filming the lieutenant and me walking down the long corridor back to the cellblock. That was fine with me. I just hoped that a lot of markets were interested in buying it.

After dinner that night I witnessed my first jail fight. Actually, no blows were exchanged, but it developed into a pretty good yelling match. And like most prison altercations, it was over something stupid—what to watch on TV.

The combatants were guys named Kim and Homer. Kim, who had been picked up hitchhiking and found to be in violation of his parole, was strong and lean. Homer was a little guy who had been in jail five or six times and was only about 24 years old. He had no smarts. His most recent arrest had come shortly after he burglarized a house in Sanford. While inside, he decided to use the phone. He called his own home in Orlando long-distance. Three weeks later, the people whose house had been burglarized spotted a peculiar call on their phone bill, and it was dated the night of the burglary. They called the cops, who had no problem tracing it to Little Homer. He might as well have left his business card on the coffee table.

Kim was mad because Little Homer had been hogging the TV watching cartoons and "Gilligan's Island" all day, and he wanted to watch the network news. The hollering got louder and louder, and it reached the point where I couldn't understand what either one was yelling. But just as Kim was getting ready to put up his fists, Little Homer backed down. He already was missing one front tooth, and I guess he wanted to keep the rest. Kim turned on the news and Little Homer went off to sulk.

Since Kim was white and Little Homer was black, I kept waiting for the other guys to take sides. Kim would have had the edge since 15 of the 21 guys in our cellblock were white. But nobody offered any help. That's the way it should be. It's when guys gang up that you have riots.

It was hard to imagine anything like that happening in Sanford. It was just a county jail, not Alcatraz or Sing Sing, and it was pretty boring most of the time. Scuffles between inmates were few and far between. Violence is inherent in the U.S. prison system, but I didn't see much evidence of that until I got to Atlanta.

I was one of the few federal prisoners in our cellblock. Most of the guys were state convicts. Like me, the other federal inmates were waiting to be sentenced or assigned somewhere else.

I was still waiting when I observed my 41st birthday March 29. I sure as hell didn't celebrate.

The day got off to a lousy start. After getting my medicine at 5:40 a.m. and drinking my breakfast milk a few minutes later, I tried to get back to sleep. But Little Homer, Little Frankie and a guy called Big Homer were downstairs arguing about the TV. They couldn't agree on which cartoon to watch. They were flipping channels and hollering back and forth. I listened for about 20 minutes before getting fed up.

I leaped off my mattress and promptly knocked my head on the bottom of the sink. After rubbing my head and cussing out the fixture, I stomped out to the balcony and glared down at the three jerks.

"What the hell is going on?" I yelled.

"None of your damn business," Big Homer yelled back.

"The hell it isn't! It's 6:20 a.m. and everybody up here is trying to sleep. Keep it down!"

"We could if these two assholes would quit changing channels."

"Look. Why don't you share the TV? Each of you can have it for 30 minutes. OK?"

"That's fine, but who gets it first?"

I went downstairs and played mediator, dealing a hand of poker. Winner gets the TV first. Little Frankie won with a full house, and I started back toward my cell. But Big Homer wasn't satisfied.

"His half-hour is from 6 to 6:30," he said. "He's got five more minutes."

Little Frankie immediately started whining. The dispute was starting all over again.

"That's it," I said. "This bullshit has to stop. Since you guys asked me to deal, will you accept my decision as final?"

"Yeah," they said.

"OK, here's my decision: Go fuck yourselves. The cartoons are over at 8 a.m., and this TV is staying off until then. Got it?"

Those three clowns were so stunned they didn't know what to say. Then they looked at each other and started laughing. And all the other guys who had been listening started clapping. Boy, that felt good. It had been a long time since I had heard applause. I removed the fuse from the back of the TV, walked proudly back to my cell and went to bed thinking that maybe my birthday wouldn't be so bad after all.

But I couldn't sleep. In frustration, I got up around 7:30, put the fuse back in the TV and turned on a cartoon. That got a few laughs, but most guys were asleep. I just sat around all morning by myself, reading the paper and watching TV.

The rest of the day was blah, too. Except for talking to Sharyn around noon and again at night, nothing of interest happened. Sharyn told me to call back at 6:30 so she and the kids could all sing "Happy Birthday," but when I did, a couple of them weren't home. So much for the McLain Tabernacle Choir. But Sharyn told me to keep my spirits up. Even though the bond appeal hadn't been approved that week, she was hopeful that we'd get good news soon. She said nobody was touching my birthday cake until I got home.

My birthday dinner was as tasteless as usual, so I gave it away. In the 14 days I had been in jail, I had eaten portions of only a couple of meals—some eggs and a piece of fish. Sharyn had brought me some money for the commissary when she visited, so I was surviving on chocolate bars and milk. I still had hopes of getting out soon, and I didn't want to start eating prison food until it became a matter of forcing it down or starving to death. Besides, I was losing weight and I just didn't have much of an appetite.

Some kind of punch was available with lunch and dinner, but I couldn't swallow it. They never put ice in this "Jim Jones juice," as I called it, so it was always warm. And it tasted awful. If Jim Jones had served this punch to his suicidal followers in Guyana, they never would have made it past the first sip. He would've been forced to shoot everybody.

I felt like shooting Big Homer when he woke me up at 8:30 the next morning. I had just started to fall back to sleep after getting my medicine when I heard Big Homer screaming down the hall. I opened the cell door and saw him standing five feet away, scratching like hell.

"Homer, what the hell is wrong now?" I asked.

"Wiggie has crabs and head lice, man! I think I got 'em, too!"

It had never occurred to me that some of these guys might be carrying diseases. Big Homer and Wiggie were cellmates, and it made sense that Big Homer might catch something because Wiggie looked filthy from the day he arrived. I didn't know whether those critters jumped from person to person, but better safe than sorry. I hustled back into my cell and shut the door.

Maybe it was psychological, but my whole body started itching like crazy a minute later. In fact, everybody in the cellblock was up within minutes. Guys were scratching and complaining that Wiggie was going to get them all infested.

Wiggie and Big Homer both got sprayed down and were given medicine to fight the lice. Their room and all of their personal effects got washed and sprayed, too. The problem eventually subsided, but everybody kept their distance from those two.

Sharyn and the kids visited me for the second Sunday in a row. I really appreciated their making a five-hour round trip for just 30 minutes of visiting time. Between visits I got so bored and depressed that I felt like I was losing my sanity, but seeing them was a tremendous lift. Everybody looked terrific. I wished they could have said the same about me. At least this time they were getting ready to leave before I started crying.

Financially, Sharyn was doing OK. My dear friend Mike Schwartz had sent her a couple thousand dollars, and the $3,500 from the interview with Rod Luck was due any day. That was enough to pay the immediate bills, but if I couldn't get out on bond and was going to be in jail for a long time, she would be broke within a month. I had to think of something to bring her a large chunk of money.

Like a book. As early as my first week in jail, people were expressing interest in an autobiography that could possibly be turned into a TV miniseries. I loved the idea. Not only could it bring in some bucks, but it also would provide an opportunity for me to let people know what abuses were taking place in our federal justice system.

I started keeping a diary of my prison experiences with reflections on the people and events that had put me there. I'd spend two or three hours a day writing furiously. Writing helped pass the time and also was therapeutic. Rather than keeping things bottled up, I was airing them out on paper.

But my main motivation, as usual, was money. I was looking for a big advance that would make life easier for Sharyn and the kids. Unfortunately, that was a long time coming. It took a while to find a publisher and work out all the details.

As if money problems weren't enough, I even lost a lower bridge from my mouth. This bridge linked four teeth, white porcelain on solid gold, and was worth several hundred dollars. Either I misplaced it or somebody stole it. With the company I was keeping, somebody certainly was capable of the latter. In any event, I needed help and word was that it was easier to get out of prison than to see a dentist.

Any hopes I had of getting out before sentencing were shot April 2 when Arnie told me the appeal had been turned down. I was upset, but not too surprised. I hadn't gotten a break in months. So, I resigned myself to the fact that I was in for at least another 2½ weeks until sentencing, when I would have something new to worry about.

Sharyn took the news hard. For the first time, she broke up on the phone. She had been counting on the appeal being successful. Sitting in jail on the other end of the line, I felt helpless. There was nothing I could do.

I was getting nervous about my sentence, too. My hunch was that I would get no more than eight years of concurrent time for all four counts. Arnie had told me that while the jury was deliberating, Kovachevich said in front of him and two other attorneys that my case was "too close to call." If she considered it a borderline case, she wouldn't come down on me too hard, would she? On the other hand, she had shown no mercy at my bond hearing. I didn't know what to expect.

I had been a convict for almost three weeks when I got my first letter from a fan. It was a dandy. This guy from Wisconsin wrote that he was sorry about my conviction but that he hoped the judge wouldn't go easy on me. He wanted me to get the maximum sentence. Then in the very next paragraph the jerk asked for an autographed picture. Can you believe that? He didn't even send me a picture to sign or a self-addressed stamped envelope, either. The whole cellblock got a kick out of the letter. I gave out countless autographs to anyone who was kind enough to ask and provide a stamped envelope, but this letter went straight in the trash.

The next two weeks went by slowly as I waited for my sentencing day. Sharyn and the kids visited me twice, but the days in between were long. I had gotten another mattress to make my bed on the cell floor more comfortable, but I had a lot of trouble sleeping. Anxiety does that to you. So when the guard came by to awaken Sy and me at 4:30 a.m. April 19 to get ready to go to Tampa for our 9 a.m. sentencing, I was already awake. I barely dozed all night. Sy said the same thing, but I knew better. I had listened to him snore like a freight train.

We traded in our blue jump suits for the same clothes we had last worn when we came to Sanford 32 days before. The Irishman in me admits to believing in a certain amount of luck, and I didn't like the idea of wearing the same bluish-gray sport coat, gray slacks, blue shirt, red-and-black striped tie, blue socks and brown shoes in which I had been convicted and then denied bond. No question, they weren't my lucky clothes.

If I was feeling unlucky, Sy and Frank Cocchiaro were feeling totally pessimistic. Sy figured he'd get 10 years, but Frank was expecting 60. For a 64-year-old guy, that would amount to a death sentence. He already had about three years to go on his mail fraud conviction before he would be eligible for parole, and unless the Hanging Judge loosened her noose, he could plan on dying in prison. I was an optimist compared to these guys. I still was harboring some hope that we'd get light sentences or even probation.

The marshals arrived at 6 a.m. They chained Sy and Frank together around their waists and then handcuffed them to the chains. I also was cuffed to a chain around my waist. Being cuffed like that allows very little hand movement, so scratching your nose is almost impossible. And believe me, your nose never itches more than when you can't reach it.

The handcuffs weren't nearly as comfortable as the ones I had worn before. These were smaller, and they barely latched around my wrists. It hurt just to wear them. By the time we got to Tampa, I looked like I had been tortured.

The good news was that we got to go outside for the first time in more than a month. We had been locked inside the building the entire time in Sanford. Simply taking a deep breath of fresh air was a great feeling.

The courtroom was packed. I guess everybody wanted to see the Hanging Judge pull the lever on the trapdoor. About the only people in the courtroom I was happy to see were Sharyn and the kids. They looked great. And sitting with them was Rick Levinson, Arnie's partner and a good friend.

As soon as the judge opened the proceedings, Arnie asked that the order of sentencing be changed. I was scheduled to go first, but Arnie wanted to go over the pre-sentence investigation report with me. She said OK, and we left with the marshals.

When Arnie showed me the PSI report, I could see why he wanted to talk to me. It was a joke. Beverly Webster had based her report almost entirely on what the people in Mad Dog Merkle's office had told her. The report was loaded with factual errors and biased opinions, especially the victim impact portion. That section details how the "victims" of my so-called crimes were affected. According to the report, people like Dale Sparks and Paul Higgins had been wiped out financially by me. That was a big crock. They wiped themselves out by borrowing too much money and failing to pay it back. Hell, when you look at how much they borrowed and how much they paid back, they came out ahead in the deal. The victim impact statement was the most flagrant misrepresentation in the whole report, which was filled with lies and mistakes.

Instead of gathering facts independently, Webster had rubber-stamped the government's view of me. I was in a bad way if that report preceded me through the prison system.

What really burned my butt was Webster's attitude. She told me to call her any time and then her office wouldn't take a collect call. In fact, Sharyn, the kids and several friends had tried to reach her, but she didn't return any of their calls. She did talk to Sharyn in person once, but after telling her to set aside a couple of hours to talk, Webster stayed only 20 minutes. She was just another pawn being moved by the government to make me look as bad as possible.

When Arnie and I returned to the courtroom, Frank Cocchiaro was standing before the judge. We arrived in time to hear his sentence: 20 years in prison.

I couldn't believe it. Frank's case never even should have gone to the jury, and she gave him 20 years. At one point late in the trial, Kovachevich had come within a hairsbreadth of dismissing the charges against him. Frank was in the case only because of one guy, Dale Sparks, and Kovachevich knew his testimony was a farce. I think Ernst Mueller was even surprised when she refused to dismiss the charges. But when the jury gave her that guilty verdict, she whacked Frank hard.

Don't get me wrong, if Frank was guilty, he deserved 20 years. And I have no illusions about the man's criminal history. Beginning in 1946, Frank had been charged with such crimes as burglary, grand larceny, stealing money orders, receiving stolen property, bank robbery, forgery, contempt of court, income tax evasion and mail fraud. Several of those charges led to convictions, and now he had been convicted of racketeering, conspiracy and extortion. He was no Boy Scout. But the evidence against him in this case was almost non-existent. A guilty verdict was ridiculous, and 20 years was outrageous. That's why I was upset.

Frank did get two breaks. One was that his 20 years would be served concurrently with his mail fraud sentence. In other words, the clock already was ticking on his 20 years. He didn't have to wait until after his other sentence was served. But more importantly, the judge classified his sentence as B-2. Arnie told me that meant that Frank was eligible for parole immediately. If he could convince a parole board that he should be released from this conviction, the board was free to do it. Frank still had hope.

Sy Sher was next. He looked terrified. After hearing Frank's sentence, he knew he was in deep trouble. And he was. Kovachevich gave him 20 years. But she also designated Sy's status as B-2.

I was devastated by their sentences. According to the government, I was the chief bad guy in this alleged conspiracy, and I could only imagine what lay ahead for me. I figured that since Mueller was asking the Hanging Judge to give me 35 years, that was what I'd get.

It was time to find out. But before the judge could get me, Arnie assailed the PSI report for about half an hour. He revealed its inaccuracies and obvious bias point by point. For instance, the report indicated that Timothy Johnston had signed a particular check in Paul Higgins' check-kiting scheme. Arnie pointed out that we had introduced the check with Higgins' signature, yet Kovachevich overruled Arnie's objection. Arnie asked that several other errors be corrected, but the judge let almost every mistake stand.

The battle was still being fought when the judge broke for lunch. I was locked up with Sy and Frank, who were still in shock over their sentences. Sy had tears in his eyes.

"It could be worse," I said.

"How?" Sy asked incredulously.

"Well, she might not have given you a B-2."

"What the hell is a B-2?"

Sy's attorney hadn't even told him about the B-2 yet. When I explained that meant he could be out on parole soon, that cheered him up a bit. But he just couldn't get over the words "20 years."

During the lunch break, a marshal brought me two large Pepsis. Those were a sight for sore eyes. I hadn't had a Pepsi in more than a month. I practically chugged the first one, then nursed the second. Sy gave me another. Seventeen more and I'd be back on schedule.

The marshal also asked me if I'd sign a couple of baseballs for him. I did, and before I knew it, I was signing autographs for everybody in the lockup. For a while, at least, my thoughts were directed to my glory days and away from my immediate problems.

When we returned to court, Arnie went over the victim impact portion of the PSI report. He argued that since Webster had merely included a victim impact report prepared by the government, it couldn't be objective. But the judge refused to strike the government's version, a decision that came back to haunt her. When the Court of Appeals later overturned my conviction, it criticized Kovachevich's refusal to investigate our claims that many of the facts contained in the report were false.

As a last resort, Arnie asked that my sentencing be delayed. He wanted time to prepare his own victim impact statement that could be added to the government's report. The report still would not be as objective as it should be, but at least it would reflect my side of the story.

Kovachevich clearly wasn't happy about putting off my sentencing, but she agreed to a postponement. She said we were to return at 11:30 a.m. April 25. For the moment, I had escaped the Hanging Judge's rope.

That made me feel good. I wanted to know my sentence more than anybody else, but I considered it a victory of sorts to throw Kovachevich off her precious schedule. It was a small triumph, but at that point I was pleased with anything at all.

Poor Sy. Kovachevich was in such a foul mood after missing out on her chance to sentence me that she made Sy her whipping boy.

After my sentencing was postponed, Sy returned to the courtroom for a bond hearing. The day before, Tom Nolan, one of Sy's attorneys, had talked to Mueller about giving Sy 30 days to take care of some personal matters before reporting to federal prison in California, where he lived. Mueller had agreed to that request.

As expected, Kovachevich refused to release Sy on bond pending the results of his appeal. But when Nolan told the judge about his agreement with

Mueller to give Sy a 30-day grace period, you would have thought that he had called her a Communist sympathizer or child molester. She went nuts. She started screaming at Nolan and Mueller and basically kicked Nolan out of the courtroom. Needless to say, she denied Nolan's request.

I was in a holding cell while this was taking place, but the marshals who told me about it were stunned. They said they'd never seen Kovachevich so bent out of shape. Was she so obsessed with the idea of nailing me that she couldn't even be rational enough to honor a prearranged agreement between the prosecution and the defense?

My mind was racing on the ride back to Sanford. I was bitter, frightened and amazed about all that had happened over the past 13 months, and I still didn't know what sentence Kovachevich had in mind for me. "Twenty years" kept ringing through my ears, but I knew my sentence would be worse.

A phone message from Rod Luck was waiting for me upon our return to jail. I called him back, and he said Lt. McCullough had approved a live TV interview with me for the 11 o'clock news if I was willing. I said sure. A couple of hours later, I was standing in front of Luck's camera with an armed guard standing behind me. Guards don't carry guns in prison for fear that an inmate will grab one, but Luck insisted on it for dramatic effect. I managed to tell Luck what had happened in court that day without going into a tirade against Kovachevich. I knew it was wise to try to get on her good side, if she had one, until sentencing was complete.

Sharyn and all the kids except Michelle came to see me two days later. That visit was even more emotional than the first one had been. Everybody knew that I probably was going to get socked with a heavy sentence and it was hard to be upbeat. I couldn't fake it at all. As I turned the corner into the visiting room and saw Kristi and Dale waiting for me, I suddenly started feeling so ashamed of the pain I was bringing my family that my eyes filled with tears. That wasn't a good start.

On the other side of the bulletproof glass, Kristi took the phone first. After telling each other how much we loved and missed each other, she handed the phone to Dale.

"Dad, you have to ground Timmy," she said.

"Why should I do that?"

"He got a D on his report card."

That was like hearing that Ronald Reagan had approved massive cuts in the defense budget. It was something I never thought I'd hear. Tim was the best student of all my kids. He almost always got straight A's or maybe an occasional B. If Tim got a D, then I knew my legal problems were really tearing up my family.

Just as Kristi was getting up to leave, our eyes met. We both started bawling. She said, "Daddy, I love you," then hurried out of the visiting room.

I was still crying when Denny and Tim came into the room.

"What the hell is going on with your grades?" I asked Tim.

"Dad, it's not your fault," he replied. "I'm just a little lazy right now."

Can you believe that? The thought of Dad spending the next 20 years in jail had to be eating away at him, but my 16-year-old son was trying to protect me. I was so proud of him.

Denny, too. His report card was super. And both boys were hanging tough. After talking with them for a few minutes, I asked to speak to Sharyn. I was still wiping away tears when she picked up the phone.

"What's wrong?" she asked.

"This is supposed to get easier," I said, "but it isn't."

"Denny, if you're going to break up like this, the kids and I will just stay home."

"I'm sorry, Sharyn. I just feel so bad about what I'm putting you through. I want to make it up to you, but I don't know how."

Sharyn started crying, too. For the longest time, we just stared at each other through the glass in silence with tears rolling down our cheeks. I looked in Sharyn's eyes and saw a woman who was in a lot of pain. But I also saw a woman who still loved me very much. Words can't describe how much Sharyn's loving gaze meant to me. It went straight to my heart and stripped my defenses. My emotions were out on my sleeve for everyone to see. And I didn't even care.

After my family had gone, I had another visitor—a chaplain. He was there, he said, to "save Denny McLain." He was one of those born-again Christians. I told him that I didn't need to be "saved" because I had never left the Catholic church. I hadn't been a good Catholic by any stretch of the imagination for a long time, but I still believed in the Catholic church and all its teachings. It was just a matter of starting to live by them again.

That wasn't good enough for the chaplain. He insisted that I needed to be reborn. He even told me that I wasn't a Christian. I know he meant well, but he just couldn't understand that I was every bit as much of a Christian as he was, only in my own way. My way left room for personal improvement, and I intended to do that. But I didn't need him telling me that his way was right and mine was wrong. The way I saw it, his way was loud and showy and mine was quiet and personal. To me, religion is a private matter. If God ever wants me to start shouting about it from rooftops, he'll give me a sign. This guy wasn't it.

Still, we had a nice chat and even prayed together before he left. My prayer skills had gotten a little rusty, but I was making a comeback in prison. And if nothing else, talking with the chaplain took my mind off my problems.

I came down with the flu that week, and by April 25 I was sicker than a dog. I was having hot flashes and cold shakes, plus my throat was sore. Arnie tried to get another postponement, but Kovachevich said the sentencing would proceed as scheduled.

That was disappointing. Defendants are allowed to address the court before they are sentenced, and I was preparing a statement more than 50 pages long that I wanted to read. I didn't see how I could do it in the shape I was in, but I didn't have any choice. I stayed up until 3 a.m. the morning of the sentencing working on my speech. The majority of my statement focused on the disreputable character of the government witnesses who had perjured themselves to do the government's dirty work, but I also wanted to tell the court that I was sorry about the shame I had brought on my family and myself. It wasn't a plea for mercy; it was a statement of fact about my guilt and my regrets.

When I awoke the next day at 6 a.m., I felt like I'd swallowed a cactus and my voice was almost gone. I could speak only in a whisper. On the ride to Tampa with the federal marshals, I realized that reading my entire statement was out of the question.

I was feeling weak and drained when I arrived at the courthouse, but Kristi and Dale gave me a big boost when they saw me and called out: "We love you, Dad! Mom loves you, too!" They came to the sentencing with Sharyn, Denny and Tim. Michelle didn't come, but only because we thought she was too young to understand what was happening.

The sentencing proceedings began with Arnie and Mueller hashing out problems over the PSI report. After those were resolved, Arnie took one last crack at getting the judge to go easy on me.

Arnie made an eloquent 30-minute speech. He started off by quoting from a Platonic dialogue. The point he was making was that one injustice should not be answered with another, and to sentence me to 35 years, as the government had requested, would be a grave injustice. Arnie was hoping that the judge would put me on probation and require so many hours of community service, but we knew that was just wishful thinking.

Arnie also addressed the fact that Mueller had told a reporter that because I was a public figure, I should be dealt with more harshly than a regular guy. Arnie pointed out that another federal judge in the Middle District of Florida had recently given a lighter sentence to a nationally known figure because "somebody with a high profile suffers more than the ordinary citizen, and that should be given consideration on his side of the ledger. The ordinary citizen who comes before you doesn't suffer that kind of long-range, continuing humiliation." In other words, this other judge had indicated that Mueller was 180 degrees off-base.

In closing, Arnie asked the judge that if she decided to send me to prison, at least give me a B-2 sentence. He said that a first-time offender like myself deserved a chance to go before a parole board in the near future, especially since Cocchiaro and Sher had been given that consideration.

Finally, it was my turn to speak. The judge offered me a chair to sit in while presenting my statement, but I chose to stand. Even if my voice prevented me from sounding forceful, I wanted to at least look strong while addressing the court. Even though I was sick, I looked more fit than I had a month earlier. My body, which had been stretching the seams on my clothes, was now about 35 pounds lighter.

Using a microphone so that my hoarse whisper could be heard, I omitted my discussion of the government witnesses and went straight to the meat of my prepared statement.

"I've gone through a lot of shame and disgrace over the last 13 months," I said, "and I will live in the shame and disgrace for the rest of my life. Wherever I go, someone will always say some very unkind words about what's occurred the last 13 months. I brought enormous shame and pain on my entire family. . . ."

I had to stop at that point for a few seconds to keep my composure. It was tough admitting to the world that I'd messed up the lives of my wife and kids, especially when Sharyn, Kristi and Dale were sobbing in the back of the courtroom. But I kept going.

"... even though they had nothing at all to do with any of my problems. ... No sentence of imprisonment can match the awful humiliation of wearing handcuffs before TV cameras. The actual degradation of that particular situation is beyond my ability to define to anyone. I don't know how you get to where I am today from where I was 17 years ago. ... I don't know how many errors and mistakes a person makes in his lifetime, but I've probably made enough for at least two people. I'm guilty of greed and avarice on many occasions, and certainly you can throw in I've certainly exercised an awful lot of bad judgment in my life. At times I've tried to make a fast buck and tried to make money overnight. I've always been selfish.

"I've also been a loving husband and father for 20 years. I guess that really says what a saint I must have married. My wife, Sharyn, and I have talked a lot about this day. Of course we have tremendous anxiety about it. I also know that people are given chances to redeem themselves, Your Honor, and I'm certainly a redeemable man. The lessons I've learned the last 13 months alone I will carry with me the rest of my life. ..."

My whole speech took about 10 minutes. I never once looked up at the judge; I just kept my eyes on my legal pad and read it straight through with my hands in my pockets, then sat down and folded my hands in my lap.

I probably looked as nervous as a one-legged man in an ass-kicking contest. My voice was awful, my face was pale and my head was covered with sweat. Many people probably chalked that up to my flu virus, but a lot of it was genuine fear. As the moment drew near for the judge to read my sentence, the tension was killing me.

I knew I was in trouble when she said, "But with regard to the drugs, I will tell you right now that this court is going to deal harshly." So much for my impassioned speech making a difference.

"As to Count One," Kovachevich said, "this court sentences you to the custody of the attorney general or his authorized representative for a term of eight years. As to Count Two, concurrent to Count One, this court sentences you to the custody of the attorney general or his authorized representative for a term of eight years. ... As to Count Three, the court reiterates its adjudication of guilt with regard to Count Three and sentences the defendant to the custody of the attorney general or his authorized representative for a term of eight years. That is concurrent to Count One, Two and Three."

Sharyn and the kids were crying even harder, but it really wasn't looking too bad at that point. For the same crimes, Sy and Frank had gotten 20 years each while I had gotten eight. But Kovachevich hadn't gotten to the drug conviction yet.

"As to Count Four, consecutive to Counts One, Two and Three—that's in addition thereto, Mr. McLain—this court reiterates its adjudication of guilt in case number 84-44-Cr-T-17 as to Count Four and sentences you to the custody of the attorney general or his authorized representative for a term of 15 years."

The word "consecutive" slipped by me at first. I thought 15 years on the drug charge was outrageous, but I figured that the most I'd have to serve would be five years, when I'd be eligible for parole.

Then it hit me. "Consecutive" meant that I had to add the 15 to the eight, giving me a total sentence of 23 years. I couldn't get out on parole for almost eight years—unless the judge gave me a B-2.

No such luck.

"I don't believe the 4205-B-2 is appropriate," she said. "It's denied."

I was shocked. She had given Sy and Frank, two career criminals, the chance to be paroled immediately. But not me. Who did she think I was? Charles Manson? I guess I shouldn't have been surprised, but I was. It was incomprehensible to me that Sy and Frank could get B-2s and I couldn't.

Twenty-three years in a federal prison, with no chance for parole until November 13, 1992. Kovachevich, the ringmaster of the circus, was still leading the parade. And I was in for a long haul.

CHAPTER 10

Spinning My Wheels

The feds finally did one thing right in 1985: They declared me broke.

There was no disputing that fact. A lot of people owed me money, but the chances of those people paying me while I was in jail were slim and none. I was expected to pay $8,900 in fines as part of my sentence, which was a drop in the bucket compared with my legal expenses of well over $200,000. I was heavily in debt and had no income and few assets. In my book, that's broke.

The government finally agreed with me. On May 1, U.S. Magistrate Paul Game declared me indigent. I wouldn't have to pay Arnie to handle my appeal. The government would pay him a token amount to represent me, but nothing close to what he was worth. Arnie knew the situation and could have told me to take a hike. But he played out the hand.

Tied into the appeal was the question of who would pay for the trial transcripts. There were 26,000 pages of transcript, and the estimated cost of getting everything prepared and copied was $52,000. I needed those copies to review while working on the appeal. It eventually was determined that the government would pick up that tab.

Being declared indigent was actually a bright spot in an otherwise bleak period of my life. I was stuck in Sanford with no idea of where I would be serving my federal prison sentence. The one thing I did know was that it wouldn't be any cakewalk.

I was very bitter about my sentence, but that was nothing compared to the indignation I felt when Kovachevich handed out sentences to my so-called co-conspirators.

The government waited until I was sentenced before sentencing Larry Knott, Mel Kaplan, Barry Nelson and Stanley Seligman. They were scheduled for sentencing the same day that Kovachevich lowered the boom on Sy Sher and Frank Cocchiaro, but after my sentence was postponed, Kovachevich put them on hold, too. It didn't take a genius to figure out why. Her Ladyship didn't want Arnie to use their light sentences as an argument against a heavy one for me. And it would've been a hell of an argument.

Knott was the first to face Kovachevich, who miraculously transformed from the Hanging Judge into the Wrist-Slapping Judge. For his role in the three-kilo cocaine transaction, Knott got five years' probation. Shouldn't a previous offender get hit hardest? Knott, a four-time loser already in jail on another drug charge, got probation. During a long criminal career that began in 1952 when he pleaded guilty to robbery, Knott had been charged with such crimes as passing bad checks, possession of stolen property, impersonating a police officer, counterfeiting, fraud, receiving stolen property and carrying a concealed weapon. I had never been convicted of anything in my life and she gave me 15 years on the same drug count. Figure that one out.

Kaplan got the same deal as Knott—five years' probation. That I could swallow. Kaplan wasn't involved in the drug deal any more than I was. We both just happened to be in the wrong place at the wrong time. But Mel didn't know how to handle his good fortune. Kovachevich warned him that if he talked to Nelson under any conditions during his probationary period, she'd throw him in jail. Less than a year later, she found out that Mel was talking to Nelson and put him in the slammer for five years. It was almost as if Mel was hypnotized. He couldn't stay away from Nelson and paid the price.

Nelson actually had to go to prison. He got a four-year sentence, which was only about 44 years less than he deserved. This degenerate who had stolen millions of dollars, taken thousands in kickbacks and tried to deal cocaine got four measly years.

What really made me barf was when Kovachevich said, "The fact that you admitted your guilt is the first step toward rehabilitation." Ha! The day Barry Nelson quits ripping people off will be the day Tampa is covered by three feet of snow. Didn't she hear the Nelson/Kaplan tapes? What it comes down to is that Knott, Kaplan, Nelson and Seligman kissed Uncle Sam's ass and protected themselves. I took him on in court and got screwed. In other words, if you plead guilty in the Hanging Judge's courtroom, you do little time. If you exercise your right to a trial and lose, you get hung out to dry. I certainly did.

It always bothered me that the judge held it against me for not admitting my guilt. Hey, I took the stand and admitted my guilt for two days. I laid it all out on the line. I guess Kovachevich was upset because I wasn't admitting the charges in the indictment. Well, that was just too bad. I thought it was my Constitutional right to profess my innocence. Why should I plead guilty when I'm not? But she made me pay for not rolling over and playing dead.

The last guy to be sentenced was Stanley Seligman, the forgotten man. He had been named in his own separate indictment, which had been kept secret until just before the trial, and then, like Nelson, he didn't even have to testify. This swindler got 18 months and had to pay back the $7,000 he took from Danny Cowart.

Kovachevich was really blowing some smoke when she sentenced Seligman, a former U.S. district law clerk. "I gave serious consideration to inviting every U.S. district law clerk to your sentencing," she said, "but I decided you've been humiliated enough." Hell, the guy was a ghost the whole time. Nobody saw him. Humiliated? The capper came when she gave Seligman almost two months to report to prison in Colorado so that he wouldn't have to spend his birthday in the can. I almost lost my lunch.

I had never been a bitter person, but that changed when I went to prison. Sitting around all day with nothing to do but play cards and watch TV gave me a lot of time to think—about the judge, the attorneys, the witnesses, the investigators and the jury. And the more I thought, the more bitter I became. The judicial system had failed me, and my family was suffering as a result. The government was so obsessed with getting me that it let about two dozen "real" criminals off the hook. Sy and Frank were thrown in for show. Knott, Nelson,

Siegmeister, Mendelson, Bertucci, Myatt, Johnson—not one of those guys served a minute in prison for their various roles in the three-kilo, 10-kilo and 400-kilo cocaine deals. Just me, and I wasn't even involved. The federal government had made me the victim of a persecution, not a prosecution.

I couldn't even go to sleep without being reminded of my cruel fate. Each night the coffin door on my cell would swing shut with that gut-wrenching slam, and the walls would start creeping in on me. I would lay there, sweating, waiting for the walls to squeeze me to death, either in terrifying agony or joyful release. Then, after falling asleep, I would awaken suddenly from a nightmare. Awaken from one nightmare into another.

I tried not to get bogged down with self-pity. I read books and newspapers, watched the TV news, wrote in my diary, talked with other inmates, plotted my legal strategy with Arnie, called Sharyn for support—anything to keep my mind active and productive. And for about 15 minutes each day, I just sat and dreamed. I dreamed most often that I was sitting on the couch at home with Sharyn, watching our big-screen TV, with a Pepsi in one hand and a Twinkie in the other. That was my idea of heaven.

For the time being, I had to cope with purgatory. I hadn't even been assigned to my federal hell yet.

One of the nice things about purgatory was the telephone. Except for the U.S. Postal Service, phones are the only daily link between inmates and the outside world. The phones in Sanford were busy almost constantly from 6 a.m. to 11:30 p.m. seven days a week. AT&T must make a fortune off prison phones.

I certainly burned up the lines. I've never had a slow finger when it comes to long-distance dialing. The telephone is cheaper than traveling and faster than writing. I'm a firm believer in the telephone being the next-best thing to being there, although in my case it was a distant second.

In Sanford, the prisoners lined up to use the phone. There was no official time limit to calls, but you had to be pretty brave to stay on the horn too long with a bunch of inmates lined up behind you.

One guy who came to Sanford just before my sentencing had reason to be brave. This guy was about 6-foot-3, 290 pounds, and not an ounce of that was fat. He was solid muscle. He did 300 push-ups every day to keep in shape. As if that wasn't enough, he shaved his black head bald. He looked like a bowling ball with an icebox for a body. His arms were like two of mine put together. This guy had been convicted of shooting a cop, and he was in Sanford to stand trial on other charges. He seemed like a pretty nice guy, but he obviously had a mean streak. I decided that if a riot ever broke out, I wanted to be on his side.

"King Kong" and I had an understanding regarding the telephone. His wife worked from 3 to 10:30 p.m. six nights a week, and he always called her at 11. They'd stay on the phone for half an hour or 45 minutes. Well, I called Sharyn every night at 11 just to say good night and tell her "I love you." It didn't even take five minutes, but it was important to both of us.

I didn't arm-wrestle King Kong to see who would get the phone each night at 11. Our deal was that he would tap me on the shoulder just before 11 and remind me to call Sharyn. He'd give me five minutes to make my call, but after that the phone was his. I was happy with that arrangement—as if I had a choice.

But one day, I forgot about that. I was standing in line to use the phone when King Kong stepped right in front of me. He decided that he deserved that spot more than I did, I guess by virtue of his biceps, triceps and any other "cep" you can imagine.

"What the hell do you think you're doing?" I asked.

"What does it look like I'm doin', motherfucker? I'm waitin' to use the fuckin' phone."

"Not until I'm through with it, you're not."

"Look, you no-good little motherfuckin' scumbag cocksucker, I'm usin' the phone next. Got that, motherfucker?"

"Hey, there's no way you're getting away with this."

"Watch, motherfucker."

That was one insult too many. Without thinking, I clenched my fist and slugged him in the face. It was just like that Burt Reynolds movie where the guy got punched in the face and his jaw never moved. If King Kong felt it, he didn't let on. He was probably more surprised than anything.

Well, I'd picked a hell of an opponent for the first fight of my life. If I'd stopped to think about it, I would've let him have the phone all week. But I reacted impulsively when he kept calling me names, and suddenly I was faced with the prospect of defending myself against a 290-pound slab of cop-maiming muscle.

Defend myself? Shit, I ran. Picture 270 pounds of white flab jiggling up the stairs at breakneck speed and you'll have some idea of the way I was moving. I don't think I ever galloped down the line to first base any faster. I locked myself in my cell and started praying.

I couldn't stay in my cell forever. Some sort of truce had to be arranged. About an hour later, I asked somebody to go downstairs and tell King Kong that I was interested in a peace summit. He was agreeable. With him standing at the foot of the stairs and me at the top, close enough to my cell that I could run back and lock myself in if he got angry, we talked things over. I told him how my trial had left me in a piss-ass mood and how the pressure of being locked up was getting to me. I spent the next hour or so getting things off my chest and trying to smooth the water. It apparently worked because we became pals for the next couple of days. Then I got transferred to another jail.

Thank God I got transferred. Our truce seemed to be working, but King Kong scared the hell out of me, and I was glad to leave him behind.

I was hoping to leave jail behind entirely. Another bond hearing was scheduled for May 16, and this time I was asking to be released pending the outcome of the appeal of my conviction.

The day before the bond hearing, I was moved from Sanford to Hillsborough County Jail in downtown Tampa. The guards told me to take all my stuff with me in case the judge decided to release me. I liked the sound of that.

I didn't like Hillsborough, though. It was a pit. The food was awful, the floors were a mess, the air conditioning was broken and the place was overcrowded. I was placed in cellblock 300-1-South, which had 29 men crammed into 16 one-man cells. Obviously, about half had to sleep on the filthy floor, including me. I made my bed, such as it was, on a narrow balcony overlooking the main area of the cellblock.

The shower area in my cellblock should have been condemned. It was disgusting. It looked as if a septic tank had backed up and spilled waste all over the floor. Two toilets were located next to the shower, and the mess around those was even worse. Everybody must have had bad aim. I had to take a shower once in the two days I spent at Hillsborough and I washed myself with record-breaking speed. It was an awful feeling to walk out of a shower and wonder if I was cleaner than when I walked in.

Nothing happened quietly in Hillsborough. The morning of my bond hearing, I was jarred from sleep at 4 a.m. by an explosion of noise that could've awakened the dead. Doors were slamming, people were screaming, guys were taking showers—it looked and sounded like a Chinese fire drill. I tried to figure out what was going on and finally realized that it was just breakfast being served. Why it had to be done at that hour and with that much commotion was beyond me. The guards seemed to delight in slamming the trap door on each cell as hard as they could. There's nothing like the sound of steel slamming on steel to get your day started off right.

I managed to fall back to sleep until about 6:15. I got up, took my medicine and waited to be taken to the courthouse. Once again I changed from my prison attire into the "lucky" outfit I had worn for my conviction, bond denial and sentencing. I figured that this bond hearing would be my last appearance before Kovachevich for a while. By the end of the proceeding, I was praying that was the case.

Just like before, we presented the only witnesses. It was a new crew this time to say the same thing: Denny McLain is no threat to flee or hurt anybody. I took the stand again and told the judge that I would agree to any conditions for bond—she could make me report to a marshal every day or even have one live with me. I just wanted to get out so that I could take care of my family. Arnie told the judge that if I couldn't qualify for bond, then no one could. The government presented no witnesses, yet the judge saw fit to deny me bond.

Kovachevich didn't stop there. Besides labeling me "a danger to the community" and "a threat to flee," she called me a "professional criminal." That stunned everyone in the packed courtroom. It was clear to all that the judge's vendetta against me had extended beyond the normal battle lines. She was using her position to attack me personally.

It still galls me that my family had to listen to that garbage. When I left the courtroom, Sharyn and Kristi were standing outside in tears. I think they were most upset because I had given Kovachevich another chance to take a cheap shot at me when I probably never stood a chance of getting bond. Arnie could have brought in Ronald Reagan to speak on my behalf and she still would have kept me in jail.

I wasn't just imagining this. When federal marshals who watch judges operate every day tell you they see it, too, you know it's for real. "She hates your guts, Denny," one of the marshals told me that afternoon. "It was never more evident than today."

Frankly, I wasn't surprised. I wouldn't have given her the chance to embarrass me again if I didn't think I had a chance of winning. But realistically, I knew the odds were against me. If nothing else, that hearing provided more proof that Kovachevich was anything but the unbiased, fair judge she was supposed to be.

Bitterness was swelling again as I was taken back to Hillsborough. I went straight to a phone and called Sharyn. As soon as she said hello, my bitterness turned to desperation. With 23 years staring me in the face and no hope of getting released on bond, I fell apart.

"It's all over," I wept. "I'm stuck. I might as well be dead."

"Denny, don't talk like that," Sharyn pleaded.

"Why not? Anything would be better than being caged up like this. I can't take it anymore."

"Don't quit!" Sharyn screamed into the phone. "Don't you ever quit. You can't let them get away with what they've done to you. Keep fighting!"

"Sharyn, you don't understand. They beat me."

"I can't believe you're talking like this. I've never seen you give up on anything in your life. You're not a quitter!"

She was right. I'm not a quitter. And I had a hell of a supporter in my corner.

"I'll be OK, Sharyn. And I want you to know, it's not jail that scares me. It's being away from you and the kids. I don't know if I can take it."

"Of course you can. You can take anything. And don't worry about us. You'll beat this thing, and when you do, we'll be waiting for you."

"I love you, Sharyn."

"I love you, too."

She did it again. The girl I thought I was carrying all those years was carrying me.

It's embarrassing now to even admit that I considered suicide. I've always lived my life to the fullest, so the thought of throwing it away is repulsive. Even in prison, I had to be alive for a reason. And the most obvious reason was the thought of one day regaining my greatest blessing—my family.

That thought gave me hope, but it also made me sad. If I were released on parole after serving the minimum amount of time, I would be 48. Kristi would be 27, Dale 26, Denny 24, Tim 23 and Michelle 20. They'd all be adults and I would have missed all those important years in their lives.

That meant I had to fight. Mad Dog Merkle had won the first round. Round two would be fought in appellate court. As soon as I got the trial transcripts, I could begin working on my appeal.

I still didn't know where my new home would be. I was hoping to be sent to the Federal Correctional Institution in Tallahassee, which was only about four hours from Tampa. That was close enough that my family could drive up fairly often. I had heard good things about Tallahassee—that it was clean, that visitors were allowed five days a week and that plenty of recreational activities were available. After being locked up in county jails for two months, I was ready for an environment with fresh air.

But I had heard rumors that my destination was the U.S. Penitentiary in Atlanta. That would not be good. Atlanta was about eight hours from Tampa, meaning that visits from my family would be unlikely. It was just too far away. If the U.S. Bureau of Prisons had any interest in helping the families of inmates stay together, they would send me to Tallahassee.

I had a feeling I'd be going somewhere the next morning. I was besieged by both guards and inmates asking for autographs. Did they know something I didn't?

I hoped so. I didn't want to stay in Hillsborough another night. At 2:30 a.m., the whole cellblock was awakened when a couple of guards came in and hollered out the names of three state prisoners who were being transferred. I fell back to sleep, but at 3:45 breakfast was served. A 110-piece band could've marched through our cellblock and made less noise. I tried to keep sleeping, but it was useless. The TV already was on, so I got up at 4:30 and watched an interview program with three other guys.

For many guys in cellblock 300-1-South, the highlight of the day was an aerobics program that came on at 6 a.m. About 20 guys got up to watch three girls do aerobic exercises on TV for half an hour. These gals were fun to watch, but nothing compared to the girls on cable TV. I was reminded of the times that I would be flipping through the channels on my big-screen TV at home and see the aerobics program on HBO. Those girls were awesome. Then Sharyn would walk in the room and start hitting me on the arms or standing in front of the TV until I changed the channel. I tried to tell her that if I ever decided to start exercising seriously again, I'd need to know how to do it properly. It was purely educational. Sharyn didn't buy that.

The funny thing about these aerobics parties was that no one exercised. Some guys might have been performing strenuous mental exercises, but nobody did a sit-up or jumping jack while the show was on.

I was deeply engrossed in mental aerobics when a guard called out, "McLain, it's time to get out of here." Even after gathering all my stuff and taking it to the check-out area to wait for the federal marshals to pick me up, nobody told me where I was going.

While I was waiting, a pretty woman about 25 years old was leaving. She had been picked up for prostitution and spent the previous night in jail. I was shocked when she told the guard, "I have to hurry to the airport this morning and pick up my husband."

"Is she really married?" I asked the guard after she left.

"She sure is," he said, "and this is the second time in six months that she has been our guest. You can't believe it, can you?"

"Hell, no."

"You'd be surprised to know about all the wives who are hookers. Some do it for the money, some for the excitement of a new man and some just because their husbands can't do the job at home. A lot of husbands even know about it and allow it."

Some of the things you learn in prison are pretty wild.

The marshals arrived at 7:30 and took me to the lockup in the federal building. I still didn't know my destination, but I knew I wouldn't be traveling alone. We were waiting for a van to arrive from Orlando with other passengers.

When the van showed up, I finally learned my immediate destination: Tallahassee. The question was whether or not I would stay there or be sent on to Atlanta. I had heard that when you're passing through Tallahassee, you're put in a 6-by-8 cell and left there until your departure. That could take several days, and all that time you're left in your cell. I prayed that Tallahassee was my final stop, not an intermediate one.

The van carrying me, two marshals and six other prisoners arrived at the prison around 4:30 p.m. I thought we were pulling into one of those fancy industrial parks until I saw a sign that indicated this was the Federal Correctional Institution. The red-brick buildings looked new, and the grounds were impeccably manicured. Trees, bushes and grass surrounded the facility. So did a fence with a locked gate.

Still wearing handcuffs, we were led from the van through an immaculate lobby to a check-in area. The first thing I noticed was how clean the place was. The floors sparkled. You could eat off them. At Hillsborough, the cockroaches would beat you to the food.

And if the sandwiches they gave us upon arriving were any indication, the food was actually worth eating. We were given two sandwiches, each of which had two pieces of meat, a crisp piece of lettuce and real mayonnaise. I hadn't seen two pieces of meat or lettuce on anything in two months of meals. Even the bread was fresh. I munched on the sandwiches while filling out paper work and completing other processing details.

It was all becoming old hat except for one new twist—a strip search. I endured a lot of humiliation and dehumanization during my 2½ years in prison, but nothing compared to the absolute degradation of being strip-searched. This was the first of many times, but I never got used to it.

First I took off all my clothes. The guard even had me take out my dentures. While I was standing in a room completely naked, the guard looked under my arms, up my nose, in my mouth, through my hair, between my toes and on the soles of my feet. He then told me to lift my testicles, I guess to see if I was hiding a helicopter or machine gun. But the worst part was when he told me to bend over and grab my ankles. That made it easier for him to spread my cheeks and look right up my asshole. I don't know what he expected to find, but he sure gave it a good look-see. I must admit, this guy was disgustingly thorough.

I tried to forget my own humiliation by putting myself in the guard's shoes. How would he describe his job to friends or his kids? Would he say he's an asshole examiner? An orifice engineer? I couldn't even imagine why someone would take such a job in the first place. You'd have to be pretty hard-up for work.

I don't mean to be cruel. But no one can tell me that a strip search is anything other than cruel and inhuman punishment. I still shudder when I think about it.

After putting on my new prison uniform of tan slacks, a white T-shirt, white socks and pink undershorts, I sat around for about three hours. I eventually was told that my stay in Tallahassee would be temporary. Atlanta was expecting me.

That was a huge disappointment. Not only was I being sent farther from home, but I also had to spend the next few days in one of those tiny cells I had heard about.

It was an honest-to-goodness jail cell. The door had round steel bars, just like they show in movies, and the off-white paint was chipping off the walls onto the cement floor. Crammed into the 6-by-8 cell were a bunk bed, a toilet and a sink. A light hung overhead. The regular prisoners stayed in dormitory rooms, but those of us who were just passing through were kept caged up like zoo animals.

I had a cellmate, and since we were locked inside our room for all but an hour or two every day, neither of us had any privacy. When one of us wanted to use the toilet, the other would stand by the door and look away. Maintaining inmates' dignity and self-respect obviously wasn't a high priority with the Bureau of Prisons.

After having daily use of the phone in Sanford, it came as a surprise to learn that phone access would be limited to every third day during my stay in Tallahassee. Sharyn had no idea where I was, and I had no way to tell her. Fortunately, the next day was a phone day and I could call her then. In the meantime, she would be worried sick. Whenever I was on the road playing ball, selling big-screen TVs, golfing or anything else, I almost always called Sharyn at night to make sure everything was OK and let her know where I was. You could feed a family of five for a decade on the phone bills we've run up over the years. She got nervous on the few occasions when I failed to call, so you can imagine how she must have felt when I was in prison and she didn't hear from me all day.

I was glad that lights out came early in that cellblock. I had no TV to watch, no cards to play, not even a book to read. I tried writing a letter to Sharyn, but it took me forever because I couldn't stop crying. I was still upset when the lights were turned out at 10 p.m. But it had been a long day, and I fell to sleep quickly.

Remember Willie Sutton? He was the famous bank robber who said he robbed banks because "that's where the money was." Well, my cellmate in Tallahassee didn't have all the notoriety Sutton did, but he was almost as accomplished. His name was Frank Smith, he was 77 years old, and he, like Sutton, robbed banks for a living.

After holding up a poker game at age 17, Frank started robbing liquor trucks, nightclubs and anything else that had a lot of money in it. He said that in 1943, he ordered the father of ABC newswoman Barbara Walters to unlock a safe containing $8,000. A few years later he started concentrating on banks. According to Frank's count, he had robbed at least 15 banks in his lifetime, some with a partner and others by himself. All told, he figured he had stolen close to half a million dollars.

Frank didn't look the part. He was about 5-6 with a ruddy complexion, white hair and a meek demeanor. He looked more like a retired bookkeeper on his way to a bingo parlor than a lifetime bank robber. But he certainly sounded like one. Speaking in his New York accent, he used phrases like "case the joint," "pack a piece" and "on the lam" when describing his many adventures. And he loved to talk about them. He even carried newspaper clippings detailing his life of crime. Egotism was rampant in prison, even in a frail old man.

Frank most recently had robbed a pair of banks in the Daytona Beach area in 1984. He got away with less than eight grand, and in the old days he never would have been caught. But a surveillance camera provided a picture that led the cops to his trailer, where they found some of the money marked with incriminating red dye. Frank couldn't compete with modern technology.

I don't think Frank really minded being caught. He said he was through with crime, but I couldn't believe him. Frank had spent about 35 years, or nearly half his life, in prison, and he seemed comfortable there. Frank said he needed the money, but I got the impression that he pulled those bank jobs because he had nothing going on the outside and he figured he'd just rob another one for the hell of it. If he got away with it, fine; if he didn't, well, he'd just go back to the slammer. And if he lived through his five-year sentence, I figured he'd try robbing a bank as an octogenarian.

Frank Smith was a sad description of what happens to people in prison. They give up on themselves. For many convicts, life becomes better for them in prison than it is on the outside. Food, shelter and clothes are provided, and in most federal institutions they can watch TV, play racquetball, read, sit around all day—whatever makes them happy. They're among their peers, so to speak, and they no longer have to try to make it in a law-abiding society. Society undoubtedly is better off without some of these guys, but others probably could become productive citizens if given the proper counseling and instruction. But our penal system emphasizes detention, not rehabilitation, and the taxpayers wind up shouldering the financial burden for all these people.

Nevertheless, my first exposure to the conditions in a federal prison was encouraging. From what I could see through the window nine feet away from my cell, the facilities and grounds in Tallahassee were super. The atmosphere was much like that on a college campus. I could see a courtyard with people walking on sidewalks lined by bushes and trees. There were no guard towers or spotlights. The guards dressed in gray or blue slacks with light blue shirts and no ties. They didn't carry clubs or guns, and they didn't seem at all abusive. It was nothing like what you see in the movies.

Except for being locked up constantly. That was bad. The guards let us out for about an hour each morning, but we still were confined to an indoor area about 90 feet long and nine feet wide. This corridor right in front of our cells was enclosed by steel bars, so it wasn't like taking a walk in the park when they let us out. It was just a chance to stretch our legs and take a shower. The shower was just another 6-by-8 cage alongside all the other cells, and when one guy went to bathe, the guards locked him inside. The first time I took a shower in Tallahassee, I was locked in for 25 minutes before the guard came back to let me out.

I really wasn't in any hurry to leave. Standing under a shower was a welcome relief from sitting in my cage all day, especially since there was no air conditioning in that cellblock. Even though a guard finally brought a book to my cell, there was nothing to do but read, write, sweat and talk to Frank for hours on end. I was starting to get stir crazy, which explains why I was so excited when a guard handed me a mop my second day there and told me to get to work. I was happy to do anything to get out of cell No. 6. The guard noticed my reaction and asked, "How would you like to go pound rocks with a sledgehammer?" When I said yes, he started laughing. "We don't do that kind of work anymore," he said. Too bad. I could've used the exercise.

Just as I finished mopping the floor, the guard said, "McLain, you have

visitors." Thank God, Sharyn and all five kids were there. And this time we
didn't have to look at each other through glass and speak on the phone. It was
a contact visit, my first ever. Except for brief hugs in the courthouse halls, I
hadn't really held anyone in my family for more than two months. I couldn't
wait.

It was even better than I had expected. I was led into a big room filled with
tables and chairs to accommodate about 125 people and immediately spotted
the six most beautiful faces I've ever seen. I practically ran over to them, and
we embraced in a big huddle. Then for the next six hours we just held on to
each other and talked. I don't think I let go of Sharyn the whole time except to
wolf down all the goodies they got me from the commissary—half a dozen
Cokes (they didn't have Pepsi), a cheeseburger, potato chips and chocolate chip
cookies. I really pigged out on junk food and affection.

The only downer was the clock. When you're in the can, time moves slower
than molasses in January. Then when you have visitors, the clock hands spin
like helicopter props. The visit was over much too quickly. And then after
everybody left, I was subjected to another strip search. But it was worth it to
spend that time with my family.

The food in Tallahassee wasn't bad. Some meals were terrific, while others
were definite throwaways. The cooks there batted about .500, which was a
pretty good average in the penal system. I had come to expect a continuous
flow of garbage after my time in the county jails.

Most of the guards were pretty nice, too. The only jerk I came across was
this guy who thought he was Sergeant Preston of the Yukon. He never missed
an opportunity to remind me who was boss around there.

One day I asked him if he could sharpen my pencils. "Ask me something
important," he snapped and refused to do it. That really blistered my butt. I
couldn't write in my diary or jot down notes on my appeal without pencils. If
we were to trade places, he'd realize how important a pencil is to a guy fighting
for his freedom.

He really pissed me off a couple of days later when he took my necklace
away. Sharyn had given me a gold chain with a holy picture, and when I
checked into Tallahassee, I was allowed to wear it in the holding cell. But this
guard asked to look at it one day and then kept it after deciding that one of the
edges was too sharp. That was ridiculous. Each day they gave me a razor and
left me in the shower for half an hour to bathe and shave, but a holy medal-
lion was considered a potential weapon. This guy said he was enforcing the
rules, but he was just being an ass.

Still, as jails go, this one was pretty nice, and I wanted to stay. Not caged up
in a holding cell, of course, but in one of those nice dormitories. The BOP
designates each federal prison according to its security level, with level one the
lowest and level six the highest, and Tallahassee was a level two prison—one
notch above minimum security. Besides being close to home, it looked like a
pretty nice place to do my time. I put in a written request to stay at Tallahassee
and eventually was allowed to discuss the matter with associate warden John
Clark.

Clark didn't think my staying there was such a good idea. He said that I
would be doing my time at a camp in Atlanta, not the maximum-security

fortress behind 37-foot walls, and I would be foolish to stay in a prison when I could live in a camp. A camp is easy and relaxed, he said, with a generally safe population and no fences. They use the honor system there; if you cross the line surrounding a camp, you become a fugitive. A camp is more like being sent to the principal's office than being incarcerated. Clark convinced me that even though Atlanta was a lot farther from home, I would be better off leaving Tallahassee.

Clark also told me that I would be leaving for Atlanta the following Tuesday, May 28. Well, the sooner, the better. I wanted to get settled into my new home and get to work on my appeal. I couldn't do anything while locked up in that cage.

I did have an opportunity to get out for longer than usual one day, but I passed. A guard came by and asked everybody in the cellblock if we had any complaints. I had nothing pressing on my mind, but almost everybody else said they did, and they were taken before a committee to air their gripes. A guy from our cellblock called Nashville Ray came back from that meeting with an interesting piece of news. He had run into Barry Nelson and Larry Knott. Small world, isn't it? Nashville Ray mentioned that he knew Denny McLain, and Nelson told him that he had been involved in my case and got a 20-year sentence. Nelson, of course, really got four years. Nashville Ray said that Knott didn't utter a sound when he heard that I was in Tallahassee.

Before leaving, I enjoyed one more visit with Sharyn and the kids. They came up on Saturday, spent four hours with me and then stayed in a motel so they could visit me Sunday, too. We spent most of our time playing "dirty hearts," a card game I taught them. The worst card to get in that game is the queen of spades, called the "bitch," and I wrote the name of my favorite judge on that card. The kids got a big kick out of that.

The kids always seemed terrific when I saw them in person, but they must have been good actors. I know they were hurting inside. Michelle sent me a letter that she titled "My World is Falling Apart," and it practically ripped my heart right out of my chest. I couldn't read it without bawling. My family was in pain, and it was my fault. Rather than put the letter out of sight, I pulled it out from time to time to remind myself why I had to fight like hell to get out of prison. And I vowed never to do anything that would jeopardize my family's livelihood and happiness again.

On May 28, the day after Michelle turned 13, I was transferred to the Federal Correctional Institution in Talladega, Ala., a podunk town 100 miles west of Atlanta. It was just a pit stop on the way to Atlanta, but it gave me another look at a modern facility in the federal prison system.

Talladega was a lot like Tallahassee. It was clean and new, and the only visible indication that it was a prison were the two fences covered with barbed wire that surrounded the facility. And it was air-conditioned to a fault. During my processing, I was left for three hours in a room that was so cold, you could have hung meat in it. I rarely get cold in an air-conditioned room, but that place was freezing.

The prison clothes in Talladega's holdover unit were a riot. Everybody wore a bright orange, one-piece jump suit. Mine was so tight, I looked like a hot-air balloon ready for takeoff. As soon as I got to my cell I unbuttoned the top and let the sleeves hang from my hips. The bottom half of my jump suit was especially tight, but I kept it on for warmth. The cell was freezing, too.

At least I wasn't being locked in a cage anymore. I was back in a regular cell with access to other prisoners and a TV. That made a big difference. No offense to Frank Smith, but our lack of mobility had made my 11 days in Tallahassee little better than solitary confinement. I liked being able to roam around and talk to people.

My cellmate in Talladega was Nashville Ray, who had made the trip up from Tallahassee. He was in on a contempt charge after refusing to turn over some records to a federal judge. He hadn't been indicted for anything, but he had sold an airplane to some guys who were trying to implicate him in a drug deal. The scenario sounded familiar. Anyway, Nashville Ray and I had some long conversations that I think were therapeutic for both of us. Inmates talk a lot, mainly because it's nice to cry on each other's shoulders. His main advice was to be patient. I'd get to Atlanta soon enough, he said, so relax. That was easier said than done.

After a day or two, Nashville Ray was moved to another cell and a guy named Holly moved into mine. Holly was this guy's last name, but it worked just as well as his first. He was gay. I knew that already since we had shared a cell my last day in Tallahassee. At first I was disgusted—homosexuality is something I'll never understand—but I grew to like the guy. He was fascinating to talk to, and he'd talk your ear off.

Holly was about 28 years old with long blond hair and a face that can only be described as pretty. That was how Holly described it himself. He was always the "prettiest" person in school, he said, "including all the girls." He certainly didn't try to hide his effeminate inclinations. When he talked about women's clothes, which was often, he used words like "lovely," "darling" and "divine." He was very feminine.

You're probably thinking this guy was in prison on some morals conviction like molesting little boys. Well, you're in for a surprise. Holly was an international jewel thief. He said he had stolen millions of dollars in jewels before getting caught. Actually, it was his partner, a woman, who got caught and turned him in. She did about a year in prison, while Holly got slapped with three sentences totaling 21 years.

Prison might seem like a great place for a guy who prefers men to women. Homosexuality is rampant in the can, so it's a smorgasbord for gays, right? Not necessarily. Holly said he had been in no less than a dozen fights already because he resisted many guys' advances. He didn't want to be raped. "They must ask," he said. But a lot of convicts just decided to take what they knew Holly had to offer. I don't condone homosexuality, but I felt sorry for Holly. He was such an easy target.

And that was a shame. Holly was a nice guy with a super personality and wouldn't hurt anybody. I enjoyed talking to him. In fact, I was rather upset when I was moved to a different cell after less than a week in Talladega. Holly figured I was moved just because he was gay. He said he was going to consult an attorney and possibly file a discrimination suit against the federal government. I don't know if that was why I was moved or not, but it did seem suspicious. We were getting along fine, yet somebody decided it was important to put me in my own room.

Most of my 13 days in Talladega were rather uneventful, but I do remember one notable incident. One day a guy in Beta unit, the dormitory I was living in, had a visitor. His girlfriend had driven 500 miles from Virginia to see him. The visit had been approved by a counselor, whose job it was to help inmates with their problems.

Unfortunately for this inmate, a different counselor was on duty when his girlfriend arrived. He told the woman that only wives were allowed to visit inmates. Since she wasn't married to the guy, she couldn't see him.

Well, the inmate was irate when he heard that. He grabbed the letter approving his girlfriend's visit and showed it to the counselor, a big black guy named Ike who never had a nice word for anybody. He was a mean sonofabitch. Ike looked at the letter and handed it back to the inmate.

"I'm the counselor of record today," he said, "and there will be no visit today for you."

"Give me a BP-9," the inmate demanded.

Those were harsh words. A BP-9 is a BOP form used by inmates when they want to file a complaint against a guard, counselor, administrative official or even the institution itself. If the grievance is upheld, a BP-9 can work against a prison employee who is up for a raise or promotion. Nobody wants a BP-9 in his file.

Now Ike was starting to get mad. "I said you're not having any visitors today," he snarled, "and I don't like your attitude. You're going to the hole."

"The hole" means segregation. Inmates in the hole are locked up by themselves for days, weeks, months on end. It's no fun. I know, because I've been there.

The inmate was beside himself with fury. He was screaming at Ike, who cuffed the guy's hands behind his back and screamed right back. Obscenities were flying everywhere. The inmate kept hollering about how his girlfriend had driven 500 miles for a visit that had already been approved, and Ike finally decided he had heard enough. With the guy's hands still locked behind him, Ike threw the inmate against the cement block wall.

I was appalled, and so were the other 30 guys who witnessed this cruelty. How much courage does it take to rough up a guy who can't even use his hands to defend himself? It was the most ignorant display of cowardice I had ever seen.

But I hadn't seen anything yet. I soon discovered that Ike was a pussycat compared to some of the guards in Atlanta, but at the time, I thought he was right up there with Idi Amin.

Ike grabbed the inmate and dragged him off to the solitary area. I don't know what happened next, but about 10 minutes later, Ike and the inmate, without handcuffs, both were back in Beta house. Ike promptly walked the inmate to the visiting room, where he spent the next three hours with his lady. I'd love to know what brought about that abrupt change, but I never found out.

That same day, I went to Mass for the first time since 1978. When the Mass started, I was the only native U.S. citizen there. The priest was an Irish immigrant and the other eight worshipers were Colombians. For their benefit, I suppose, the priest said the entire Mass in Spanish, even after a couple other Americans showed up. I didn't understand a word, but the Mass was a very moving experience for me. I had tears in my eyes almost the whole time. I'm not sure why. But I felt really good about celebrating Mass, and I hoped to do it regularly in Atlanta.

My emotional state must have been pretty frazzled back then because it didn't take much to start me crying. Later that night, I watched a movie called "Sixteen Candles" on TV, and I cried through practically all of it. It was a stupid movie about teen-age crushes, but one scene in particular really got to me. The father was telling his teen-age daughter how special she was and talking about falling in love. It reminded me so much of a similar talk I had had with Kristi that I got all choked up. Maybe it was because a lot of guys had had visitors and I was too far away for my family to come, but all I could do was think about how much I wanted to be home.

On June 10, I was transferred to Atlanta, which gave new meaning to the saying "There's no place like home." In the case of the U.S. Penitentiary, I prayed that there was no other place on earth like that hellhole.

CHAPTER 11

The Big A

Maybe it was the first time you walked into Yankee Stadium and saw the hallowed grounds upon which such legendary heroes as Babe Ruth, Joe Di-Maggio and Mickey Mantle toiled. Or when you first gazed at the Grand Canyon or Niagara Falls. Or when you saw the ground 30,000 feet below you on your first airplane ride.

At some point in life, everybody witnesses an awe-inspiring spectacle that just blows them away. That happened to me the first time I laid eyes on the "Big A."

This was a real prison. Not just a house of detention, but a genuine joint, just like you see in a Jimmy Cagney movie. Going from Talladega to Atlanta was like traveling through a time warp.

The first thing I noticed was the wall. It looked like the Great Wall of China, and was just as imposing. Made out of concrete and steel, it was 37 feet at its highest point and several feet thick. Before the Boulder Dam was built in 1936, this wall was the largest piece of concrete masonry in the world. It surrounded the entire penitentiary—all 27 acres—and was a stark contrast to the wire fences that surrounded the other prisons I'd seen.

Everything about the Big A looked old. The prison had been built at the turn of the century and had all the features you'd associate with an old-time pen. There were 11 watchtowers manned by real, live guards with loaded guns. There were spotlights that swung back and forth against the walls at night. Cells were stacked on top of each other in tiers. And the first building I was taken to had tremendous stone walls and marble floors. I honestly expected to see Pat O'Brien walking down the stairs in a three-piece suit and introducing himself as the warden, or Edward G. Robinson running around in striped pajamas, trying to escape over the wall. It was strange seeing this black-and-white image in living color.

I was surprised when I was led inside the same walls that Al Capone had once called home. I wasn't supposed to be there. I was supposed to go to the camp next door. I was hoping that everybody had to go inside the main prison for starters, and that those bound for the camp would be taken there after being processed and enduring another damn strip search.

Well, it didn't work out that way. A guard led me to dorm No. 1, room No. 8 in the basement of a building and pointed to bed No. 1. "Welcome to your new home," he said. I wasn't going to the camp.

Why? I wish I knew. Nobody ever told me. It just tore me up that somebody had decided that I was so dangerous that I had to be kept inside a maximum-security prison, even though I had never committed a violent act in my life.

And they didn't even have room for me. When I went to Atlanta, about 2,200 men were living in an institution built to accommodate about 1,200. My room measured 12 by 20 feet and had 10 men crammed in it. Five bunk beds and a desk took up most of that area. And if more than one guy wanted to move around inside the room, forget it. There wasn't enough space. All socializing had to be done in the halls or one of the two TV rooms.

At least the bathroom facilities were not crammed into our room. But that had its bad points, too. Everybody in the dorm used a community bathroom, which reminded me of the one in Hillsborough. The toilets, showers and sinks were always getting stopped up, forcing sewage to spill all over the floor.

This was a strange dorm. It was located in the basement of the hospital building, with the top two floors populated by sick people. I was told that the basement once had been used as a research facility for the study of malaria. I don't know if that was true. But supposedly, inmates who volunteered to be used as guinea pigs were given "good time" toward the reduction of their sentences.

Living below the hospital provided a unique perspective on the prison as a whole. When somebody got beat up, knifed or otherwise abused, we often saw the result right above us.

A lot of the patients in the hospital were Cubans. That was because there were so many Cubans in the Big A to begin with. Of the 2,200 or so prisoners there when I arrived, about 1,900 were Cubans. They were caged in five huge cellhouses, while the Americans lived in one of two dorms adjacent to a cellhouse or in the hospital basement with me.

I had barely gotten settled in my room when a guard came by and announced that it was time for the 4 o'clock count. That was an actual count of inmates taken every day at 4 p.m. If for some reason a guy wasn't in his cell when the guard came by, he was thrown in the hole. And anybody who wasn't standing at attention also ran the risk of being locked in segregation. Almost without fail, the critical moment in a TV show or a football game came at 4 p.m.

After the count I went to the mess hall for dinner, where I ran into Frank Cocchiaro. For a 64-year-old convict, he looked terrific. He had a tan that would have made my daughter Kristi jealous, thanks to his job taking care of the rose gardens for the prison's recreation department. Working outside all day had turned his skin darker than George Hamilton's. It was hard to believe that a guy in prison could have a better tan than most people on the beach.

I had worried about how I might be treated by the other inmates, especially when I realized I wasn't leaving this maximum-security hellhole. But Frank assured me that I had a friend. And it quickly became apparent that Frank was a good friend to have. As much as an inmate can have control, he ran that place.

"Anything you need, you tell me," he said. "Any problems you have, you tell me. If you need anything at all, let me know. I'll take care of it."

Frank also suggested that I stay away from gambling. I gambled anyway, but it was good advice. If you lose money to a convict and can't pay him right away, you can be in serious trouble. Even if it's just five bucks. To a guy in prison, five bucks looks like 500, and he'll do anything to get it.

The biggest problem for gamblers was money not arriving in the mail when they expected it. A losing bettor would tell a guy he'd pay him when his check arrived, but inevitably it would be lost in transit or delayed in the mail room, which was notorious for that. I once saw a guy get beat up when that happened. He owed somebody a $6 case of Twinkies after losing a football bet, and when his check from home didn't arrive on time, he got hurt bad. It was a petty thing to get beat up for, but that's what prison does to people. And I saw guys get beat up for a lot less.

Bets were never paid off with cash. Nobody had any. Inmates had been allowed to hold cash before the Cubans arrived, and I was told that there used to be big poker games involving thousands of dollars that started every Friday night and ended early Monday morning. But cash was taken away after the Cubans showed up. Anybody caught with cash was thrown in the hole. Any money we had was registered in an account at the commissary, and it was to be used for commissary purchases only.

Our "currency" was cigarettes and stamps. You can get just about anything in prison if you have those. I had no use for cigarettes, but I was happy to win a few cartons playing cards or betting on football. The Cubans got five free stamps a week, unlike the Americans, and I could trade them three 60-cent packs of cigarettes for $4.40 in stamps. I wrote more letters than Vanna White turns, so I hoarded stamps. Guys who neither mailed letters nor smoked could always trade for food or anything else of value.

I spent the rest of my first day in Atlanta getting acclimated. I discovered that of the three dormitories housing American inmates, mine was the only one that was air-conditioned. But it also was crowded, filthy and infested with cockroaches, spiders, mosquitoes, flies, rats and mice. As usual, I had been assigned an upper bunk, which put my face about two feet below the ceiling. The tile above my face had a hole in it, and I could just visualize 100,000 cockroaches pouring through that hole. I'd have had a heart attack.

The real horror story of our dormitory was the telephone situation. There was one phone for 78 inmates. And it didn't even stay on all day. The phone came on at 12:30 each afternoon and was supposed to stay on till about midnight, although it often was turned off at 10 p.m. This situation resulted in daily fights and verbal arguments and probably was more responsible for prisoner unrest than any other grievance. To keep guys from killing each other, a sign-up sheet was used. Each inmate could sign up for one 15-minute block of phone time every other day. Even the inmates who didn't use the phone would get a block so they could sell their time for food, cigarettes or whatever they could get.

That situation gave me some serious headaches. For me, the phone was medicinal. It helped take away the pain of being locked up. I couldn't even imagine not talking to Sharyn every day. I usually managed to squeeze in a call a day to her by using another guy's time when he didn't use his full 15-minute block, but not always. And that situation made it harder than hell to get in touch with Arnie, Mike Schwartz and other friends. Remember, they couldn't call me; I had to call them collect. If they weren't there when I called, I was out of luck until my next shot at the phone. Fortunately, Sharyn sent me an MCI card after a few weeks. That allowed me to call people direct and have the calls billed to our home phone. This was illegal because inmates are only supposed to make collect calls. But it saved the McLain family a lot of money.

My family came to visit my first weekend in Atlanta, which happened to be the weekend of Father's Day. Inmates were allowed to have visitors from Friday through Sunday and on holidays, and Sharyn and the kids stayed for the full three days. We were together in a big cafeteria-like room from 12:30 to 8 p.m. on Friday and from 8:30 a.m. to 3:30 p.m. on Saturday. We were supposed to have the same hours on Sunday, but our visit was cut off at 11:30 a.m. Without any warning, a guard just walked up and said, "The visit is terminated." The guard said the room was so crowded, somebody had to leave, and he nominated the McLains.

I was outraged, Sharyn was shocked and the kids felt as if they had done something wrong. The normal procedure in such cases was that the families that had traveled the farthest got preference over the families that lived in the immediate area. This guard evidently was just showing the new inmate who was boss. I complained to one of the dorm counselors, and that visiting day eventually was restored. But it sure put a damper on Father's Day to see my family leave four hours ahead of schedule.

Still, we had spent more time together than on any other occasion since the conviction. And it was time well spent. After they got over the initial shock of seeing me behind the walls of a facility that really looked like a penitentiary, we played dirty hearts, ate goodies from the commissary and talked. We talked a lot. One of the few positive things I can say about being imprisoned is that it forced us to deal with some family-oriented issues that we had never talked about before. We were thrown into a visiting room together for almost eight hours, and we had to talk about something. That's tough to do for three days in a row. Sit down with your family at the dinner table for four or five hours sometime and try keeping a conversation going. It's tough. But my being in prison really taught us how to do that. Now we can spend hours together just talking.

Inevitably, one of the things we talked about was money. With motel rooms, gas and food, it cost about $400 each time my family came to Atlanta. That was $400 they really didn't have to spend. Mike Schwartz often picked up the tab for the rooms. That was in addition to checks he sent Sharyn every month or so. Without his help, I don't know what Sharyn would have done.

Kristi, Denny and Tim already had jobs. Kristi was working in day care, Denny was doing surveying and a number of other jobs, and Tim was a caddie at Avila Golf and Country Club. They brought in enough money to buy groceries, but the rent and utilities were a continual problem. It looked as if Sharyn, who hadn't worked outside the home in more than 20 years, would have to get a job.

I was doing what I could to rustle up money. I managed to get an $8,000 advance on my baseball pension, which helped a lot. I was hoping that a book contract would be our gold mine, but that took months to arrange. Most of Sharyn's support came from Schwartz, a longtime friend named Harold Warren and her parents.

I finally had an income—a whopping 11 cents an hour. On June 24, I started my first job in the Big A—taking inventory on a warehouse for the kitchen. When I walked in, the warehouse looked like Hiroshima after the atom bomb. Boxes and supplies were scattered everywhere, and the room was filthy. It looked as if it hadn't been cleaned since Al Capone's days. My job was to clean the room and count everything in it.

The guards who supervised me said there was no hurry. These cops—also known as "hacks"—told me that this was one of the best jobs in Atlanta and I could do very well if I kept my mouth shut and my profile low. Well, keeping a low profile has always been a tall order for me, but I did my best. I didn't feel like ruffling any feathers. Not yet anyway. And besides, the inmates got paid for a 40-hour workweek regardless of how many hours we spent on the job. I was hauling in a king's ransom—about $19 a month. Unfortunately, I had no choice but to spend it all in one place.

That first morning, I went to work at 7:30 and spent much of my time talking to a cop named Pat Reams. Pat was from Detroit and was a super nice guy. He said he was working seven days a week at the prison while also working on his master's degree in nutrition. Sometimes he would fix me a big breakfast. He was planning to complete his studies and find work in his field. He said he hated his job, mainly because it was hard dealing with a few of the other cops, whose mentality levels hovered somewhere around their shoe size. Too many had trouble remembering that inmates are people, too, and should be treated as such.

After talking for almost two hours, I started cleaning up the warehouse. To my surprise, Reams pitched in and helped. There we were, convict and cop, working side by side. I couldn't believe it. Later, he and the other cop, Roger Colley, brought me some watermelon. In addition to my 11 cents an hour, I got all the watermelon and cantaloupe I could eat.

That taught me a lot about cops. For the most part, they were good guys. There were some bad apples, and the Big A had more than its share. But most cops were just ordinary guys doing a thankless job in order to feed their families or put themselves through school. I have all the respect in the world for guys who are working to make ends meet. The real bad guys were a group called the TDY, short for temporary duty cops. They were cops from other institutions who were sent to Atlanta to help keep order. They would come in like storm troopers and just look for trouble. They succeeded in making life miserable for everybody.

I could have finished this warehouse job in a day or two, but Reams told me to drag it out as long as I wanted. I worked till about 10 a.m. each day, then spent the rest of the afternoon tackling a more ambitious project—fielding a baseball team.

When I first arrived, Frank Cocchiaro told me that I could manage the prison's baseball team, the Cardinals. After all, I was the only former major leaguer in the Big A. That sounded like fun.

Well, politics exist in the slammer, just like anywhere else. The guys running the Cardinals told me they didn't want any outside interference. I don't know how a fellow convict could be considered outside interference, but the message was clear: Get lost.

So much for my managerial career.

But one day a guy named Juan came to me and said he knew about 10 guys who wanted to form their own team to take on the Cardinals. Would I be the manager? I loved the idea. Baseball talent was in low supply in the Big A, but I figured we could come up with a team at least as good as the Cardinals. I even said I'd pitch.

That was a mistake. I quickly learned that pitching isn't quite like riding a bicycle. You can't just pick up a baseball after 12 years and throw it like you used to—especially when you're 41 years old and weigh 275 pounds. We practiced every day for about two weeks, and my arm felt like it was going to fall off. I had to get a pain-killing shot just to make it out to the mound for the big game.

It was scheduled for July 6, but I got a reprieve. It was rained out. The game was rescheduled for July 14, which gave me a chance to recuperate and gave my players more time to practice. We sure as hell needed it. My players, most of whom were my age or older, had all the desire and intensity in the world, but only four or five had any real talent. If I couldn't pitch, we were in trouble.

The game was played on one of two diamonds in "the yard," the prison's big recreational area. The yard also had an elaborate weight-lifting area, an oval track, a dozen tennis courts and about half as many racquetball courts. All the equipment for the baseball teams and other sports was provided, including double-knit Cardinal uniforms that looked just like the ones the big boys wear. This equipment, of course, was top-notch, courtesy of the American taxpayers. My players had named our team the Detroit Dennys, so I tried to get some Tiger hats for them. But the prison officials wouldn't put my request through. That was their way of reminding me that I was just another convict.

The prison's athletic facilities really weren't bad, although I didn't make much use of them. I stayed indoors a lot just so I wouldn't have to look at that monstrous wall. Even after living there a few weeks, it still was unbelievably intimidating.

A big crowd was on hand to see Denny McLain make his first pitching start since 1974, when I hurled a couple of games for that semipro team in Ontario. No reporters were there, but only because the prison administration turned down the numerous requests for permission to cover it. I heard that all three major networks and a couple of the cable networks, not to mention lots of newspapermen, wanted to record this momentous encounter between the Cardinals and the Detroit Dennys.

It was absurd that anybody would find this game newsworthy. But it was just as ridiculous that the prison kept the media out. What a perfect PR gimmick! The warden could talk proudly about how the inmates were staying active, not just wasting away behind bars. That wasn't the truth of the matter, but the networks weren't interested in a segment on prison reform. They just wanted to show the major leagues' last 30-game winner pitching in this unusual setting. Not too many positive stories came out of the Big A, and the administration was turning down a rare opportunity.

I think the powers that be were making every effort to keep from showing me any favoritism. They wanted everybody to understand that I was no better than any other inmate. And since no other inmate commanded the kind of attention that I drew, they tried to screen it out. Well, I could have told them that the publicity was inevitable. I'd been trying to dodge the press for years, but it was a losing battle.

As it turned out, I was glad we played without fanfare. It wasn't a pretty sight. I gave up a three-run homer in the first inning, but recovered to strike out six batters in the next three innings, all on fastballs, one of which broke my catcher's thumb. I left the mound with the game tied, 4-4, in the sixth. I played shortstop the rest of the game, which we ended up losing, 25-5. I went 3 for 3 with two walks, and one of my hits bounced off the left-field wall. But all I could think about after the game was my arm. It hurt so bad, I couldn't raise my hand. And then I slipped in the shower and hurt my back. By the time I went to bed, even my eyebrows hurt. I was feeling more pain than I ever experienced in my career, and my next five days were spent in bed and in the hot showers, trying to work the kinks out of my body.

But the most painful experience was probably the one I avoided—by the skin of my teeth. Everybody was betting on the game and I couldn't resist getting in on the action. Two guys I knew were absolutely convinced that the Cardinals would take us apart, Denny McLain or no Denny McLain. I was convinced that a two-time Cy Young winner could handle a bunch of ragtag convicts. The talk got out of hand and we settled on a $3,000 wager. Fortunately, the two guys backed out at the last minute, and I was glad they did. At that point I would have killed for $3,000, and vice versa.

After that fiasco, I knew it was time to quit pitching. I decided to devote my free time to working on my appeal. For the next several months, I spent at least three or four hours a day reading case law.

The Big A had a terrific law library. It was up to date with all the books that provide ammo for an appeal, plus it had electric typewriters and a copy machine. At first it took me forever to find cases worth noting. It would take me a week to read through 30 cases. But I moved a lot faster—say, 30 cases in about two hours—after a little Jamaican attorney taught me how to Shepardize cases. The Shepard's index provides a cross-reference of cases that have some bearing on the one in question, so if I found one case that applied to me, Shepard's would lead me to more. It was a real timesaver.

While learning a lot about the law, I also was becoming increasingly aware of the tragic situation involving Cubans in the Big A—a situation that led to a massive riot in 1987.

Though the Big A's population was more than 80 percent Cuban, I didn't see many of them. They lived in different buildings and were rarely let out of their cells. A few dozen Cubans were allowed to work in the mess hall kitchen or Unicor, the prison manufacturing center that made brooms, gloves, mailbags and other items for federal government use. But most of them were confined to their cells.

I got a kick out of the Cubans I did run across early on. Baseball is very popular in Cuba, and most of these guys seemed to have heard of me. I'd walk by and hear them say, "There goes Deeny McLain." But there was nothing funny about the way Cubans were treated in the Big A.

Their nightmare began in April 1980, when President Jimmy Carter opened the doors of the United States to any Cuban wanting to flee the dictatorship of

President Fidel Castro. Almost 125,000 Cubans took him up on that offer, leaving by boat from the Cuban port of Mariel in what became known as the "freedom flotilla." Their dream was a life of freedom in America, and I think Carter showed courage and compassion in letting them pursue that dream.

The vast majority of Cubans seeking asylum have blended into American society. But U.S. immigration officials discovered too late that Castro was emptying his prisons and shipping off criminals and mental patients to the American shore. They were detained immediately upon arriving in the United States and sent to the Big A, which became the holding tank for all these undesirables. Congress had ordered the Big A closed in 1980 because it was so outdated and dilapidated, but when the Cubans arrived, it had to be kept open. Since the Big A was an "administrative facility" with no specific security-level classification—it could handle drunk drivers and armed robbers alike—it was convenient to put the Cubans there. But only temporarily, it was hoped. The United States wanted to deport the undesirables, but Castro refused to take them.

The number of Cubans in Atlanta grew rapidly as they ran afoul of the law. Any time a Mariel Cuban was convicted on a criminal charge, no matter how minor, he was sent to a federal prison, usually the Big A, after serving his state sentence. Some were there because of traffic citations. Like the 600 or so hardened criminals and mental patients awaiting deportation, these guys were detained indefinitely.

That was the crux of the problem. The Cubans were in limbo. They had no idea when, if ever, they would be deported or set free. They feared deportation more than anything because they figured they'd be tortured and persecuted in Cuba. But their future in the United States was almost as dismal. Even though they already had done their time for crimes as minor as shoplifting and disturbing the peace, they were in federal custody for the rest of their lives—as far as they knew. In the land of the free and the home of the brave, where immigrants are welcomed with open arms, unsentenced men were imprisoned indefinitely. It reminded me of the detention of Japanese-Americans in World War II, another episode most Americans would like to forget.

In October 1984, after many of the Cubans had been detained more than four years, the natives started getting restless. They could see that their jailers were in no hurry to do anything with them, despite the fact that they were costing U.S. taxpayers more than $30 million a year. One day about 50 Cubans organized peacefully in the yard and held up two bed sheets with the word "freedom" written on them. They marched peacefully into the main corridor of the prison, where guards told them to stay put. The cops returned with riot gear, told the demonstrators to line up against the wall, handcuffed them and took them to the hole. That night the entire prison was locked down. No one, including the American inmates, could leave his cell.

The lock-down of the Americans ended after two days, but the Cubans remained confined 24 hours a day. In addition, prison officials started taking away all of their personal property—family photographs, books, Bibles, clothes, you name it. Virtually everything they owned was swept into piles and dumped into trash bags. A few items were recovered later, but most were destroyed. The water in their cells also was turned off much of the day, making the use of toilets and sinks impossible. The Cubans were even deprived of toilet paper. They were left to live in their own filth for at least 10 days, when the administration started letting a few Cubans out of their cells.

The Cubans had demonstrated peacefully and the result was a lock-down, the destruction of their only reminders of freedom and physical degradation. Now they were in an ugly mood.

On November 1, about 500 Cubans rioted in cellhouse B. The riot started when guards used tear gas in an attempt to disperse a group that had formed around a Cuban who was being taken to the hole. The Cubans set fires, smashed windows and tore apart anything they could reach. No one was seriously hurt, but after eight hours of rioting, they did more than $1 million of damage.

The administration promptly locked down the entire Cuban population. When I arrived in Atlanta in June 1985, they were still locked down. Some Cubans were freed from their cells over the next few months, but not many. And in January 1986, when a jury acquitted the two men accused of inciting the riot, jurors said that in addition to finding the men not guilty, they were "ashamed of our government" for the way the Cubans were being treated. Ironically, I saw those two Cubans months later when I spent time in the hole at Talladega.

Robert W. Kastenmeier reached the same conclusion about the Cubans' plight three weeks later. Kastenmeier was a U.S. representative from Wisconsin and the chairman of the House subcommittee on courts, civil liberties and the administration of justice. He inspected the Big A in February 1986, and even though the administration had spent days feverishly cleaning up the place, he found the Cubans' plight absolutely deplorable.

Kastenmeier was appalled. In a report describing the problem and listing various solutions, he detailed how the Cubans were locked for 23 hours a day in 10-by-21 cells housing eight men each. He discussed how they suffered from lack of exercise, lousy and unsanitary food, poor medical care, limited access to showers and items of personal hygiene and a complete lack of privacy.

"The current living situation for Cuban inmates at the Atlanta federal penitentiary is intolerable considering even the most minimal correctional standards," he wrote. "These detainees—who are virtually without legal rights— are worse off than virtually all other federal sentenced inmates. They are required to live in conditions which are brutal and inhumane. They are confined without any practical hope of ever being released."

Small wonder they rioted. The hopeless predicament they found themselves in had created an explosive situation that made violence inevitable. Kastenmeier reported that in the five years preceding his visit there had been nine murders, seven suicides, 158 serious suicide attempts, 2,000 serious incidents of self-mutilation, 4,000 other incidents of self-mutilation and a monthly average of 15 inmate-on-inmate assaults. These guys were slashing themselves and each other with knives out of sheer frustration.

Believe me, it happened. While I was in Atlanta, numerous Cubans were stabbed by other Cubans and at least three were killed. One guy named Lazaro Calero-Ramos was murdered while being led to the shower with his hands cuffed behind his back. Calero-Ramos had been having trouble with another

Cuban and tried to kill himself a couple of times. On February 17, 1986, somebody did the job for him. He was between his cell and the shower when the guy he feared came at him with a homemade knife. Only one cop was with Calero-Ramos at the time—there were supposed to be two—and he ran away. The cop eventually returned, but not until Calero-Ramos had been stabbed 10 times. Ironically, his suspected murderer was killed a year later while in the custody of several guards. He, too, was handcuffed behind his back, but he died by strangulation.

This violence, an almost daily occurrence, was pretty much isolated among the Cubans. They were hurting each other, themselves and the cops. But as more and more Cubans were released into the general population, the greater the threat of injury to the Americans. The Cubans were desperate, and the dumbest thing anybody could do was tangle with them. They were in the worst possible situation imaginable, so they had nothing to lose by fighting. And they were among the most ingenious people I've ever seen. They could make a knife out of butter if nothing else was available. I felt sorry for the Cubans because they were treated like garbage, but I was afraid of them, too.

The entire situation was stupid as well as tragic. By mixing hundreds of non-violent men with a bunch of hoods, stripping all of them of their rights and dignity and then reducing their hopes of freedom to almost zilch, the United States was creating a time bomb.

I could feel the tension building the whole time I lived in the Big A. I expected another riot to break out any time. And it finally did on November 23, 1987, when the Cubans responded to a new U.S.-Cuban agreement that called for the return of 2,500 detainees to their homeland. Many of these Cubans already had been approved for release, so they had reason to be upset. They took 89 hostages and held control of the prison for 12 days. Fire destroyed three buildings, and one inmate was killed early in the uprising. Several more were injured. Fortunately, I was a free man working in Indiana when I read about it in the newspaper.

The Cubans, many of whom were in their eighth year of captivity, finally surrendered after a pact was reached. The agreement promised amnesty for most activities during the riot, case-by-case reviews of the inmates' immigration status and parole for those who were found not to be dangerous to society. Many of the more hostile Cubans were transferred to Talladega, where they remain under lock-down.

Funny, the whole mess could have been avoided if anybody had listened to a certain federal judge who had his head on straight. Even before I was sent to Atlanta, U.S. District Judge Marvin Shoob tried to help the Cuban inmates. Shoob pointed out that the United States was kidding itself if it thought Cuba would ever accept these people back. Castro didn't want them. They were Uncle Sam's problem, and Shoob said imprisoning them indefinitely was wrong. That kind of injustice takes place in other countries, but it's not supposed to happen here. For a nation that prides itself on its support of human rights, we were way off-base with the Cubans.

Shoob proposed a case-by-case review of each inmate's status. While the hardened criminals had no business walking the streets of this country, he said, most of the Cubans presented no threat to society. If they were a threat, then the government should have to prove it in court. Otherwise, they deserved to be free. And the terrible overcrowding problem in the federal prisons, particularly Atlanta, could be eased tremendously.

Makes sense, doesn't it? But the 11th Circuit Court of Appeals repeatedly shot down Shoob's rulings. The appellate court insisted that the Cubans had no Constitutional rights, even though President Carter had invited them to this country. One of the three judges on the panel, Robert S. Vance, told a lawyer representing the Cubans in a class-action suit that "the government can keep them in the Atlanta pen until they die."

I'm sure that was what our Founding Fathers had in mind when they drafted the Constitution.

I was glad that Kastenmeier came to the prison and made known the Cubans' problems. But the scary thing was, he didn't even see the worst of it.

Like the hunger strikes. One time there were as many as 300 Cubans refusing to eat for days on end, hoping to bring attention to their plight. They would rather starve to death than live like animals. But inmates starving themselves make a prison look bad, so the administration responded by force-feeding the Cubans. The cops cuffed a guy to a hospital bed, hands to the top and feet to the bottom, and held his arm still while someone shoved a needle in it to feed him intravenously. Less fortunate guys got fed through tubes in their noses. Milk was poured through the tubes, which were oversized and gave the Cubans bloody noses. Their blood mixed with the milk and drained into their stomachs. Some guys almost drowned in their own blood.

The Cubans tried to resist the force-feeding, but they were defenseless against the cops, who were not averse to throwing them against a wall or knocking them around. It was hard to believe that the Cubans put up with all this abuse just to make a point, but I saw them being led up to the hospital right above my dormitory for force-feedings time and again. In fact, the hunger strikers eventually had to be moved to segregation, presumably so the manhandling wouldn't be so obvious.

I can't blame the cops for getting rough now and then. Attacks on guards were both numerous and serious, and they had to defend themselves. It probably got old being pelted by excrement and urine tossed from the Cubans' cells. But some of those attacks were guard-provoked. And to beat the hell out of them while they were handcuffed? I believe in a fair fight, and all the cards were stacked against the Cubans.

I saw Cubans get locked to their beds for long periods of time, including one guy for three days. Three times a day a cop would unlock one arm so he could eat. I saw cops throw water on these guys so they would get sick and vomit on themselves. And since they were immobile, they had no choice but to lie in their own waste. This treatment of the Cubans was the most revolting thing I've ever seen.

Cubans weren't the only people mistreated in the hospital. So were the Americans. Nobody hurt us intentionally, but our medical care was a farce.

Shortly after arriving in Atlanta, I developed a severe numbness in my right leg that extended from my kneecap up close to my hip. I went to the doctor, who told me not to worry; a neurosurgeon would be dropping by the prison in eight to 10 weeks and he could run some tests then. Hey, no hurry! Take your time! If my leg rotted away, what difference did that make? I was just a convict.

The doctor wasn't kidding, either. It took at least 10 weeks to see the neurosurgeon. And when I hurt my back, I waited several weeks before getting to see an orthopedist. While waiting on specialists, I survived by eating Tylenol like raisins.

A lot of guys had it worse than I did. A guy named Chuckie, one of my roommates, suffered a stroke in January 1985 and was promised that he would be examined by a cardiologist every two or three weeks. It was June before he saw one. An X-ray revealed that another roommate, J.C., had a growth the size of a baseball in his chest, and he waited about five months before anyone did a biopsy. The poor guy had cancer and was dropping weight faster than Elizabeth Taylor, but nobody was in a hurry to look at him.

Locking up guys in filthy, cockroach-infested cells was bad enough, but denying us proper medical care was atrocious. We didn't volunteer to live in the can. We were forced to be there. That being the case, it was Uncle Sam's responsibility to take care of us. He didn't.

On the lighter side, I once saw a guy get terrific treatment for an imaginary ailment. This kid decided he wanted a few days off work, so he went to the doctor. He must have been convincing because when he came back, he had a full cast on his right leg. There wasn't a thing wrong with him. I think the doctor just enjoyed putting on casts. If my leg had been broken, I guess I would've gotten better service.

When I first got that numbness in my leg, I asked to be moved to a lower bunk. As heavy as I was and with a bum leg, it was hard climbing up there. And there just wasn't enough space in that room to stand around. If I was in the room, I had to be in bed.

In prison, even a simple request can be turned into a major hassle. One cop said he couldn't get me a lower bunk without a doctor's excuse. I told him I already had a doctor's excuse, and he told me to get another one. I finally went to a counselor in my dorm, who took care of the problem and blistered the guy's ears for a while.

This guy was just plain bad news. He was one of those cops who enjoyed giving the inmates trouble and acting like somebody important. He once refused to let me go to the law library on a day when it was open. I had a work idle because of my back, and he said that made me ineligible for use of the library. That was bull. I asked to see the policy statement that said that, and he couldn't find it. Nobody could. He also liked to go through my locker and take my potato chips and Cokes. I guess stealing is OK if you're doing it from convicts.

This hack was bad, but there was another guy who was worse. In fact, this guy was probably the most hateful person I ever had to deal with in the federal penal system.

He was a case manager, and that automatically put him in a position to cause trouble. There were three levels of authority in a dorm, and a case manager was in the middle. First there were the counselors, who were there to handle your everyday, nickel-and-dime requests like getting moved to a different bunk or acquiring stamps. Then came the case managers, who were in charge of the legal files. If you had any problems working on your appeal, parole or anything like that, you went to your case manager. Overseeing the counselors and case managers was a unit manager, who supervised the whole dorm.

It took all of 30 seconds to get a clear picture of this clown. The first thing he ever said to me was: "You might as well sit down and enjoy yourself. You're going to be here a long, fucking time. You're in the stupidest place in America, so that has to say something about you."

Nice to meet you, too! I replied that the difference between me and him was that he chose to be in this pigsty, and that said more about his character than mine. After that, we spoke only when absolutely necessary.

About the only times we talked were when he called me into his office to bitch about something. I was getting a lot of requests for interviews, and he told me I was making too many waves. I can't even swim, but I've always managed to make a few waves wherever I've been. He didn't like that.

What really irked me was that I'm not a hard guy to get along with. I had nothing against the cops, counselors, case managers or anybody else. They were just doing their jobs. And I certainly didn't expect the red-carpet treatment from anybody. I just wanted a little respect, which I would give them in return. It was a two-way street. But this guy was unhappy with me because I wouldn't kiss his ass or stay out of sight.

Case managers were there to help the inmates, but he made it clear to me that he didn't want to hear any requests. It seemed to me that he never did a thing to help anybody and even went out of his way to make things miserable for guys who already had enough misery in their lives.

I guess I shouldn't have expected much from the guy. You know what he did before becoming a case manager? He was a locksmith. Terrific credentials, huh?

A few other guys gave me problems now and then, but it was usually over something trivial. One day I went to the hospital to get a work idle approval, but the physician's assistant on duty refused to get it from my file. He told me that if I wanted the idle bad enough, I'd have to see the doctor himself. Some of the physician's assistants actually thought they were doctors. When I went over his head and got the doctor involved, the PA got mad, called one of the kitchen employees for whom I was now working and told her to give me a hard time. Pat Reams finally straightened out that mess.

Petty little annoyances like that did nothing to help rehabilitate inmates and made no sense. Instead of aggravating us for no good reason, why not be nice? A little trust, understanding and cooperation could go a long way toward helping inmates become decent members of society again. By insulting, harassing and degrading us, prison workers were just breeding contempt for the system. That result is 180 degrees away from the government's supposed goal of rehabilitation.

Fortunately, there also were a lot of nice guys in the system. And my morale got a big boost when a guy named Hill, the assistant kitchen manager, offered me a new job. He wanted me to set up and staff a diabetic food line.

Now you're talking! It meant a lot to have somebody show some faith in me and put me in charge of something. And being able to run a food line meant one thing for certain: I was going to start eating right. The food in Atlanta was awful—I can't even guess how many times we were fed rice, beans and some unidentifiable piece of bulletproof meat—but cooking it myself was a heart-warming thought.

The stuff that went on in the kitchen was disgusting. The Cubans thought a great way to get back at the system was to defile it. I saw them shit in the freezer and urinate in the food. They also dropped rats and mice in the food. Guys would stick a spoon in their bowl of soup and scoop up a dead mouse. The Cubans thought that was hilarious. They didn't mess with their own food —just ours. Some days I would tell everybody not to even bother eating because all of our food had been messed with.

Sanitation obviously wasn't a big priority in the kitchen. Two gay Cubans iced cakes and mixed the jam and butter every day with their bare hands. Neither one wore gloves. It made me sick to think where their hands had been before they came to work. I even saw one of them take off his shoes and mash tuna salad in a huge bin with his feet. He looked like he was stomping grapes. The guys who fixed salads didn't wear gloves, either. They didn't even wash the produce. They just sliced the lettuce, tomatoes and carrots and tossed them in a bowl. One day a rat was spotted running across a table before the lunch meal. It scurried across the potatoes, corn and bread before disappearing from sight near a pot of piping-hot gravy. The gravy was served for lunch—until the rat was found at the bottom. The rodent had been scalded to death.

Needless to say, I ate as many meals in my room as I could. It wasn't that hard to sneak bread, meat and fruit out of the kitchen and into the dorm. Occasionally, a couple of the cops would actually escort me to the dorm with bags of groceries. Most of the cops didn't care. They just helped themselves to the food, too.

The mess hall became a much more popular place after I created the diabetic line in August 1985. This line was designed for people on special diets and included a menu of hard-boiled eggs, toast, cereal and fruit for breakfast and rice, hamburgers, baked fish and fried foods for lunch. I didn't handle dinner. The food was always good for those meals. I made sure the Cubans didn't mess with it.

The only meal I actually prepared personally was breakfast. Working in three-day shifts, I got up before 4 a.m. and went to the kitchen. I cooked the food, helped serve it and supervised everything connected with the preparation of that meal. By 9 a.m. I was usually back in my dorm, through working for the day. I also scheduled guys to handle the lunch line and the breakfast line on mornings I didn't have to get up myself. If they didn't show up, it was my job to get everybody's rears in gear.

The hours were good, but the food was phenomenal. At least compared to what we'd been getting. I cooked a mean breakfast, and I made sure the cooks on the other shifts did a good job, too. I also was able to munch on doughnuts and drink milk while working and then sneak a bunch of groceries back into the dorm. So much for losing more weight.

Besides the food, the filthy living conditions and the treatment of the Cubans, my biggest gripes with the Big A were the phone and mail situations.

The mail room was slow. Some letters would have arrived quicker if the sender had walked to Atlanta and delivered them personally. I couldn't count the number of times that I went more than a week without getting a thing and then 10 pieces of mail would arrive on one day. The guys in the mail room seemed to enjoy hoarding the mail. They had to read it first, of course, because everything except legal mail was inspected before being delivered. And some of my legal mail was opened, too, which really irritated me. That was a flagrant violation of the rules. I raised hell about it, but it didn't do any good.

Slow mail service often caused delays in legal proceedings as well as problems at home. Not everybody used the phone like I did, and these families depended on efficient mail service. Say an inmate's wife has a problem at home and writes her husband a letter, hoping it gets to him in a day or two. It takes a week. When the wife doesn't get a quick response, she thinks her husband doesn't care. Communication starts to break down, fights develop and before you know it, the guy gets papers in the mail informing him that his wife is filing for divorce. Things like that happened all the time. I don't have any figures, but the divorce rate among convicts must be phenomenal.

The BOP claims to support the idea of keeping inmates' families together, but its actions indicate otherwise. First a guy is moved hundreds of miles away from his family so visits are difficult or impossible. Then his mail gets read and delayed. On top of that, the use of the phone is a nightmare. How is a convict supposed to keep the lines of communication open? Under those circumstances, the family structure is bound to fall apart.

Prison officials were constantly messing with the phone. As if it wasn't enough to monitor and record our personal calls, they seemed to get a big kick out of shutting it off early and making it as difficult as possible to call anybody. Phone use was limited to five days a week for a while, and I even heard rumors about inmates being allowed only one call per month. That would've been cruel.

The whole idea of telling grown men when they could use the phone was absurd. We were treated like children. But I made the best of the situation by grabbing as much phone time as possible. I always kept an eye open for the phone being available, and when it was, I jumped on it. That proved to be a bad move on one occasion.

On Friday night of the week I started the diabetic line, I noticed the phone on the hook. A guy named Joe Marrow, who also had been represented by Arnie Levine, had signed up for the 15-minute block from 7:45 to 8 p.m., and I had it from 8 to 8:15. Well, Marrow didn't show up at 7:45 because he was running the projector for a movie that ran long, so I grabbed the phone. It was fair game if a guy missed his starting time, and I was looking at almost 30 consecutive minutes of uninterrupted phone use. Or so I thought.

At 7:55, I was chatting with Sharyn when Marrow came by.

"Hey, motherfucker, you're on my telephone time," he said.

"I am not on anybody's phone time," I said, "and I am not a motherfucker. Don't talk to me like that."

Marrow, who looked to be about 55 years old, supposedly was a gopher for organized crime. He thought he was pretty tough. He proceeded to drill me with about a dozen profanities, which made it difficult to continue my conversation with Sharyn.

"Go fuck yourself," I shouted.

"Fuck you, you fat cocksucker," he yelled back and then walked away. So much for Joe Marrow. I turned my back and started talking to Sharyn again. A few seconds later I was on the floor and blood was everywhere.

My blood.

Marrow had whacked me over the head with a 25-pound fire extinguisher. A couple of guys who saw what happened said he took the fire extinguisher off the wall, lifted it over his head and slammed it down on me. Had it not glanced off one of the partitions on either side of the phone, my skull would have been crushed.

I picked myself off the floor as Marrow ran away. I grabbed the phone and heard Sharyn screaming, "What happened?"

"Honey, I'll have to call you back in a couple of minutes. Everything is all right."

"Are you hurt?"

"No, not really. I'll call you back."

Actually, I was hurt. I was dizzy and my head was throbbing. I put my hand up there and it was drenched with blood. I walked over to Doc, one of my roommates, and asked him to take a look. He said there were two gashes in my head, one about four inches long and the other about three inches. I went to my room, got a towel, filled it with ice and applied it to the wounds. It was still bleeding like crazy about an hour later when I decided I'd better call Sharyn and tell her what had happened. She had been terrified waiting all that time, of course, and she was still crying when I had to get off the phone a few minutes later.

I went through four towels before the bleeding finally stopped. I didn't want to go to the hospital because that meant Marrow would get locked up, and I didn't believe in snitching. I had every intention of getting even, but not that way. I just cleaned myself up, took a bunch of Tylenol and started playing cards. By the time I went to bed at 2:30 a.m., my headache was almost gone.

Frank Cocchiaro was furious the next morning when he heard about the attack. He summoned Marrow to our breakfast table and ate his ass out. Seeing that Frank was on my side, Marrow suddenly wasn't so brave anymore —if it takes any courage to blind-side a guy with a fire extinguisher. He apologized a hundred different ways and asked me over and over again if I was going to forget about it. The only thing I said was that I wouldn't go to the cops. And I didn't. I had another form of vengeance in mind.

A few days later, Frank set Marrow up for me. He told me that Marrow would be in the weight room at 7 p.m., and if I had any business I wanted to take care of, that would be a good time. I went there at 7, and Marrow was waiting for me, all by himself.

"Hey, we need to talk," I said.

"Look, I'm sorry, Denny," he said. "I didn't mean it."

"You didn't mean it? You almost fucking killed me!"

"Well, if you don't accept apologies, fuck you."

For the second time in three months, I punched a guy. I just reached back and socked him in the face. But this time the guy fell down. One punch and Marrow was lying on the floor. He started to get up.

"If you get up," I said, "I'm going to hurt you. That's all I'm going to tell you, Joe. If you get up, I'll hurt you. I'll hurt you bad."

He didn't get up. And it was a good thing. I was serious about hurting him. But he remained on the floor, a beaten man. That was how I got even with Joe Marrow.

It amazed me that I almost got killed because a guy wanted to use the phone. It was so petty. But that's how it is in prison. When you take away a man's freedom and dignity he doesn't have much left, and what little he has suddenly becomes worth fighting for. Or it seems worth it. I saw Doc, a little nerd who made Pee Wee Herman look tough, get beat to a pulp once because he changed the TV channel. No way you can justify that.

Sharyn and the kids had planned to visit the weekend after my brush with death, but they couldn't afford it. And with school starting soon, Denny and Tim couldn't work full-time anymore. That put Sharyn under a lot of pressure to find a job.

The pressure was really starting to get to her. Being broke was the main problem, but she also was beginning to realize that my appeal would be a slow process and it would be some time before I had any chance of getting out. She got very depressed and suffered some severe migraine headaches. That made it even more difficult to look for work, and she already was nervous enough about that.

I fully understood her apprehension. After we got married, she devoted herself to being a full-time wife and mother. That was what she wanted to do, and she did it very well. She had no intention of working outside the home anymore. Then all of a sudden, she was faced with the prospect of reentering the work force after more than 20 years. That would be scary for anybody. And for the wife of the Tampa area's most famous jailbird, it was terrifying. It embarrassed her to be recognized as my wife because she had no idea how people would react. Job-hunting meant she would be meeting a lot of strangers who would ask questions, and even though she had nothing to be ashamed of, she felt stigmatized, like the words "convict's wife" were tattooed on her forehead. She just wanted to keep a low profile.

Sharyn did have a couple of jobs while I was in the can, but neither lasted very long. She worked at the University of South Florida on a temporary basis when help was needed, but nothing long-term ever worked out. She had enough on her mind trying to cope with five kids and a husband in prison. I tried not to press her on the subject of employment.

With a book and possibly a movie deal in the works, I still was hoping that I'd strike oil. But until I did, my wife and kids were eating spaghetti, some nights without sauce, and macaroni and cheese almost every night. And without the regular generosity of Sharyn's parents, Mike Schwartz, Harold Warren and others, they wouldn't have had a roof over their heads. I was lucky that most of my friends never deserted me.

I may sound like a leech for accepting all these gifts and loans, but my friends wouldn't call me that. There have been plenty of other times when the tables were turned and I was the one signing checks. I'm a firm believer in the saying "What goes around, comes around." It all balances out in the end.

There was a long dry spell after my family's third visit to Atlanta in late July. Except for one visit at the end of October, I didn't see all of them again until after Christmas. In the meantime, I did whatever I could to get out of the Big A—not just because it was a pigsty and one of the most violent prisons in the country, but also to be closer to my family. I tried to get transferred to Tallahassee.

That trail led me to Herbert Shafer, an Atlanta attorney who was good friends with the prison warden, Jack Hanberry. Shafer had even represented the warden in a criminal case. In 1981, four years after he became warden, Hanberry had been arrested for shoplifting a $1.10 hairbrush from a local Kroger supermarket. Shafer was able to get Hanberry, an ordained Baptist minister, acquitted of the charge. The word on the grapevine was that for $5,000, Shafer could put his influence with the warden to good use and arrange a transfer anywhere.

The weekend I met Shafer was a busy one. Sharyn came up by herself on September 13, which happened to be a very lucky Friday the 13th. We spent 6½ hours together just talking, holding each other and watching the soaps on TV. It was a great day. Then we spent several hours together the next day before she headed back to Tampa.

Sharyn and I also met Shafer that Saturday. Ironically, he was a big fan of Sharyn's dad. He said he thought Lou Boudreau and Ray Mack formed the best double-play combination he'd ever seen. It was nice to get the conversation off to a good start. I figured that maybe my baseball ties would earn me a discount.

Not hardly.

"What'll it cost me to get to Tallahassee?" I asked Shafer in the visiting room.

"For everybody else it's five grand," he said. "All these guys are low profile, so that's all it takes. But you pose more of a problem."

"How much more?"

"For you it'll cost $10,000. Pay that and you should be in Tallahassee within 60 days."

"Ten grand? That's ridiculous!"

"Well, that's it. Take it or leave it."

Shafer made it quite clear that the warden would be in on the deal. He said Hanberry had plenty of contacts in Washington, D.C., and all the good Reverend had to do was pick up the phone and the transfer would be approved. Hanberry would be retiring sometime in the next couple of years, Shafer said, and the $10,000 would be part of a little retirement fund.

I told Shafer that Sharyn and I had to talk it over before I could get back to him, although I didn't really think a deal was possible. Five grand would be hard enough to scrape up, but 10 seemed out of the question, especially with my family barely getting by. It meant a lot to all of us to be closer together, but the price was too stiff.

I didn't junk the idea entirely. Over the next few weeks I kept in touch with Shafer, who said the warden would approve a transfer as soon as I came up with the dough. But that day wasn't coming anytime soon.

In early October I was visited by an attorney who was helping Frank Cocchiaro with some post-conviction work. I had been talking to her about a number of matters, particularly the phone situation. She was a bright, energetic woman who was outraged by what was happening in the Big A. She seemed like a fighter who could help change a few things around that pigsty.

While we were talking, I mentioned the deal Shafer was offering. Her eyes perked up.

"They've been trying to get this guy for a long time," she said. "Everybody knows he takes extortion to move guys, but no one has come forward yet."

She paused. "Would you talk to the FBI?"

"I don't think so," I replied. "I didn't mind working with the FBI outside the walls, but in here is a different story. You can get hurt doing something like that."

"Well, nobody has to know. . . ."

"No way. Forget it. I'm not interested."

The attorney came back a few days later and brought a friend. She said this woman was from her office. This new woman immediately started asking me about the Shafer thing—had I contacted him recently, would I talk to him again soon and so on. I said I still was dealing with Shafer and told her everything that had happened so far.

After spilling my guts, I got a surprise. "She is from the FBI," the attorney said.

"You've got to be kidding," I responded.

"I'm afraid not."

"Well, terrific. I've just told you everything and now when I walk out of this room, somebody is going to whack me because they recognized her as an FBI agent."

"No they won't," the agent said. "I haven't put anybody in this institution. I just came to Atlanta a month ago."

"So what?" I asked. "How do you know that one of the people that you nailed in New York or Ohio or wherever the hell you're from, isn't in here?"

"I'm almost positive," she said.

"Almost isn't good enough."

I was scared, but the damage had already been done. Even if I cut off the conversation right there, somebody might believe that I was doing business with the cops. I might as well see what their game plan was.

"What do you want from me?" I asked.

"We want to nail Shafer and Hanberry," the agent said. "You can do it for us. We want to wire you. We want you to set up another meeting with Shafer and we'll get him. We'll get them both."

One other thing: The agent said that if I cooperated, she'd get me transferred to a camp somewhere. Now she was talking. I decided to go along for the ride.

Sharyn was visited in Tampa by a couple of FBI agents a few days later. These two men apparently had the bright idea that Sharyn needed to wear a wire, too. They said it would be too tricky to sneak a wire inside the prison, so they thought the best plan was to give Sharyn $10,000, have her set up a meeting with Shafer and then record the actual transaction. The feds would then step in and nab him.

That plan didn't suit me at all. I could just see word leaking out that Sharyn was helping the FBI and either Shafer or Hanberry calling some ex-con to do them a favor. Sharyn's life could be in danger. She was willing to help, but I vetoed it.

With Sharyn working as an intermediary, I kept in contact with the FBI agent and the attorney over the next few months. We tried to work out a plan whereby I could get a wire and nail Shafer right there in the prison visiting room. But nothing ever came of that scheme and Shafer never was charged with any wrongdoing, despite the fact that two inmates signed affidavits in which they accused him of offering to arrange transfers for a fee. Another dozen or so inmates, both Cuban and American, said the same thing in interviews. When questioned by reporters, Shafer vehemently denied the allegations.

I was sorry to see that possible avenue out of Atlanta hit a dead end, but I hadn't been comfortable working with the FBI anyway. Word started getting around that I supposedly was a snitch, and one guy actually came to my room to fight with me. Thank God he was drunk. I managed to knock him down and I threatened him with a chair. He later apologized to me.

It finally became obvious to the other inmates that I was no snitch. It was the prison administration I was after.

In the fall of 1985, I became McLain, P.I. Magnum would've been proud of the job I did digging up dirt on that rathole. Enough dirt to fill a graveyard.

The first thing I started looking into was the hospital. Besides the fact that we received poor medical care, many guys were worried about AIDS. We had strong reason to suspect that at least a couple of guys in the hospital had the incurable disease. This was back before everybody knew that it could not be transmitted by casual contact. The most likely people to contract AIDS are homosexuals, and since the Big A had tons of them, particularly among the Cuban population, we were scared. Nobody worked more closely with the Cubans than the inmates, and for all we knew, we could get AIDS by handling the same kitchen bowl.

The key phrase was "for all we knew." Nobody bothered to tell us the facts about AIDS. I found a private memo to the prison administration detailing how hospital employees should be careful when coming in contact with patients suspected of having AIDS, but not one word of the memo dealt with recommended precautions for inmates. No literature was ever distributed to us. No condoms, either. The big thing now is "safe sex" to prevent the spread of AIDS. Well, making condoms available to inmates makes a lot of sense. The gays are going to do their thing one way or another, so they might as well protect themselves—and everybody else.

I also was concerned about asbestos. I came across a report prepared in 1984 that showed the walls between rooms in a dorm like mine contained 50 to 60 percent asbestos. That is an incredibly high percentage of asbestos, which causes lung cancer and other diseases. Breathing the stuff is deadly. The same walls sampled in 1984 were standing when I lived in the Big A, and at the rate that pigpen was decaying, there had to be asbestos particles flying through the air. It wouldn't surprise me to learn someday that I have lung cancer. And since I've never smoked, I'll know exactly where I got it.

It wasn't hard being an investigator in that prison. As word got around that I was looking for examples of abuse, neglect, waste and anything else of interest, inmates and even prison employees started coming to me with information. Other inmates were always happy to let me know what shady goings-on they had witnessed. I also got a lot of cooperation from employees who wanted the ripoffs and abuses exposed. Gene Webster, a friendly cop who was vice president of the guards' union local, was doing some investigating of his own, and we used to compare notes. And I did a lot of poking around in officials' offices and desks. Nosy inmates have access to just about anything they want unless they're locked up constantly.

I don't know whether I felt more like Bob Woodward or Rona Barrett, but it was fun snooping around. And I figured that since I had been imprisoned wrongly, it must have been for a reason—to expose the institution and the people who ran it. I pursued that mission vigorously.

I looked around the kitchen and found purchase orders for produce that came from "any available source" on a cash basis. Why wouldn't the prison write the vendor a check? Was it trying to hide something? And what did "any available source" mean? Maybe that explained why the produce we got was so bad. Pat Reams told me that one day he refused to accept delivery of the garbage being passed off as produce and then was told by the assistant kitchen manager to mind his own business. Something was fishy, but I never found out exactly what.

I heard from a couple of guys that inmates taking the GED test to earn their high school equivalency diploma were being supplied with the correct answers before taking it. The prison supposedly received a fee for each inmate who passed the test, so the motivation for providing the answers was obvious. I was all in favor of guys who didn't graduate from high school having the opportunity to take the test, but what good did it do if they left prison still unable to read or write? It looked like another scam to me.

Frank Cocchiaro all but admitted that was true when he came into my room and sat down on the corner of my bed the morning of November 5. It was the first time he'd ever been angry with me.

"I hear you had a talk with Carlucci," Frank said. Carlucci, a former physician who had been convicted of giving out illegal prescriptions, administered the GED test to inmates. I had asked him about the rumors I'd heard, which he denied.

"Yeah, I talked with him," I said. "So what?"

"So that's not something you should be asking about. Leave it alone. Forget you ever heard that information."

"What's the big deal, Frank? It looks like the prison is getting paid to award diplomas to guys who can hardly spell their name."

"If that's happening, it's no concern of yours. Drop it." His tone was icy.

"Frank, I'm looking for anything that can get me out of this pigsty. By exposing this place, they'll have to move me. And this GED thing may go all the way up to the warden."

"Don't even think about it," Frank hissed. "The Reverend knows and is respected by some very good people." I knew exactly what he meant.

"Frank, I can hardly believe he's with organized crime."

"He's with *good people* and that's all you need to know. Leave him alone. If you want something, I'll make sure he gets it for you."

"Then tell him to transfer me."

"I'll work on that."

"Frank, I want out of this fucking place."

"You leave the warden out of it and something good can happen."

"OK, Frank. Just get me out of here."

That night, Frank was out of there. He died of a massive heart attack.

Don't read too much into that. I doubt my investigation of the warden caused Frank so much stress that his heart gave out. I think Frank died from complications after a hernia operation the previous June. The timing of our conversation was coincidental.

Ever since the surgery, Frank had been in quite a bit of pain and discomfort. Five days before he died, the prison doctor told Frank that something was wrong. The hernia operation was a simple procedure, and the pain should have been gone by then. Frank told me that he would be sent to the U.S. Medical Center for Federal Prisoners in Springfield, Mo., for additional tests.

Less than nine hours after our little chat, Frank was in the yard working out in the weight area with a couple of friends called Ralph and Country. Frank had been on a physical fitness kick and spent time every day lifting weights. He looked really fit and trim, too. If you didn't know his gut was bothering him, you would've thought that 65-year-old man was the picture of health.

About 6:30 p.m., Frank said, "Boy, I feel dizzy," and fell to the ground, unconscious. Country told me that a guard, who was supposed to be trained in CPR, saw Frank collapse but didn't try to revive his heart. He just waited for the doctor to show up. But the doctor wasn't on duty, and the physician's assistant was waiting for Frank to be brought up. The wait lasted 20 minutes. Twenty valuable minutes. Frank eventually was taken to Grady Memorial Hospital, a real hospital in downtown Atlanta, but never regained consciousness. He died at 8:03 p.m.

Well, the BOP had its ultimate trophy—an inmate who dies of natural causes in the can.

I was bitter about Frank's death. With proper medical care, he might be alive today. And it hurt to lose a friend.

Yes, I considered Frank my friend. He had scared the shit out of me by warning me about messing with the warden, but I think he was doing that for my own good. And even though he had a long rap sheet that detailed a life of crime, all I knew was that he treated me well. When we got locked up in Sanford, he helped me make the transition to prison life. He did it again in Atlanta. He gave me food when I didn't have any money and he watched out for me. He couldn't have been any nicer. I really missed him.

After Frank's death, I was even more determined to get out of the Big A. It was too easy to die there, and I had no intention of taking my last breath in that hellhole.

But as the holidays rolled around, I became very depressed. Besides feeling sorry for myself, I was worried about my family. They were really struggling. They ate hot dogs for Thanksgiving dinner. I couldn't help but think of Kovachevich and Mad Dog Merkle enjoying big turkey dinners while my family ate hot dogs and I sat in the slammer.

The Christmas season was much better for all of us. Jim Campbell sent $1,500 to go along with several other checks from friends, so Sharyn and the kids started eating a little better. A number of friends sent me Christmas cards and letters, which were almost as good as money. It was a big lift to know that they were still thinking about me.

I got two terrific Christmas presents just before December 25. My bad-news case manager resigned and the prison priest either quit or was fired. We called that priest the "hack in black" because he carried handcuffs with him in his boots. I even heard horror stories that he turned in inmates for sins he heard in confession. I never went to Mass or confession in Atlanta because of the hack in black.

Christmas Day in the Big A was cold and lonely. It was about 11 degrees and snowing outside. But as much as I like warm weather, I would've been happy to sleep in the snow if it meant freedom. Anything was better than being in prison.

The first thing I did Christmas morning was shave. I had been growing a beard, but a cop told me that all convicts do that as they go through a stage in which they try to lose their identity. I refused to lose mine.

I also had a few presents from the Salvation Army to open. I received a handkerchief, some candy and a magazine on prisons. Just what I wanted to read.

The rest of the day was spent playing cards, watching TV and talking to a couple of people on the phone. I also cried like a baby for about 10 minutes. The holidays and special dates like birthdays and our wedding anniversary were the toughest for me. I remain to this day something of a chauvinist, but one thing I learned in prison was how to cry without feeling ashamed.

I might have gone crazy if my family hadn't visited me the weekend after Christmas. It was the first time I'd seen them in two months. Dennis, who already stood well over 6-foot, looked even taller than the last time I had seen him. He thought it was funny that I had to look up at him. Michelle was looking more and more like a woman all the time, and Kristi and Tim looked great, too. Sharyn was beautiful, as always. We had an enjoyable 2½ days before they returned to Tampa.

The hardest parts of these visits were always the beginning and the end. I was always so happy when my family arrived, but within minutes I would get mad as hell. The damn cops watched us like vultures in the visiting room and seemed to be eavesdropping, which annoyed me something awful. I would simmer down after an hour or so, and everything would be fine until the last day. Then I would get uptight, knowing that as soon as my family walked out the door I would be left with another devastating empty feeling.

The new year brought with it a new job. Running the diabetic food line was great, but the early hours were getting to me and I was working too hard for just 11 cents an hour. I applied for a job with Unicor, the prison factory, which offered wages of something like 44 cents an hour. I was hired and put to work in the cotton lab five days a week. It was incredibly boring—I either stretched, pulled and tore cotton or sat there with absolutely nothing to do for seven hours a day—but the extra money was nice. It's not every day you get to quadruple your salary.

Ironically, Unicor had been the focus of another one of my many investigations. Several weeks earlier, I had learned from a number of people that hundreds of thousands of dollars in equipment from the factory was being destroyed and trashed. One guy told me that he had personally demolished three dozen typewriters and adding machines with a sledgehammer. Another guy told me he had seen two dozen electric motors being hauled off to the junkyard. Also tossed in the garbage or sold as scrap were new and old tools, desks, file cabinets, calculators and all kinds of machine parts, including brand new ball bearings worth more than $100,000. One guy gave me a list of model and serial numbers of all the stuff that was being destroyed. Though I never saw any equipment being thrown away myself, I had that list and plenty of sources, including prison employees, who saw what was happening.

Why all this waste? One theory was that a new manager was throwing this perfectly good equipment away because it was easier to empty a warehouse than to inventory it. If so, then somebody's laziness was costing U.S. taxpayers some big bucks. Another theory was that it was being done for budget reasons. It's a well-known fact of government life that if you don't keep increasing budget requests, your department's budget will be cut. By tossing equipment out the back door, the Big A could keep citing a need for more money to buy new equipment.

It was about time to go public. I met with Gary Leshaw, an attorney with the Atlanta Legal Aid Society. Besides helping the Cubans with their class-action suit, Leshaw was helping a group of Americans with another class-action suit against the prison regarding our living conditions. I had been supplying Leshaw with all kinds of material that prison officials would have liked to keep secret.

Like the porno tapes story.

This was great stuff. I found U.S. Penitentiary purchase orders for dozens of videotapes, including the films "Emmanuelle" and "Little Miss Innocence." Somebody at the Big A was buying X-rated tapes.

And that wasn't all. Somebody was in love with the Dallas Cowboys. The prison had ordered videotapes of Super Bowls V, VI, X, XII and XIII, all of which featured Dallas, plus almost two dozen historical highlight tapes on both the Cowboys and the NFL in general. The prison had ordered enough football footage to keep the most die-hard fan entertained for weeks.

If football wasn't your cup of tea, maybe you'd prefer to watch "Gone With the Wind," "The Royal Wedding," "Flashdance," "An Officer and a Gentleman," "The Outlaw Josey Wales," "The Joy of Natural Childbirth" or a couple of "Star Trek" movies or Elvis Presley tapes. All that and more, to the tune of $2,300, was ordered by the Big A.

And not one was ever shown to inmates.

Where were the tapes? Who was watching them? We didn't know. We just knew that the only movies we ever saw were shown on 35-millimeter film projectors, not videotape recorders. The obvious assumption was that somebody at the prison—apparently a cinema buff who liked watching naked women and the Dallas Cowboys—purchased the tapes for his personal use.

I directed all these purchase orders to Leshaw, who gave them to a reporter for the Atlanta Journal and Constitution. On February 22, 1986, the paper ran the story under the headline, "Porno tapes ordered at Atlanta pen."

That was a Saturday. On Monday I was locked up in the hole.

About 10 a.m. February 24, a couple of cops shook down my room. That meant they looked through everybody's personal property, including the stuff in our lockers. During this shakedown a cop found three government documents on a desk we all shared. It wasn't anything particularly juicy; just a couple of accounting spreadsheets and a sentence computation sheet belonging to another inmate. Despite the innocuous nature of the documents and the fact that they could have belonged to anybody, an incident report was written up on me for possession of unauthorized documents.

The administration was really reaching. Those documents had little bearing on anything important, and I don't believe the cops really cared that they were in my room. They were just a means to an end. The warden figured I was behind the porno tapes story and needed an excuse to throw me in the hole. He got what he wanted.

About an hour after the shakedown, I was taken to segregation in cellhouse C, a five-floor cellhouse where the mentally disturbed Cubans were housed. Most of them were free to roam the bottom four tiers of cells, with Americans on top.

I was locked in a cell about 5 feet wide and 10 feet long. It was tiny. I was crammed into that bathroom-sized cell with a metal sink, toilet and bunk and all my personal gear. The front of the cell had bars across it, while the other walls were solid. If I wanted to talk to a guy in another cell, I had to hold a mirror outside the bars to see him.

My first impression of segregation was that it was anything but isolated. All those Cubans walking around downstairs kept the place hopping. Guys were screaming, banging on walls and tables, blasting their TVs and radios, dancing and crying all day long. The noise was incredible. I was given earplugs, but they didn't help much. I felt surrounded, even though I was alone and no one was in the cells on either side of me.

It was a creepy feeling. I knew that I was in the hole because of the porno tapes story, but I had no idea how long I'd stay there or what else might happen. It even occurred to me that if somebody wanted to send up a goon to beat me up or kill me, that was an ideal place to do it. Most of the guys in that cellhouse were loony, so there was little chance that anyone with credibility would witness an attack.

Fortunately, the two cops in segregation were friendly. They let me use a phone to call Sharyn. I told her to call Gary Leshaw and anybody else who could raise some hell and get me out of there. The confinement and noise were bad enough, but I was worried about my safety.

The prison went ahead with plans to discipline me. On February 27, the Unit Discipline Committee found me guilty and recommended a punishment of 15 days in the hole, the loss of 15 days of "good time" toward an early release and a disciplinary transfer to another prison. I didn't like the first two ideas, but a transfer sounded great. A hearing before the Institution Discipline Committee to settle the matter was scheduled for March 4. Until then, I remained locked in the hole, out of sight but certainly not out of mind.

Especially the warden's. Hanberry and I waged a spirited debate in the newspapers. I decided it would be wise to publicize my predicament so that if the warden or anybody else had any ideas about messing with me, the media would be right on top of it.

On February 28, the Atlanta paper published an article quoting a statement I had given to Leshaw when he visited me in the hole. "I feel my being locked in seg is 100 percent retribution for an article that embarrassed and/or exposed this administration," I said in the statement. ". . . I will not be made a scapegoat for administrative misconduct." I wanted everybody to know that I hadn't ordered the tapes and that I certainly didn't appreciate taking the heat for it. The Reverend responded that he knew nothing about the videotape orders, that the questionable purchases were a result of either bad judgment or someone's innocent mistake and that the other tapes were to be used to build a tape library for inmates.

Yeah, and the Titanic is still sailing the North Atlantic on an extended voyage. If these tapes were for inmates' use, why didn't we ever see them? Many of them had been ordered as far back as October 1984. A couple of prison staff members were even quoted anonymously as saying that the prison didn't have the equipment to show videotapes. And if they were purchased with the idea of a library in mind, why did so many of the tapes focus on football and the Cowboys? A little variety would've made that explanation easier to swallow. The real killer was "The Joy of Natural Childbirth." There weren't any women in the Big A! Somebody clearly was buying these tapes of personal interest for personal use.

It seems to me that Hanberry had to know about the purchases. It wasn't like somebody tried to sneak in one tape with a bunch of legitimate ones. Somebody was ordering page after page of videotapes. And I can't believe anybody would be so bold without the boss' approval.

As for the whole thing being an honest mistake, how could anyone order "Emmanuelle" and "Little Miss Innocence" by mistake? The names of the movies were typed quite clearly on the purchase order. So was an order for a book called "Erotic Aerobics." Some horny little devil was looking to get his jollies at the U.S. government's expense.

That was a strange situation—a convict in the hole and a warden going at it in the newspapers. I was just glad to have my say. Being the most famous inmate in the Big A did have its occasional advantages.

Living in the hole wasn't one of them. The food was actually better than the food in the mess hall, but that was the only good thing you could say about it. I hated being locked up 23 hours a day. The hour break was for a brief exercise period and a shower, and I wasn't even allowed to shower over the weekend. I was allowed to get out and use the law library on occasion, so I did that as much as possible. The rest of the time I was confined to my little box. I passed the hours reading, working on my case and listening to the radio. Radios were supposed to be off-limits in the hole, but the cops let me bring mine with me. Atlanta had lots of radio talk shows and news programs that kept me entertained and informed.

I never felt the despair in segregation that I felt that first night I was locked up in Bradenton. After almost a year, I had become a fighter. Hell, I figured I had more dirt on the prison than the U.S. government ever had on me, so I knew the fight wasn't over. And I didn't spend much time feeling sorry for myself. I was surrounded by too much pain and turmoil to do that. Most of the Cubans in cellhouse C had been locked up for years, and if they weren't crazy before they arrived, they were now. I could see in their faces and actions that they had lost all direction and meaning to their lives. They had accepted their fate and given up hope. It was tragic.

I saw an American in the hole whose situation was pitiful. Joe had been such a nice guy when he lived in the dorm. He was friendly, sociable and quiet—a big, handsome guy who got along with everybody. But for some reason his mental health was questioned, and he was put in the hole. The doctors juiced him up with Thorazine, a tranquilizer used on some mental patients, and turned him into a vegetable. He was totally incapable of taking care of himself. He'd make a mess on his cell floor and the cops would have to come in and mop it up. He'd stay up all night yelling at the Cubans to be quiet and beating on his cabinet and the walls of his cell. Then he'd cry for hours on end. I tried to talk to Joe, who was six or eight cells away, but he wouldn't answer. He just kept crying.

Joe belonged in a hospital, not segregation. I told every cop I saw about his behavior, and they all swore that they had passed the information along to the physician's assistant. But nobody came to help this poor man. They wouldn't even let him out of his cell to walk around because they were afraid he'd hurt someone. They just ignored him and let him rave like a maniac.

The scariest thing was that Joe was scheduled to be released in two months. They couldn't let him out in that condition. He'd hurt himself or somebody else. He'd been fine when he lived in the dorm, but now he couldn't even function normally. It was so sad.

But not as sad as the story of little Mike Olson. He was the 4-year-old son of Bob Olson, one of the officers in charge of cellhouse C. His plight had nothing to do with the prison, but it affected me more than any of the many abuses I had witnessed or heard about. Mike was terminally ill with an upper respiratory infection.

Men and women all over the world are inflicted with all kinds of pain and injustice. But why a 4-year-old boy? Children come into this world innocent. They deserve more out of life than a disease that ends that life so early. Why would God punish a sweet little boy? Why would God take him away from his family? Is there a God?

I found myself asking a lot of tough questions while listening to Mike's father tell me this story. And the more I thought, the more I realized that God does exist and does work in mysterious ways. I don't always understand them, but I believe that they are neither senseless nor cruel. He has a plan; we just don't know what it is all the time.

I never even met little Mike, but I prayed my heart out for him. Though I was in no position to be asking for favors, I hoped that God would listen to my pleas for mercy. God must have heard because last I heard, Mike was still hanging in there.

Thinking about Mike made me think about my family, too. Could I handle the death of my wife or one of my children? I don't think so. The thought really shook me up. I can't even imagine losing a member of my family. They are so wonderful. God has blessed me with a terrific wife and four marvelous, healthy children. I couldn't have asked for more. In return, I gave my family a lot of grief for a lot of years. As I sat in my cell, I realized that it was time to shape up—to stop thinking of myself first and them next. They deserved better. I prayed a lot for them, too, and for another chance at making it up to them.

Unlike my trial, my March 4 hearing before the prison's Institution Discipline Committee was short and sweet. But they were similar in another way—they both were kangaroo courts.

I was charged with the possession of unauthorized documents. I didn't deny that the documents were mine, but they weren't confiscated from my locker. They were taken from a communal desk used by all seven guys in my room. (Three guys had left several weeks earlier.) I certainly wasn't hiding the documents. Inmates and staff had brought me more stuff than I ever wanted to read, and some of it wound up on that desk. What was the big deal?

The big deal was Denny McLain embarrassing the warden. In the days preceding the hearing, cops had questioned me about the documents, but they spent most of their time asking about the porno tapes article in the Atlanta newspaper. It was obvious why I had been written up. Hanberry wanted to punish me. But he couldn't prove that I had leaked the porno tapes story, so he had to get me on some trumped-up charge.

The only prosecution witness was Louis Watley, the cop who found the documents in the shakedown. Watley admitted that he found a number of documents on the communal desk, but he insisted that they were just copies of what he had found in my locker. That wasn't true. I didn't have any copies. Everything he found was on that communal desk. I don't think Watley ever even looked in my locker. I guess he was saying he found the documents there to make it look as if I was trying to hide something. But I had nothing to hide. And I even offered to take a polygraph test to prove it. The IDC said no, which goes to show that truth was not the issue. Protecting the warden was.

I told the committee up front that I had mailed copies of other documents to senators, congressmen, judges and lawyers to make known some of the penitentiary's problems, particularly the health-related ones—AIDS, asbestos, overcrowding and so on. I had every right to be concerned about those problems, and I wanted people in powerful positions to know about them. I also encouraged the prison administration to appoint an impartial committee to investigate the waste and fraud I had discovered. It was unlikely that a prison-appointed committee would expose the warden, but there was no question that an investigation was necessary.

In my own defense, I said that the documents I was charged with possessing were insignificant and that my having them certainly didn't harm the prison. All I had done was collect information from people who knew I was concerned about our physical welfare. And I had been a good prisoner with no disciplinary problems in the past. There was no reason to lock me up in segregation any longer.

I presented no witnesses other than myself, but I was represented by a staff member, recreation director Fred Smith. Smith told the committee that he had interviewed four inmates who confirmed that documents were piled high on the communal desk and that nobody recognized the documents as having been in my locker.

I could've had Honest Abe testify on my behalf and it wouldn't have mat-tered. Almost without hesitation, the IDC found me guilty and sentenced me to 15 days in the hole and the loss of 10 days of good time. Nothing was said about a disciplinary transfer. A cop later told me that the papers spelling out my punishment had been prepared before the hearing. The committee mem-bers obviously had determined my guilt in advance.

Well, that made me mad. I had spent an hour with my hands cuffed tightly in front of me for nothing. And why was I really being punished? For taking on Hanberry. The Reverend had his revenge.

But that didn't keep him out of the news. My statement to the committee that the prison should be investigated for wrongdoing was reported not only in Atlanta, but also in such papers as USA Today and the New York Times. A week later, the story quoting prison employees as saying the videotapes never were shown to inmates came out. I was in the hole, but the warden was losing the battle of credibility. In fact, Hanberry announced two weeks after my IDC hearing that he would retire right after his 50th birthday in June. Coincidence? You be the judge.

The eight days I had spent in the hole prior to the hearing did not count toward my 15-day sentence, so I braced myself for a long stay. Ironically, I bid farewell to the Big A two days later.

CHAPTER 12

Talladega

I was sleeping soundly the morning of March 6 when a cop rapped on the bars of my cell.

"Let's move it, McLain," he said. "Start packing."

"What time is it?" I asked, rubbing my eyes.

"It's 5:30 and all's well. That's because you've got your wish. You're getting out of here."

"The President finally decided to pardon me?"

"Not quite. You're being transferred to Terre Haute."

So, the rumors were true. I had heard the day before that I might be headed to Indiana. And in typical BOP fashion, nobody gave me any warning. It was just pack 'em up and move 'em out, and don't forget to write.

Well, the cop's news that morning came as a mixed blessing. I was thrilled to be getting out of Atlanta, but why wasn't I going to Tallahassee? Beds were available, and it made all the sense in the world to put me there. Terre Haute? The BOP might as well have assigned me to Bolivia. Indiana seemed almost as far from Tampa.

But it had to be better than Atlanta, right? I had visions of a big, open prison with clean rooms, good food, friendly inmates, meaningful work and a big law library. My luck had to be changing.

It was, but not like I thought. Just before leaving Atlanta, Gene Webster burst my bubble.

"Let me warn you, Denny," he said. "You're not going to Club Med. The guys behind the walls in Terre Haute are mostly multiple offenders for serious, violent crimes. It's a tough place full of young warriors."

Wonderful. Out of the frying pan, into the fire.

When a U.S. marshals van came to pick me up that morning, my wrists were cuffed to a waist chain and my ankles were locked in leg irons. The government still had this idea that I was going to try to escape. Even if I had had an inclination to run, I sure as hell couldn't hide.

Rather than heading north on Interstate 75 to Indiana, the van rolled west on I-20 to Alabama. The marshals were taking me back to Talladega, but only temporarily. My final destination was Terre Haute.

Upon arriving in Talladega, I immediately was tossed back in segregation. My being transferred didn't change the fact that I had to complete my 15-day sentence in the hole. I had 13 days to go, regardless of where the BOP happened to put me.

Segregation in Talladega beat the hell out of Atlanta's hole. My cell was much bigger, about 10 by 14 feet, and clean. But then everything in Talladega seemed clean. After Atlanta, the men's room at a Texaco station would look like a hospital's operating room.

Talladega's hole was much more quiet and isolated. Every cell was occupied, but the doors were solid rather than crossed with bars, making communication with other inmates difficult. But I was able to talk to the guys in the cells on either side of me through small gaps in the walls. The guy on one side was very nice and we talked quite a bit, but the other guy seemed to be missing a few screws. I left him alone.

One strange thing about Talladega was that inmates in solitary who wanted to write were given only half a pencil. Somebody actually thought that would help minimize the number of suicide and assault attempts. Is that crazy or what? If somebody is wacky enough to attack a guy or himself with a sharpened pencil, then he'll do it with half a pencil, too.

My freedom was just as limited as in Atlanta. For 23 hours a day I was confined to my cell, left alone with my books, papers and thoughts. The only time I left my cell was to shower and stretch, and the cops took all the enjoyment out of taking a shower. When my turn came every other day, I was told to back up against the cell door and put my hands through the food slot. Only after my hands were cuffed behind me would the cop open the door. Then I was led to the shower room and locked inside. Again I had to back up against the door and put my hands through a slot so the cop could unlock the cuffs and free my hands. After showering, I had to endure the handcuff procedure in reverse in order to get back to my cell. It all seemed ridiculous. In less than two weeks, I would be free to roam the compound without cuffs. Would I suddenly become non-dangerous? The cop in charge of the showers finally realized I wasn't dangerous to begin with, so after the first week he dispensed with the handcuff nonsense. That made showering less of an ordeal.

I was still mad about being assigned to the hole by the Atlanta IDC. On my fifth day in Talladega, I filed a BP-9 requesting that my conviction be overturned and my good time returned. I even asked that the Atlanta officials involved in the unauthorized documents scam be reprimanded. Talladega Warden Robert L. Martin denied my request. I later filed a BP-10 to take my gripe to the regional level, but that request for administrative relief also was denied. I could have filed a BP-11 and gone straight to Washington, but by that time I decided to just drop the whole thing.

Getting that situation resolved was less important than staying the hell away from Terre Haute. My first night in Talladega, I told the manager of Alpha unit, the segregation building, that I wanted to stay.

"You don't have a chance of staying here," the guy said. "This is a quiet little place. Nobody wants waves, nobody wants rumbles, nobody wants a guy who causes problems."

"You don't understand," I said. "I never. . . ."

"I don't need to understand. You're going to Terre Haute."

"Well, I'm going to put a cop-out in with the warden." A cop-out was a request for something.

"Fine," he said. "I'll give it to him, but he won't sign it. No way."

"I'm putting it in anyway."

"Well, good luck."

The next day, Martin approved my request. I was staying in Talladega.

Why? I have no idea. The warden obviously had something to do with it, but if the approval went beyond him, I was never told. I'm just grateful to whoever was responsible.

I really felt like I had pulled one over on the government. Taking on Jack Hanberry had gotten me thrown in the hole, but it also got me out of that pigsty and into a clean, modern facility. I'd won the battle.

But not the war. I was in neither Tallahassee nor a camp, and I was even farther away from home—about 10 hours—making visits even more impractical. And I was a hell of a long way from being free. Talladega was a level four facility, just like Terre Haute. There was no monstrous wall dotted with lookout towers encompassing the prison, but we were surrounded by two fences about 20 feet high and 10 feet apart. Both sides of each fence and the ground between the fences were covered with barbed wire. Four or five patrol trucks manned by armed guards constantly circled the perimeter outside the fences. In many ways Talladega was a country club compared to the Big A, but the words "maximum security" still fit.

Don't get me wrong. I was thrilled to be out of Atlanta and to have avoided going to Terre Haute. But it really scared me that at the drop of a hat, the BOP could move me anywhere in the country.

Precisely for that reason, I gave up my crusading. I had no intention of looking for scandals in Talladega. I had seen how easy it was for the BOP to move me, and I didn't want to get lost in another shuffle. It was time to count my blessings and play it safe. Somebody came up to me about a week after I got out of the hole and asked if I wanted to look into some payoffs in the kitchen, the laundry area and Unicor's shipping department. I begged off, saying I didn't want to know anything about anybody. Other guys came to me with evidence and rumors about corruption, but I just looked the other way. Had the system intimidated me? Absolutely. I was too comfortable in Talladega to risk getting shipped to some hellhole.

Just to be on the safe side, the officials in Talladega gave me a job as a dorm orderly. I was hoping to get a job in Unicor because of the better wages, but they had no intention of letting me work where I could snoop around. In fact, I was repeatedly turned down for jobs that would have put me in the vicinity of prison records. The administration was that scared of me. So, I spent 18 months working as a custodian. I got paid 11 cents an hour to scrub and mop the halls in my dorm and to keep the TV rooms clean. If it took me half an hour a day, I was slacking. But I still got paid 88 cents for a full day's work.

My dorm was called Sigma unit and had about 160 men in it. It had four TV rooms, which wasn't enough but was double the number in Atlanta, and four phones, which was enough so that guys weren't hitting each other over the head with fire extinguishers. No more major headaches over the telephone.

Sigma was a lot like Gamma and Delta units, the other two dorms for regular inmates. Alpha unit was used for segregation and Beta unit, where I had stayed my first time through Talladega, housed holdover inmates en route to other prisons. The population of the entire prison, including as many as 250 holdovers at a time, fluctuated around 800.

One obvious difference between Beta and Sigma units was our apparel. In Beta I had worn that orange jump suit, but Sigma residents wore military garb—khaki-colored pants and white T-shirts. We'd laugh and say "Here come the carrot people" whenever the Beta residents filed into the mess hall.

The adjustment to Talladega was easy because almost everything about the place was an improvement. Every building was modern, clean and air-conditioned. The rooms were too small—two guys were stuffed into rooms designed for one—but they were clean. As prison cuisine goes, the food was excellent. But most of all, the staff, as a whole, was friendly. Most of the guards, case managers, counselors and so on treated the inmates like people. That made a world of difference.

There were exceptions, of course, such as Shitty Smitty, a cop. Shitty Smitty was so named because he was an asshole. He went out of his way to go through everybody's rooms, looking at family pictures, reading personal mail and just generally putting his big nose where it didn't belong. He'd look in lockers, and if he found what he considered too many pencils, stamps or Twinkies, he'd take them. He was just one of those cops who thought it wasn't enough to take away a guy's freedom; he thought convicts were there to be harassed and aggravated. He did more than his share of that.

Shitty Smitty got his name from a memorable incident in Sigma unit. Everybody disliked him, so a guy in our dorm called Khadafy decided to set him up. Khadafy was our so-called executioner—the practical joke kind. While Shitty Smitty was on duty one night, Khadafy took human excrement, smeared it on the officers' telephone and hung up the receiver. Along with a bunch of other guys, Khadafy went in a TV room that had big glass windows and provided an excellent view of the phone. I was in there, too, waiting for the phone to ring. When it did, Smitty quickly picked up the receiver, put it to his ear and said hello. But before the word was all the way out, Smitty dropped the receiver and slapped his face frantically, just like Curly on "The Three Stooges." He had shit in his ear and mouth and all over the side of his face.

Everybody in the TV room went bonkers. Guys were laughing so hard, tears were rolling down their faces. I must have laughed for two hours. Shitty Smitty got what he deserved.

But most of the cops were decent. They were either nice or they left you alone to go about your business.

My immediate business was getting out of prison. That meant spending a lot of time in the law library, the one area in which Atlanta clearly beat Talladega. The biggest problem was the absence of any electric typewriters and copy machines. It was a real pain in the ass to prepare a brief or motion and to keep track of vital research. When I needed something typed, I had to find an inmate who had access to a typewriter at his workplace and pay him to do it. These hired typists charged hefty fees because they ran the risk of being thrown in the hole if caught. My favorite typist was a guy named John, who could rip off 90 words per minute, nice and neat and in the proper form. I'd like to hire him as a secretary if he ever gets out on parole from his sentence for robbing banks. John, incidentally, was transferred to Terre Haute after getting caught with unauthorized documents. Sound familiar?

I usually worked in the library about three hours in the afternoon, took a break for the 4 o'clock count and dinner and then headed back for another three hours of research. The library wasn't current with all the updates on federal cases and regulations, but I devoured everything that was available. That kept me busy until May 1986, when I sent the last of the trial transcripts off to Levine. I had located dozens of cases that I thought might support my appeal, which was being prepared by Arnie and Stevan Northcutt, an attorney in Arnie's firm who specialized in appellate work. The written brief of my appeal, citing at least eight cases I had uncovered, was filed in June 1986. The government filed a response in August, and Arnie filed our final reply brief in September. It would be four months before Arnie could argue it in court.

All that work in the law library had made me a pretty good jailhouse lawyer. Thanks to the valuable instruction of my attorney friends, Mike Schwartz and Arnie, I had learned how to conduct research, which is half the battle, and put legal motions in writing. Other inmates started coming to me and asking if I could help them with legal problems. If they had questions about whether a certain issue was appealable, I'd hit the law books and find out. Then I'd do what I could to advise them and put it on paper. I didn't handle anything as big as my own appeal, but I helped a lot of guys with BP-9s, BP-10s and BP-11s. Those were interesting because the inmate was usually right. I enjoyed seeing a guy take on the establishment and win. I helped guys with about half a dozen grievances that wound up in court. The inmate won in two cases, including one guy who got out of prison five years early, and the other four were still pending by the time I got out.

I really enjoyed working on other inmates' cases. I'm the type of guy who has to stay busy, and researching law is a great way to pass the time. It's also easier to be objective about another guy's case as opposed to your own. My advice eventually became so popular that I practically kept office hours. Guys knew when they could come to my room and I'd sit down with them, talk about their cases, help them draft motions or go with them to the library to do research. I never charged anybody for my help, unlike some other inmates with and without legal experience, but most guys were kind enough to say "thank you" with candy bars, cases of Pepsi, tennis shoes and any number of things. The most expensive gift I received was a tennis racket from the guy who got out five years early. I sure appreciated it because I couldn't afford one.

So, McLain, private investigator, became McLain, public defender. It worked right into my daily schedule. The doors to my room were unlocked at 5:30 a.m. I skipped breakfast and got up at 7:27 to be at work at 7:30. I was usually through in time to watch all of "Donahue" from 8 to 9. Then I watched Cable News Network for an hour. After that I had office hours to work on other cases until about 11:30, which was lunch time. The afternoon was open to play tennis, which I started doing a lot, until about 3 p.m. We had a body count at 4, followed by dinner at 5:30. I was available for legal consultation again in the evening. We had another body count at 9:30, and lights out and lock-down was an hour later. As you can see, I had plenty of spare time to read, write letters, talk on the phone and relax. My schedule was busy enough to keep my mind occupied, but not so rigid or overloaded that I wore myself out.

Another weekly event was the dorm inspection. Sigma, Delta and Gamma units were inspected for cleanliness, and the cleanest dorm was allowed to go to dinner first. That was a nice privilege because those who went first spent less time standing in line and were able to eat their meals leisurely. Well, the guy who inspected the dorms was buddies with the Sigma unit manager, so we usually went first. He had to let the other dorms go first now and then to make it look good, but I couldn't complain, even though the whole concept was rather goofy.

On Sundays my routine included Mass. A week or two after getting out of the hole, I went to a Monday-night meeting conducted by the priest, Father O'Reilly. These weekly meetings provided inmates an opportunity to discuss their problems in a group setting with the priest. I went that first night just as a way to kill a couple of hours.

"Denny," Father O'Reilly said, "I understand you play the organ."

"I used to play quite a bit, Father," I said, "but it's been a long time. I still know how."

"Well, our guitar player for Mass is leaving in a couple of weeks, so we'll be without a musician. Would you be interested in playing the organ at Mass?"

"I sure would."

"Denny, I knew it. Your being here, I believe, is a result of divine intervention. We need a musician, and here you are. You've been sent from heaven."

Not everyone would second that notion, but it was nice to feel wanted. And useful. It wasn't like playing the Riviera Hotel—the congregation usually consisted of about 40 to 50 inmates in a little chapel—but I think it meant more to me. I found a certain peace playing such religious favorites as "How Great Thou Art" and "Amazing Grace." Because of the large Latin population in Talladega, I usually played each hymn twice as we sang first in English and then in Spanish. The Scripture readings also were done in both languages.

Father O'Reilly was a terrific man. He really cared about us. But less than a year later, he was replaced by a new priest who quickly alienated a lot of Catholic inmates. He removed the wine from our Holy Communion celebration and treated us with much less respect. I continued to play the organ and attend the Monday-night meetings, but only because a nun named Sister Veronica got involved with us. The new priest was there only for Mass on Sundays and holy days, and Sister Veronica ran the show the rest of the time. She brought back to the chapel the spirit that was missing after Father O'Reilly left.

My spirit definitely needed a lift after my first few weeks in Talladega. The lack of money and distance from home had prevented my family from visiting, and it looked as if it would be several months before they could make it.

The money problem was reaching crisis proportions. And as the pile of unpaid bills mounted higher, Sharyn's depression deepened. Some days she would be fine, but other days she had migraines so bad she couldn't function. The predicament I had put her in was literally making her ill.

There were times, talking to her on the phone and reading between the lines of her letters, that I thought Sharyn might be hinting that she wanted out. She talked about moving the family to Chicago to live with her parents or to Arizona, where her brother Lou lived. I think she was just letting off steam, but I was afraid that if she moved, I'd lose her. And if that happened, I'd have nothing to live for. The only things keeping me going were her love and the hope of being able to make amends.

I couldn't have blamed Sharyn if she wanted out. She was hungry, unhappy and lonely, and she didn't deserve to live that way. I just prayed that she'd hang in there. And she did. My family moved twice while I was in prison, but each time it was to less-expensive housing in Tampa. She stuck it out.

Sharyn had her hands full with the kids. Not just feeding them, but also keeping them in line. With me away, they were tempted to get a little rebellious. The older ones spent a lot of time away from home, but they said it was because staying busy kept their minds off me. That was fine, but sometimes they got into trouble. The boys got involved in the beer-drinking scene for a while, Kristi started dating guys who concerned Sharyn and Michelle got a little sassy. They were normal, everyday problems that all families have, but Sharyn had it tough because I wasn't there to help with the discipline.

I was there in spirit, though. Sharyn really kept the family together by leaving me in charge, even when I was locked up more than 500 miles away. If one of the kids did something wrong, Sharyn told me. The kids hate to disappoint me, so my presence was still felt. They knew that if they messed up, I'd hear about it and determine their punishment. I've never been one for physical discipline, so I'd make a ruling and Sharyn would enforce it.

When it came to birthdays, holidays and other special occasions, everybody tried to carry on as if nothing was different. On birthdays, Sharyn would bake a cake and everybody would sing. It was a nice try, but usually they were just going through the motions. I really missed out on Denny's graduation from Chamberlain High School in June 1986 and Tim's graduation a year later. My absence was painfully felt, and it still hurts to think about missing my sons' high school commencement ceremonies. Those moments are lost forever.

Everyone had their own ways of coping. With Sharyn's encouragement, the kids just tried to carry on like everything was normal. In the back of their minds, they always believed that I would be home soon. I absorbed myself in my appeal, helping other people with their cases and playing a lot of tennis. And Sharyn, besides praying a lot, tried to think of my incarceration as a long road trip. Unfortunately, she couldn't look at a baseball schedule and see when I'd return.

Sharyn had one job while I was in Talladega—for half a day. She was hired by an answering service and was really excited about working. Before she went in her first day, she gave Michelle her telephone number in case of emergency. Sharyn started at 8 a.m., and by noon Michelle had called four times. Her boss asked if that was going to happen a lot, and when Sharyn said it might, her boss said, "No way, Jose." End of job.

Let's face it: Some people just aren't meant to work outside the home. Sharyn is one of those people. She loves being a homemaker, and the kids count on her being there. The only reason Michelle was calling was because she felt insecure knowing her mom wasn't at home. Sharyn wanted to work, but she was committed to being a full-time mother.

And wife. She was always there when I needed a word of encouragement or a kick in the butt. Actually, we all drew support from each other.

In the summer of 1986, I was offered a couple of jobs outside the prison.

Unfortunately, I still had to do the work inside. Two monthly magazines in Detroit—Metropolitan Detroit and Sports Fans Journal—asked me to write sports columns. I jumped at the opportunity. I've never been hesitant to express my opinion, so a forum to discuss sports was ideal. Metropolitan Detroit paid $125 a column and $500 for in-depth features, while Sports Fans Journal paid $100 a column. The money went directly to Sharyn, and Lord knows, she needed it. I genuinely enjoyed writing both columns, which seemed to go over well, and the money was a godsend.

The editors let me choose my subject matter, as long as it tied in with sports. My topics included contract negotiations, player agents, drug use, the NCAA, the baseball pension plan and even the prison softball team. I was free to work in my prison experiences, which I considered important. My columns certainly provided an unusual perspective on the world of sports.

For instance, have you ever watched a World Series from inside the slammer? Neither had I before I saw the Kansas City Royals beat the St. Louis Cardinals in 1985. And in 1986, when the New York Mets defeated the Boston Red Sox, I shared that experience with the people of Detroit.

It wasn't quite like having box seats. For each game, 25 guys crammed into a TV room that wasn't much bigger than a closet. Everybody could see the TV because it was attached to the wall about five feet off the floor, but there was little room to move around. All the guys eating shelled peanuts—at 45 cents a pack from a vending machine—were hard-pressed to find empty floor space to toss the shells.

Of the 25 men watching the Series, 21 were Mets fans. The only Red Sox rooters were Moose the Greek and Baseball Bobby, a couple of baseball nuts whose rooms were packed with just about every issue of The Sporting News ever printed; Big Joe, a scary-looking guy who used to ride with a motorcycle gang, and me—a staunch American League booster. We were feeling great when the Red Sox won the first two games in New York before heading to Fenway Park. All those Mets fans got stuck sweeping up the peanut shells while we boasted about how Boston would sweep New York.

Somebody should have knocked on wood. The Mets won the next two games. The Red Sox won the fifth contest, so we looked forward to Boston clinching it in front of all those obnoxious New York fans—not to mention those 21 guys in our TV room.

I set my chair in the middle of the second row for Game 6. I wanted to be in a central position to gloat. Even when the Red Sox blew leads twice and had to go to extra innings, I was confident. The New York fans were pretty loud when their team tied it up each time, but they got awfully quiet when the Red Sox scored two runs in the top of the 10th to take a 5-3 lead. And when Calvin Schiraldi retired the first two Mets batters in the bottom of the inning, they were almost silent.

And then it happened. The Mets pulled off their unbelievable rally, and after Mookie Wilson's ground ball went through Bill Buckner's legs, they tied the Series with a 6-5 victory.

The reaction of the 21 Mets fans was deafening. It was like sitting in front of a speaker at a Ted Nugent concert. If those guys had all been given their releases, they couldn't have cheered any louder. For the third time, Moose the

Greek, Baseball Bobby and I were left to sweep up the peanut shells and confetti. Nobody had the nerve to ask Big Joe to help.

If you're a baseball fan, then you know what happened in Game 7. The Mets won. But you probably don't know why—because of the body counts at the Federal Correctional Institution in Talladega.

We had a body count at 9:30 every night. It took about 20 minutes, and during that time we all had to vacate the TV room and return to our cells. Leaving in the middle of a ball game wasn't as bad as leaving during a TV show or movie because we could monitor the game on the radio. You can't do that with "Crime Story." Problem was, it seemed as if every time we left to be counted, the Mets scored a bunch of runs and either tied the game or took the lead.

A case in point: When we left for the 9:30 count during the seventh game, Boston had a 3-0 lead. I sat dumbfounded in my room, listening as New York scored three runs in the sixth inning to tie it up. By the time we got back to the TV room, the Mets were in the process of scoring three seventh-inning runs to move in front. The Boston Chokers never caught up.

I'll go to my grave believing that Boston would have won the 1986 World Series if not for those body counts.

Earlier in that 1986 baseball season, I had become aware of an interesting movement that was growing in Cincinnati. The "Free Denny McLain" movement.

That campaign actually was born in 1985, shortly after I was sent to prison. A sports nut named Dennis Walker, better known to his WEBN-FM radio listeners as Wild Man Walker, launched this drive. Wild Man had interviewed me when I was playing ball, and he apparently remembered me fondly because when I went to the slammer, he got mad. He was watching a Cincinnati Reds game one night when he shouted: "Free Denny McLain! Free Denny McLain!" Wild Man's buddies, who with Walker formed a group known as the Rail Gang at Riverfront Stadium, joined his cry for mercy. Before long, Wild Man and his pals were passing out buttons, wearing T-shirts and unfurling banners bearing the catchy slogan. The Cincinnati sports public knew all about it because these guys publicized my plight at every Reds and Bengals game during my incarceration. The Rail Gang carried my torch on road trips, too. Wild Man said the movement counted among its members such baseball stars as Pete Rose, Dave Parker, Buddy Bell, Bill Gullickson, John Franco and even rock star Bob Seger, who took home 20 "Free Denny McLain" buttons after his last concert stop in Cincinnati.

I had myself one hell of a fan club. Wild Man wore his "Free Denny McLain" button every day until I was released. Too bad he wasn't the foreman of my jury. In any event, it was nice to know that people still cared and remembered.

My first roommate in Talladega wasn't that thrilled to know me. In fact, when I moved in, he asked the unit manager to move me out.

He thought I was a rat. A rat was a guy who snitched on other inmates. And based on his limited knowledge of what had happened in Atlanta, he thought I'd been thrown in the hole to protect me from guys I'd ratted on.

I was no rat. As far as I'm concerned, rats are the worst scum in the world.

How can anybody rat on a guy who is in just as lousy of a position as he is? It's not like rats will get out of the can any quicker. They may get an extra break here and there, but they won't get a single day knocked off their sentence, no matter how many times they kiss a cop's ass. All rats do is prostitute themselves for some favor that doesn't amount to a hill of beans.

I just couldn't understand why some guys found it necessary to squeal on other inmates just because somebody was smoking a little marijuana or getting an extra sandwich from a friend in the kitchen. So what? He wasn't hurting anybody. But guys ratted anyway.

One guy in Talladega ratted on me for getting too many stamps. We were allowed to buy only three books of stamps a week, although I managed to get more by giving other guys money to buy them for me. But that wasn't the problem. A guy in the mail room was passing along self-addressed stamped envelopes from collectors who wanted me to sign baseball cards. Technically, since the stamps had not yet been used, I was exceeding my quota. But this mail room employee knew that I wasn't using the stamps for personal reasons, so he let them in. Otherwise, I couldn't sign the cards and return them. I couldn't afford to pay for the stamps myself.

Somehow, this rat named Marty found out. I don't know how because I never told anybody; it wasn't something I wanted to publicize. But Marty told a cop that I was getting too many stamps, and for two weeks, those stamped envelopes were cut off. Whoever sent cards during those two weeks never got them back.

That ticked me off. Most guys cheered for a fellow inmate who caught a break, but not Marty. He figured if he couldn't get the stamps, then no one should. It wasn't like I was getting passes to go to downtown Talladega or Birmingham for the weekend. I was just using the stamps to grant little kids' requests for autographs. Was that too big of a favor to ask? That's how low rats will sink to try to get on the cops' good side.

Well, I couldn't blame Johnny for wanting me out of his room. He didn't know I wasn't a rat. And it could be dangerous to live with a rat. Their rooms always seemed to be catching on fire. Guys would take paper bags, light them, throw them in a rat's room, close the door and walk away. Those little "fire messages" usually caused enough damage to warn a guy that if he didn't check himself into the hole, he'd get hurt. Guys also would set rooms on fire to let the occupants know that someone else really wanted their room. That shows the ignorant mentality of a lot of guys in prison.

I'm not saying most convicts are stupid. Far from it. Many of the guys I came across were doctors, lawyers, executives and other guys who had plenty of intelligence. But they got caught breaking the law. I had expected to be locked up with a bunch of 20-year-old killers and heroin dealers, but it came as a pleasant surprise to find that the majority of guys in the can were middle-aged and non-violent. Guys like me.

We had no business being in prison. There is no way society can benefit by putting non-violent people in jail. The No. 1 reason is cost. It's a waste of taxpayers' money. Instead of locking up non-violent criminals, make them repay their victims or put them to work in the community doing something constructive. Or both. Pay them 11 cents an hour, just like in prison, but let them live at home with their families so the innocent ones don't have to suffer. By doing that, families are preserved, the guilty are punished and society comes out ahead. Now if a guy given this form of punishment fails to comply with the court-ordered sanctions, I'm all in favor of tossing him in jail. The dummy must want to be in prison if he can't take advantage of favorable treatment. But my guess is that most guys would go along with any plan that keeps them out of prison.

Understand, I'm not saying rapists and murderers should be free to walk the streets. I want my family protected, just like you do. But people who represent no physical danger to the community should be allowed to serve their sentences without draining the public coffers. Taking away a guy's freedom isn't always the answer.

You know what happens when you put non-violent criminals in with the violent ones? You create new violent criminals. It's absolutely sinful to put a 19-year-old car thief in prison with a guy who has been robbing liquor stores and raping women for 30 years. The old pro teaches the kid how to fire shotguns, burglarize houses, do drugs, steal drugs and everything else. That becomes the kid's education. And when he gets out, he puts that education to work. Then he winds up back in the slammer, and the whole thing snowballs.

There's no rehabilitation in prison today. It's purely a human warehouse. Even worse, it's a fertile breeding ground for future serious criminals.

You can learn a lot about drugs, too. Anything you can buy outside the walls is available inside, and drugs are no exception.

Inmates are pretty clever when it comes to getting drugs into the can. In Atlanta, guys used to sneak them in in fire extinguishers. The fire extinguishers were changed periodically, and the drugs were stashed inside the fresh ones. Whoever arranged this deal, which required the cooperation of a cop or two since only they had access to the equipment, would then sell the dope for the going market price. Heroin came in this way, and I saw guys shooting up in Atlanta. They had no problem stealing syringes from the hospital.

Inmates had another, more disgusting, way of getting drugs inside—by swallowing balloons of dope. Everybody was strip-searched when they entered a federal prison or returned from the visiting room to the dorm, so guys swallowed balloons to get the drugs past the strip search. There are two potential problems with this method. If the balloon breaks inside your stomach, the drugs will make you convulse and die. I saw that happen to a guy in Atlanta, but he was lucky. He lived. Still, it was terrifying seeing him writhing on the ground in agony. Then on the next visiting day, he did it again. The balloon didn't break this time, which brings us to the second problem with this method: You must wait for your body to apply its daily function and then go through your own waste to retrieve the balloon. But a lot of guys did it, and some guys who didn't even use drugs got paid to do it for others. That's a shitty way to make a buck.

It wasn't always that complicated. Some guys just paid a cop to sneak the stuff in under his coat or whatever. Inmates got bottles of liquor the same way. I remember a couple of guys getting drunk as skunks on Johnny Walker Red. Almost anything was available—for a price. Of course, there was always the risk of getting caught, which would result in a few months in the hole.

I never had to worry about getting caught since I don't drink or take drugs. I haven't taken anything other than a prescribed drug since I played ball, and even then my involvement with drugs was limited. I popped a few "greenies," or amphetamines, but they never seemed to give me much of a lift. I also swallowed something called "red juice" a couple of times when I was with the Braves. This red juice tasted worse than liver—and nobody hates liver more than I do. But it made me feel like Superman. The first time I tried it, I was all fired up to pitch—and the game was rained out. I couldn't lie still for the next two nights. I decided to try it again a few weeks later and I felt like a million bucks—until I got my butt kicked by Tom Seaver and the Mets. I never touched the stuff again.

The only time I ever tried marijuana was when I played for the Senators. I was playing cards in the visitors' clubhouse in Milwaukee one day when one of our pitchers lit up a joint and said: "Do you want a puff? It's grass and it won't kill you." I had never so much as inhaled tobacco smoke in my life, but I decided to try it. I took one drag, and 15 minutes must have gone by before I stopped coughing and gagging. It nearly *did* kill me. That was it for my smoking career.

I had no interest in drugs, but I had no problem with other inmates using them—as long as they didn't get crazy or blow their smoke at me. In fact, the mood of the inmates always seemed pretty peaceful as long as they had access to drugs. But when they ran out, they got nasty.

Talladega wasn't as violent as Atlanta, but only because we didn't have the Cubans there. The amount of violence among the Americans in both places was probably pretty close.

Most people think of rape when they discuss prison violence. It happens, but not as much as you might expect. Homosexuality is widespread, but I don't think rape is. I knew of only three rape incidents while I was in prison, and in two cases it was pure violence. There was nothing sexual about it. The victims had it coming because they had ripped off somebody. When they got caught, they were in for a beating. They got raped in the process.

The third incident was different because the victim hadn't done anything to any of the guys who attacked him. This little white kid who had just arrived in Talladega happened to be in the TV room by himself one day. Three black guys came in and raped him. If anybody had been in the room with him, it never would've happened. But he was alone and frightened, making him an easy target.

Fortunately, those incidents were rare. There was a lot of homosexual activity, but from what I could tell, the guys who participated in it chose to do so. Many of these guys had been straight on the outside, but they took whatever they could get inside prison. Some guys even sold sexual favors for cigarettes, food, Cokes and clothes. As long as they kept their hands and everything else to themselves, they didn't bother me. To each his own. The problem was that prison administrators knew about this promiscuity, yet refused to make condoms available. The situation was tailor-made for an AIDS epidemic. And remember, most of these potential AIDS carriers will be back on the streets someday.

I was involved in three fights at Talladega, including one shortly after leaving the hole. It was another stupid TV room incident. I was watching the news by myself during dinner one evening when this guy named Gerald walked in and changed the station. I wasn't going to let this guy walk all over me, so I switched it back to the news. Gerald, who was about 6-foot, 225 pounds, got up and changed stations again.

"This TV is mine," he said. "Don't fuck with it again."

Without saying a word, I got up and turned it back to the news. This time I remained planted in front of the TV. Gerald took a step toward me.

"One more step," I said, "and you'll wish you'd gone to dinner with every-body else."

Gerald didn't back down that easily. He came at me and took a swing that wasn't even close. I grabbed him and knocked him to the ground. That should've been the end of it, but he grabbed for my balls. I got pissed and whacked him about three times, splitting his lip.

"If you get up," I said, "I'll kick your ass all over the compound. Got it?"

He got it. Gerald never messed with me again. That was an important con-frontation for me because I established myself as someone who wouldn't take any crap. If you allow yourself to be intimidated, you can pretty much bet on becoming somebody's wife.

I had only two other altercations in 18 months at Talladega, and they result-ed from guys pushing me too far. Fighting certainly isn't in my nature, but even I have a boiling point.

One fight was with a guy named Ray, who had a bad habit of hitting me on the shoulder or jabbing me in my protruding tummy whenever he walked by. I finally warned him to stop, but that just prompted him to poke me even harder. One day when I was in no mood for games, Ray did it again. I avoided his jab and managed to grab him from behind, squeezing his rib cage tightly. He was about 6-4 but very slim, so I had him gasping for breath. I picked him up and carried him into the phone room, where I tossed him on the cement floor and stuck my foot on his chest.

"Ray, I dare you to get up," I said. He didn't even try. "And I hope you'll think twice about jabbing me again."

I left the room with Ray still lying on the floor. He later apologized, and I even helped him with a legal motion. Not that it did any good. Ray contracted AIDS, and I heard that the disease eventually took his life.

Marty, the guy who ratted on me about the stamps, also went too far one day. He started yelling and screaming at me about a tennis match, and I let him carry on until he spat in my face and called me a pussy. Either one was enough to set me off, but both left no doubt. I knocked him off his feet with a tremendous right hook that left him crying on the floor. He looked pathetic. I'm glad he didn't want to keep fighting because my hand hurt like hell. I never spoke to Marty again.

I met every kind of criminal at Talladega, from murderers to money wash-ers, and the ones who really amazed me were the career criminals. Not the guys who messed up once, got caught, went to prison and learned their lesson; I'm talking about guys who had been breaking the law since they were 14 and never learned any other way to make a living. These guys were quite comfort-able with their chosen professions. They devoted themselves to crime the same way most people pursue their own careers.

"There's no difference between us," one guy told me. "Me and you are the same. You go to work; I go to work. The only difference is, you go to work for $4 an hour; I go to work for a score."

To them, going to prison is just part of the job. They get caught, do their time and return to work. If they get caught again, then it's just a few more years in stir, all expenses paid by the U.S. government. It was really frightening to see how little freedom mattered to them.

Freedom sure as hell mattered to me. It was all I thought about, especially as the months dragged by without seeing my family. After their Christmas visit in 1985, I didn't see them again until just before Christmas in 1986. It seemed like an eternity.

The week preceding their visit, I had fresh clothes all set and ready to go. When I heard they were there, I literally ran to the visiting room. I wasn't even detained long in the strip-search room. The cop on duty was so nice he just said, "Count to 25 and then go in and see your family."

Everybody looked super. The girls were tanned and slim and as pretty as Hollywood starlets. The boys were so much taller I could hardly believe it. Denny was pushing 6-5, although he looked like a 7-footer, and Tim had grown about six inches in the year we were apart. And Sharyn looked wonderful. I could tell she was tired and felt a lot of stress, but she still was the prettiest thing I'd ever seen.

We had a great time. We talked, laughed and held each other until they had to leave. As usual, we spent too much money on goodies, but that was my fault because the food in the visiting room tasted better than the mess hall chow. Maybe it was just the presence of my family that made everything taste so good.

When they came up, they were planning on going right back to Tampa. But I knew the holidays would be a tough time, so I suggested they drive to Chicago to visit Sharyn's folks. It took some talking, but she finally agreed to do it. They arrived in Chicago with few clothes and no coats, but Sharyn's family welcomed them with open arms.

Their going to Chicago had a nice side benefit for me. On the way home, they visited me again. It was the last time they'd ever see me in a prison outfit.

We had a lot to be optimistic about when I sent Sharyn and the kids on their way back to Tampa. Within a couple of weeks, my appeal was scheduled to be heard by the 11th Circuit Court of Appeals in Atlanta. We were sure it was a winner. I had sent a copy of the appeal to Mike Schwartz, who in July 1986 had become a circuit court judge in the State of Michigan, and he told me there was no way we could lose.

Most of the work was done by Stevan Northcutt. He took my research, combined it with his own and prepared a 55-page brief that outlined, argued and documented the reasons for my appeal. There were several.

Our main argument was that the whole trial had been a carnival. We contended that the long hours and lack of courtroom decorum had made it impossible for me to get a fair trial. Other issues in the appeal included Ernst Mueller's repeated attacks on Arnie's character; the introduction of the guilty pleas of Barry Nelson, Stanley Seligman and Mel Kaplan; the introduction of hearsay evidence attributed to Nelson and Seligman, and the judge's refusal to grant severance when she admitted in evidence that lawsuit Dale Sparks had filed against me and First Fidelity.

We didn't address the whole severance issue as completely as we could have. The appeal was limited to 55 pages, and we just didn't have space. And besides, Sy Sher, who had been sitting in the slammer in California, was appealing with me, and he covered that issue in depth. We didn't need to go into it.

We provided plenty of evidence that I had been denied a fair trial. It was Arnie's job to convince the appellate court. On January 15, 1987, he and Northcutt went to Atlanta along with Sy's attorneys to present our cases. The government sent one attorney to argue its position.

The presentation of an appeal is quite a bit different from a trial. Each side is limited to a 20- or 30-minute speech and then it's over. The process is so structured that the attorneys are alerted when to start by a green light on their podium, when they have two minutes left by a yellow light and when to stop by a red one. The three appellate judges on the panel then render a decision based on the oral presentations, the briefs prepared by each party and an examination of the trial transcripts.

In his speech, Arnie contended that my right to a fair trial had been denied by numerous judicial and prosecutorial blunders, the largest being the circus atmosphere Kovachevich had created. He even remarked that the colored lights on the podium reminded him of my trial—not just because he was being timed, but also because a lighted Christmas tree had stood in Kovachevich's courtroom. Arnie wasn't being flippant; he was just telling it like it was. Judges don't like to hear that fellow judges messed up, but Arnie came on pretty strong. He told me that while he was discussing Kovachevich's poor performance at my trial, none of the three appellate judges looked at him or flinched. They just stared down at their bench. It was almost as if they'd heard that story before.

After presenting my appeal, Arnie was optimistic. He had always been positive, saying he'd get me out, but he never sounded more confident than after he and Steve went to Atlanta. I called him at home that night and Arnie said: "It's just a matter of time, Denny. We've won the appeal. I guarantee it." It was the best news I'd heard in months.

Unfortunately, it would take a few months for the appellate judges to make up their minds. In a way, that was encouraging because they could have dismissed the appeal quickly. The longer they took, the more it became apparent that they were writing an opinion. We just hoped that the opinion went my way.

They aren't kidding when they say the wheels of justice turn slowly. That's especially true when you're sitting in your prison cell. The months really dragged by as we awaited word. Even when things were looking up, being in prison never got easier. It got harder every day. I'd hear a plane flying overhead and wish I was on it, regardless of where it was going. I never got used to my freedom being restricted. No one should.

I spent a lot of time thinking about my family. Especially Denny when I heard about his enlistment in the Air Force in February. My initial reaction was that he was nuts, but as time went on, I started to see some advantages. He had been voted "class clown" after a senior year in high school in which he spent too much time drinking and too little time studying. He obviously needed some discipline. The letters and phone calls we received indicated that he was starting to get his act together.

I kept busy. I played tennis every day. All that exercise was helping me drop a lot of weight and feel a lot better. Talladega didn't have very good recreational facilities, but all I needed was one tennis court to start getting into shape. I also had other inmates' legal cases to handle, plus my magazine columns to write, books to read and a color TV to watch. I watched a lot of sports, especially Braves baseball in the summer, and a lot of movies, although I always seemed to get back from the 9:30 body count just in time to read the credits. I even got hooked on a soap opera or two. "General Hospital" was my favorite, while Andrea Evans, who plays Tina on "One Life to Live," was my favorite soap star.

Oh yes, I added one other activity to my schedule: Softball. And I'm glad I did. In the summer of 1987, I played in a softball game that rivaled the 1968 World Series for personal satisfaction and excitement.

Talladega had four inmate softball teams. Sigma, Delta and Gamma dorms each had a team, and the guys who worked in Unicor formed another. I didn't work in Unicor, but the guys on that team asked me to play with them before anybody in Sigma did, so after sitting out the first half of the season, I became the Unicorns' first baseman.

The season was split into two halves, kind of like the split-season format used in 1981 when the major leaguers went on strike. The Gamma Goons won the first half of the season running away, but the Unicorns had a chance to win the second half. If we could beat the Delta Dogs in our last game, we'd be second-half champs and would play the Goons in a best-of-three series for the season championship.

The setting for this game was unlike anything I'd ever seen. Of the 550 or so inmates who could attend the game, at least 300 were there. They filled the bleachers along both base lines and the grass in front of them all the way up to the chalk. If a batter popped up a ball in foul territory, he could rest assured that no one would be able to run after it.

The place was packed with guards, too. They constantly walked around and through the crowd, reminding everybody that they were being watched. Prison officials get kind of touchy when convicts start to look organized, and the cops wanted to make sure that we didn't get any dumb ideas, like trying to knock over an outfield fence and run away. That would've been dumb because the outfield fences were laced with rolls and rolls of razor wire. Even outfielders as bold as Kirby Puckett weren't inclined to go crashing into the fences. And had we been able to knock down a fence, the armed cops in trucks were out there, just waiting for some fool to make a run for it.

The Talladega softball diamond did not have an organist, but it did have a marimba band. A group of Cuban, Colombian, Venezuelan and Puerto Rican inmates had assembled a bunch of boxes, cans and sticks to create a sound that really did resemble a marimba band. Convicts aren't supposed to have sticks, but my guess is that somebody probably discovered a few brooms missing the next day. These musicians sang, danced, yelled, chanted and banged away to set a festive mood. They played before the game, between innings and even while guys were pitching and batting. It was all in fun, unlike that organist years ago in Oakland who made me balk home a run.

A ton of money was riding on this game. Not just cigarettes, stamps and Twinkies, but cold, hard cash, too. We were allowed to have up to $20 in coins—no folding money—in our lockers at any one time, and guys were wagering as much as $500. Guys with less money and bigger biceps were betting push-ups. The winner got to watch the loser do the number of push-ups wagered. One guy I knew bet 2,000 push-ups and lost. By the time I left Talladega, he was still paying off and was on his way to becoming the next Arnold Schwarzenegger.

The biggest bettor was a black guy called Money Man. He reminded me of Louie, the Danny DeVito character on "Taxi," because he was always hustling around, trying to get an edge, and usually losing. The action before that game looked like business as usual for Money Man. Despite the fact that we had been 14-1 losers in our previous game, he was taking action from anybody who wanted to bet on the Dogs. And when we fell behind early and the margin grew steadily wider, he kept taking more and more bets. Money was acting like someone who wanted an early release from prison—in a casket.

Just before the game, the Dogs' roster was trimmed by two players. Phil the Pizza, the Dogs' 46-year-old player/manager, and Mr. Muscles Ken, a 28-year-old body builder who *already* looked like Arnold Schwarzenegger, had a major argument about the starting lineup. Pizza, whose left leg was frozen at the knee after an incident in which somebody took batting practice on it, was like Billy Martin—tough, scrappy, ornery and ready to fight at the drop of a hat. When Muscles challenged his managerial wisdom, Pizza responded with a few swings. The jabs didn't seem to bother Muscles, who was prevented from retaliating by the intervention of several cops. Both guys missed the game and were tossed in the hole. Pizza got 45 days for throwing the punches, while Muscles got 15 for absorbing them.

The Dogs were actually better without those two. Neither one could run worth a damn, Pizza because of his bum knee and Muscles because of his overdeveloped legs.

Our manager was a guy called Mad Man Mike. It would be kind to call him intense. He was more like a raving lunatic. He was a physical fitness buff, and I think all that running in circles for 15 years in the can was starting to get to him. He meant well, but he'd bite your head off for missing a ground ball, scream for 15 minutes and then come over and apologize. Mayo Smith he was not.

The way things were going for the Unicorns that game, he looked as if he might go off the deep end. We couldn't buy a break. The Dogs were catching the ball, running the bases and getting base hits. We were hitting the ball just as hard, but right at people. As the Dogs ran up the score, the crowd was getting louder, Money Man was turning paler and Mad Man Mike was getting hoarser. When we came to bat in the bottom of the seventh and last inning, we trailed, 8-1.

After our leadoff man singled, the next two batters flied out. It was looking grim for the Unicorns. But Mad Man wasn't ready to quit. He was fuming as he sent up a pinch-hitter—himself—and smoked a single. We had two on and two out, still down by seven.

Fireplug Flanagan was next. This guy was about 5-10, 185 pounds, and had no legs. His inseam couldn't have been longer than 18 inches. But he was a great athlete, and his double knocked in both runners to make the score 8-3. Squeaky Carlisle, a guy with a voice like fingernails on a chalkboard, then punched a single to right to drive home our fourth run. That brought up Jesus. A guy named Jesus couldn't let our rally die, right? He singled, sending Squeaky to third.

When yours truly walked up to the plate, the crowd was going wild. The marimba band was still playing, but I could hardly hear the music over the crowd noise. Tiger Stadium never sounded like this.

I was batting lefthanded to take advantage of the short right-field fence about 210 feet away. It was about 360 feet down the left-field line and just as far to straightaway center. I worked the count to two balls and two strikes while waiting to get the pitch I wanted. It finally came, and I blasted it over that short fence for a three-run homer to make it 8-7. As I circled the bases, the stands erupted like Mount St. Helens. I could see Money Man grinning from ear to ear, still taking bets, and Mad Man Mike hopping around like a kangaroo in heat.

Our next hitter was Gene, Gene the Pitching Machine, another lefty. He took a few practice swings, dug in at the plate and waited for the pitch. All of a sudden, the place got quiet. The crack of the bat could be heard for miles when Gene launched a towering fly ball that barely stayed fair as it sailed over the fence. The game was tied.

The place was beyond riot conditions; it was mass hysteria. Mad Man was even hugging guys. He must've been delirious. And besides getting louder, the crowd was quickly getting bigger. It was like everyone dropped what they were doing and came to watch this softball game. Inmates, cops, case managers—everybody was lined up to watch this miracle comeback.

Our rally stopped with the next batter, but we had forced the game into extra innings. The game ended two innings later, and the way it happened was almost anticlimactic. We won in the bottom of the ninth, but the decisive run was scored by a runner who had reached third on an error. Squeaky Carlisle's single brought him home.

Money Man was happy to take it any way he could get it. Last time I saw him, he was laughing, jiving and looking for a wheelbarrow to collect all the change he won.

I was happy, too. I jumped around with the rest of the guys. It had been a long time since I had felt that kind of euphoria. For a while, I was in another world. What I saw was a bunch of men, not convicts, playing a children's game and forgetting where we were. It was baseball in its purest form. And even though we wound up losing the three-game season championship series to the Gamma Goons, I'll always cherish the memory of being part of the greatest game ever seen in Talladega. I loved every minute of it.

That feeling was really something, but it was nothing compared to my reaction to the news I received on August 7, 1987.

At about 2:20 p.m., I was in my room writing somebody a letter when I was told that my attorney had just called. It was an emergency, the guy said, and I should call him back immediately. I did.

"Hi, Arnie," I said. "It's Denny. What's up?"

"We got the whole thing reversed," he said.

"What whole thing?"

"Your case, Denny. It's been reversed."

"Meaning what?"

"Meaning you can go home soon. The appellate court agreed with us. Your trial was a sham. And now you're about to become a free man."

I must've asked Arnie 65 different ways exactly what he meant. And no matter how I asked it, the answer was always the same: I won. When it finally dawned on me that I really would be going home, I started crying, right there on the phone. My nightmare finally was coming to an end.

After talking to Arnie, I called Sharyn. I was so wound up I could hardly talk, but when she finally figured out what I was saying, she went crazy. She was so excited, she wanted to drive right up and get me. She knew it would be a few days before the loose legal ends could be tied up and I could be released, but she said she'd sleep in the parking lot until I got out. It took all the persuasiveness I could muster to keep her from grabbing the kids and hopping in the car that minute.

Before long, everybody in Talladega knew I was getting out. I was jumping up and down, running into people, screaming in the halls, "I'm going home! I'm going home!" People didn't even have to hear me to figure out what had happened. They could see it in my face. I hadn't had a rush like that since my wedding night. It was unbelievable.

The unlucky victim in all of this was my roommate, Billy Davies. He was OK as long as I was free to roam the prison, but after we got locked into our room at 10:30, I was a terror. My adrenaline was pumping so fast, I couldn't sleep for two nights. Not a wink. And poor Billy was trapped with me in that 8-by-15 room.

"You have to go to sleep, Denny," he pleaded. "You have to let *me* sleep."

"Billy, I can't," I said. "I'm going *home.* You understand? I'm going to eat real food again. I'm going to make phone calls whenever I want. I'm going to open my own mail. I'm going to send Christmas cards. I'm going to make money again. Billy, I'm going to be able to make love with my wife! Don't you get it?"

Billy got it the first time, but he had to listen to it over and over. I felt so bad about it later because he was a walking zombie for two days while I was walking on air. I finally let him sleep the third night, but I couldn't. As quietly as I could, I read the appeal again and again, admiring its beauty. What an appeal!

It was a dandy. Judges Lewis R. Morgan, Peter T. Fay and Phyllis A. Kravitch were unanimous in their decision that my conviction be reversed and my case be remanded to the district court for retrial. They found my trial to be such a farce that if the feds wanted to convict me, they'd have to start all over again. The court gave Sy Sher the same deal—reversed and remanded.

In its 14-page written judgment, the court called my trial "a classic example of judicial error and prosecutorial misconduct combining to deprive the ap-

pellants of a fair trial." It said Kovachevich "allowed the discipline and decorum, inherently necessary to the proceedings, to unravel before her. . . . (Her)
efforts to speed up the pace not only rushed the attorneys, but also allowed the
proceedings to get out of hand, seriously impeding appellants' rights to a fair
trial." The point, the court said, was this: "A case involving a defendant facing
a prison sentence is much more important than an overcrowded court docket.
Consequently, this case was deserving of more patience than the judge gave it,
and the appellants' case was prejudiced by this lack of care."

It was encouraging to find that the appellate court agreed with us that
Kovachevich had presided over a circus, not a legal proceeding.

Ernst Mueller got nailed in the decision for prosecutorial misconduct. "The
prosecutor continuously made critical remarks about the character of appel-
lant McLain's counsel," the court stated. ". . . To discredit defense counsel in
front of the jury is improper, and even subsequent jury instructions aimed at
rectifying this error may not ensure that these disparaging remarks have not
already deprived the defendant of a fair trial. Such remarks are plain error as
they affect substantial rights of the defendant."

While the court decided that the admission of Barry Nelson and Stanley
Seligman's plea agreements did not constitute judicial error, the admission of
Mel Kaplan's did. "It was clear error," the court said, "to admit co-defendant
Kaplan's unredacted plea agreement into evidence. . . . The plea not only tend-
ed to show that Kaplan had lied on the stand, saying he had no knowledge of
drug transactions among himself and his co-defendants, it also included information harmful to McLain's defense with no probative value concerning
Kaplan's veracity. To allow the jury to take the whole plea into deliberations
was clear error and requires reversal."

This probably sounds like a lot of legal mumbo jumbo, but it was music to
my ears. The ruling went on to discuss other topics, including the fact that Sy
Sher's motions for severance should have been granted, but the gist of it was
simple: The government had botched my trial.

The only bad thing about the ruling was that it didn't take me off the hook
entirely. The government still could retry me. And knowing Mad Dog Merkle,
I figured he'd probably try to do it. But my immediate concern was my freedom, which I expected to get within four or five days.

It took four weeks. Arnie filed a motion to get me out right away, but Mad
Dog Merkle's henchmen fought it. Sy Sher got out in about a week, and we
later learned why: He was cooperating with the feds. I wasn't, so they made it
tough on me by filing motions to keep me in the slammer until my new trial.
They were still using that "danger to the community" crap as a reason to keep
me in, and the appellate court almost bought it. It was a 2-1 vote by the judges
that granted me a release on bond. I couldn't believe the harassment I was still
enduring after my conviction had been tossed out. Wasn't 2½ years in prison
enough for an erroneous conviction? Not for Merkle.

The delays were annoying, but I was on such a high that I didn't brood
about it. I just went about my everyday routine with extra vigor, from mopping floors to hitting tennis balls. I even played the organ at Mass with more
enthusiasm. It would take more than a delay to get me off cloud nine.

A hunger strike almost did it. And this time it was guys like me, not Cubans, who were refusing to eat.

This hunger strike started about the same time U.S. Magistrate Paul Game finally set my bond to pave the way for my release. The whole thing was stupid. A bunch of guys in Sigma unit were upset with the new phone policy. The phones were still on all day, but the administration had instituted a sign-up sheet system like we had used in Atlanta. It was an extra hassle, but it wasn't that big of a deal. Considering that some guys were tying up the phone for hours on end, I kind of liked the new policy.

The smart thing would have been to consult Jim Fleagle, our unit manager. He was a hell of a guy, perhaps the best I came across during my prison term. He was friendly, the type of guy inmates could joke around with, and he didn't want to see guys sitting in the can any longer than necessary. As long as a guy was straight with him and really seemed to be cleaning up his act, Jim was willing to help him out any way he could—including going to bat with the parole board. That really showed his faith in the convicts.

Well, these clowns in Sigma decided to bypass Jim and the entire prison administration. Instead of going through regular channels, they decided the whole dorm would go on a hunger strike. We were allowed to eat as much as we wanted from the vending machines and our stock of commissary food, but no one was to touch the meals served by the prison. The idea was to get the administration's attention by letting all the food go to waste. It was a stupid idea, but like with any other strike, those who dared to cross the picket line risked retaliation.

The strike accomplished zilch. Everybody got sick of Snickers bars and Hostess cupcakes, which were becoming scarce anyway because vendors were prohibited from restocking the machines, and then the phones were shut off. The whole thing had exploded in our faces. We had taken two giant steps backward and none forward.

Then the warden did something I never thought I'd see: He turned the phones back on. It was the most logical thing I had seen a warden do in 2½ years. There was no rule requiring inmates to eat, so why punish us? I was impressed.

That didn't end the strike, though. It took me and about half a dozen other guys to do that. The hunger strike continued the third day, but some of us decided we weren't going to keep missing meals on account of mass ignorance. We rounded up about 40 or 50 guys who said they wanted to eat and when that dinner bell rang, we hit that mess hall in one collective bolt. All of a sudden, the place was packed. Almost everybody followed us in. It turned out that only a few morons were serious about the strike, and they kept it up for a few days. But it was a waste of time and food because the administration wasn't about to change things over a ridiculous hunger strike.

The administration was more tolerant during the strike than after it. About 70 guys suspected of organizing this movement were thrown in the hole, and Jim Fleagle told me I would've been in there with them if not for the fact that I was getting released soon. I had been clean as a whistle in Talladega, but my history of rabble-rousing in Atlanta made me a prime suspect in any shenanigans with the administration. But Jim knew I wouldn't be messing around when I was due to get out any day.

That day finally came September 4. That was a Friday, and it would've been the following Tuesday or Wednesday before I got out if not for the kindness of Walt Olender, a man I'd never even met.

Walt is a delicatessen owner from Bayonne, N.J., who collects and sells baseball memorabilia. When I was in Atlanta, he sent me a couple of baseball cards to be signed. I returned them, and we started corresponding. Besides exchanging letters weekly and talking on the phone now and then, he sent me more cards and knickknacks to sign. He sold these items, but if he kept any of the money, I'd be surprised. He was sending me money to use in the commissary every week, plus he sent Sharyn $1,500 at Christmas in 1986. We continued to correspond the whole time I was in prison.

On September 1, Game had set a $200,000 bond for me to get out, and I obviously didn't have it. Mike Schwartz ordinarily would have handled that for me, but he was out of town and couldn't help until the following week. I called Walt and asked him if he could do me a big favor. That was a huge understatement, but Walt didn't hesitate. He flew to Tampa and pledged his assets as collateral to sign my note for bond, making it possible for me to get out. Harold Warren also signed my bond. I finally met Walt at a baseball card show in New York three months later, and he is a super guy. I'll always remember the kindness of the man who sprung me from prison, sight unseen.

I was in a daze the day I got out of the slammer. It was about half past noon, and I know everybody was saying goodbye and wishing me well, but I can't remember walking from the dorm to the front door of the prison. I do remember taking my first step into the bright sunshine, looking back at the prison and thinking: "My God! I'm out!" For the first time in 902 days, I was free to walk away. There were no handcuffs, chains, locked doors or guards to tell me to stop. The feeling was incredible. The joy I felt after winning my 30th game in 1968 didn't even compare.

I was even happy to meet the press. A group of reporters and photographers was waiting behind a barrier outside the front door, and I stopped to answer questions for a while. If I've ever smiled more during an interview, I don't know when. And I was happy to have my picture taken. I was down to about 235 pounds and looked pretty damn good, if I do say so myself.

When I first heard that I had won my appeal, I had hoped that Sharyn and the kids would be waiting for me when I walked out the door. That didn't work out, but I had arranged a deal that was even better. WTVT-TV in Tampa agreed to send them up on a chartered plane in return for an exclusive interview. They couldn't make it to Talladega until a couple of hours after my release, but it was worth it to have them fly up and then all of us fly back together.

Sharyn had worked out another deal that was nice. A few days before my release, a Detroit Free Press sportswriter named Eric Kinkopf had interviewed Sharyn. He mentioned that he would be in Talladega the day I got out and offered to help out with my transportation if necessary. When the charter plane was lined up, Sharyn enlisted Eric's help in getting me to the airport, which was several miles from the prison. That was a great deal for both of us. Eric got a one-on-one interview, and I got a free lift.

After talking with the handful of reporters at the prison, I hopped into

Eric's car and we took off. Eric and I had just met, but I was so pumped I talked his ear off like we'd been buddies for years. I couldn't help but rattle on about all the things I wanted to do when I got home. I suppose it gave him a lot of good material for his story.

To kill some time before going to the airport, where a pack of reporters was waiting, we drove all over Talladega. We visited Sister Veronica, who was pleased to know that I had found an inmate to replace me as organist. The guy weighed about 350 pounds and probably wound up crushing the organ bench, but he sure could play. Then we went to a Burger King, where I sank my teeth into a couple of bacon double cheeseburgers and french fries. All told, we spent almost two hours eating, driving around and talking before going to the airport, where I had another impromptu press conference. That ended after about five minutes when, at last, my family arrived.

I was standing at the bottom of the steps as Sharyn, Kristi and Michelle stepped off the plane. It had been eight months since I had seen them, and believe me, they were a sight for sore eyes. As usual, all eyes were moist. I hugged each of my daughters and Sharyn for a long time, especially Sharyn. I can't tell you how wonderful it felt to hold my wife, knowing that nothing anybody might say could make me let go until I was good and ready.

It took about 20 minutes for the plane to refuel. As soon as it was ready, we jumped inside and flew home. What a flight. The plane was a Beechcraft Super King Air 200, one step above my Cheyenne II, and it was pure heaven to be flying in style with my wife and daughters.

It was a shame my boys couldn't enjoy that flight, too. Denny was stationed in London with the Air Force, and Tim had just started his first year of college at Embry-Riddle Aeronautical University in Daytona Beach. But Tim came home that night to join us for an incredible homecoming dinner.

I had been looking forward to one of Sharyn's famous meals for 2½ years, and it was one to remember—for everybody. The whole time I was away, Kristi refused to let Sharyn fix pork chops. I love pork chops, and Kristi just decided that as long as I wasn't there to enjoy them, no one in the family should. That first night I was home, Sharyn fixed a pork chop dinner that couldn't be beat. It was the best meal I ever ate.

But then, Sharyn could've fixed liver and I would've enjoyed it just as much. The menu didn't matter. I was just thrilled to be home.

CHAPTER 13

Freedom

How do I love freedom? Let me count the ways.

I love getting up in the morning to the sound of an alarm clock or Sharyn's gentle nudge—not the sound of my door being unlocked at 5:30 a.m.

I love going to the refrigerator and pulling out a Diet Pepsi.

I love driving my car.

I love comfortable furniture.

I love using the bathroom—in private.

I love opening doors for myself.

I love seeing a clock that shows 4 p.m. and not having to move a muscle.

I love watching TV—and choosing the channel and volume myself.

I love opening mail that hasn't already been read.

I love talking on the phone without a guard listening in.

I love wearing my choice of clothes.

I love walking in the country—as far as I want to go.

I love eating real food.

I love seeing Sharyn the moment I wake up in the morning, the moment before I fall asleep and as many moments as possible in between.

I love life.

I took all this for granted before being sent to prison. But not anymore. Every time I answer a ringing telephone or dig into a plate of Sharyn's Polish sausage and pork chops, I'm reminded that for 2½ years, I couldn't do that. We have so much freedom in this country, we tend to forget how lucky we are. But if there's anybody who really appreciates his freedom, it's me. I thrive on it.

For about two weeks after getting out, I just kicked back and enjoyed myself. We needed money, so I brought in five or six thousand dollars by making a number of personal appearances and doing an exclusive magazine interview. All of a sudden I was flying across the country, staying in first-class hotels and eating the finest food again, and all this without handcuffs or guards. The change was so dramatic it was almost frightening. I loved it, but I was just as happy hanging around the house and soaking up the joy of being home.

Then on September 17, I accepted a job. In Indiana, of all places.

David Welker, who had just purchased the Fort Wayne Komets of the International Hockey League, called me one day and asked if I'd be interested in working for him. He remembered that I played the organ, and he thought it would be a great publicity gimmick to get Denny McLain to play the organ at his minor league club's home games.

Well, I had no appetite for being paraded around like a circus animal. I passed. But Welker really wanted me to come up to Fort Wayne. After meeting and talking further, we reached an agreement. He hired me as marketing director of the hockey club and made me a partner in his newly formed distributorship for Koala Koolers, a new non-alcoholic wine cooler from Australia.

I've never been much of a hockey fan, but those wine coolers really piqued my interest. I saw an incredibly wide-open market. They taste just like regular wine coolers, but without the alcohol. A lot of people would love to enjoy the taste without running the risk of driving drunk or waking up with a hangover. I saw those coolers as my ticket back into the business world.

The deal Welker offered me wasn't bad. He agreed to pay me $27,000 a year and provide me with a condominium, a car, health and life insurance, a loan and a country club membership. I viewed the package as a good starting point for a guy who had just been released from the slammer.

Moving to Indiana wasn't easy. First I had to get the judge's permission to leave Florida. Then came the matter of uprooting the family. Denny was in London, but everybody else was pretty comfortable in the Sunshine State. Tim already was attending school in Daytona Beach and Kristi had a job in Tampa. They decided to stay behind while Sharyn, Michelle and I moved north.

After calling Florida home for 10 years, it came as quite a shock to return to the Midwest. I am not a cold-weather person. I grew up in Chicago and played ball in Detroit, but I had long since gotten used to mild winters and hot summers—the type of climate that permits a year-round golf schedule. Putting up with snow and subzero temperatures isn't exactly my idea of fun. But even though the climate wasn't ideal, I was fired up to start promoting David Welker, Koala Koolers and the Komets.

It's funny how some things work out. The wine coolers deal never amounted to anything. It could have, but to introduce the product the way we had in mind—selling it to major distributors who would put Koala Koolers on every supermarket shelf in the country—required several million dollars. Welker didn't have that kind of money. He had never even examined the club's financial records before buying the Komets, and as a result the team was costing him quite a bit more than he had anticipated. He just didn't have enough left over to give the coolers a fighting chance.

Had I known that, I never would have gone to work for Welker. Once again, somebody had gotten me involved in a deal under false pretenses. How could I let that happen again? Well, I was broke and needed a job. Welker painted a pretty picture and I bought it. It turned out to be a fraud.

Welker didn't even live up to the terms of our original agreement. I never got a car or loan from him, and instead of living in his condo, he put us in his house in Roanoke, about 15 miles southwest of Fort Wayne. The house is gorgeous, but it's way too big for three people. The cost of utilities alone during the winter months was more than most folks' mortgage payments.

After the wine coolers deal was put on ice, I found myself knee-deep in the world of minor league hockey. That wasn't so bad. I actually enjoyed promoting the Komets. I looked at the team like any other product: People have to know about it and have a reason to buy it. I'm good at making the product visible.

The key was getting people into Allen County Memorial Coliseum, and I came up with lots of attractions. One of my first was Turkey Night. The Komets always gave away about 15 turkeys at a game around Thanksgiving, but that wasn't much incentive to fill an 8,000-seat arena. As usual, I started thinking big. I went out and talked to a local turkey farmer, who agreed to provide 1,000 turkeys at a cut-rate price in exchange for some free publicity. We advertised the hell out of the promotion, gave away the birds and wound up with a crowd of 7,358—about double our normal crowd.

That was just the start. I arranged baseball card shows that brought in the largest consecutive hockey crowds Fort Wayne had seen in years. The club paid such stars as Pete Rose, Bob Gibson and even myself to come and sign autographs for three hours before and during a game. The fans got free autographs for the price of a ticket, which cost less than the price they'd pay for an autograph at a card show. I also brought in the San Diego Chicken one night and sponsored big giveaways of used cars and trips to such places as San Francisco, Las Vegas and Miami.

The way I saw it, I had to keep things hopping. Welker was paying me to generate interest in the team, and I was coming up with more than enough ideas to give him his money's worth. For instance, after seeing how bored everybody looked between periods while the Zamboni resurfaced the ice, I thought it would be fun to have some kind of giveaway to break the monotony. Before long, I had a gal wearing a bear costume skating between periods, tossing out Frisbees that were redeemable for a free dinner at a local restaurant.

The old-timers around the Komets' offices were amazed when they saw me go to work. They'd never seen such a whirlwind. I think I provided a breath of fresh air there, and I know I had a good time coming up with fresh ideas to sell the club.

All these promotions and gimmicks involved cash outlays or trade-offs, but everybody knows you have to spend money to make money. The bottom line is boosting attendance. Once you have the fan interest, everything just snowballs from there. And my marketing scheme worked. After averaging 3,835 fans a game the year before I arrived, the Komets drew an average crowd of 4,053 with me involved. That was an increase of more than 5 percent. Nothing earth-shattering, but a good start.

Unfortunately, Welker had made such a mess of the front office that the club was doomed to lose money. He didn't know anything about running a hockey team. His business was cement and pipes. But some of his decisions made no sense, regardless of the business. For example, he let a woman who was well trained in marketing handle the books. Then when the books got fouled up and a team of accountants had to come in and try to straighten them out, he fired her. The books weren't even her fault because no one knew what was going on. Welker refused to use daily spreadsheets, which are crucial to the success of any business. They let you know where you stand at all times. But when I suggested that he use spreadsheets, Welker said: "I expect to lose a little money. There's no need for such controls." When I heard that, I should've packed up and left. It was a crazy way to run a business.

One nice thing about my job with the Komets was that I had a lot of latitude to pursue other deals. I wasn't tied down to the office 40 hours a week. As long as I had all the promotions running smoothly, I was free to come and go as I pleased.

I participated in a lot of card shows. I was kind of leery at first because I didn't know how people would react, but the shows have been a lot of fun. I've enjoyed signing autographs and meeting people, including many of the hundreds of people who wrote me letters of encouragement during my ordeal. Very few have asked rude questions or told me they wished I was still in prison. The great thing about baseball fans is that they remember me for what I did on the diamond, not off it. I've had so many people tell me how grateful they are for my contributions to the Tigers' World Series championship and for the other good years I had. That really says something nice about the game of baseball.

My name still must mean something in Detroit because shortly after my release, a local car dealer named Dan Scenga asked me to appear in some TV commercials. They're really cute. All three commercials play off my prison sentence and bookmaking background. In one ad, I'm acting like a football coach with my clipboard, talking to my "team" of car salesmen. These guys all get this shocked look on their faces when I say, "And even *I* can bet on this." The one I like best ends with one of the salesmen closing a car trunk, which knocks the license plate to the ground. I pick it up, look at it and say, "You know, I made this one."

In return for the commercials, the dealer gave me the use of a brand new red Corvette. It's awesome. For a guy who enjoys life in the fast lane, that car is perfect. I even worked out a deal where I got a phone installed in it. Now I can take care of business while zipping back and forth between Fort Wayne and other cities. I also managed to hook up with a car dealer in Huntington, Ind., named Bernie Nelson, who provided a second car. All he asked in return was that I drop by his dealership once in a while. I have to be one of the world's few ex-cons whose name is actually good for business.

I wasted no time getting started wheeling and dealing again. That may sound crazy, but I still get off on making deals. The difference now is that I've got Judge Schwartz looking over my shoulder. Before I proceed with anything, I apprise Mike of the situation and get his opinion. If I'd had him watching out for me years ago, I never would've gotten into trouble. I'll try to avoid shady characters and situations like the plague from now on, but just in case, Mike will be working overtime to keep me on the straight and narrow.

We may even go into business together. We were presented with an idea for a new product that could revolutionize the drum industry. It's a metal gadget that fits on a drum and eliminates the unwanted reverberation caused by a drumbeat. We've shown this gadget to dozens of professional drummers, and everybody says it's the best thing they've seen in years. This deal could flop or it could make us rich, but if Mike says go, we'll go. We're also considering the purchase of a radio station. Wouldn't that be interesting?

Since getting out of prison, I've been approached with more deals than you could imagine. Most go in one ear and out the other, but a few have stuck with me. I'm already busy promoting concerts of small bands around the Midwest, and don't be surprised if you hear my name connected with some other products somewhere down the line.

On the other hand, I wouldn't mind keeping a lower profile. So far, that hasn't been possible. The media have shown amazing interest in me since my release and Mad Dog Merkle still seems dedicated to the task of making my life miserable.

After my conviction was reversed, Merkle could have let me get on with my life. But no. He was adamant about retrying me. True to form, he wouldn't quit. Rather than be satisfied with the 2½ years he'd already taken away from me and my family, he decided to spend more of the taxpayers' money to do it all over again. A new trial would be shorter because I wouldn't have any co-defendants and I'd already been acquitted of the 400-kilo drug charge, but we're still talking about thousands and thousands of dollars.

After we realized that Merkle was going to keep after me, Arnie Levine tried to work out a plea bargain. We were willing to discuss an arrangement in which I pleaded guilty to some minor charge, and the government would sentence me to the time I'd already served. I didn't like the idea of pleading guilty to anything, but I just wanted to get the whole mess behind me. Well, Merkle's office wanted me to plead guilty to the remaining drug charge, which I absolutely will not do. We reached a stalemate. My efforts on behalf of the FBI in the Atlanta money-for-transfers scam apparently didn't carry much weight with Merkle.

While these discussions were taking place, Judge Kovachevich set a trial date for January 4, 1988. That date was later postponed indefinitely because Ernst Mueller was tied up with another case, and then in March she set a September 7 trial date.

It shouldn't come to that. I believe an agreement can be worked out whereby I don't have to go back to trial or prison. With the exception of Merkle and perhaps Kovachevich, I think everybody agrees I've paid my dues. Merkle got his pound of flesh and I did some time. Enough is enough.

Or is it? I discovered that Elizabeth Kovachevich hadn't changed much while I was away. She still enjoys taking jabs at me.

On December 18, Kovachevich held a hearing to see whether everything was on schedule for my January 4 trial date. I didn't attend because it was a brief proceeding that was fairly dull and routine—if anything in my life fits that description—and it would've cost me about $500 to fly down to Tampa. The court order didn't require my attendance, but Kovachevich called me "inconsiderate" and "irresponsible" for not being there. Mueller joined the parade, calling my conduct "outrageous" and "ludicrous."

Hadn't these people learned anything from the appellate decision? Kovachevich even admitted that the notice I received did not state that I had to appear. But she made it clear that at all future hearings, no matter how minor, my presence is mandatory. So every time she gets the notion to hold a status hearing, I'm out $500.

After my release from prison, I was fortunate enough to become associated with a man who has done a lot to restore my faith in the federal justice system. Denny Meadows is my U.S. probation officer in Fort Wayne and one hell of a guy. As long as people like him are involved, there's hope.

The bottom line is that he cares. He is genuinely concerned about me and the many other people who report to him. He listens to my problems and works with me, not against me. When the Fort Wayne airport got snowed in the day before I was scheduled to attend a March 4 hearing in Tampa, Denny called the U.S. Probation Office in Tampa to explain that it would be impossible for me to make it. He not only saved me $500, but also kept me out of hot water with the judge. Denny also treats me like a decent person, not a lowlife. If more people in the Department of Justice had his attitude, you'd see a lot more guys coming out of prison rehabilitated.

Besides checking in with Denny once a week as a condition of my bond, I'm working with him in the community. He suggested that I go to local high schools and talk to kids about my experiences. The idea is to give them a firsthand account of what can happen if you mess with the law or hang around with the wrong crowd. I've had a great time doing that. The kids are attentive and ask good questions. They are too young to remember me as a pitcher, but their teachers must brief them well because they ask as many questions about my baseball career as they do about prison. But the point doesn't get lost. With the stories I can relate about getting thrown in the hole and bashed over the head with a fire extinguisher, I think I make an impression.

I know I have in a couple of cases. Denny Meadows said that after my first talk, a student called him and expressed his appreciation for my advice, which had helped him "make some important decisions." During my second speech, a girl in the front row started crying. I talked to her afterward, and she said I had frightened her because a friend of hers was in trouble. I didn't mean to scare her, but maybe it prompted her to get her friend to straighten up. I plan to keep talking to kids as often as Denny can arrange it, and if I can help even one kid make the right choices, then my time is well spent.

On March 7, I found myself with a lot more time on my hands. David Welker fired me.

Why? Because he was through using me. He admitted as much when he told the Fort Wayne Journal-Gazette, "I did it (hired McLain) for publicity." Welker is running for Congress, and he needed to hire somebody who would help him get his name in the papers.

His plan worked. I made him a star. Welker ran a poll to find out how many people in the community recognized his name, and thanks to me, the poll indicated that he and the front-runner were running neck and neck in that department. That's what happens when you get your name and picture in Sports Illustrated, Newsday and a bunch of other publications. It must have been pretty exciting for a pipe and cement magnate who had never been in the spotlight before.

Then, for some crazy reason, Welker told me that I had become a liability in his campaign for Congress and he dumped me. I was bitter at first, but I'm not dwelling on it. I've never had any shortage of job offers, so that doesn't worry me. What bothered me was the man's lack of honor. He made lots of promises, got me to move my family more than a thousand miles away and then canned me after getting the headlines he craved. I was grateful for the initial opportunity he provided, but that didn't give him the right to renege on our deal.

The world is full of dishonorable people, and it seems as if I've been used by half of them. David Welker was the latest in a long line. It was a shame we ever got involved, but it was partly my fault. I should've thought twice about Welker when he told me that he planned to run for President if his campaign for Congress was successful. Remember Paul Higgins and his pal Timothy Johnston, the other guy I came across who wanted to be President? You know where that got me. The next time somebody tells me his goal is to be President of the United States, I promise I'll run like hell.

Life goes on. Like a cat, I have a tremendous knack for always being able to land on my feet. I'll bounce back.

I still intend to use Fort Wayne as my launching pad. We really enjoy living here. The people are terrific, and we really feel like an accepted part of the community. The location is ideal—just a couple of hours from Chicago, Detroit and Indianapolis, where I conduct a lot of business. The only real drawback is living so far away from Kristi and Tim. But they are growing up, and I can't expect them to stay at home with Mom and Dad forever.

As I put the finishing touches on this book in the spring of 1988, Kristi is working as a computer operator and completing her studies at Hillsborough Community College. Dale also is working and is back home living with her mother. Denny is in London with the Air Force, keeping the peace. Tim is completing his freshman year at Embry-Riddle, where he is studying aeronautical engineering. And Michelle is a sophomore at Homestead High School in Fort Wayne. The older kids have left the nest, but I still have my baby.

And my wife. Every time I wake up in the morning and see her lying next to me, I count my blessings. It still amazes me that after all the grief I put her through, she stuck with me. She is truly a remarkable woman.

I'll never hurt her again. The one genuine benefit of my going to prison was that it forced me to think. To think about how Sharyn has never done a thing to hurt me, yet I broke her heart again and again. To think about how my selfishness and greed put my wife and kids through hell. To think about how, through it all, they kept loving me anyway. Their capacity for forgiveness runs deep. I owe my family so much. It will take the rest of my life to make it up to them.

Most guys don't get a second chance, but I was lucky. A lot of guys leave prison and find their families gone and their friends out to lunch. But my family and such friends as Mike Schwartz and Arnie Levine have stood by me every step of the way. They've really helped me pick up the pieces. My new lease on life is all the proof I need that God answers prayers. When I was in prison, someone sent me a medal of St. Jude, the patron saint of lost causes. Let me warn you: If you're trying to reach St. Jude right now, he's probably on some beach in Florida, recuperating after being overworked.

I'm a changed man. I enjoy helping Sharyn in the kitchen, working around the house, walking the dog, grocery shopping. I never used to do those things. Now I love it. Every night when I go to bed, I can't wait to get up the next morning and start a new day. Being in prison helped me recognize that life is too precious to waste on things that don't matter. My family matters.

Naturally, Sharyn was a bit leery when she first saw the "new" Denny. I can't blame her. After all, I'd been self-centered for a long time, and it probably came as a shock when I got out of the slammer and started acting like Heathcliff Huxtable, Model Husband. But I'm for real. That's because I finally realize that Sharyn isn't just my wife. She's my best friend.

This may sound like so much rhetoric, but it's the truth. I suffered a lot, but Sharyn endured 10 times that. And I'm constantly reminded of our ordeal, even when I sleep. I have nightmares in which I'm in prison, waiting desperately for someone to get me out. I have even stranger dreams in which I'm trying desperately to get back *into* prison so I don't miss the 4 o'clock count.

Dreams aside, I've learned my lesson. I may be thickheaded, but I'm not stupid. One tour of our federal prison system was enough. You'll never find me anywhere close to a criminal situation again.

This book is titled "Strikeout" for a reason. I have gone down swinging a few times in my life. But as far as I'm concerned, it's a whole new ball game for me now. At age 44, it's the first inning of the rest of my life. And this time I'll go the distance.

Even I can bet on that.